BRITISH COMPOSER PROFILES

The British Music Society

BRITISH COMPOSER PROFILES

third edition

A biographical dictionary
of past British composers
1800 – 2010

by

Gerald Leach

Revised and edited by

Ian Graham-Jones

Front cover photographs, top (L-R):
Sir Lennox Berkeley, Sir John McEwen, Doreen Carwithen

Front cover photographs, bottom (L-R):
Maude-Valérie White, Sir Arthur Sullivan, Sir Arnold Bax, York Bowen,
William Alwyn

Back Cover photographs (L-R): Sir Malcolm Arnold, Gwirne Creith, Ruth Gipps,
Frederick Hymen Cowen

Cover background:
A page from Sir Malcolm Arnold: *Salute to Thomas Merritt,* op. 98, ms. in the
composer's hand, reproduced by kind permission of the Malcolm Arnold
Estate.

Cover design by Lynette Williamson.

British Composer Profiles (3rd Edition 2012) is published by the
British Music Society
(Registered Charity No. 1043838)

British Library Cataloguing in Publication Data
A catalogue record of this book is available from the British Library
ISBN 978 1 870536 99 8

Printed by Biddles, part of the MPG Group Bodmin and King's Lynn

Contents

Preface

When the twelve founders of the British Music Society first met in 1979, it was obvious at the time that little information was available about British composers between the Jacobean period and the twentieth century. It seemed that amateur promoters and performers of concerts that included British music often had little to help them prepare programme notes. Thus it was that the first edition of *British Composer Profiles* was published in 1980, which provided brief biographical notes on British composers. A second, enlarged edition followed in 1989. Since then the information revolution brought about by the internet has made so much more available, but it is often too detailed and fragmented to be easily assimilated. It is to be hoped that these profiles will be sufficiently condensed and, at the same time, informative enough, to fill the void.

The present edition has been greatly expanded and readers will find many new names. The inclusion of a greater number of women composers is also a welcome addition. The choice of photographs and illustrations may seem random; it was felt best to include a few thumbnail portraits of composers where they might not be readily available elsewhere. Considerations of page layout were also another factor in their choice.

As in previous editions, living composers have not received attention. They can now offer to the general public their own websites and their work can be promoted by their publishers, and organisations such as the British Academy of Songwriters, Composers and Authors, and Sound and Music. Sadly there are so many of them that would warrant inclusion, but where can one draw the line between the twenty-two-year-old who has had two works performed to critical acclaim and the eighty-year-old who is still struggling to be heard?

Inclusion in the *Profiles* is not necessarily an indication of worth, nor is the length of a profile an indication of importance; some are just more interesting than others. By and large value judgments have been avoided, though the reader may occasionally sense an enthusiasm on the part of one of other of the authors. We hope that the reader will forgive these lapses.

The choice of the year 1800 as a starting point may seem arbitrary. But those composers that brought about the English Musical Renaissance from the last decade of the nineteenth century onwards owed much to the previous generation that taught them, a generation who would have been born in the early years of that century.

A wide variety of sources has been useful in the preparation of these profiles and, where there have been insoluble discrepancies, the authors have had to use their judgment. We apologise for any errors that may have crept in. There will be composers that have not been covered in this much expanded new edition. We wish to assure their surviving relatives or fans that, wherever we have made a decision not to include a composer, it has been because the information at hand has been inadequate. Undoubtedly some may have been simply overlooked or constrained by practical considerations. For these we offer heartfelt apologies.

As in the previous edition, a Chronology of the composers has been provided. New lists of the dates of formation of some British societies, institutions and concert venues, as well as dates of the main Conservatories of Music mentioned in the *Profiles* have been added. Readers will also see a new section of Appendices compiled by the authors. These list some of the main foreign teachers, a note on some of the major universities and their degrees which have been referred to in the *Profiles*, and an index of significant articles that have appeared in the publications of the British Music Society to date.

Gerald Leach
Ian Graham-Jones
October 2011

Introduction

Lewis Foreman

I first started exploring British music when I was at school, especially the music of the first half of the twentieth century. It was then still new; even Elgar, Delius and Holst had been dead less than 25 years. When I first started, Vaughan Williams was still alive! There were recordings, but much of the music even by the big names was unavailable, and lesser names were almost completely unknown. Indeed one was constantly encountering names which did not appear in reference books, even the generally excellent Fifth Edition of Grove's Dictionary of Music. Much of Elgar was thought below par, while Imogen Holst by her trenchant criticism ensured that the full range of her father's music remained unperformed. Thus, in the late 1950s, acquiring a second-hand copy of the 10-inch LP of Rubbra's Fifth Symphony revealed a glimmer of a wonderful musical world whose promise could not be explored because most of Rubbra's music was unrecorded. Yet there *were* performances, and in those days it was far cheaper to attend a concert than purchase an LP – whereas today the opposite is true. And then there was the mystery of Victorian music, largely belittled by one's musical superiors, but in fact often fascinating and intriguing as one investigated musty scores picked up from dealer's remainder trays or library basements.

This was a musical world dominated by a received canon of major or 'important' names in which most of the others, especially those in a tonal idiom, were suspected to be below par. This attitude has only slowly been eroded. It has been challenged by allowing a wide conspectus of music lovers to hear the music in live performances, broadcasts or recordings. To be assessed music has to be heard, preferably several times. Yet the fact that a work is recorded does not mean that we are necessarily hailing a forgotten masterpiece. What we are being given is the means of exploring it – when we have a work of ambition it needs assessment over time in a way impossible for most of us from the score. Our most recent example of the re-evaluation of a really big name who had never received his due, came with the recording of the symphonies and other orchestral music of the composer Richard Arnell, himself a celebrated teacher of composition. Yet the Royal Scottish National Orchestra's superbly played cycle of Arnell's symphonies, directed by Arnell's pupil Martin Yates, must all too vividly demonstrate how we need to evaluate our music and assess it from personal experience.

Learning instruments – first recorders, later viola and clarinet –
one began to discover composers whose names were almost forgotten and
tended to be associated with small pieces for these specialist instrumental
repertoires. No teacher ever encouraged one when, say, playing the
Christopher Edmunds Sonatina or Herbert Murrill's Sonata for treble
recorder. Nor did one ever encounter these composers in the regular
repertoire, though we now know Herbert Murrill, sometime Director of
Music at the BBC, particularly for his Second Cello Concerto *The Song of
the Birds*, and Chris Edmunds for three symphonies, the Second a notable
example of music responding to the challenges of the war in 1939 and
1940.

When the British Music Society first started I remember Geoffrey Bush
being very ambivalent about its activities, feeling that worthless or very
minor names were being given an undeserved platform. As this came from
Geoffrey it deserved the most serious consideration. But ultimately, largely
owing to the British Music Society's activities, over a span of time what
became apparent was the extent of worthwhile composition in our time;
we became aware of the phenomenal range of talent and personal voices.
This was activity not given voice by the established mechanisms of concert
life and BBC assessment. In this third edition of a remarkably useful
reference book we find a notable range of names – and if you have just
come across an unfamiliar name of a British composer of our time ten to
one you may be able to broaden your knowledge of them in these pages.

In his pioneering first edition of this reference work in 1980 –
another world – Gerald Leach rather hedged his bets when he wrote
'inclusion in this list is not necessarily a guarantee of musical worthiness,
and some of the names presented here may expediently be left at the
bottom of the music pile in the organ loft'. After thirty years of exploring
it is remarkable how worthwhile some of that forgotten music has turned
out to be. Remarkable, too, is the sheer extent and number of names that
we find documented here. The big names of the earlier part of our period
now seem even larger and more established – Elgar, Vaughan Williams,
Britten. Others that we now know to be important (and, measured by
available recordings, now have a substantial following) have been rescued
from being known by one or two works – notably Bax, Bridge, Bantock
and Moeran. If there was no room for Bax, Bridge, Finzi, Moeran and the
rest, what space might there be for lesser names?

Much of this music was rediscovered by a small but dedicated band
of amateur promoters and performers – student and amateur orchestras,
sometimes of remarkably high achievement. Choral societies and amateur
and municipal opera companies provided a ready stream of revivals, often
featuring young artists some whom would later become famous. Thus the

activities of such groups as the Kensington Symphony Orchestra and Opera Viva directed by Leslie Head, Fulham Municipal Opera and the Fulham Municipal Orchestra directed by Joseph Vandernoot, the Broadheath Singers conductor Robert Tucker, all explored the repertoire. By helping to select music for these programmes they fed one's own curiosity at music that one had read about, had even seen in the score or on the piano, but had never *experienced* on the orchestra in performance. What revivals they were, a wonderful education discovering music by many of the composers featured in this book.

Soon there came specialised entrepreneurs, smaller enterprises and one man bands, who wanted to record the repertoire at a time when the major record companies dominated the world and tended to dictate what constituted acceptable international repertoire. Thus appeared now well-known record labels: Lyrita run by Richard Itter, Argo by Harvey Usill, and later Unicorn the inspiration of John Goldsmith. Soon followed Hyperion and Chandos founded respectively by Ted Perry and Brian Couzens. Yet even here EMI with their encyclopaedic traversal of Elgar and Vaughan Williams, and Decca with Britten and his contemporaries, showed us the wonderful unique musical experiences to be found in this repertoire when played by top-line artists. The process continues with more recently founded labels such as the Dutton Epoch series for which I have been delighted to act as repertoire adviser.

Music by unfamiliar names would appear often, say, in mixed recitals of instrumental or organ music, and wanting to fill in their background a quick reference to Grove would draw a blank. I once had the idea of producing a reference work to be called 'Not in Grove' which would include interesting figures not thought apposite for that august reference book. It never came to fruition under that title, and yet here we have a worthy and very wide-ranging compilation fulfilling that very function. May I commend it to all my readers, and encourage listening and performance of this wonderful rich repertoire – maybe not always up there with the greats but often a worthwhile enterprise in their own right. Music lives in performance – Enjoy!

Profiles

ADAIR, Yvonne Madeleine
1897 – 1 Jan. 1991
By origin a Guernsey girl, Yvonne Adair studied at the Royal Academy of Music before specialising in rhythmic and aural training. She produced vocal works, pieces for piano, and for percussion groups, including many arrangements, some of which were published under the pseudonym of Ella Fairall. She also wrote several books on music.

ADAMS, Stephen
31 Jan. 1844 – 25 Aug. 1913

Michael Maybrick was born in Liverpool. He studied at Leipzig with Ignaz Moscheles, Carl Reinecke and Louis Plaidy and later in Milan with Gaetano Nava for singing. He appeared as a baritone singer in many prestigious London and provincial concerts. Under the pseudonym 'Stephen Adams' he composed a great number of songs, many gaining widespread popularity. *The Holy City*, *Thora*, *Nirvana*, *Nancy Lee* and *Star of Bethlehem* may still be familiar. Maybrick was at some time Mayor of Ryde in the Isle of Wight. He died in Buxton, Derbyshire, where he was staying, but is buried in Ryde.

ADAMS, Thomas Julian
28 Jan. 1824 – 10 May 1887
Adams introduced the harmonium into Britain and furthered its adoption by writing tutors for the instrument. He was born in London and studied with Moscheles and privately in Paris. In 1851 he founded his own orchestra, touring extensively with it. Having organised several other orchestras in the North of England (Scarborough, Tynemouth and Buxton), he eventually settled at Eastbourne in 1887 as conductor of the Devonshire Park Concerts. He remained in Eastbourne for the rest of his life. Adams composed fantasias, studies, marches and concert pieces for orchestra.

ADDINSELL, Richard Stewart
13 Jan. 1904 – 14 Nov. 1977
Addinsell was born in London and studied law at Hertford College, and music at the Royal College of Music, later continuing his musical studies in Berlin and Vienna. At the age of twenty-four he wrote music for Clemence Dane's play, *Coming of Age*. He became well-known as a composer of film scores (*Fire over England, Blithe Spirit, A Tale of two Cities, Love on the Dole, Goodbye Mr Chips, Waltz of the Toreadors* and many more) and incidental music to plays, much of it in collaboration with Clemence Dane. He worked for a time in Hollywood, and his *Warsaw Concerto*, an occasional but stirring Rachmaninovian piece (orch. Roy Douglas) written for the film *Dangerous Moonlight,* is still highly popular; it won him the Polish Cross of Merit.

Addinsell composed several works for piano and orchestra (notably *Festival* and *The Smokey Mountains* concertos), preludes for orchestra and light songs, some of the more successful being settings of words by Joyce Grenfell for her comedy revues. Much of his work was orchestrated by Roy Douglas. Addinsell died in Chelsea.

ADDISON, John Mervyn
16 Mar. 1920 – Dec. 1998

'Jock' Addison was born at West Chobham in Surrey and was a pupil at Wellington College. He studied piano, oboe and clarinet at the Royal College of Music, where he read composition with Gordon Jacob, war service interrupting his studies. He was a professor of composition at the RCM in 1951-58. Addison's music often had a light texture and his orchestral works – a Partita, Trumpet Concerto, Bassoon Concertino, Variations for Piano and Orchestra, a ballet (*Carte Blanche*), *Conversation Piece, Wellington Suite* for horns, piano, strings and percussion – usually demanded more chamber-like forces.

He wrote much chamber music, especially for brass and woodwind, choral miniatures, incidental music for the stage, and musicals. But Addison may best be remembered for over sixty film scores, which included *Private's Progress, Lucky Jim, The Entertainer, Tom Jones,* and *Reach for the Sky.* Addison died in the USA, where he had spent his latter years.

AGATE, Edward
1880 – 18 Oct. 1940

Born in Manchester, Edward Agate was well-known for his translations of opera libretti from a variety of languages (some 350 songs, thirty operas, and Rimsky-Korsakov's *Principles of Orchestration*). He was younger brother of James Agate, the drama critic. Agate composed sparingly but with originality. Among the songs and piano music his *Five Songs* (dedicated to Delius) and his *Three Interludes* for piano (premiered in 1940 by Franz Osborn) were performed as recently as 2001 to some appreciation. He is buried at the Unitarian Church in Monton Green, Manchester.

AGER, Laurence Mitchell
1904 – 17 Dec. 1989

Born at Polegate in Sussex, Laurence Ager studied at the Royal Academy of Music. He was an organist and choirmaster at several churches, directed other choirs, contributed articles to the Musical Times and Musical Opinion, and was a committee member of the Composers Guild of Great Britain. He composed about 120 part-songs, other songs, carols and church anthems, organ music, and piano pieces such as *A Book of Birthdays.*

AGUILAR, Emanuel Abraham
23 Aug. 1824 – 18 Feb. 1904

Of Spanish parentage, Aguilar was born in Clapham, London. He was a skilled pianist who gave many concert performances in London as well as in Germany. His compositions include three symphonies (the last of which was written in 1854), overtures, two operas – *Wave King* and *The Bridal Wreath* (the overture of which was performed in 1863), cantatas, chamber music, songs and a number of piano pieces. He also published *The ancient melodies of the liturgy of the Spanish and Portuguese Jews.*

AITKEN, George Benjamin Johnston
1868 – 11 May 1942
George Aitken was born in London, where he spent most of his life. He went to St Andrew's Choir School, later becoming a sub-organist there. After training at the Royal Academy of Music he was organist at St Mary's, Berkeley Square, then at Hampstead Parish Church. From 1904 he taught at the Guildhall School of Music. Aitken penned *Tobias Matthay and his Teaching* and some music criticism. He composed church services, anthems, songs, pieces for piano and for violin, and some organ works.

d'ALBERT, Charles Louis Napoleon
25 Feb. 1809 – 26 May 1886
Charles d'Albert's vast output of dance music – waltzes, polkas, quadrilles, and so on – acquired or him some not inconsiderable fame in his time. He was born at Nienstetten, Hamburg, and studied piano at the Paris Conservatoire before coming to England to study dancing at the King's Theatre, London. He became dancing master there before moving to Covent Garden, and eventually left to set up his own dancing school. Charles d'Albert settled in Liverpool, sired his more famous son Eugène in Glasgow, and died in London.

d'ALBERT, Eugène Francis Charles
10 Apr. 1864 – 3 Mar. 1932
Eugène d'Albert, whose father was of French Italian stock and whose mother was German, was born in Glasgow and studied at the National Training School for Music (later the Royal College of Music) with Ernst Pauer, Prout, Stainer and Sullivan. After a brief period with Liszt at Weimar, Eugen d'Albert (as he was professionally known) made his name as a concert pianist (he gave the premiere of his first Piano Concerto at the age of seventeen) and composer of operas, *Tiefland* being his most famous. In 1907 he succeeded Joachim as director of the Hochschule für Musik in Berlin.

As well as nineteen operas, d'Albert composed a symphony, two piano concertos, a cello concerto, several overtures and two string quartets. He died at Riga in Latvia while working on a further opera, *Mister Wu* (later completed by Leo Blech), having earned some claim to notoriety by having had six wives.

ALBERT, Prince Consort
26 Aug. 1819 – 14 Dec. 1861
Albert (Prince of Saxe-Coburg-Gotha) was unequalled in his time as a promoter of music. He improved the bands at Buckingham Palace and Windsor where many first performances of Mendelssohn, Bach and Wagner were given in this country. His name is honoured in the dedication of the Royal Albert Hall. Albert himself sang, played the organ, and composed an opera, anthems and church services, choruses, lieder, romances and canzonettes. He was born at Rosenau in Germany where he received his musical training, and married Queen Victoria in 1840. He died at Windsor Castle and his body lies in Frogmore Mausoleum.

ALCOCK, Walter Galpin
9 Dec. 1861 – 11 Sep. 1947
Organist at the Chapels Royal and assistant at Westminster Abbey, Alcock officiated at several coronations. He was born at Edenbridge in Kent and studied at the National Training School for Music with Sullivan, Stainer, J.F. Barnett and Eaton Faning. He was also organist at Salisbury Cathedral for a period and professor of organ at the Royal College of Music, being much in demand as a recitalist. He played at the coronations of Edward VII, George V and George VI. Alcock composed anthems and church services (notably a *Sanctus* for the 1911 Coronation), organ works and piano pieces. He was knighted in 1933 and died fourteen years later in Salisbury.

ALDRIDGE, Amanda Christina Elizabeth
16 Mar. 1866 – 5 Mar. 1956
Amanda Aldridge followed a successful career as a contralto singer with her brother, Ira Frederick, as accompanist. She composed under the name Montague Ring. She was born at Upper Norwood in London, her father, Ira, an African-American tragic actor and her mother the Swedish opera singer, Amanda von Brandt. After schooling in a Belgian convent Amanda won a scholarship to the Royal College of Music, where she studied singing with Jenny Lind and Georg Henschel, and harmony and counterpoint with Frederick Bridge and F.E. Gladstone. As an established performer she did much to help young, visiting African-American singers. Aldridge's music is populist, often using syncopated dance rhythms; her most famous is *Three African Dances* of 1913. She wrote several other dance suites for piano, often arranging them for other media. Many of her songs gained popularity and were often a splendid vehicle for African and African-American poets. She broadcast on radio and appeared on television into her 80s.

ALEXANDER, Arthur
25 Nov. 1891 – 1967
Arthur Alexander was born at Dunedin in New Zealand, but came to England to study at the Royal Academy of Music with Tobias Matthay and Frederick Corder, winning prizes and awards. In 1920 he became a professor of piano at the Royal College of Music and toured abroad as a piano recitalist and examiner, though his main interest lay in teaching. He married the composer Freda Swain, with whom he performed piano duets. In London he gave several first performances including Bax's second Piano Sonata and Scriabin's fifth. His own output was mainly for piano but also encompassed some chamber and orchestral works.

ALFORD, Kenneth Joseph
21 Feb. 1881 – 15 May 1945
Kenneth Alford was the professional name assumed by Frederick Joseph Ricketts, a Londoner by birth. He enlisted as a bandboy in the Royal Irish Regiment in 1895, playing cornet. After serving in India he studied at Kneller Hall and in 1908 became bandmaster of the Argyll and Sutherland Highlanders. Under his pseudonym he began to write military marches, many of which, such as *Colonel Bogey*, became very popular. It was written in response to an overheard whistled fragment and its theme was used to great effect by Malcolm Arnold in the music for the film *Bridge on the*

River Kwai. In 1927 he was appointed director of music to the Royal Marines. Alford also composed pieces for various instrumental groupings and some church music. He died in Reigate, having dedicated nearly fifty years of his life to military music.

ALLEN, George Benjamin
21 Apr. 1822 – 30 Nov. 1897
Born in London, George Allen was a chorister at Westminster Abbey and received a Mus.Bac. at Oxford. He originated and executed a scheme for building the Ulster Hall in Belfast and spent some time in Australia, dying in Brisbane. Allen established a comic opera company and produced some Gilbert and Sullivan operas. His compositions include operas, cantatas, church services, over 800 songs, part-songs and pieces for organ and for piano. Allen also wrote about the relationship between musical scales and colour.

ALLEN, Henry Robinson
1809 – 27 Nov. 1876
Henry Allen was born in Cork, Ireland. After settling in Notting Hill, London, he taught singing and achieved some fame as an operatic tenor and baritone. He composed *The Maid of Athens* and many other popular ballads.

ALLEN, Hugh Percy
23 Dec. 1869 – 20 Feb. 1946
Born in Reading, Hugh Allen went to Kendrick (now Reading) School and studied music with a local organist, Dr F.J. Read. On leaving school he was appointed assistant organist to Dr Read, who had by then moved to Chichester Cathedral. In 1892 he won an organ scholarship to Christ's College, Cambridge, following this with doctorates at both Cambridge and Oxford. Allen was organist at St Asaph Cathedral, Ely Cathedral, then New College Oxford, succeeding Parratt as Professor of Music at Oxford and Director of Music at the Royal College of Music (later also at Reading University). He played an important role in the English Musical Renaissance, championing British composers as a highly successful conductor of the London and Oxford Bach Choirs. Allen composed a few hymn tunes, a *Magnificat* and some organ voluntaries. He was knighted in 1920. He died three days after being knocked down by a motor bike.

ALLIN, Steuart
13 Apr. 1915 – 13 Dec. 2002
Steuart Allin worked in the Educational Music Department at J. & W. Chester before retiring in 1985. Though born in Brighton, his early years were spent in Leeds and Ipswich, where he studied with Stanley Wilson. A talented painter, Allin's work was exhibited. He was also a gifted poet and many of his poems were set to music by composers such as Ian Kendall, as well as by himself. He was a singer and performed several of his own songs. Allin composed chamber works, piano pieces and music for cello and piano. His best known works are *Celtic Legends* for piano and orchestra and *Psalm of Praise* for choir and orchestra. Allin died at Swanage.

ALLINGTON, Rex.   See **BESLY**, Maurice

ALLISON, Horton Claridge
25 Jul. 1846 – 1926
Allison, a London organist and a skilled pianist renowned for his memorising skills, studied at the Royal Academy of Music at at the Leipzig Conservatoire. He took both his Mus.B. (Cantab.) and Mus.Doc. (Durham) in 1877. He composed cantatas, a symphony (1875), two piano concertos, a suite for orchestra and an organ sonata.

ALLITSEN, Frances
30 Dec. 1848 – 30 Sep. 1912
Frances Allitsen was the pseudonym of Mary Frances Bumpus, born to a London bookdealer. After dabbling unsuccessfully with writing she overcame parental opposition and enrolled at the Guildhall School of Music, paying her way by giving music lessons. Some of her student compositions were well received there. Later many of her songs were to become very popular and were sung by such as Hayden Coffin and Clara Butt (both her jingoistic *There's a land, a dear land* and her reputation were given a boost by the Boer War when Dame Clara Butt adopted the song). Sacred songs like *The Lord is my life* and *Song of Thanksgiving* were equally popular. Allitsen composed an opera (*Bindra the Minstrel*), a dramatic cantata (*For the Queen* – first heard at the Crystal Palace in 1911), a 'scena' (*Cleopatra*, written for Dame Clara Butt), a *Suite de Ballet*, some other orchestral pieces that have not survived, a few piano pieces, and nearly 150 songs (*England, my England* and *The Lute Player* are still worthwhile). Mary Bumpus died in London.

ALLON, Henry Erskine
1864 – 13 Nov. 1897
Henry Erskine Allon was the son of Henry Allon, a Congregational minister who by his various publications and hymn-book editions, contributed greatly to the music of his church. The younger Henry Allon was born and died in London. He studied at Reading and at Trinity College, Cambridge with Frederick Corder. During his brief life he composed comic operas, cantatas, songs, and chamber and instrumental pieces.

ALWYN, William
7 Nov. 1905 – 11 Sep. 1985

A writer, poet, artist (and authority on the pre-Raphaelites), linguist and professional flautist, William Alwyn found time to compose five symphonies, four operas (including *Miss Julie* and *The Libertine*), two string quartets, three concerti grossi, a harp concerto, song cycles and instrumental works, all in a romantic though personal idiom. Alwyn was born in Northampton, where his father was a grocer. At the age of fifteen he entered the Royal Academy of Music as a flautist but soon found that, as far as composition was concerned, the climate was stiflingly 'academic'. As a result, Alwyn took up lessons with J.B. McEwen who opened up a new world for the young composer. At eighteen when his father died, Alwyn had to leave the RAM to earn a living. He played the flute in theatres, cinemas and symphony orchestras and composed a vast quantity of music including fourteen string quartets, a piano concerto and a massive oratorio. All these were later rejected as juvenilia in a cathartic reappraisal of his compositional techniques, as Alwyn only acknowledged those works written after 1939.

In 1926 McEwen replaced Sir Alexander Mackenzie as Principal of the RAM and Alwyn was appointed as professor of composition. In 1935 he wrote the film music for *The Future is in the Air*. This was the first of over sixty film scores (including *Odd Man Out*, *History of Mr Polly*, *The Fallen Idol*, *Desert Victory* and *The Way Ahead*) and, in acknowledgement of his contribution to the genre, he was made a Fellow of the British Film Academy in 1958. Alwyn was a founder-member of the Composers' Guild of Great Britain and was its chairman in 1949, 1950 and 1954. He was awarded the CBE in 1978. [See also Carwithen, Doreen].

AMERS, Henry Gellon
1877 – 10 Aug. 1936
Henry Amers studied with his father and grandfather, both professional musicians, and later had organ lessons with James M. Preston and in Germany. While still a boy, he performed solo for King Edward VII. Although he was born in Newcastle upon Tyne, Amers moved to Brighton, where he conducted concerts on the Palace Pier. In 1914 he enlisted in the Northumberland Hussars, served in France and rose to the rank of Captain before being wounded in action. Returning to Brighton, Amers was soon appointed conductor to the Municipal Orchestra in Eastbourne, where he stayed from 1920-30 (Eileen Joyce and Cyril Smith made their first appearances here with him). In 1923 he initiated an annual series of festivals, which continued until World War Two, and attracted conductors and performers such as Elgar, Bantock, Eric Coates, Beecham, Sargent, Holst, Ethel Smyth, Josef Holbrooke, Quilter and Grainger. Amers composed some light musical novelties or, rather, compilations, best known being *All on a Christmas Morning*, *The Wee MacGregor*, *A Highland Patrol* and *Bhoys of Tipperary*. (He should not be confused with Flt Lt John Henry Amers (1866-1946), who conducted for the RAF and the Metropolitan Police bands.)

AMES, John Carlowitz
8 Jan. 1860 – 21 Jul. 1924
Ames was born at Westbury-on-Trym, near Bristol, and was educated at Charterhouse and Edinburgh University. He studied music at Stuttgart with Immanuel Faisst then at Dresden under Franz Wüllner. Ames was a prominent member of various musical societies and performed as a concert pianist. He wrote an opera (*The Last Inca*), three comic operas, two piano concertos, a violin concerto and incidental, choral and chamber music.

ANCLIFFE, Charles
1880 – 20 Dec. 1952
Son of a bandmaster in Kildare, Ireland, Ancliffe studied at Kneller Hall, later becoming bandmaster to the South Wales Borderers in India, then to the Scarborough Military Band. Most of his musical works were for the medium of the military band: marches like *Ironsides*, *Castles in Spain* and *The Liberators* were hugely popular, as were his waltzes (*Nights of Gladness* became the signature tune for the eponymous BBC programme). He also wrote a great many other short works for the medium, and

some longer suites (*The Purple Vine*, *Below Bridges* and *Southern Impressions*). Many of his songs were also at one time popular, including the song cycle *Ask Daddy*.

ANDERSON, William Henry
21 Apr. 1882 – 12 Apr. 1955
W.H. Anderson was born in London and sang tenor in several London churches, and made a few operatic appearances before emigrating at the age of twenty-eight to Canada. His job as a draughtsman for Canadian National Railways seems to have left him time to compose over 150 songs and much church music. He also collected and arranged folk-songs. Some of his music appeared under the pseudonyms of Hugh Garland and Michael Bilenko.

ANDERSON, William Robert
7 Dec. 1891 – Jan. 1979
A composer of many anthems and part-songs, W.R. Anderson was born in Blackburn and died in Bournemouth. He had music lessons with a Cuthbert Whitemore, A.J. Osborne and Dr F.H. Wood and became organist and choirmaster successively in Accrington, Londonderry and Highgate. He taught music, edited the publication Music Teacher, and lectured at London University and for Trinity College of Music. He also wrote several books on composers and teaching, and was a radio and music critic.

ANDERTON, Howard Orsmond
20 Apr. 1861 – 1 Feb. 1934
Anderton was born at Clapham in London and studied at the Royal Academy of Music with G.A. Macfarren and Ebenezer Prout. He taught in London, Folkestone, and at the Midland Institute and was a choral conductor and adjudicator. In 1923 he became librarian at the London headquarters of the British Federation of Musical Competition Festivals. He composed an opera, various orchestral works (some with incidental music to plays by Euripides and Sophocles), piano quintets and other chamber works, songs and part-songs. Anderton worked for many years as Granville Bantock's personal secretary and in 1915 published a biography of Bantock.

ANDERTON, Thomas
15 Apr. 1836 – 18 Sep. 1903
Thomas Anderton was born and died in Birmingham – a man who spent all his life devoted to work in his home city. As well as conducting an orchestra in the city, he was part owner and editor of The Midland Counties Herald. He retired from the musical profession in 1874, although he continued to compose a few works. His cantata to Longfellow's words, *The Wreck of the Hesperus*, is still known, as are the songs *My love is so pretty* and *Come to my fairy home*. He wrote many more songs, glees and part-songs. His works also include a symphony, several overtures and piano pieces.

ANDREWS, Jenny
1817 – 29 Apr. 1878
Née Constant, Mrs John Holman Andrews taught singing and composed chamber music and songs, best known of which, and still sung occasionally, is *Prince Charley's Farewell to Scotland*. Jenny Andrews died in London.

ANDREWS, Richard Hoffman
22 Nov. 1803 – 8 Jun. 1891
Richard Andrews was a music publisher, violinist and an organist in Manchester, where he was born. Having started life as a child actor, at the age of nine he was apprenticed to the leader of the Manchester Theatre Band. As well as author of *Music as a Science* (1885), he edited and arranged a large number of works for piano. He also composed songs and glees, best known being *I'll lo'e thee, Annie*. And we'll probably never know who Annie was.

ANGEL, Alfred
1816 – 24 May 1876
Born in East Anglia, Alfred Angel composed church music, part-songs (*Arise my fair, and come away* was popular in his day) and organ works. He was a chorister and assistant organist at Wells Cathedral, then from 1842 a sub-chanter and organist at Exeter Cathedral until his death.

ANSELL, John
26 Mar. 1874 – 14 Dec. 1948
John Ansell was a successful composer of light orchestral music in the first half of this century. His music is now forgotten except for occasional performances of the Overture *Plymouth Hoe*. He studied at the Guildhall School of Music with MacCunn and played viola under Sullivan's baton before following a career as a theatre conductor in London, particularly at the Playhouse, where he wrote incidental music for all productions during his tenure. He spent a few years on the staff of the BBC and conducted the Queen's Hall Light Orchestra. In 1930 he was briefly assistant conductor of the new BBCSO. Ansell composed operettas (including *The King's Bride*, *Medora* and *Violette*), incidental music, dance suites and other orchestral works, usually characterised by a tuneful, easy, flowing style. He died at Marlow.

ANSON, Hugo Vernon
18 Oct. 1894 – 4 Aug. 1958
Though born at Wellington, New Zealand, Anson came to England at the age of eighteen to study at the Royal College of Music. After dabbling with economics, medicine and law he settled down to music in the 1920s and eventually became Director of Music at Alleyn's School, Dulwich, then joined the teaching staff of the RCM. Anson wrote texts on improvisation and composed a Concerto for Two Pianos and strings, a string quartet, incidental music, pieces for violin, for cello and for flute and piano, solo piano pieces, songs and part-songs and some church music.

ANTHONY, Evangeline
28 Nov. 1885 – 1913
Evangeline Anthony made her debut as a violinist with the London Symphony Orchestra in 1904. She was born in Hereford, daughter of the owner of the *Hereford Times*, and studied with the local violin maker, Donald Heins, then with August Wilhelm. She toured abroad, impressing audiences and critics but died in Germany at the age of twenty-seven after an operation for appendicitis. She is buried at Tupsley, Herefordshire. During her tragically short career she composed works for violin.

ApIVOR, Trevor Denis
14 Apr. 1916 – 27 May 2004

Not many consultant anaesthetists have become recognised composers (though dentistry can claim a few). Denis ApIvor studied medicine at Aberystwyth and at University College London, as his parents were unsympathetic to his own choice of a career in music. He was born in Collinstown, Eire, to Welsh parents who, five years later, moved to Caernarvon in Wales. He gained a boy choristership at Christ Church, Oxford, then at Hereford Cathedral, where his father was chaplain at the cathedral school, also studying clarinet, piano and organ. In his twenties he was encouraged by Cecil Gray to study music, and he took lessons with Patrick Hadley and Alan Rawsthorne. An early friendship with Constant Lambert plus encounters with the music of such disparate composers as Bernard van Dieren, Warlock, Delius, Berg and Webern influenced ApIvor's musical aesthetic and, by 1949 after he had spent some time in India in the army, and after the fatal illness of his first wife, he adopted serial techniques. Several Royal Ballet commissions resulted in *A Mirror for Witches* (1952) and *Blood Wedding* (1953). A Sadler's Wells opera commission, *Yerma*, was never staged, though the BBC broadcast an unstaged version. For his stage works, ApIvor was particularly drawn to the works of Lorca and Dylan Thomas, though his first major opus, *The Hollow Men*, was a setting of T.S. Eliot.

Denis ApIvor composed five symphonies, concertos for guitar, piano, violin, and for cello, an orchestral suite and an overture, string quartets, many other chamber and instrumental works, especially significant being his output for guitar. He also wrote several songs. His last work was the operatic scena *The Trixter* (2002), the libretto being from a poem by Peter Warlock. ApIvor died at Robertsbridge, Sussex.

APRIL, Elsie
14 Dec. 1884 – 16 Mar. 1950
Elsie April lived in Manchester and is believed to have had a career on the stage and as a musical assistant to Noel Coward. She composed some light orchestral works, including a suite, *The Village Green*, and several ballads, such as *Here Lies a Vagabond.*

ARCHER, Frederick
16 Jun. 1838 – 23 Oct. 1901
Frederick Archer was an organist at Merton College, Oxford, the city of his birth, and at Alexandra Palace, where he later became conductor. The latter part of his life was spent in the United States of America, in Brooklyn, then at New York. For three years he was conductor of the Pittsburgh Orchestra, in the city where he died. Archer composed a cantata (*King Whitlaff's Drinking Horn*), an overture *King Lear*, and piano pieces. He wrote several books on music and founded a magazine, The Keynote.

ARDLEY, Neil
26 May 1937 – 23 Feb. 2004
A consummate communicator, Neil Ardley wrote over a hundred books, many for children, on topics ranging through music, birds, flight, light, magnets, human

biology, computers, and a science encyclopaedia. He was born in Carshalton, Surrey, attending Wallington Grammar School before reading chemistry at Bristol. Ardley's career began in children's publishing before he turned to professional writing. Though a pupil of composition and arranging with Ray Premru and Bill Russo, he was largely self-taught as a composer, developing his skills in jazz orchestras such as the John Williams Big Band and the New Jazz Orchestra as a pianist, and occasionally saxophonist. His music, always approachable, blended through-compositional artistry with improvisation and he became a distinctive voice on the British jazz scene. His major works included a trilogy: *Greek Variations* (a suite for chamber jazz ensemble and soloists), *A Symphony of Amaranths,* and *Kaleidoscope of Rainbows.*

In the late 1980s Ardley, together with Ian Carr, John L. Walters and Warren Greveson, formed the electronic jazz orchestra, Zyklus. After joining a local choir he was inspired in 2001 to write a *Creation Mass*, a setting of poems by Patrick Huddle. Two years later the Bakewell Choral Society commissioned *Cantabile*, premiered in June 2004.

ARKWRIGHT, Marian Ursula
25 Jan. 1863 – 23 Mar. 1922
Born in Norwich, Marian Arkwright studied at Durham University and was instrumental in forming the Rural Music Schools Association in the early 1920s. Her brother Godfrey wrote extensively on early English music. Marian composed orchestral suites, notably *Winds of the World* (the winning entry in a competition set by 'The Gentlewoman'), a Requiem Mass, choruses, an operetta *The Water Babies*, songs and part-songs, and music for woodwind.

ARMES, Philip
15 Aug. 1836 – 10 Feb. 1908
Philip Armes was born in Norwich and was senior chorister at the cathedral before becoming a pupil of J.L. Hopkins in 1850. He sang 'Where the bee sucks' for Jenny Lind at the Bishop's Palace and was presented with the gift of a grand piano as a result of his solo work. He received his Mus.Doc. at Oxford in 1864 and was appointed organist at Chichester Cathedral for a year, then at Durham Cathedral, also accepting the chair of music at Durham University in 1897. He composed oratorios (*Hezekiah, St John the Evangelist, St Barnabas*), church anthems and services, madrigals and organ works. His hymn-tune, *Galilee*, is still widely used. Armes died in Durham.

ARMSTRONG, Thomas Henry Wait
16 Jun. 1898 – 26 Jun. 1994
Thomas Armstrong was born into music: his father was music master at King's School, Peterborough and conducted the Operatic Society, the Choral Union, and the Orchestral Society as well as being a church organist in Peterborough. Thomas's earliest training was in the Chapel Royal choir under Walter Alcock at St James's Palace. He entered King's School, Peterborough, and became assistant organist there. An organ scholarship at Keble College, Oxford, was interrupted by service with the British Expeditionary Force in France. After graduation Armstrong was appointed assistant organist at Manchester Cathedral, later returning to London, where he studied composition with Vaughan Williams at the Royal College of Music. From

1928 to 1933 he was organist at Exeter Cathedral and became a very active Director of Music at the University College of the South West.

Armstrong is best remembered, however, as organist at Christ Church, Oxford, where he taught many organ scholars who would later become well-known. At Oxford he conducted the Bach Choir. In 1944 Armstrong joined the new Faculty of Music at Oxford. Eleven years later he became Principal at the Royal Academy of Music, where his considerable energies were again apparent. He was given an Honorary Fellowship at Keble College, and in 1958 he was knighted for his services to music.

Thomas Armstrong composed church anthems (*Christ whose glory fills the skies*, *Creator Spirit* and *The Eternal Gifts of Christ* are the best known) and other choral works (especially *Never weather beaten sail*), and many songs and part-songs. He also wrote books on Mendelssohn's *Elijah* and Richard Strauss's tone poems.

ARNELL, Richard Anthony Sayer
15 Sep. 1917 – 10 Apr. 2009
'Tony' Arnell's music found early fame with the championship of Sir Thomas Beecham and a few other conductors, though his works were neglected after Beecham died and the BBC under Glock couldn't countenance British works that didn't bow towards atonality and serialism. In fact, Arnell was a pioneer, in particular of mixed media performances, as shown by his *Combat Zone* which involved a poet reading, a narrator, two singers, two electric guitars, a brass group, chorus, electronic tape and himself on piano. Later came *Nocturne, Prague 1968* followed by *I Think of All Soft Limbs* and *Astronaut I* for a science fiction festival in Sunderland. This last employed a rock group ('Sticky George'), a poet (Edwin Lucie Smith) reading his own work, a film, cello, horn, piano and electronic tape. All performers were to improvise at some points in the work.

Arnell, son of a builder, was born in Hampstead and attended University College School before being accepted at the Royal College of Music, where he studied with John Dykes Bower and John Ireland. At the outbreak of World War Two he was in the United States for the New York World Fair. He was advised to stay and became a musical consultant to the BBC's North American Service. His ballet *Punch and the Child,* three string quartets, *Ceremonial and Flourish* for brass (for a US visit by Sir Winston Churchill), the first three symphonies and other works were written in the US and it was there that his interest in mixed media was nurtured.

Returning to England, Arnell taught composition at Trinity College of Music, eventually becoming Principal Lecturer. His works were regularly performed and he received many commissions. For a time he lectured at the Royal Ballet School, having already written three ballets. He was also an influential composer of film scores, to the extent that he taught at the London School of Film Technique, then became Music Director at the London Film School. Not content with all this he pioneered jazz studies and electronic music at Trinity College, he edited 'Composer', the journal of the Composers' Guild of Great Britain, published a volume of poetry and married eight times, an achievement just beating that of his symphonic output (seven symphonies). Recently Arnell's work has found a new champion in Martin Yates, and at least six of the symphonies are recorded. But there is much other orchestral music waiting to be given an airing.

ARNOLD, George Benjamin
22 Dec. 1832 – 31 Jan. 1902
Born at Petworth, Sussex, Arnold studied with S.S. Wesley and obtained a Mus.Bac. degree at Oxford in 1855 (his doctorate followed in 1861). He was organist at St Columba's College, then St Mary's, Torquay, and New College, Oxford. In 1865 he succeeded Wesley at Winchester Cathedral, remaining there until his death. Arnold composed church music and some secular works. His cantata *Sennacherib* was performed at the Gloucester Festival in 1883.

ARNOLD, Malcolm Henry
21 Oct. 1921 – 23 Sep. 2006
Any brief profile of Malcolm Arnold and his music is doomed to failure. As a British composer who assimilated jazz and folk-dance, who wasn't afraid of a 'big tune', who incorporated three vacuum cleaners, a floor polisher and four rifles into his *Grand, Grand Overture* for a Gerard Hoffnung Festival, who shot himself in the foot to ensure a discharge from the army at the end of World War Two, and who was abandoned in the 1960s by the musical establishment and the BBC despite the popularity of his music, Arnold was never a man to be pigeon-holed. For all his sense of fun and his spurning of fashionable trends, he composed much deeply moving and technically accomplished music.

   Malcolm Arnold was born in Northampton. From the age of twelve, after hearing Louis Armstrong, he developed a passion for jazz and moved to London for trumpet lessons with Ernest Hall, principal trumpet of the BBCSO. In 1938 an open scholarship took him to the Royal College of Music, where he studied composition with Gordon Jacob and William Lloyd Webber. He left the RCM to join the London Philharmonic Orchestra, soon becoming principal trumpet. His experiences in orchestral playing resulted in his extraordinary talent for orchestration. In 1948 a Mendelssohn Scholarship took him to Italy for a year. As a conscientious objector Arnold joined the National Fire Service, but finally volunteered for military service and joined the Buff's band.

   Returning to civilian life and composition he won many important commissions and several prizes. In 1953 his ballet, *Homage to the Queen*, was performed at Covent Garden on the night of the coronation. Many successes followed, including more than eighty film scores (*Bridge on the River Kwai, Badger's Green, Whistle Down the Wind* and *Inn of the Sixth Happiness* among them). Arnold wrote nine symphonies; the last, the most tragic, was completed after his second divorce, a suicide attempt and a partial recovery from alcoholism. He had also been most unjustifiably passed over for the position of Master of the Queen's Musick in favour of Malcolm Williamson.

   In 1966 he moved to Cornwall, where he took an active part in the amateur musical life of the county, and in 1969 was made a bard of the Cornish Gorsedd. He then moved to Dublin, before settling in his home town of Northampton for his final years. During these most difficult times he was looked after by Anthony Day. Arnold was awarded a CBE in 1970 and was knighted in 1993, years too late.

   A prolific composer, Malcolm Arnold produced, in addition to the symphonies and film scores, orchestral overtures, divertimenti and dances, concertos for clarinet, flute and horn (two each), guitar, organ, trumpet, harmonica, oboe, two pianos, two violins, and viola. He wrote a great deal of chamber and instrumental music, works for brass band, a cantata *The Return of Odysseus*, three more ballets and an opera *The Dancing Master*.

ARNOLD, William.   See **SANDERSON**, Wilfrid

ARNOTT, Archibald Davidson
25 Feb. 1870 – 1910
Born in Glasgow, he moved to London at the age of ten. Having taken his Mus.Bac. (Durham) in 1891, he studied at the Royal College of Music with Parry and Stanford, and later with Frederick Corder. Works include *Young Lochinvar* for chorus and orchestra, *The Ballad of Carmilhan* (Longfellow) for baritone and orchestra, two operas, concert overtures, song cycles and chamber music.

ARUNDELL, Dennis Drew
22 Jul. 1898 – 10 Dec. 1988
Dennis Arundell may be better remembered as an actor rather than as a composer, especially for his role of Dr Morell on the radio; he played many parts on the stage, in films and on television. Born in Finchley, he went to Tonbridge School, then St John's, Cambridge. He produced operas for radio, TV and the theatre and translated over twenty operas into English. He also wrote a history of Sadler's Wells Opera. He wrote much incidental music, a couple of children's operas with A.P. Herbert, a TV opera (*Don Procipio*), and several songs.

ASCHER, Joseph
4 Jun. 1831 – 20 Jun. 1869
Joseph Ascher was born in London of German parentage. He studied under Moscheles and lived mostly in Paris. He was pianist to the Empress Eugénie and composed numerous piano works, arrangements and a few songs. *Alice, where art thou?* is still a well-known ballad. He died in London.

ASHFIELD, Robert James
28 Jul. 1911 – 30 Dec. 2006
An impressive and energetic organ recitalist, Robert Ashfield was organist at Southwell Cathedral from 1946, moving ten years later to Rochester Cathedral, where he could perform with some mischief when called for. He was born at Chipstead in Surrey and went to Tonbridge School, then the Royal College of Music, later gaining his FRCO. He conducted the Rochester Choral Society from 1956 onwards and was appointed professor of theory at the Royal College of Music in 1958. Ashfield was also Director of Music at London University. He composed a choral suite (*Cantiones Roffenses*), much church music, an organ sonata and other works for the instrument.

ASHTON, Algernon Bennett Langton
9 Dec. 1859 – 10 Apr. 1937
Born in Durham, Algernon Ashton claimed to be a descendant of Richard III. He was a compulsive and prolific writer of letters to the press, many regarding the disrepair of the graves of the famous. His father was principal tenor at Lincoln and Durham

cathedrals and his mother was a pianist. At the age of three, when his father died, he was taken to live in Leipzig, where he later studied with Heinig, Knorr and Raff, then with Reinecke, Jadassohn, Richter, Papperitz and Coccius at the Conservatory. By 1879 he had already reached his compositional half-century, though he was to dismiss these early works as immature. He returned to England in 1881 and four years later was appointed a professor of piano at the Royal College of Music. His many works, progressive  for their time, include four symphonies (all lost), piano and violin concertos, concert overtures, string quartets (twenty-four in all the major and minor keys), two quintets, three trios, sonatas for cello, violin and viola, a suite for two pianos, 248 piano pieces, other chamber and instrumental works, organ music, 220 songs, duets, some part-songs, and English and Irish dances. Ashton died in London.

ASPA, Edwin
6 May 1835 – 17 Aug. 1883
Aspa's cantatas, *Endymion* and *The Gipsies*, were well-known during his life, as was his operetta, *The Statue Bride*. He was born in London and was nephew of the Italian composer, Mario Aspa. He spent much of his life in Leamington Spa, where he was organist at St Peter's Church and conductor of the Leamington Choral Society. Aspa also composed church music and organ pieces. He died in Lincoln.

ASPULL, George
Jun. 1813 – 19 Aug. 1832
A native of Manchester, George Aspull was a renowned pianist who had played to Clementi at the age of nine and for King George IV at Windsor two years later. During his very brief life he composed many piano pieces, all of which were published posthumously. Aspull died at Leamington of pneumonia, said to have been contracted at Clementi's funeral. British Musical Biography (1897) says that 'he was everywhere hailed as a precocious genius of exceptional ability'.

ASTLE-ALLAM, Agnes Mary
b. 1857
Born in Reading, Agnes Astle-Allam became a well known singer who usually accompanied herself in performances ranging widely throughout England and Wales. She studied with Adolf von Holst (Gustav's father), F. Atkins, Dr Scott, Francis Pritchard, Mr Aylward and Dr Haydock. She composed songs and pieces for piano.

ATHERTON, Robert
9 Dec. 1916 – 1997
Father of the well known conductor David, Robert Atherton was born in Blackpool. He studied at Durham University and the Royal Academy of Music and in 1947 became conductor of the Blackpool Symphony Orchestra, a position he held for over fifty years. In 1956 he conducted the Burnley Municipal Choir – another long-standing appointment. He composed *Sine Nomine* (an orchestral overture), an *Intermezzo* for orchestra, string quartets, anthems and organ music.

ATKINS, Ivor Algernon
29 Nov. 1869 – 26 Nov. 1953

 Dedicatee of Elgar's *Pomp and Circumstance March No. 3*, Ivor Atkins was born in Cardiff. Son of an organist, Ivor studied with G.R. Sinclair before being appointed assistant organist at Truro, then Hereford cathedrals. After a stint at Ludlow Parish Church he rose to the organ loft at Worcester Cathedral and conducted regularly at the Three Choirs festivals. Responsible largely for reviving these festivals after World War One, he was awarded a knighthood in 1921. Atkins' cantata, *Hymn of Faith* of 1903 received many performances. He also wrote a *Magnificat and Nunc dimittis*, part-songs, church anthems and several songs. Atkins died in Worcester.

AUSTIN, Ernest
3 Dec. 1874 – 24 Jul. 1947

Brother of Frederic Austin (see below), Ernest was born and lived all his life in London, though he died at Wallington in Surrey. He started a career as a businessman and was largely self-taught as a musician, though he took some lessons with F.W. Davenport. His most popular composition was *Pilgrim's Progress* for organ, but he also wrote a symphony, *Variations on The Vicar of Bray* for strings, chamber music (including five piano trios), and choral music, piano pieces, many songs and some works for children. His *Stella Mary Dances*, an orchestral suite, was premiered at the Proms in 1918. Ernest Austin also wrote *The Story of the Art of Music Printing*.

AUSTIN, Frederic
30 Mar. 1872 – 10 Apr. 1952

Frederic Austin was born in London and lived there, as did his brother Ernest, all his life. He studied music with his mother and with his uncle Dr W.H. Hunt, later taking singing lessons with Charles Lunn. He followed a varied career as an organist in Birkenhead and Liverpool, a highly regarded baritone singer (especially as an interpreter of Wagner), artistic director of the British National Opera Company, arranger and composer. He was also a professor of singing at the Royal Academy of Music. It was his arrangement of *The Beggar's Opera* in 1920 that ran for over 1,400 performances at the Lyric in Hammersmith. His own works include a Symphony in E, incidental music, orchestral overtures and other works, church music, chamber, piano and other instrumental pieces, and many songs. Austin had a broad knowledge of contemporary music and he was not afraid to experiment. In his rhythmically exuberant *Rhapsody: Spring* he interposes $\frac{3}{2}$ and $\frac{7}{4}$ time into a basically $\frac{6}{8} - \frac{9}{8}$ rhythm, later asking the violins to play in $\frac{18}{8}$ against $\frac{6}{4}$ in the rest of the orchestra. A great deal of Frederic Austin's time and energy was spent encouraging and helping other musicians and musical organisations.

AYLWARD, Florence
10 Mar. 1862 – 14 Oct. 1950

Florence Aylward wrote many popular ballads, best known of which are *Beloved, it is morn* and *Love's Coronation*. Her first song, *Daydawn*, was composed in 1888. She was born at Brede in Sussex and died in St Leonards on Sea.

Bache, Francis Edward
14 Sep. 1833 – 6 Nov. 1858

F.E. Bache was born in Birmingham, where he died at the age of twenty-four. As a thirteen-year-old pupil of Alfred Mellon, the conductor at the Birmingham Theatre Royal, he played violin there for the Birmingham Festival performance of Mendelssohn's *Elijah* in 1846. During his brief life Bache was a prolific composer and an accomplished pianist, and his music was held in high regard by his teachers Plaidy, Hauptmann and Schneider on the continent, and Sterndale Bennett in England. His compositions include a piano concerto and other orchestral works, two operas (*Rübezahl* and *Which is Which*), songs, piano and instrumental pieces.

BACHE, Walter
19 Jun. 1842 – 26 Mar. 1888

A younger brother of Francis Edward (see above), Walter Bache was an enthusiastic and renowned exponent of Liszt's piano music. Bache studied organ with James Simpson in Birmingham, then with Plaidy, Moscheles, Hauptmann, Reinecke and Richter in Leipzig. In Rome he had lessons with Liszt. Back in London Bache achieved distinction as a pianist and taught at the Royal Academy of Music, where he founded the Liszt Scholarship. He composed a variety of works for the piano. Bache was born in Birmingham and died in London.

BAGA, Ena Rostra
1906 – 15 Jul. 2004

One of four musical sisters, whose father was leader of a cinema orchestra, London-born Ena Baga excelled at the Hammond and the great Wurlitzer. Privately educated, she became an accomplished accompanist for silent films, playing piano and organ at several of London's celebrated film and stage venues, such as the New Gallery and the Tivoli in the West End. She entertained at Lyon's Corner Houses in the 1930s and stood in for Reginald Dixon at Blackpool's Tower Ballroom, while the incumbent was away during the war. She toured South Africa and featured in command performances in Britain. Baga composed several works for organ, including her own signature tune, *Bagatelle*. She broadcast regularly and made many recordings. She spent her later life in London and died there.

BAINES, Francis Athelstan
11 Apr. 1917 – 4 Apr. 1999

Francis Baines demonstrated extraordinary musical versatility, playing double bass in London orchestras, and hurdy-gurdy – *not* in London orchestras. A specialist in early instruments, he directed many performances in the genre, leading the Jaye Consort of Viols. Born in Oxford, Baines studied at the Royal College of Music, later becoming a professor there. His compositions include two symphonies, a violin concerto, string quartet, oboe quartet, a concertino for trumpet, *Grounds* for unaccompanied double bass, sonata for viola, other works for trumpet and some for trombone. His sense of humour is testified to by his contributions to the Gerard Hoffnung concerts, a Fanfare and *Rigmarole* for six trumpets, six trombones and four percussionists. Francis Baines died in County Cork, Ireland.

BAINES, William
26 Mar. 1899 – 6 Nov. 1922

William Baines, born at Horbury in Yorkshire, died in York at the age of twenty-three. He came from a musical but poor family and his musical education was limited to an occasional lesson with a Mr Albert Jowett of Leeds. Baines was never a robust child and a bout of pneumonia following the commencement of his army training at the age of nineteen left him weaker still, though he was accompanying silent films on the piano when he was thirteen. He took a lively interest in literature and in the music of Ravel, Debussy and Scriabin, and his own music was influenced particularly by that of Scriabin.

Baines worked long hours at his composition, even towards the end of his life when he was suffering from tuberculosis (Eaglefield-Hull's claim that William was confined to the garden shed at this time is incorrect, and was probably the result of a recommendation that his brother Teddy be so confined. Teddy died within eight months of William's death). Most of Baines's works remain unpublished though several piano pieces were accepted by the publishing firm of Elkin. In addition to the piano pieces Baines wrote a symphony and some shorter orchestral pieces, a string quartet and many other chamber and instrumental pieces. His compositions show a competence and originality rare in such a young composer. Of his 216 works, now all in the British Museum, there are many that merit a rehearing.

BAINTON, Edgar Leslie
14 Feb. 1880 – 8 Dec. 1956
Bainton was born in London and studied at the RCM with Walford Davies, Stanford and Charles Wood. In 1912 he became Principal of the Conservatory of Music at Newcastle upon Tyne and worked there as a teacher and pianist. He was interned in Germany for the duration of World War One at Rühleben camp near Berlin, where he composed his *Three Pieces for Orchestra* and a string quartet. Edgar Bainton's music has been well represented at music festivals and includes two symphonies and a choral symphony (*Before Sunrise*), a Concerto-Fantasia for piano and orchestra, two operas (*Oithona* after Ossian, and *The Pearl Tree*, and a one-acter, *The Crier by Midnight*); several works for chorus/soloists and orchestra, piano and instrumental pieces and songs. In 1933 Bainton settled in Australia, and became director of the NSW State Conservatorium of Music at Sydney, where he died while swimming in the sea.

BAIRSTOW, Edward Cuthbert
22 Aug. 1874 – 1 Apr. 1946
Edward Bairstow, born in Huddersfield, was an organ pupil of Frederick Bridge at Westminster Abbey, and later held posts as organist at Wigan, Leeds and York Minster. He conducted the Leeds Philharmonic Society, York Musical Society and

Bradford Festival Chorus Society, and in 1929 became Professor of Music at Durham University. Bairstow composed songs, part-songs, anthems (notably *Blessed city, heavenly Salem* and *Let all mortal flesh keep silence*) and organ pieces. The liturgical *Lamentations* are surprisingly adventurous. Several of his hymn-tunes are still used and copies of his texts, *Counterpoint and Harmony* and *The Evolution of Musical Form* may still be found. In 1932 Bairstow received a knighthood. He died in York.

BALFE, Michael William
15 May 1808 – 20 Oct. 1870

Michael Balfe, who learned the violin and piano with his father, began composing when he was only ten years old. He had already made his debut as a violinist two years earlier. After the death of his father in 1824 he moved to London from his home city of Dublin to make his own career as a musician. Attempts at operatic singing were a failure through nervousness, and Balfe found a position in the orchestra of Drury Lane Theatre, at the same time taking lessons in composition with K.F. Horn, organist of St George's Chapel, Windsor. In 1825 Balfe's work so impressed Count Mazzara (it is said that Balfe also bore a striking facial resemblance to the Count's dead son) that he became a generous patron of the musician. The Count took Balfe to Italy to study composition with Paer and Frederici and singing with Galli; and within a year his first ballet, *La Pérouse*, was performed in Milan. On the way through Paris he was introduced to Cherubini and Rossini, on both of whom he made a lasting impression. The latter engaged him as a baritone. After a first appearance in *Figaro* which gained him considerable success as a singer, he gave this up this occupation in 1835 in order to compose opera. His first, *The Siege of Rochelle*, played successfully for three months and established his fame.

Balfe spent six years as conductor at Her Majesty's Theatre in London until it closed, when he moved to St Petersburg, becoming quite a celebrity. He amassed a great fortune and in 1864 he bought Rowney Abbey in Hertfordshire, where he retired to practise farming, and where he eventually died. Balfe married the Hungarian singer Lina Rosa. He composed nine operas (as well as *The Siege of Rochelle, The Maid of Artois, Joan of Arc, Falstaff, The Bohemian Girl* and *The Rose of Castille* all achieved popularity, the cosmopolitan nature of the operas reflecting Balfe's familiarity with English, French and Italian literature), a ballet, cantatas, ballads, some works for orchestra, a piano trio and a cello sonata. A tablet in Westminster Abbey is dedicated to Balfe, though he is buried at Kensal Green Cemetery, London.

BALL, Eric Walter John
31 Oct. 1903 – 1 Oct. 1989

Eric Ball may have been one of the most influential figures in the brass band movement, contributing a great deal also to choral music. He was born in Kingswood, Gloucestershire, and grew up into a Salvation Army background, one which presumably led him towards brass band and choral music. He became editor of the *British Bandsman* journal and was highly influential in the brass band movement, as well as devoting a lifetime to the Salvation Army and his Christian faith.

He conducted in and composed test pieces for the Open Brass Band Championships, and wrote many more pieces for the medium: marches, overtures, suites, and three rhapsodies on negro spirituals. Ball also made many arrangements for brass band, including Arthur Bliss's *Checkmate Suite* and Elgar's *Enigma* Variations. He died in Bournemouth.

BALY, William
28 Jun. 1825 – 4 Jun. 1891
Baly was born at Warwick and studied at the Royal Academy of Music with Sterndale Bennett and Cipriani Potter, where he was elected FRAM. He taught at Harley Street College for Ladies, later moving to Exeter, where he was professor at the university and conductor of the Exeter Orchestral Society and Madrigal Society. Baly composed a symphony, overtures, a string quartet, piano pieces and part-songs.

BANISTER, Henry Charles
13 Jun. 1831 – 20 Nov. 1897
Born in London, Banister studied at the Royal Academy of Music with Cipriani Potter, later becoming a professor of harmony and composition there in 1853. In 1880 he was appointed a Professor at the Guildhall School of Music and taught also at the Royal Normal College for the Blind. His many compositions include four symphonies, a fantasy for piano and orchestra, concert overtures, chamber music, cantatas, songs and piano pieces. He also lectured and wrote music texts, *Musical Art and Study* and *The Harmonising of Melodies*. Banister died in Streatham.

BANKS, Don
25 Oct. 1923 – 5 Sep. 1980
Born in Melbourne, Australia, Don Banks followed in his father's footsteps as a jazz musician until he came to England in 1949, where he spent the rest of his professional life as Director of Music at the University of London and at Goldsmith's College. Banks studied composition with Mátyás Seiber and Luigi Dallapiccola, but his admiration for the serial techniques of Milton Babbitt considerably influenced his work. He consistently strove for an original tonal palette and was a master of orchestration and light music arrangement. Banks also did much to introduce and disseminate the techniques of electronic music composition in this country, and was active as a composer of 'third-stream' music (classical/jazz hybridisation). His works include a violin concerto, horn concerto and other orchestral pieces, much chamber music, works for electronic tape and orchestra, piano music, songs and part-songs, and incidental music to films and TV. Don Banks died in Sydney.

BANTOCK, Granville
7 Aug. 1868 – 11 Oct. 1946
Granville Bantock was born in London, where he studied at the Royal Academy of Music with Frederick Corder, and where he won the Macfarren Scholarship. He founded the New Brighton Choral Society (Merseyside) and toured the world extensively as a conductor of musical comedies before settling down as Principal at the Midland School of Music in Birmingham and Professor at the University. His next appointment was as Chairman of the Corporation of Trinity College.

Bantock was a modest, selfless man, who encouraged and supported many younger British composers. His own musical output was vast and was held in very high regard by his contemporaries. His most remarkable works are probably the massive choral and orchestral work *Omar Khayyam* and the orchestral tone-poems, among which may be counted the *Pagan* and *Hebridean* Symphonies. He also wrote the *Celtic* symphony, suites and other orchestral pieces, three operas (*Caedmar*, *Pearl of Iran* and *The Seal Woman*), piano and chamber music, songs and church anthems, and several pieces for brass band. Literature was one of Bantock's great loves and he was conversant with many aspects of eastern cultures, a predilection reflected by his settings for his songs and choral works. His wife, the poetess Helena Von Schweitzer, also provided material for his songs. Bantock was knighted in 1930. He died two weeks before a long-awaited performance of his *Hebridean* symphony. Bantock's ashes were scattered on Moelwyn Mawr, Wales.

BARBIROLLI, John
2 Dec 1899 – 29 Aug. 1970
As a conductor and arranger, Sir John Barbirolli needs no introduction, but he also composed a few works, notably an Oboe Concerto based on themes by Pergolesi, and an *Elizabethan Suite* for strings and voices. Barbirolli was born in London. He studied piano and cello at Trinity College and at the Royal Academy of Music. As a cellist he won high acclaim as a soloist (making his first appearance at the age of eleven) and chamber musician. His debut as a conductor was with the British National Opera in 1925, and he was soon working with the London Symphony Orchestra. He succeeded Toscanini as conductor of the New York Philharmonic, then returned to England in 1943 to rejuvenate the Hallé Orchestra. It was in this role that his fame was assured, and he was still at the rostrum in 1970, just before he died in the Middlesex Hospital. During his lifetime Barbirolli conducted orchestras all over the world to win lavish praise and a great many honours. He was knighted in 1949.

BARCLAY, Arthur
16 Dec. 1869 – 12 Oct. 1943
Arthur Barclay Jones (he later dropped the patronymic) was born in London. For many years director of music at Brompton Oratory, Barclay composed a Symphony in C minor, orchestral overtures, choral and church music, organ pieces and works for solo piano. He was born in London and studied at the Guildhall School of Music with Thomas Wingham. For a time he was himself professor at the GSM, teaching piano. He died at Purley in Surrey.

BARKER, George Arthur
15 Apr. 1812 – 2 Mar. 1876
George Barker was well known as an operatic tenor and recitalist. He was also a prolific composer of ballads and songs, most popular of which were *The Irish Emigrant* and *Exelsior*. He also wrote many waltzes and other piano pieces. Barker was born in London and died in Aylstone, Leicestershire.

BARLOW, David
20 May 1927 – 9 Jun. 1975
David Barlow, Senior Lecturer in Music at the University of Newcastle upon Tyne, was born at Rothwell in Northamptonshire, and was a pupil at Kettering Grammar School. He studied at Emmanuel College, Cambridge, at the Royal College of Music with Gordon Jacob, and privately with Nadia Boulanger. At the RCM he won the Cobbett Chamber Music Prize. Barlow's early music showed the romantic influences of Ireland, Bax and Vaughan Williams, but in his later works he adopted a brand of serialism. His compositions include two symphonies, two operas: *David and Bathsheba* and *The Selfish Giant* (the latter written for schoolchildren), works for orchestra and for chamber orchestra (including the beautiful and contemplative *Variations* for cello and orchestra), a string quartet, trio and quintet, pieces for organ and for piano, and songs.

BARNARD, Charlotte Alington
23 Dec. 1820 – 30 Jan. 1869
'Claribel', as Charlotte Barnard thought of herself, was perhaps the most popular and successful song and ballad composer of the 1860s. Born in Louth, Lincolnshire, Charlotte Pye was a solicitor's daughter. This may have given her the gateway to financial success but was ruinous to her early love life. She was sent away on a European tour to escape the clutches of a suitor, wedding a clergyman on her return. Her early music lessons seem to have been from local musicians, but she nevertheless made several hits as a songwriter (a ballad, *Janet's Choice*, ran to several editions) before further classes with Althaus and W.H. Holmes. Consequently her songs were adopted by singers like Charlotte Sainton-Dolby, Parepa-Rosa and Sims Reeves. *Come back to Erin*, *Golden days* and *Five o'clock in the morning* will be remembered. More ballads and some sacred music followed, with a few piano pieces. In 1868 Claribel's father went bankrupt and the Barnards, financially afflicted, fled to Belgium, where she wrote a few French songs. She returned to England a year later and died in Dover.

BARNBY, Joseph
12 Aug. 1838 – 28 Jan. 1896
Sir Joseph Barnby is mostly remembered for his hymn tunes, 256 altogether, and for his songs, of which *Sweet and Low* achieved a perennial popularity. He also composed anthems and services, an oratorio *Rebekah* and part-songs. He was born in York and studied at Eton, then at the RAM with Cipriani Potter. He was appointed an adviser to the publisher Novello, which in 1867 set him up with his own choir. In 1871 he gave the first complete church performance in England of Bach's *St Matthew Passion*, and two years later the *St*  *John Passion*. Barnby was organist at various London churches, then became Director of Music at Eton College and Principal of the Guildhall School of Music in 1892. In 1871 he was appointed conductor of the Albert Hall Royal Choral Society and his five years' service was so appreciated by the choir that they commissioned a bronze bust of him for the Royal Albert Hall. Barnby was knighted in 1892. His work brought about a resurgence of many of the sacred masterpieces of the eighteenth century after years of neglect. He died suddenly at the age of fifty-seven in London.

BARNES, Frederick Edwin Lucy
1858 – 21 Sep. 1880
Frederick Barnes spent the last part of his short life in New York and Montreal, where he died. He was born in London and studied at the Royal Academy of Music and at the Chapel Royal under Rev. Thomas Helmore. Barnes composed an opera, operetta, a setting of the *23rd Psalm* for voices and orchestra, songs and pieces for piano and for organ.

BARNETT, John
15 Jul. 1802 – 17 Apr. 1890
Born in Bedford of German-Hungarian extraction and second cousin of Meyerbeer, John Barnett displayed considerable musical ability at an early age. In 1813 he became a singer (alto) at the Lyceum, receiving lessons in return for his services. He began composing while still a boy and continued his musical education with piano and harmony lessons, the latter with Ferdinand Ries, who had been a friend of Beethoven.

Barnett wrote a musical farce, *Before Breakfast*, in 1825 and the success of this work dictated his future career as a writer of popular musicals, ballads and operas. His best known work, *The Mountain Sylph*, was regarded as the best opera since Arne and it established the English dramatic school. He toured France and Germany (where he married) in 1837 and wrote a symphony and two string quartets. On his return to England in 1838 he opened the St James's Theatre, intending to found an English Opera House, but the project failed. In 1841 Barnett moved to Cheltenham where he taught singing and wrote treatises on music. His output of songs numbered over 2,000, though he rejected many as 'pot boilers'. He died at Leckhampton near Cheltenham.

BARNETT, John Francis
18 Oct. 1837 – 24 Nov. 1916
J.F. Barnett was the son of the famous tenor and singing teacher, Joseph Barnett, and nephew of the composer John Barnett (see above). He was born in Kentish Town in London and received his initial musical education from his mother before studying with Dr Henry Wylde. In 1850 he won a King's Scholarship at the Royal Academy of Music and pursued a successful career as a concert pianist, spending some time at Leipzig Conservatorium under Reitz, Hauptmann, Plaidy and Moscheles, and playing at the Philharmonic Society's concerts. A Fellow of the RAM and later a professor at the Royal College of Music and Guildhall School of Music, Barnett composed a symphony (1864), piano concerto, other orchestral works, two oratorios, chamber music, flute sonatas and solos, piano solos and songs. His most successful work was the cantata *The Ancient Mariner*, first performed at the Birmingham Festival of 1867. Esteemed in his time, his compositions in all genres were regarded as a model of craftsmanship. J.F. Barnett died in London.

BARNS, Ethel
5 Dec. 1874 – 31 Dec. 1948
Ethel Barns was born in London and studied with Herr Kummer at the School of Music in Watford. She was advised by Joachim to go to Berlin but, at her parents' insistence, she went to the Royal Academy of Music in 1887 for lessons with Prosper

Sainton, Emile Sauret, F. Westlake and, for harmony and composition, Ebenezer Prout. She received several awards and was appointed a sub-professor at the RAM. She made her debut as a violinist at the Crystal Palace in 1899, though she had appeared on the concert platform as a pianist seven years earlier. She played violin at all leading London and many provincial concert halls.

With her husband, the baritone Charles Phillips, she founded the Barns-Phillips Chamber Concerts. Her compositions include a *Concertstück* for violin and orchestra, a *Fantasie Trio* for two violins and piano, five violin sonatas, two trios, works solo violin and for piano (noteworthy is a dramatic *Cri du Coeur*), and songs. Her *Humoreske* for piano has been said to rival that of Dvořák. Barns died at Maidenhead in Berkshire.

BARRY, Charles Ainslee
10 Jun. 1830 – 1915
Born in London, Barry was educated at Rugby and studied theology at Cambridge University. After a brief period of musical study in Germany, he returned to London to take a position as organist and choirmaster at Forest School, Leytonstone. His many writings on music included programme notes for various London concerts. Influenced by the style of Wagner's music, his works include a symphony, two overtures and marches (which were given trial performances at the Musical Society of London), a cantata, chamber music, piano works (including transcriptions) and songs. From 1881-94 he lived in Lewisham.

BARSOTTI, Roger
17 Sep. 1901 – 1 Jan. 1980
Of Anglo-Italian parentage and born in London, Roger Barsotti's early musical career began in military bands and as a flautist with the Hastings Municipal Orchestra. As a young man he enlisted in 'The Buffs' and studied at Kneller Hall. He was bandmaster of various regimental bands until the end of World War Two. From 1946 to 1968 he was Musical Director of the Metropolitan Police Band. Over a hundred of his works were published, mostly for brass band, military band and orchestra and comprising suites, dances, marches, and some instrumental solos. His best known work was the *Neapolitan Suite*.

BART, Lionel
1 Aug. 1930 – 3 Apr. 1999
Lionel Bart, a Londoner from beginning to end, won nine Ivor Novello awards for his many successes as a writer of musicals. This recalcitrant Eastender, expelled from school and loath to take music lessons seriously, was born Lionel Begleiter, youngest of a large Jewish family that had escaped the pogroms in Galicia. As a youngster he played skiffle in various groups, including 'The Cavemen'. He did his national service in the RAF, then set up in printing. He joined the Communist Party and wrote lyrics and music for several left-wing productions. His success as a songwriter began with the comedy songs he wrote for Billy Cotton, and he followed these with numbers

for pop stars such as Tommy Steele and Cliff Richard. He composed a film score for *The Tommy Steele Story* and a TV score for *Dr Jekyll and Mr Hyde*, but his crowning successes were the musicals: *Wally Pone, King of the Underworld, Fings ain't what they used t'be, Lock up your Daughters, Blitz!, Maggie May, Twang!, La Strada*, and *Oliver!* The last ran for 2,618 performances in London and 774 on Broadway. Bart's song *From Russia with Love* will strike a nostalgic chord with all Bond fans.

BARTHOLOMEW, Ann Mounsey. See **MOUNSEY**, Ann

BATE, Stanley Richard
12 Dec. 1911 – 19 Oct. 1959
Plymouth-born Stanley Bate studied locally with Harold C. Lake for composition and with Douglas Durston for piano. A local philanthropist paid for some lessons with Felix Swinstead in London. Bate began his career as a pianist, but later turned to composition, winning a scholarship at the Royal College of Music to study with Vaughan Williams (composition), R.O. Morris (counterpoint), Gordon Jacob (orchestration) and Arthur Benjamin (piano). He also studied privately with Nadia Boulanger in Paris and with Hindemith in Berlin, having won a travelling scholarship.

Bate composed four symphonies (Glanville-Hicks claims he penned a dozen), two operas, several ballets, five piano concertos, other concertos for harpsichord, viola and cello, three violin concertos, incidental and film music, chamber music, songs and many piano works. He became associated with the London stage, for which he wrote much of his incidental music, and had some success as a painter. Though neglected in Britain, Bate's music has been successful in the USA and Australia.

He was, in fact, married to the Australian composer, Peggy Glanville-Hicks, whom he'd met at the RCM. After a divorce, he re-married some years later. He travelled widely in the USA, South America and Europe, performing much of his own music to some acclaim. Stanley Bate died in London, after which his music was largely forgotten.

BATH, Hubert
6 Nov. 1883 – 24 Apr. 1945
Hubert Bath was born at Barnstaple in Devon, where his first musical experiences were in the church choir. He studied piano with Oscar Beringer and composition with Frederick Corder at the Royal Academy of Music. Among his fellow students were Arnold Bax and York Bowen, Myra Hess and Harriet Cohen. While still at the RAM his setting of Longfellow's *Spanish Student* won him the Goring-Thomas Scholarship.

As Music Adviser to London County Council, and a successful operatic conductor, Bath became known as a composer chiefly for his stage works (*Bubbole, Young England, The Three Strangers, The Sire de Maletroit's Door, Trilby*, etc.) and for his film music, working for Gaumont-British and MGM. His *Cornish Rhapsody* from the film *Love Story*, starring Margaret Lockwood and Stewart Granger, is still very popular. Bath also wrote symphonic poems, orchestral variations, a *Freedom* Symphony for brass band, cantatas, chamber music, choral works (*The Wedding of Shon Maclean* being the most successful), several marches and over 200 songs. He became an authority on 'barbaric music'. Hubert Bath died at Harefield in Middlesex.

BAX, Arnold Edward Trevor
8 Nov. 1883 – 3 Oct. 1953

Arnold Bax was born at Streatham in London and studied at the Hampstead Conservatory, then at the Royal Academy of Music with Tobias Matthay and Frederick Corder. A self-confessed romantic with a penchant for anything Celtic, he spent much of his life in the west of Ireland and wrote three volumes of Irish stories under the pseudonym Dermot O'Byrne, though he had no Irish ancestry. After a brief liaison with a Russian girl and a failed marriage, Bax maintained a close relationship with pianist Harriet Cohen.

He composed seven fine symphonies, a violin concerto, many other orchestral works, five string quartets (two of them unnumbered) and other works, four ballets, film music (*Oliver Twist* and *Malta G.C.*), a great many pieces for various instruments with piano, much solo piano music, and songs. He rejected many of his early orchestral works. Recognition of his services to music was marked by a knighthood in 1937 and appointment as Master of the King's Musick in 1942. Bax's autobiography 'Farewell my Youth' provides valuable and entertaining reading. He died while on holiday in County Cork, Ireland.

BAYNES, Sydney
1 Feb. 1879 – 3 Mar. 1938

Born in London, Baynes began his career as an accompanist for singers: Edward Lloyd, Ben Davies and others. He was also an organist at various London churches. He worked for the BBC for many years as an arranger and became well known as a theatre conductor, appearing at the Theatre Royal, Adelphi, and Drury Lane. From 1928-38 he broadcast regularly with his own orchestra. Baynes's best known work is his *Destiny Waltz*, one of his many waltzes ending in the letter 'y'. He also wrote a *Miniature Ballet Suite*, an overture *Endure to Conquer*, marches, many songs, piano works and church music. His arrangements and original writings display an inordinate fondness for the saxophone.

BEAZLEY, James Charles
1850 – 27 Jun. 1929

Born in Ryde, Isle of Wight, Beazley studied composition with Sterndale Bennett. After a brief appointment at the King's School, Sherborne, he returned to Ryde through ill health. He composed the cantatas *Drusilla* and *Josiah*, piano pieces and works for violin and flute. He continued to teach in Ryde until his death there.

BECHER, Alfred Julius
27 Apr. 1803 – 23 Nov. 1848

Becher was born in Manchester to German parents, and studied in Heidelberg, Gottingen and Berlin. He edited the *Radikale*, issued in Vienna, and was a music critic. He also composed a symphony, string quartets, other chamber works, piano pieces, a *Fantasie* for cello and piano and some songs. In 1846 he published a monograph on the singer Jenny Lind. Webern was killed by three shots from a GI's rifle, one of the accidents of war. Becher's death was a little more calculated. After publishing a revolutionary paper in 1848 in Vienna he was arrested, tried for treason, found guilty and condemned to die by firing squad.

BEDFORD, Herbert
23 Jan. 1867 – 13 Mar. 1945
Herbert Bedford was born and died in London and received his musical training at the Guildhall School of Music. He lectured, painted miniatures and in 1894 married the composer Liza Lehmann. The first English composer to be awarded the Brahms Medal, Bedford wrote operas (*Kit Marlowe* is best known), a ballet, works for voice and orchestra, a symphony and other orchestral pieces, chamber works and songs. He championed a new form of song in the 'sprechgesang' idiom and was one of the first British composers to write specifically for military band. Also within the military context, and perhaps with greater effectiveness, he invented an anti-aircraft range-finder that was used in World War One.

BELL, William Henry
20 Aug. 1873 – 13 Apr. 1946
Bell was born in St Albans where he became a cathedral chorister. Winning a Goss Scholarship in 1893 to the Royal Academy of Music to study piano, organ and violin, his teachers included Alexander Mackenzie, Reginald Steggall, Alfred Burnett, Alfred Izard and Frederick Corder. He was later taken on as a professor of harmony at the RAM. Bell was appointed organist at St Albans, moving on to Oswestry in Shropshire, then to a London church. In 1912 he emigrated to South Africa to become director at the South African College of Music, Cape Town. Six years later the college was incorporated into Cape Town University, and Bell became Dean of the Faculty of Music there. His pupils included Hubert du Plessis and John Joubert. On retirement in 1935 Bell and his wife moved back to England, but returned to Gordon's Bay near Cape Town two years later. Bell stayed there for the rest of his life. After his death his wife moved back to Sleaford in Lincolnshire.

Bell's main interest was in the stage, and he composed operas (*Hippolytus*, *Isabeau*, *The Duenna* and the Japanese Noh-play *Tsuneyo*), five symphonies, symphonic poems, a viola concerto, incidental music works for chorus and orchestra, violin sonatas and a great many songs. W.H. Bell was probably the first South African ethnomusicologist, and he incorporated African folk music into his *South African Symphony* of 1929.

BENBOW, Charles Edwin
1904 – 1967
Edwin Benbow was born at St Leonards and studied music with Gustav Holst and Horace Kesteven, and at the Royal College of Music. He taught music at Winchester and then became a professor of piano and examiner at the RCM. He was also a pianist and conductor on the staff of the BBC, holding several awards. Benbow composed music for string orchestra, pieces for organ and for piano, church music and songs.

BENEDICT, Julius
27 Nov. 1804 – 5 Jun. 1885
Though born in Stuttgart to Jewish parents, Julius Benedict spent the last forty years of his life in England, where he was celebrated as conductor of opera and oratorio. Benedict studied with Hummel and with Weber, whose biography he later wrote. His first opera was produced at Naples in 1829, followed closely by his second opera.

Eight years later, having moved to England, he became conductor at Drury Lane and soon wrote his first English opera, *The Gypsy's Warning*. He conducted the Liverpool Philharmonic Society, the orchestra at Covent Garden, and at all the major festivals.

From 1845 he began a 35-year stint as conductor of the Norwich Festival. In 1848 he conducted the London premiere of Mendelssohn's *Elijah* and in 1850-51 toured as accompanist to Jenny Lind in the United States. Knighted three times by different European monarchs, he also received many lesser decorations. Benedict's compositions include several operas (only one, *The Lily of Killarney* is remembered), two oratorios, four cantatas, symphonies, piano concertos and songs. His most outlandish composition is a piece for eight harps and four pianos! He died in London and is buried at Kensal Green cemetery.

BENJAMIN, Arthur
18 Sep. 1893 – 10 Apr. 1960
Born in Sydney, Australia, Arthur Benjamin came to England at the age of eighteen to study with Stanford and Frederic Cliffe at the Royal College of Music. He served in the infantry, then in the Royal Flying Corps during World War One, and was eventually shot down and captured by the Germans. After the war he returned to Australia for a few years as a professor of piano at the Sydney Conservatorium, but in 1921 he came back to England and five years later joined the staff of the  RCM. After a period as conductor of the CBR Symphony Orchestra in Vancouver and a lectureship in Portland, Oregon, he finally settled in London, where he died.

Benjamin made his name as a composer of light music, but he also composed a symphony, several concertos, operas (*The Devil Take Her*, *Prima Donna*, *A Tale of Two Cities, Mañana* – written for TV, and *Tartuffe*), as well as various orchestral and instrumental pieces, often displaying the influence of jazz. His film music included *Conquest of Everest*, *An Ideal Husband* and Hitchcock's *The Man who Knew Too Much*. He is now best known for his *Jamaican Rumba,* one of several Caribbean pieces.

BENNETT, George John
5 May 1863 – 20 Aug. 1930
Bennett was born at Andover and sang in Winchester College Choir. He studied at the Royal Academy of Music with G.A. Macfarren and Charles Steggall, at the Hochschule in Berlin, and at Munich with Rheinberger. He was appointed a professor of harmony and composition at the RAM and in 1895 became organist of Lincoln Cathedral. While in this post he conducted the Lincoln Music Festivals. He conducted the Lincoln Musical Society and was an examiner for several universities. George Bennett composed a serenade, suite and overtures for orchestra, chamber music, church music, songs and piano pieces. He died in Lincoln.

BENNETT, Frederick James Wentworth
1856 – 25 Jun. 1908

Bennett was born in Somerset. After conducting local choral societies, he studied the flute at the Royal Academy of Music and then taught the instrument at Brighton School of Music. He wrote booklets on both conducting and flute playing. His works include a mass, several cantatas, a flute concerto, a symphony, songs and part-songs. He later became a JP, and died in Bournemouth.

BENNETT, William Sterndale
13 Apr. 1816 – 1 Feb. 1875

Born into a musical family in Sheffield, though orphaned at the age of four, W. Sterndale Bennett demonstrated musical abilities at an early age. At eight he was a choirboy at King's College, Cambridge, and at ten he went to the Royal Academy of Music, where he studied with Crotch, W.H. Holmes and Potter. At the age of seventeen he greatly impressed Schumann and Mendelssohn, who invited him to Leipzig, where he studied with Moscheles. On his return to England he held several posts – conductor of the Philharmonic Society's concerts, Professor of Music at Cambridge University, a professor and later Principal at the RAM, – and in 1849 he founded the Bach Society, introducing the *St Matthew Passion* to Britain.

Sterndale Bennett devoted considerable energy to all of his duties and it is possible that his compositions may have suffered as a consequence. Of his forty-seven published works, the most frequently performed have been the sacred cantata *The Woman of Samaria*, the secular cantata *The May Queen* and the fourth Piano Concerto. He also composed five symphonies (four of them youthful works and unpublished in his own lifetime), five other piano concertos (one of them lost), overtures (incl. *The Naiads*, *The Wood Nymph* and *Paradise and the Peri*), chamber music, church music, songs, and some splendid works for solo piano. His only oratorio, *Zion*, remained unfinished. He was knighted in 1871, died in London, and is buried in Westminster Abbey. The neglect into which Sterndale Bennett's music has fallen is all the more surprising in the light of the very high regard accorded him by Stanford, Mendelssohn ('the most promising young musician I know') and Schumann, though there has been a modest revival of his music since the 1980s.

BERGER, Francesco
10 Jun. 1834 – 26 Apr. 1933

Born in London of an Austrian father and Bavarian mother, Berger was a piano professor at the Royal Academy of Music and the Guildhall School of Music. He studied at Trieste with Ricci and Lichl and at Leipzig with Hauptmann, Plaidy and Moscheles. For twenty-seven years he was Honorary Secretary of the Philharmonic Society, London (for which he commissioned Dvořák's seventh and Saint-Saëns' third symphonies). Berger composed the overture and incidental music to two plays, *The Lighthouse* and *The Frozen Deep* (acted by Dickens and his circle in 1856-57), over a hundred piano pieces and a similar number of songs. He died in London.

BERINGER, Oscar
14 Jul. 1844 – 21 Feb. 1922
A pianist of some distinction and founder of the 'Academy for the Higher Development of Pianoforte Playing' in London, Beringer premiered the first British performances of Brahms's second piano concerto and Dvořák's piano concerto. He was born at Furtwangen, Baden in Germany and, when he was five, his father fled with his family to England as a political refugee. The young Beringer had no formal lessons until he returned to Germany, though his older sister's tuition had prepared him for some successful performances at the Crystal Palace. In Germany he studied with Moscheles, Richter, Reinecke and Plaidy at Leipzig, and with Tausig, Ehlert and Weitzmann in Berlin. He taught for a time in Germany before being appointed a professor at the Royal Academy of Music. Beringer composed an *Andante and Allegro* for orchestra, piano pieces and songs. He died in London.

BERKELEY, Lennox Randall Francis
12 May 1903 – 26 Dec. 1989
Born at Boars Hill near Oxford and a pupil at Dragon School and at Gresham's School, Holt, Lennox Berkeley was a composer of integrity and wholly unjustified humility. His music is deeply felt, yet suffused on occasions with a refreshing Gallic wit. He escaped from the English pastoralism and folk-song movement that influenced many of his contemporaries by studying in Paris for five years with Nadia Boulanger, after reading French and philology at Merton College, Oxford. In Paris the Gallic influences on him were strengthened further by his acquaintances with Ravel and Stravinsky. It was Ravel who had recommended him to study with Boulanger. During the war years Berkeley worked under Sir Arthur Bliss as a musical director at the BBC and in 1946 married a colleague, Elisabeth Bernstein. One of their three sons, Michael, is a well-known broadcaster and composer.

As a professor of composition at the Royal Academy of Music, Lennox Berkeley was held in high regard and affection by his pupils, many of who became themselves highly successful: David Bedford, John Tavener, Richard Rodney Bennett, Nicholas Maw and William Mathias, to name a few. In 1928 he converted to the Roman church and his many religious works led to his being awarded the Papal Knighthood of St Gregory (1973). He received many honours and was knighted in 1974. As a member of an aristocratic family, he narrowly missed inheriting an earldom and the magnificent Berkeley Castle in Gloucestershire. Berkeley met Benjamin Britten in 1936 and they forged a worthwhile musical friendship, collaborating at once on the orchestral suite, *Mont Juic.*

Of Lennox Berkeley's other works, the *Serenade* and the *Divertimento* for string orchestra are perhaps his best known and most characteristic works, though the many, highly polished, piano pieces must rank highly. He also wrote four symphonies, many suites, overtures and other orchestral works, concertos for flute, guitar, piano, and violin among other concertante works. Among the works for voice and orchestra are the notable *Four Poems of St Teresa of Avila* and the *Ronsard Sonnets*. He wrote three string quartets and many other chamber works, pieces for solo instruments, especially for piano, and many splendid songs. His operas comprise *Castaway*, the highly successful *A Dinner Engagement, Faldon Park, Nelson* and *Ruth*. He wrote many choral works, some hymns, carols and church anthems, and film and incidental music. Sir Lennox was the first President of the re-formed British Music Society, a position he held with some pride until his death in London.

BERNARD, Anthony
25 Jan. 1891 – 6 Apr. 1963
Born in London, Anthony Bernard studied piano with Josef Holbrooke and L. Borwick, organ with T. Haigh, and composition with Bantock and Ireland. He held various positions in London churches as an organist and choirmaster. In 1921 he founded the London Chamber Orchestra, and nine years later became Musical Director at the Shakespeare Memorial Theatre in Stratford. He composed much incidental music for the theatre, including *In Parenthesis*, also adding to the organ repertoire and writing some songs, such as *The Cherry Tree*. Bernard died in Kensington, London.

BERNERS, Gerald, Lord
18 Sep. 1883 – 19 Apr. 1950
Gerald Hugh Tyrwhitt-Wilson was born at Apley Park in Bridgnorth, Shropshire. He went to Eton, entered the diplomatic service in 1909 and succeeded to the baronetcy of Berners in 1918. A gifted painter (his miniatures exhibited in several major European galleries) and an author as well as a composer, Lord Berners' wit and eccentricity caught the public eye. At Faringdon in Berkshire he built the last English folly and he was the model for Lord Merlin in Nancy Mitford's novel *The Pursuit of Love*. Gourmet, wine  connoisseur and linguist, Lord Berners acknowledged before he died that there was nothing left for him to try his hand at.

As a composer Berners was largely self-taught, though he later studied with Stravinsky and Casella, retaining the friendship and respect of the former for the rest of his life. This 'English Satie' composed brilliant musical parodies, an opera (*La Carrosse du Saint-Sacrement*), four ballets and some orchestral pieces, film music (notably *Nicholas Nickleby*), songs and instrumental pieces, all highly original and, especially much of the piano music, in a progressive idiom, and often with considerable wit. Berners wrote five highly entertaining novels, some of them blatantly caricaturing his friends and acquaintances, and a two-volume autobiography. He often designed the sets and costumes for productions of his ballets. He died in London, leaving his considerable estate to his life-partner, Robert Heber-Percy.

BESLY, Maurice
28 Jan. 1888 – 1945
Born in Yorkshire, Maurice Besly went to Tonbridge School before gaining a BA at Cambridge in 1910 and an MA at Oxford nine years later. He took early lessons with Dr H.C. Stewart and spent two years at the Leipzig Conservatorium under Teichmüller, Schreck and Krehn. In 1919 he became organist at Queen's College, Oxford, conducting the Oxford Orchestra and the Oxford Bach Choir. Besly was also guest conductor at times for the London Symphony Orchestra, the Royal Albert Hall Orchestra, and the Scottish Orchestra. He taught for a time at Tonbridge, practised as a solicitor, and was Director of the Performing Right Society. Besly's best known

work was the popular ballad *The Second Minuet*, though much of his light orchestral suites, such as *Cheslsea China* and *Suite Romantique*, were popular. He also wrote choral works, pieces for chamber orchestra, songs and piano music, sometimes using the name Rex Allington.

BEST, William Thomas
13 Aug. 1826 – 10 May 1897
W.T. Best did more than anyone else in his own time to familiarise the public with the organ works of J.S. Bach. Undoubtedly the finest organist of his generation, he served at St George's Hall, Liverpool, and St Martin-in-the-Fields, London, and gave organ recitals in Paris, Rome and in Sydney, Australia. It was Best who gave the opening recital on the Albert Hall organ in 1871. He was born at Carlisle and trained as a civil engineer, but only decided to take up music later. He studied under Kohn Norman. His compositions include church services and anthems, organ pieces, two overtures and a march for orchestra, and piano pieces. He also wrote seminal texts on the techniques of organ playing, and edited organ works by Bach and Handel (twenty volumes of the latter).

BEVAN, Frederick Charles
3 Jul. 1856 – 27 Mar. 1939
Most of Bevan's life seems to have been spent in Australia, where he died. But he was born in London. He was a singer and composed ballads and songs, best known of which are *Flight of Angels*, *The Admiral's Broom* and *The Merry Monk*.

BEXFIELD, William Richard
27 Apr. 1824 – 29 Oct. 1853
W.R. Bexfield was born at Norwich and studied with Zechariah Buck at the Cathedral there. He then gained his Mus.Bac. at Oxford University and three years later a Mus.D. at Cambridge in 1849. A lecturer and organist, first at Boston, Lincolnshire, and later in London at St Helen's, Bishopsgate, he composed church anthems, an oratorio *Israel Restored* (1851) – which was performed at the Royal Albert Hall in 1880, a cantata (*Hector's Death*), songs and organ pieces. Bexfield died in Norwich.

BINGE, Ronald
15 Jul. 1910 – 6 Sep. 1979
Binge's *Elizabethan Serenade* has achieved an almost unparalleled popularity though his other works in the same relaxed, graceful vein are seldom heard. He was born at Derby and followed a career as a conductor for gramophone and broadcasting. He had early lessons in piano, organ and harmony, but was largely self-taught as a composer. By 1930 Binge had moved to London, where he was composer, arranger and organist at a silent theatre with a small orchestra. He also arranged music for Mantovani, a role that widened his horizons so that he began writing light orchestral music as a freelance. His own radio series, *String Song*, ran from 1955-63. His works include a *Thames Rhapsody*, *Saturday Symphony*, a saxophone concerto, film scores (including *Desperate Moment* and *The Runaway Bus*), music for some fifty TV shows, many songs, and pieces for brass (*Cornet Carillon* for four cornets and brass band was hugely popular) and military bands. Ronald Binge died at Ringwood in Hampshire.

BLACK, Stanley
14 Jun. 1913 – 26 Nov. 2002

As a conductor Stanley Black achieved over 3,000 broadcasts with the BBC Dance Orchestra and other groups. He also composed, arranged and directed music for over 200 films, such as *It Always Rains on Sunday* (1947), *Laughter in Paradise* (1951), *The Naked Truth* (1957), *Too Many Crooks* (1958), *The Long and the Short and the Tall* (1960) and *The Battle of the Sexes* (1960). But perhaps best known was his score for Cliff Richards's *Summer Holiday*. Other works included *Breakfast at Tiffany's*, an Overture to a Costume Comedy, the *Three Blind Mice* Variations, and *Strike up the Band*, used in the film *Exodus*.

Born Solomon Schwartz, Black started life in Whitechapel, London, son of a shoemaker. He began piano lessons early and attended the Matthay School of Music. The BBC Symphony Orchestra broadcast one of his compositions when he was only twelve. A career as a concert pianist seemed likely, but at the age of sixteen he was given a season at Margate with a Dixieland jazz band. From then on Black stuck to jazz and light music, playing with many well-known bands. Latin American music also informed much of his own performances after a tour of South America in 1938 with Harry Roy. During World War Two Black served briefly with the RAF, then took the baton of the BBC Dance Orchestra for eight years. During this period he provided the signature tune and the music for the first five series of 'The Goon Show'. Black was later employed by Decca, and was Resident Musical Director of the Associated British Film Studios. He was awarded an OBE in 1986.

BLEZARD, William
10 Mar. 1921 – 2 Mar. 2003

William Blezard was primarily a piano accompanist who worked with some of the top stars: Laurence Olivier, Max Wall, Marlene Dietrich, Joyce Grenfell, Joanna Lumley, Patricia Hodge, Ian Ogilvy and Honor Blackman. He was born at Padiham, near Burnley, to mill workers, though his father was a semi-professional tenor. His early talents were displayed at a local cinema and were recognised and encouraged by a local mill owner who paid for Blezard to have lessons. In 1938, while at Clitheroe Royal Grammar School, he won a scholarship to the Royal College of Music, where he studied piano with Arthur Benjamin and Frank Merrick, composition with Herbert Howells and orchestration with Gordon Jacob. His studies were interrupted between 1940-46 when he served with the RAF in North Scotland as a morse code operator.

After winning the Cobbett Prize for his *Fantasy String Quartet* back at the RCM, Blezard was invited to work with Muir Mathieson at J. Arthur Rank's Denham Film Studios. There he composed music for films and documentaries, also arranging and orchestrating Noel Coward's *The Astonished Heart*. His work in theatre included the Peter Brook productions of *Titus Andronicus* and *The Tempest*.

As pianist for the BBC 'Play School' Blezard demonstrated prodigious talents at improvisation. In addition to film and theatre music he composed orchestral works (*Battersea Park Suite*, *Caramba*, *The River* and *Duetto* for strings being particularly successful), chamber music, piano and other instrumental works, and some songs. He died in Barnes, London.

BLISS, Arthur Edward Drummond
2 Aug 1891 – 27 Mar. 1975

Arthur Bliss was born in London and studied with Charles Wood at Cambridge and with Stanford at the Royal College of Music. This latter course of studies was interrupted by World War One, and Bliss was wounded on active service. After the war he returned to music and may have studied with Vaughan Williams and Holst. Some of the experimental procedures adopted in his works of this period (particularly *Madame Noy*, *Rout* and *Rhapsody*) led to his reputation as an 'enfant terrible'. (In 1918 he conducted the first performance of Stravinsky's *Ragtime*. His later music, however, became conservative, though retaining a rhythmic vitality and a cosmopolitan flavour. In 1923 the Bliss family moved to the United States where Bliss met his future wife, Trudy Hoffmann. They were married in 1925 and returned to London. The outbreak of World War Two saw them in America again and Bliss accepted an offer of a lectureship at the University of California, a position which he held for two years before returning to England as musical director of the BBC; it partly was at his suggestion that the BBC Third Programme was established. Nine years later he was knighted and in 1953 was appointed Master of the Queen's Musick following the death of Sir Arnold Bax.

Perhaps best known for his ballet scores and film music (most notably H.G. Wells' *Things to Come*), Bliss also composed a *Colour Symphony*, concertos for piano, violin and cello, two operas (including *The Olympians* to a libretto by J.B. Priestley), choral and vocal works with orchestra, many orchestral pieces, music, songs, piano pieces and some brass band scores. One of his finest works is *Morning Heroes*, a choral symphony written in memory of a brother killed in action.

BLOCKLEY, John
1800 – 24 Dec. 1882

Blockley lived all his life in London. He was a publisher, issuing many of his own songs and ballads. Many were highly successful, like *The Arab's Farewell to his Steed*, *Jesse's Dream* or *The Relief of Lucknow*, and *The Charge of the Light Brigade*.

BLOWER, Maurice Sibley
27 Sep. 1894 – 4 Jul. 1982

Blower was born in Croydon and began his musical career as a choirboy in London. After a stint at the National Bank of India, the war intervened and he joined the East Surrey Regiment, and was taken prisoner in 1917 at St Quentin. He studied music at the RAF School of Music with Sir Walford Davies and was attached to the Guildhall School of Music for two years. He obtained his D.Mus. in 1929, submitting two choral works, The *Lady of Shalott* and *Message of the March Wind*. It is thought that his *Symphony in C* was started around that time, though it was not finished until 1939. He settled at Rake, near Petersfield, Hampshire, where he was long associated with the Petersfield Music Festival, and taught at a local school.

His published works consist mainly of part songs and works for strings. His arrangement of Purcell's *Come, ye Sons of Art* (for SSA and piano) is still popular. His *Horn Concerto*, composed in 1950 for horn and strings, was given its first performance by Dennis Brain, and his *Symphony in C* received its first performance in 2009 in Havant, Hampshire. He died at Petersfield.

BLYTON, Carey
14 Mar. 1932 – 13 Jul. 2002

A nephew of the children's writer Enid Blyton, Carey was born at Beckenham in Kent and attended Beckenham and Penge Grammar School. At fifteen he contracted polio, and two years of convalescence gave him the time to learn to play the piano, not having shown much interest in music before then. Soon he was composing songs and chamber music. In 1950 he was accepted at University College, London, where he co-founded the Beckenham Salon group under Arthur Bliss' presidency. Three years later Blyton entered Trinity College of Music, studying with William Lovelock. By 1957 he won a scholarship to Copenhagen's Royal Danish Academy of Music to study with Jørgen Jersild.

On his return to England Blyton became an editor at Mills Music, then at Faber Music. In these posts he was associated with publications of works by Richard Rodney Bennett, Roberto Gerhard, Holst and Britten. In 1963 he joined the staff of Trinity College of Music, ten years later moving to the Guildhall School of Music and Drama as a professor of composition for film, television and radio.

Carey Blyton's works are often light-hearted, like the orchestral pieces *Cinque Ports*, *On Holiday* and the overture *The Hobbit*. He composed works for piano, guitar and other instruments, music for wind, vocal pieces (*Lachrymae in Memoriam John Dowland* and *Lyrics from the Chinese*) and stage, film and TV scores. But his best-known work is a children's ditty *Bananas in Pyjamas*, a thirty-second miniature that spawned a whole theme industry in Australia! Blyton died of cancer at Woodbridge in Suffolk, where he spent his last few years with his family.

BODMAN, Christopher
1948 – 22 Jun. 2004

Christopher Bodman strived to encapsulate the sounds and sights of nature into his music, as exemplified by his *Woodlands* Concerto for two pianos and strings, his *Woodlands* Symphony, *Seven Waterfalls* for piano solo, and *Songs of the Humped-Backed Whales* for trombones, written for a BBC TV wildlife documentary. Bodman also composed three piano concertos, an orchestral modern dance score (*Rupert Brooke*) for tenor, piano, woodwind, percussion and strings, *Soundscape Tranquillity* for piano and percussion, an organ concerto, a double piano and string concerto, and other orchestral and instrumental works. Five string quartets, a work for four trombones, two electronic music soundtracks (for *Another World* and *The Alien who Lived in the Sheds*) and some choral music testify to Bodman's range.

Bodman was born in Northampton, was a chorister at Christ Church Cathedral, Oxford, and attended Warwick School before entering Lancaster University, where he studied composition with Anthony Gilbert. After graduating with a BA Hons. in 1973, Bodman won an International Music Scholarship from Illinois to study for an MA in composition at Rosary College in Florence, then an Italian Government Major Scholarship to the Guiseppe Verdi Conservatory in Milan to study contemporary compositional techniques with Franco Donatoni. Back in England Bodman took a post as an advisory music teacher in London special schools. He later became musical director of the LPDA Singers in London and was an editor of Après-Midi Editions. Bodman died at Chalfont St Peter.

BONAVIA, Ferruccio
20 Feb. 1877 – 5 Feb. 1950
Violinist and critic, Bonavia was born at Trieste. He studied in Milan and in Germany with Willy Hess. In 1898 he settled in England and became music critic for the Manchester Guardian; then, in 1920 for The Daily Telegraph. After playing under Richter for ten years he turned to composition, producing an opera, violin concerto, string octet, several other chamber works, violin pieces and songs. He wrote biographies of Verdi, Mozart and Rossini. Bonavia died in London.

BOROWSKI, Felix
10 Mar. 1872 – 6 Sep. 1956
Born at Burton in Westmorland, Felix Borowski emigrated to the United States, where he became a music critic and a professor of violin and composition. Eventually he was appointed Professor of Music at Northwestern University. He composed three symphonies, an opera, ballets, a piano concerto and many other orchestral works, three string quartets, motets, pieces for organ, violin and for piano, and songs. Borowski died in Chicago.

BOTTING, Herbert William
29 Mar. 1869 – 1898
A born and bred Brighton man, Botting, after gaining his FRCO, ventured to Leipzig to study at the Conservatory, where he was organist and choirmaster at the English Church. On his return to England, he ventured north to Southport for four years, but returned to his home town to take up various posts as organist and to conduct the local choral and orchestral society. His works include an ode, *Christ's Nativity,* for soprano chorus and orchestra, various other works for chorus and orchestra, and pieces for organ, piano, cello, and songs.

BOUGHTON, Rutland
23 Jan. 1878 – 25 Jan. 1960

Born at Aylesbury, Rutland Boughton left school at an early age and was apprenticed to a firm that promoted brass band concerts. Thanks to the generosity of a group of local admirers he was able to become a pupil of Stanford and Walford Davies at the Royal College of Music. On leaving he had a difficult time until a job as reviewer for the Daily Mail turned up. Boughton then became conductor and accompanist at the Haymarket Theatre, then in 1905 joined the staff of the Birmingham School of Music to teach singing and composition. Boughton lived a romantic life, divorcing twice and finally marrying one of his students. He wrote courageously about social problems of his time, adopting a left-wing political stance which lost him a great deal of popularity; and this, together with his love affairs, may have played a part in the failure of his greater ambitions. He admired the music of Wagner and conceived a cycle of operas paralleling those of his idol and based on the legends of King Arthur. To this end he founded an annual festival at Glastonbury, hoping eventually to build a festival theatre there. This ambition was never realised owing to a lack of financial support. He died, disappointed, in London.

One of Boughton's operas, *The Immortal Hour*, achieved enormous success and received more performances than any other English opera. He wrote many other operas (among them *The Birth of Arthur*, *Bethlehem*, *The Round Table*, *Lily Maid*, *Agincourt*, *Galahad*, *Avalon*, *The Moon Maiden*, *Alkestis*, *Queen of Cornwall*, etc.), choral dramas, three symphonies, concertos for flute, strings, trumpet, and two for oboe, other orchestral works, ballets, chamber music, song cycles and songs.

BOWEN, York Edwin
22 Feb. 1884 – 23 Nov. 1961
A Londoner from birth to death, York Bowen demonstrated considerable musical talent at a very early age. He studied at Blackheath Conservatoire for two years with Alfred Izard until he won the Erard and Sterndale Bennett scholarships to the Royal Academy of Music. He was a pupil there of T. Matthay, F. Corder and W. Battison Haynes and gained many distinctions. As a horn and viola player he served in World War One in the band of the Scots Guards. Famed as a pianist, Bowen was also a highly prolific composer, whose works include three symphonies, orchestral suites and overtures, four piano concertos and concertos for horn, viola and violin. He wrote much chamber music and pieces for the viola and viola d'amore. Among his many piano works the twenty-four *Preludes* for piano, Op. 102, have been described as the finest pieces for solo piano ever written by an Englishman. Bowen died in Hampstead.

BOYCE, Ethel Mary
5 Oct. 1863 – 3 Feb. 1936
Daughter of a JP and a close friend of Dora Bright, Ethel Boyce was born in Chertsey and studied at the Royal Academy of Music with Walter Macfarren for piano and F.W. Davenport for composition, where she won several prizes and scholarships. She was briefly engaged to Edward German, but this was broken off, and she never married. She composed a number of cantatas, notably *The Lay of the Brown Rosary* for soli, chorus and orchestras, pieces for violin and piano, and a quantity of songs, some of which were published by Novello & Co. She died at her home in Chertsey.

BRAHAM, Philip
18 Jun. 1882 – 2 May 1934
Philip Braham was Musical Director at Wembley Studios in the early days of talking films. He was a prolific composer of scores for early British films, including *Rats* (1923), and *Up With the Lark* (1927). His most famous song, still available today, is *Limehouse Blues*. It was included in the revue *A to Z* (1921), and became very popular, being sung by Gertrude Lawrence in the USA. Braham was born in London.

BRAITHWAITE, Sam Hartley
20 Jul. 1883 – 13 Jan. 1947
Though born at Egremont in Cumbria and deceased at Arnside in the same county, Sam Braithwaite lived most of his life in Bournemouth, where the majority of his works were first performed. He studied piano and clarinet at the Royal Academy of Music, later joining the staff there. He composed some piano pieces and a great deal of light orchestral works. His *Military Overture* was written for a Pageant of Empire

at the Crystal Palace. Among his other works are another overture (*The Fighting Temeraire*), a tone-poem (*Night by Dalegarth Bridge*) and *Near an Eastern Bazaar.*

BRENT-SMITH, Alexander
8 Oct. 1889 – 3 Jul. 1950
This educationalist, author and composer was born and died at Brookthorpe in Gloucestershire and went to King's School, Worcester. For twenty-one years he was director of music at Lancing College in Sussex and his music was represented on several occasions at the Three Choirs Festivals. His compositions include two symphonies and a symphonic study, four operas: *The Gentle Tyrant, The Captain's Parrot, The Age of Chivalry* and *Catherine Morland* (the last after Jane Austen's 'Northanger Abbey'), large scale choral works, five concertos (for piano; violin; five woodwind and strings; two violins and strings; two pianos and strings), chamber and instrumental music. Brent-Smith wrote *Studies and Caprices: Essays on Musicians and Music* and a book on Schubert. He was reputedly a brilliant organist.

BREWER, Alfred Herbert
21 Jun 1865 – 1 Mar. 1928
Born at Gloucester, Herbert Brewer studied at the Cathedral school there with C.H. Lloyd. He went to Exeter College, Oxford, then the Royal College of Music, where he studied with Walter Parratt. He held posts as organist at Gloucester, Oxford and Coventry and at the cathedrals of Gloucester and Bristol, also conducting several musical societies. In 1922-23 Brewer was High Sheriff of the City of Gloucester. He was knighted in 1926. His compositions include choral works, an operetta, orchestral pieces, songs, anthems and services, organ solos and pieces for violin and piano.

BRIAN, Havergal
29 Jan. 1876 – 28 Nov. 1972
The son of working class parents from Dresden in Staffordshire, Havergal Brian lived to the age of ninety-six, dying at Shoreham-on-Sea as a result of a fall just four years before the Centenary Festival which was to bring to an end the neglect his music had suffered throughout his life. His first musical training was as a church chorister, and at twelve he was very much in demand as a church organist, broadening his experience by playing in local bars. Starting his working life as a carpenter's apprentice, he was mainly self-taught as a composer and largely

Bust of Havergal Brian by Robert Thomas (1967)

followed his own musical dictates, able to devote time to his work through the support of a local wealthy businessman. This support was lost when Brian moved to London and for a time he suffered hardship until he accepted the post of assistant editor of Musical Opinion.

His earlier works were distinctly in the European symphonic tradition – his favourite composers included Bruckner, Strauss and Sibelius – but Brian's later music is highly characteristic. He composed thirty-two symphonies, thirteen of them after his eighty-sixth birthday. The first symphony, the *Gothic*, is probably the largest symphony ever written and is inspiring in its range and intensity, Part 2 being an extended setting of the Te Deum. Brian also wrote operas (the first, *The Tigers*, was an iconoclastic satire poking fun at war and patriotism in a manner which could only be suspect at the time), a violin concerto, dramatic cantatas, large-scale choral works (including a massive setting of Acts I and II of Shelley's *Prometheus Unbound*, the full score of which is lost), chamber and instrumental works, songs and part-songs.

The revival of interest in Brian's music in the 1980s may be attributed largely to Reginald Nettel and Robert Simpson who, as a young BBC music producer in the 1950s, discovered the composer and broadcast several of his works. The Havergal Brian Society continues to promote his music. Brian died at Shoreham-by-Sea in Sussex.

BRIDGE, Frank
26 Feb. 1879 – 10 Jan. 1941
Bridge was born at Brighton in the same year as John Ireland. Like Ireland he studied with Stanford at the Royal College of Music. Shortly after completing his course Bridge joined the Grimson String Quartet as a violinist, but soon turned to the viola and played with the English String Quartet for several years. Bridge's father was conductor of a theatre orchestra and young Bridge helped as a violinist and arranger. Later he became a conductor himself, deputising for Sir Henry Wood and touring the United States to conduct his own works.

Bridge's early music was romantic in idiom, but in his later years he adopted more progressive techniques, not always satisfying the critics. Though his music has been neglected, Frank Bridge is remembered as a successful teacher, to whom Benjamin Britten acknowledged a debt. As a composer Bridge was most at ease in chamber music, and was awarded the Cobbett Gold Medal by the Worshipful Company of Musicians for services to the genre. He also wrote an opera (*The Christmas Rose*), a work for piano and orchestra (*Phantasm*), orchestral suites, film music, the magnificent *Oration* for cello and orchestra, much piano music and songs. Four string quartets form the landmarks in his output. Frank Bridge died at Eastbourne.

BRIDGE, John Frederick
5 Dec. 1844 – 18 Mar. 1924

Frederick Bridge was born at Oldbury near Birmingham. As a young child he became a chorister at Rochester Cathedral, where his father was vicar-choral. He took organ lessons from Sir John Goss and in 1868 completed his bachelor's degree at Oxford. He was appointed organist of Manchester Cathedral, then Westminster Abbey, officiating at coronations and state occasions. Bridge also conducted and lectured with renowned wit. He finally became Professor of Music at London University. He was a keen antiquarian and edited Elizabethan music as well as writing educational books. His compositions include several oratorios (*The Repentance of Nineveh* being the best known), a cantata (*The Rock of Ages*), other church works, songs and some orchestral works. He was knighted in 1897 and in 1911 was created Commander of the Royal Victorian Order. J.F. Bridge died in London.

BRIDGE, Joseph Cox
16 Aug. 1853 – 29 Mar. 1929
Brother of John Frederick Bridge, Joseph was born in Rochester, Kent. He studied at Exeter College, Oxford, where he later became organist. On his appointment to Chester Cathedral he revived the Chester Music Festival. His other posts included that of Professor of Music at Durham University from 1908, and director of studies at Trinity College of Music from 1925. He died at St Albans. Joseph Bridge composed a Symphony in G minor (1894), an oratorio, cantatas, an operetta, requiem mass, church music, songs, and organ and piano pieces.

BRIDGEWATER, Ernest Leslie
31 Aug. 1893 – 19 Mar. 1975
Leslie Bridgewater was born at Halesowen in Worcestershire and studied at the Birmingham School of Music with York Bowen. He became musical director of the Shakespeare Memorial Theatre at Stratford and composed incidental music to nineteen of the Shakespeare plays. He also wrote a piano concerto and much light music in addition to several film scores, including *Against the Wind* and *Train of Events*. He founded the Leslie Bridgewater quintet and served on the music staff of the BBC for many years, conducting the BBC Salon Orchestra from 1939-42. This became a vehicle for championing eighteenth-century composers such as Arne, Scarlatti and Eccles. He died in Hong Kong.

BRIGHT, Dora Estella
16 Aug. 1863 – Dec. 1951
Dora Bright, who later became Mrs Knatchbull, was born at Broomhill, Sheffield. She studied piano and composition with Walter Macfarren and Ebenezer Prout at the RAM, gaining the Potter Exhibition in 1884 and the Lucas Medal for composition in 1888. She was the first woman to win the Lucas Medal, for which she entered a work for string quartet, her *Air and Variations*. After a short period travelling in Germany and Switzerland, Dora Bright began her career as a concert pianist with a series of recitals in London, and was the first to give concerts wholly of English music.

In the 1890s she married a Crimean War veteran and more or less gave up concert performance, though she continued to compose. She also founded an amateur operatic society at Babington, her home near Bath. More composition lessons in Paris with Moszowski led to her writing a series of ballets for Adeline Genée, who had earlier danced in Bright's first ballet, *The Dryad*. Dora Bright wrote three operas, eight ballets, mime plays, several works for piano and orchestra, a *Concertstück* for six drums and orchestra, orchestral suites, songs, chamber music and piano pieces. The conservatism and romanticism of her own works were buttressed by the series of articles she wrote for Musical Opinion in the 1940s lambasting the music of her more progressive contemporaries. She died at Babington, Somerset.

BRITTEN, Edward Benjamin
22 Nov. 1913 – 4 Dec. 1976
Britten's music has attained a world-wide popularity unrivalled by that of any other British composer. He was born at Lowestoft on St Cecilia's Day and started to

compose at the age of five. While still a boy he took lessons with Harold Samuel and composition with Frank Bridge, later paying tribute to the latter with his *Variations on a Theme of Frank Bridge*, the work which first brought Britten to the public's notice. The composer won a scholarship to the Royal College of Music to study with John Ireland and Arthur Benjamin. He supported himself for the next few years by writing scores for documentary films, and it was during this period that he came to know W.H. Auden, an association which resulted in his lifelong interest in the stage. Several of Britten's more important settings were to words by Auden.

In 1939, disillusioned with the political scene in Europe, Britten with his friend Peter Pears, left England for the United States, remaining there for three years. In 1946 Britten, John Piper and Eric Crozier founded the English Opera Group and, two years later, the Aldeburgh Festival was established. In 1953 Britten was made a Companion of Honour. In 1965 he received the Order of Merit and, in 1975, a life peerage.

Britten's music covers a wide range of forms and is often difficult to categorise. It includes a cello symphony, a superbly exciting *Sinfonia da Requiem*, concertos for piano and violin, several operas (*Peter Grimes*, *The Rape of Lucretia*, *Albert Herring*, *Billy Budd*, *Gloriana*, *The Turn of the Screw*, *Midsummer Night's Dream*, a version of *The Beggar's Opera* and one for children – *Let's Make an Opera*), cantatas and parables for church performance, the latter influenced by Japanese Noh plays. *Noyes Fludde*, based on a Chester miracle play, was designed for performance by children, with a core of professional singers and instrumentalists. He wrote a great deal for chorus or voice and orchestra, including the *War Requiem*, considered to be his finest work; as well as songs and song cycles, string quartets and other chamber music, and pieces for solo instruments, notably the piano, cello and guitar. Britten died at Aldeburgh and is buried there in the parish churchyard of St Peter and St Paul.

BROCKLESS, Brian
21 Jan. 1926 – 18 Dec. 1995
Organists surviving from the 1960s will remember Brockless for his rather adventurous organ works published for Novello's Organ Music Club. Born in London, where he spent much of his life, he studied at the Royal College of Music and privately in Italy with Mátyás Seiber. He was also a pupil and devotee of Sergiu Celibidache. Organist at the church of St Bartholomew the Great, West Smithfield, Brockless conducted several chamber orchestras. In addition to the organ works, he wrote an *English Elegy* for strings, some chamber works and songs.

BRODSZKY, Nicholas
1905 – 24 Dec. 1958
Composer of revues and many film scores such as *Quiet Wedding* (1940) and *The Way to the Stars* (1945), Nicholas Brodszky also wrote a great many songs, often in collaboration with lyricist Sammy Cahn. A number of the songs were popularised by Mario Lanza. *Be my love*, *Because you're mine* and *Wonder why* are typical of his style. Brodszky was born in Odessa, Russia. He studied in Rome, Vienna and Budapest and worked successfully in films in Germany, then in Austria, before settling in England in the late 1930s. He always kept one step ahead of the spread of Nazism. Brodszky died in London.

BROOME, William Edward
1868 – 10 May 1932
Broome was born in Manchester, though he spent his early life in North Wales, a chorister and assistant organist at Bangor Cathedral and conductor of the Penrhyn Male Chorus. In 1893 he crossed the Atlantic and held various appointments as organist, first in Montreal, then ending up in Toronto, where he also conducted the Toronto Operatic Society. He composed motets, cantatas (*The Siege of Cardiff Castle* gained some success) and songs, and won eight National Eisteddfod prizes for his works.

BROWN, Henry Albert
c. 1864 – 3 Mar. 1925
H.A. Brown's main claim to fame is that his *Valse Septembre* of 1909 was featured in the film *Titanic* (1997). He led his own orchestra and wrote several other waltzes (*Anticipation Waltz*, *Lorraine Waltz*, and others named after months of the year) under the pseudonym 'Felix Godin'.

BROWNE, John Lewis
18 May 1864 – 23 Oct. 1933
Though born in London, where he studied with his father and with S.P. Warren and Frederick Archer, Browne spent most of his musical career as an organist in San Francisco, Atlanta, Philadelphia and Chicago. With over 500 organ recitals to prepare for, he still managed to compose an opera (*La Corsicana*, 1923), an ode (*The Granite Walls Rise Fair*, 1911) a *Missa Solemnis*, and many songs and organ pieces. Browne died in Chicago.

BROWNE, William Charles Denis
3 Nov. 1888 – 4 Jun. 1915
Denis Browne, killed in action at Achi Baba in Turkey shortly after the burial of his schoolfriend Rupert Brooke on the island of Skyros in March 1915, showed early promise as a composer. Of Irish descent, he was born in Leamington Spa and went to Rugby School. While studying classics at Clare College, Cambridge, he became a pupil and close friend of E.J. Dent, who often referred to Browne and his fellow student Clive Carey, as 'my disciples'. After a brief period of teaching at Repton, Browne moved to London to teach, assisting Holst at Morley College. He succeeded Clive Carey as organist and choirmaster at Guy's Hospital. As critic for The Times and  New Statesman between 1913 and 1914 he displayed an enviable musical perception.

His compositions include songs and part-songs (two songs in particular, *Diaphenia* and *To Gratiana, Singing and Dancing*, are among the best English songs of their period), a ballet (*The Comic Spirit*), *Two Orchestral Dances* and some choral works. The date given above as that of Denis Browne's death is the date he was wounded in the shoulder, then in the stomach. His fellow officers, retreating under severe attack, had to leave him in the trenches as the enemy advanced. Though he was reported wounded and missing, Browne's body was never found.

BRUCKSHAW, Kathleen
5 Jan. 1877 – 10 Oct. 1921
Born in London, where she lived most of her life, Kathleen Bruckshaw made her public debut at the age of twelve in a performance of Rubinstein's Piano Concerto in D minor, with August Manns at the Crystal Palace. She studied with Stavenhagen and Busoni and played with all the major English orchestras and with the Berlin Philharmonic Orchestra. Her compositions include a piano concerto, a piano quintet, violin sonata, and solo piano pieces.

BRYDSON, John Callis
1900 – 1 Sep. 1977
Brydson is probably known only as a composer of organ works and church anthems, but he also wrote concerti, sonatas for various instruments and part-songs. He was born at Kegworth in Leicestershire and attended Loughborough Grammar School before gaining his Mus.B. at Loughborough Training College and an external Mus.Bac. at Durham University. He held several appointments as organist, choirmaster and musical director, mostly in Loughborough, Leicester and Derby.

BRYSON, Robert Ernest
31 Mar. 1867 – 20 Apr. 1942
Ernest Bryson was born in Liverpool and followed a career in the cotton industry, music being purely an amateur interest. He studied privately and composed two symphonies (first performances by Bantock and Harty), an opera, (*The Leper's Flute*) other orchestral pieces, works for chorus and orchestra, two string quartets and organ music and songs. He died at St Briavels in Gloucestershire.

BUCALOSSI, Ernest
27 May 1867 – 15 Apr. 1933
Ernest Bucalossi was born in London, son of Procida Bucalossi, who was a conductor at several London theatres. The latter made many arrangements of numbers from Savoy-related operettas, and it is possible that some of his popular pieces have been misattributed to his son. Ernest was taught by his father before studying at the Royal Academy of Music. He had already deputised for his father as conductor at the Prince of Wales theatre and was subsequently appointed to the D'Oyly Carte opera company to tour the provinces with the Gilbert and Sullivan operettas. By the age of eighteen Bucalossi had already composed his famous waltz, *La Gitane*. He may have written a number of operas himself, but is best remembered for his many orchestral waltzes, marches, serenades, and other dances (*The Grasshopper's Dance* is still performed by brass bands, and a brief snatch has been appropriated for a TV advert). He also wrote the incidental music for *A Kiss for Cinderella*.

BUCK, Percy Carter
25 Mar. 1871 – 22 Aug. 1947
Percy Buck was born at West Ham and studied at the Guildhall School of Music and at the Royal College of Music with Parry, Walter Parratt and C.H. Lloyd. He went to Worcester College, Oxford, where he was organist, then played for a time at Bristol Cathedral. He left Bristol for Wells Cathedral, and in 1901 became Director of Music

at Harrow School. The remainder of Buck's teaching life was spent as Professor of Music at Trinity College, Dublin (succeeding Ebenezer Prout), and at London University. He composed an orchestral overture, string quartets, choral works and organ pieces and wrote didactic works on organ technique, harmony and acoustics, contributing also to the Oxford History of Music. In 1935 he was given a knighthood. He died in London.

BUCKLEY, Olivia Dussek
1801 – 29 Dec. 1847
Daughter of the pianist and publisher J.L. Dussek, Olivia was born in London. She took music lessons with her mother and first appeared in public at the age of eight. She was appointed organist at Kensington Parish Church, and also played harp and piano. Author of *Musical Truths*, she composed two books of *Fairy Songs*, several ballads, and some piano pieces.

BULLER, John
7 Feb. 1927 – 12 Sep. 2004
In any consideration of John Buller's life and work one has to begin with *Proença*. Not that the audience knew where to start at its premiere in 1977, as the work emerges from the orchestra's tuning up. *Proença* was his first major orchestral work and it defined his status as a major composer. Buller had composed little before then, having followed a career in the family business as an architectural surveyor. After his father died in 1955, he had studied at Morley College before qualifying with a B.Mus. at London University in 1964. A year later he attended a summer school at Wardour Castle in Wiltshire, run by Harrison Birtwistle with Alexander Goehr and Peter Maxwell Davies, the last becoming Buller's lifelong friend. The school was a major and lasting influence in his development as a composer, but it was not until 1972 that a performance of *The Cave* for flute, clarinet, trombone, cello and tape brought the composer to the critics' attention. In 1974 *Le Terrazze* for woodwinds, brass, strings and tape reinforced his standing and he was made composer-in-residence at Edinburgh University shortly afterwards. He was given an Arts Council bursary in 1978 and took up another residency at Queen's University, Belfast, in 1985.

Buller's work was unashamedly intellectual and drawn from a wide variety of cultural stimuli. But most important of these were James Joyce and classical Greek drama, the former eliciting *Two Night Pieces from Finnegan's Wake, Finnegan's Floras* and *The Mimie of Mick, Nick and the Maggies*. His opera, *The Bacchae* (Buller preferred *Bakxai*), a setting of Euripides, was an immediate success in 1992. Also of note during his relatively short career as a composer was *The Theatre of Memory,* based on a mnemonic constructed by the 16th-century Giulio Camillo. Buller's last significant work was the orchestral *Illusions*, written for the 1997 Cheltenham Festival. By this time he may already have been suffering from the first signs of Alzheimer's disease. John Buller was born in London and died in Sherborne, Dorset.

BULLOCK, Ernest
15 Sep. 1890 – 24 May 1979
As organist of Westminster Abbey for thirteen years, Ernest Bullock directed the music for several important State occasions, including the coronation of King George

VI. He was born in Wigan and received his doctorate at Durham University. His various posts included those of organist at St Michael's, Tenbury and at Exeter Cathedral, Professor of Music at Glasgow and Principal of the Scottish Academy. Between 1952 and 1960 he was Director of the Royal College of Music. Bullock composed anthems and church music, songs and part-songs, organ works, fanfares and ceremonial pieces. He was knighted in 1951 and received a CVO in 1977.

BUMPUS, Mary Frances. See **ALLITSEN**, Frances

BUNNETT, Edward
26 Jun. 1834 – 5 Jan. 1923
'Bunnett in F' will be familiar to all church musicians. In addition to this setting of the *Magnificat* and *Nunc dimittis*, Edward Bunnett composed church anthems, hymn tunes, cantatas (*Rhineland, Lorz* and *De profundis*), songs and some organ pieces. He was born near East Dereham, Norfolk, and was a boy chorister at Norwich Cathedral, where he sung 'Lift Thine Eyes' with Jenny Lind in 1849. He later served as organist at several churches in Norfolk. He was conductor of the Norwich Musical Union and his works were often performed at the Norwich Festivals. From 1890 he was also in charge of the pier concerts at Lowestoft, Suffolk. Bunnett died in the city of his birth.

BUNNING, Herbert
2 May 1863 – 25 Nov. 1937
Herbert Bunning was born in London and went to Harrow School and Brasenose College, Oxford. He studied music with Schurig in London and Engel in Hanover, and also in Italy and France. In 1884 he was given a commission in the Queen's Own Hussars. Bunning became musical director at the Lyric Theatre, Hammersmith in 1892 and subsequently at the Prince of Wales Theatre. He composed operas (*Princess Osra*), overtures and orchestral suites, a 'scena' for baritone and orchestra, and various vocal and instrumental works. Herbert Bunning died at Thundersley in Essex.

BUNTING, Christopher Evelyn
8 August 1924 – 28 July 2005
Christopher Bunting gave up an engineering course at Bristol University when he was accepted for a music degree at Cambridge, under Thurston Dart. Bunting was to become an internationally renowned cellist. He was born in North London, son of a civil engineer who had worked in India. Both parents were talented amateur musicians. He had piano lessons as a child at the Hampstead Conservatory, then studied cello with Ivor James. During World War Two, when his studies were interrupted, he joined the Air Training Corps and then the Home Guard. He also served with the Norfolk Regiment and was assigned to the Stars in Battledress entertainment unit, playing alongside William Pleeth. A scholarship in 1952 enabled him to study with Pablo Casals, after which his own performances took him all over the world.

His frequent broadcasts took him even further afield, and he championed contemporary composers such as Henze and Shostakovich. He premiered Finzi's Cello Concerto as well as Alan Rawsthorne's. Bunting was also an exemplary teacher of cello and worked extensively with children. He taught for six years at the Menuhin

School and was professor of cello at the Royal College of Music for many years. In addition to studies for cello Bunting composed a *Concerto for Cello and Strings,* a *Fugue for Six Cellos*, an *Elegy* for cello and piano, and *Three Pieces for Cello Ensemble*. In 2000 he was awarded an MBE, by which time an undiagnosed illness had already confined him to a wheelchair.

BURGESS, Anthony. See **WILSON**, John Anthony Burgess

BURGON, Geoffrey
15 Jul. 1941 – 21 Sep. 2010
In 1979 Geoffrey Burgon's *Nunc Dimittis* from the film *Tinker, Taylor, Soldier, Spy* made the popular music charts, a rare vernacular accolade for the composer of some highly regarded 'classical' works. Burgon also achieved popular acclaim for his many scores for television: *Brideshead Revisited, The Chronicles of Narnia*, Monty Python's *The Life of Brian, Terror of the Zygons* and *The Seeds of Doom* (both *Doctor Who* mini-series), *Testament of Youth, Cider with Rosie, Martin Chuzzlewit, Silent Witness*, and *Bleak House* among others.

Burgon was born in Hambledon, Hampshire and went to Pewley Grammar School in Guildford. As a teenager he began to play jazz trumpet before entering the Guildhall School of Music and Drama to study composition with Peter Wishart. He later studied privately with Lennox Berkeley. After a few years as a jazz and orchestral trumpeter he began to compose in earnest, gaining early successes with the *Five Sonnets of John Donne*, a *Requiem* for the Three Choirs Festival of 1976 and *The Fall of Lucifer*, a musical drama. Then followed concertos for trumpet, percussion (for Evelyn Glennie), and piano, and important works for solo voice with orchestral, chamber or instrumental accompaniment. Burgon also wrote several ballets, some chamber works and many significant choral pieces. As if he wasn't busy enough as a composer, he also played cricket for his local team, wrote detective novels and indulged himself in old cars, in particular the Bristol marque.

BURROWS, Benjamin
20 Oct. 1891 – 28 Jan. 1966

A Leicester musician, Benjamin Burrows was also a precision engineer, skilful in microbiology. He was a pupil of Charles Kitson and the teacher of Charles Lovelock. Ben Burrows ran a postal tuition system which achieved considerable success in his day. He also devised his own machine for music printing, and published his music under the title Bodnant Press. He was born in Leicester and his first music lessons were from his parents before he took up organ studies with H. Bell, whom he succeeded as organist of St Mary's, Leicester.

Burrows gained his doctorate from London University and an FRCO. He lectured at Leicester University for thirty years. His works include five *Psalms* for chorus and orchestra, a string quartet, two cello sonatas, piano and organ pieces, and over 150 songs (ninety-three of them written within a space of twenty-one months for student Jane Vowles). Ten of his works are now available from Green Man Press (Bodnant imprint).

BUSCH, William

25 Jun. 1901 – 30 Jan. 1945

During a short adult life that ended in Woolacombe in Devon, William Busch composed a *Prelude* for orchestra, concertos for piano and cello, a piano quartet and other chamber and piano music and songs. He was born in London to parents of German origin, and studied in New York and Berlin (piano with Leon Kreutzer and composition with Leichtentritt). In England he had piano lessons from Mabel Lander and composition classes with John Ireland, Bernard van Dieren and Alan Bush. He taught music at Highgate School in London and was well-known as a pianist, making his debut in London in 1927. Towards the end of his life, illness turned him more towards composing.

BUSH, Alan Dudley

22 Dec. 1900 – 31 Oct. 1995

Alan Bush's life, philosophy and music were informed to a great extent by his deeply-felt political faith and unending commitment to improving social conditions. His espousal, in 1935, of communism stayed with him for the rest of his life. Sadly, this did not help his musical career in Britain.

Bush was born in Dulwich, London, and went to Highgate School before entering the Royal Academy of Music in 1918, studying with Tobias Matthay and F. Corder. During his time there he became a friend of Michael Head, whose sister Nancy he married ten years later. Nancy wrote the libretti for three of his operas, and the words for many other works. He took private lessons in composition with John Ireland and in piano with Mabel Lander, Benno Moiseiwitsch and Artur Schnabel. While still a student, Bush and Florence Lockwood played several of his works in Berlin, leading to his eventual studies in philosophy and musicology at Humboldt University. He witnessed first-hand the rise of Germany's National Socialist Party.

After returning to England he became active in many socialist areas, co-founding the Workers' Musical Association and leading the London Labour Choral Union (following Rutland Boughton). His *Towards Tomorrow*, a Pageant of Cooperation, was written for International Cooperative Day at Wembley Stadium in 1938. Two years later he was involved with the founding and the progress of the Birmingham Clarion Singers. During the war Alan Bush was a private in the Army Medical Corps. In 1947 he took over from Boughton the running of the Workers' Music Association summer schools, which he ran for thirty-one years.

A brilliant student at the RAM, Bush was quickly appointed Professor of Composition there, retiring in 1978. For many years he was an examiner for the Associated Board. During his long life he wrote four operas (*Wat Tyler, Men of Blackmoor, The Sugar Reapers* and *Joe Hill*), four symphonies, a piano and a violin concerto, *Dialectic* for string quartet and other chamber works, three operettas for children, choral works, two ballets, film scores and incidental music, pieces for piano and for organ, songs, and music for military and for brass band. Much of his music was performed and received warmly behind the Iron Curtain. Rigorous in its craftsmanship, his later works were more approachable than his earlier and more modernistic *oeuvres*. Alan Bush died in Watford General Hospital after a short illness.

BUSH, Geoffrey
23 Mar. 1920 – 24 Feb. 1998

Geoffrey Bush will be remembered with most affection by the many amateur musicians in whom he took such an active interest, writing many of his own works for amateurs and encouraging others to follow his example. He was born in London, and his only early musical training was as a boy chorister at Salisbury Cathedral, a period which cemented his Christian faith and informed his musical outlook. At the age of thirteen he entered Lancing College, where he was overlooked by Alexander Brent-Smith, but later encouraged by Jasper Rooper. He gained the Nettleship Scholarship at Balliol College, Oxford, and stayed to achieve a doctorate. During the war, as a pacifist, he became assistant warden at a hostel in Monmouthshire for difficult, evacuee pupils from deprived backgrounds. He returned to Oxford, joining the staff of the university's extra-mural department in 1947, then moving to London University five years later. For several years he took private lessons with John Ireland.

Geoffrey Bush wrote a great deal about English music, especially about neglected composers, many of whose music he arranged. He was a regular broadcaster, both as pianist and as contributor to 'Music Magazine' on BBC radio. He did much for the Composers' Guild of Great Britain and represented it in the USSR in 1964. He was also an active and effective worker for the Performing Right Society. As a university teacher he is remembered for his warmth and his ability to inspire, but he could be a stickler for accuracy and would always insist on high academic standards.

Bush edited many English songs by earlier composers (Parry and Stanford were prominent), and his own compositions are dominated by that genre, including about a dozen song-cycles. But he also wrote six operas (*The Equation*, a setting of the play 'X + O' by John Drinkwater, *The Blind Beggar's Daughter, If the Cap Fits,* the highly entertaining *Lord Arthur Savile's Crime, Love's Labour's Lost,* and a summer school musical theatre piece, *The Cat who Went to Heaven*), two symphonies and other orchestral works, secular and sacred choral works, chamber music, instrumental works for piano, organ, etc. Much of this was written for amateur or children's forces. Bush penned *Musical Creation and the Listener* in 1954, and two volumes of essays. In *Left, Right and Centre* appears one of the most concise and cogent arguments against the proliferation of nuclear weapons to be found anywhere.

As a pianist Dr Bush accompanied the soprano Sophie Wyss, and as an organist he served at St Luke's in Chelsea. A fan of detective fiction (his father had written detective stories), he had a short story anthologised and collaborated with a friend, Bruce Montgomery ('Edmund Crispin') in *Who Killed Baker?*. He also collaborated in the 1950s with John Elliott on a thriller for TV, *Never Die.*

BUTTERWORTH, George Sainton Kaye
12 Jul. 1885 – 5 Jun. 1916

Butterworth's tragically short life – he was killed at Pozières at the age of thirty-one while a Second Lieutenant in the Durham Light Infantry, at the battle of the Somme – has bequeathed us a mere handful of works. Of these the orchestral *Banks of Green Willow, Two English Idylls* and *A Shropshire Lad* are still deservedly popular. His mother was a professional singer in London and George's musical talent was apparent

at an early age. He studied at Eton with Dunhill, at Trinity College, Oxford, and at the Royal College of Music with Charles Wood. At the RCM, or even before, while at Oxford (where he taught at Radley College), he came under the influence of Cecil Sharp and Vaughan Williams and became active in the English Folk-song movement. It was Butterworth who suggested the idea of the *London Symphony* to Vaughan Williams, and to whom that symphony is dedicated. In addition to orchestral pieces Butterworth wrote many songs, a violin sonata, and a suite for string quartet. He collected and arranged many tunes. He was posthumously awarded the Military Cross.

BYE, Frederick E.
4 Jun. 1901 – 11 Feb. 1978
Born in Birmingham, Frederick Bye was a student at the Birmingham School of Music. He taught for two years at Bromsgrove School and conducted the Solihull Society of Arts, the Bourneville Orchestra and the Barfield Grand Opera Society. His works include a concerto for cello and strings and *Netherlands Suite* for strings.

BYNG, George W.
1862 – 29 Jun. 1932
A Dubliner by birth, George Byng, also known as David George, was musical director of the London theatre the Alhambra, for which he composed the music for thirty ballets. He also wrote incidental music for many stage shows, an orchestral suite (*A Dog in Naples*) and many songs, best known of which is *My sword and I*.

CALDICOTT, Alfred James
26 Nov. 1842 – 24 Oct. 1897
Alfred Caldicott became assistant organist at Worcester Cathedral at the age of fourteen. After studies in Leipzig with Moscheles and others, and having taken a Mus.B. degree at Cambridge, Caldicott worked as a professor of harmony at the Royal College of Music from 1882-92. Born in Worcester, Caldicott died nearby at Malvern. He wrote thirteen operettas, many glees and several cantatas, of which *The Widow of Nain* (1881) and *A Rhine Legend* (1883) were most successful.

CALKIN, John Baptiste
16 Mar. 1827 – 15 May 1905
Born in London, John Calkin held organ posts in Ireland and London, including at Woburn Chapel. He taught at the Guildhall School of Music and was a council member of Trinity College. He composed some chamber music, anthems and church services, glees, songs, and part-songs, hymn tunes and organ and many piano pieces.

CALLCOTT, William Hutchins
28 Sep. 1807 – 5 Aug. 1882
Born in Kensington, Callcott was the son of John Wall Callcott, the prolific composer of songs and glees. W.H. Callcott composed songs, of which *The Last Man* is best known, and church anthems, including *Give us peace in our time, O Lord*. He also made numerous arrangements of classical pieces for piano and piano duet and, like his father, composed a number of glees. He was organist at Ely Place in London.

CAMPBELL, Colin MacLeod
12 Mar. 1890 – 24 Jun. 1953
Conductor and accompanist, Colin Campbell was born in London. He studied at the Royal Academy of Music and gained a music degree at Oxford. His compositions include a musical drama (*Thais and Talmae*), a ballet (*Princess Gioia*), a children's ballet, instrumental music, piano duets and songs.

CARDEW, Cornelius
7 May 1936 – 13 Dec. 1981

Cornelius Cardew was the focus of the British musical avant-garde in the 1960s and '70s, though he later turned towards a more approachable idiom as a vehicle for overt Maoist political polemic. He was born at Winchcombe in Gloucestershire and sang as a chorister at Canterbury Cathedral before entering the Royal Academy of Music to study cello and piano with Howard Ferguson. Winning a scholarship to Cologne, he assisted Stockhausen, then studied with Petrassi in Rome. Cardew taught composition at the RAM from 1967, and worked largely with experimental music groups, playing cello and piano with AMM (the free improvisional ensemble) from 1965; and in 1969, together with Michael Parsons and Howard Skempton, he founded the Scratch Orchestra, for instrumentalists of any ability. These groups used aleatoric techniques, often involving random activity.

Cardew's music employed a form of serialism rather than indeterminacy. As a trained graphics designer he scored his own works in striking graphic notation. They include vocal works, two string trios, three piano sonatas and many experimental pieces for orchestra and for various instrumental combinations. Cardew died in London a a result of a hit-and-run accident.

CAREY, Francis Clive Savill
30 May 1883 – 30 Mar. 1968
Baritone singer, opera producer at Sadler's Wells, folk-song collector and teacher, Carey was born at Sible Hedingham in Essex. He was a pupil at Sherborne School before studying at Clare College, Cambridge, then entered the Royal College of Music, where he took singing with James H. Ley and composition with Stanford and Jean de Reszke. He toured the world as a member of the English Singers. He composed many songs.

CARMICHAEL, Mary Grant
17 Jul. 1851 – 17 Mar. 1935
Born in Birkenhead on the Wirral, Mary Carmichael went to school in France and Switzerland before studying music in Munich with Heinrich Porges for harmony and with Oscar Beringer and Walter Bache for pianoforte. At the Royal Academy of Music she had lessons in harmony and counterpoint from Ebenezer Prout. Carmichael made her name as an accompanist, only later becoming known as a composer of rather rhythmic piano pieces, which were first published under the name of M.G. Carmichael.

She went on to write songs, duets and part-songs. Her song-cycle, *Songs of the Stream* (1887), was the first of its kind in England. Most of Carmichael's latest works were religious in nature, though she did produce an operetta, *The Frozen Hand, or The Snow Queen* to a theme by Hans Christian Andersen. She also composed a setting of the Mass for male voice choir as well as marches for military band dedicated to Lord Kitchener and Lord Roberts. Her interest in the revival of eighteenth-century English music resulted in the publication of arrangements of English songs by such as Boyce, Shield, Arne and Hook. She died at her Hampstead home.

CARR, Frank Osmond
23 Apr. 1858 – 29 Aug. 1916
Known for a number of burlesques, light operas and musical comedies, Frank Carr conducted at various theatres. He was born near Bradford and gained a Bachelor's degree in music at Oxford in 1882, capping this with a doctorate nine years later. The operetta, *His Excellency*, was to a libretto by W.S. Gilbert. In 1907 Carr wrote the music for a ballet, *Sir Roger de Coverley*. He died at Uxbridge in Middlesex.

CARR, Howard
26 Dec. 1880 – 16 Nov. 1960
Howard Carr came to the public notice as a conductor in London theatres between 1903 and 1906, after which he worked in Australia for two years. In 1921 Carr succeeded Julian Clifford as conductor of the Harrogate Municipal Orchestra, then returned to Australia in 1928 to head the NSW State Conservatorium in Sydney. He came back to England in 1938. Carr composed two symphonies, an orchestral overture (*Sir Walter Raleigh*) and other short orchestral works (*The Jolly Roger* of 1940 is a typical example), operettas (*Under the Greenwood Tree* was popular for a time) and musicals, songs and part-songs.

CARR, Michael
11 Mar. 1905 – 16 Sep. 1968
Son of a pugilist, Michael Carr fought his way to late fame in the 1950s with two hits by The Shadows, *Man of Mystery* and *Kon Tiki*, though he was known to an earlier generation for songs such as *Did your mother come from Ireland?*, *Hometown*, *Ole Faithful* and *South of the Border*. His march *The Spice of Life* opened BBC radio's 'Music Hall'. Carr was born Maurice Cohen in Leeds and was brought up in Ireland. He began his musical career in the United States from 1924 to 1930, then came to London, writing songs for Gracie Fields and often collaborating with Jimmy Kennedy.

CARRODUS (Carruthers), John Tiplady
20 Jan. 1836 – 3 Jul. 1895
One of the most famous of nineteenth century English violinists, Carrodus was born at Braithwaite, near Keighley in Yorkshire, and died in London. After studying the violin at Stuttgart he returned to England to play in the Covent Garden Orchestra. He became leader of the Philharmonic Orchestra and a professor at the National Training School for Music, and was well known as a soloist and quartet player. He composed a fantasia and a romance for violin, and edited a collection of violin duets.

CARSE, Adam
19 May 1878 – 2 Nov. 1958

Born Adam von Ahn at Newcastle upon Tyne, Adam Carse went to school in Germany before entering the Royal Academy of Music to study with Frederick Corder, later becoming a professor of harmony and counterpoint there. He taught for a time at Winchester College. Carse composed five symphonies and other orchestral works, light orchestral pieces, an overture for brass band, a cantata, chamber music and songs, and wrote simple violin and piano pieces for teaching purposes. He also wrote books on the history of the orchestra and edited eighteenth-century symphonies. Adam Carse died at Great Missenden in Buckinghamshire. His collection of 350 wind instruments is housed at the Horniman Museum in South London.

CARWITHEN, Doreen
15 Nov. 1922 – 5 Jan. 2003
Born in Haddenham, Bucks of a musical family, Carwithen studied composition at the Royal Academy of Music with William Alwyn, whom she eventually married in 1976. After the war she began to make her name as a film composer, producing thirty-five scores, including *Boys in Brown, The Stranger Left no Card* and, importantly, *Elizabeth is Queen* (1953). Orchestral works include the overture *ODTAA* (One Damned Thing After Another), a concerto for piano and strings, the overture *Bishop Rock* and *Suffolk Suite,* as well as two string quartets and a sonatina for piano.

After her marriage she moved to Blythburgh in Suffolk, where she became known as Mary Alwyn. On the death of her husband in 1985 she was instrumental in forming the William Alwyn Foundation. She suffered a stroke in 1999 and died near Norwich.

CARY, Tristram Olgilvie
14 May 1925 – 24 Apr. 2008
The Daleks first trundled into Doctor Who's life to a soundtrack by Tristram Cary, one of the earliest British pioneers of electronic music. Third son of the novelist, Joyce Cary, he was born in Oxford and went to Westminster School before reading science at Christ Church, Oxford. His studies were abandoned when he joined the Royal Navy in 1943 as a radar engineer. Three years later he returned to Oxford, changing to politics, philosophy and economics, and, with a BA under his belt, he enrolled at Trinity College of Music, where he composed his first conventional work

to be performed, the *Piano Partita*. In 1955 his first electronic commission was for the radio play 'The Japanese Fishermen'; this was followed by many more commissions from the BBC and for films. Among the latter were *The Ladykillers*, *Quatermass and the Pit*, *Madame Bovary* and *Jane Eyre*. Cary also created the music for the British pavilion at Expo '67. The same year he co-designed the portable VCS3 synthesizer and founded the electronic music studio at the Royal College of Music, having already created his own private studio.

In the early 1970s Tristram Cary emigrated to Australia to work at the University of Adelaide, and was eventually promoted to Dean of Music there (1982-86). In 1992 his 'Illustrated Compendium of Musical Technology' was published and nine years later he was awarded a Doctorate. He died in Adelaide.

Cary's works cover conventional and electronic genres and include: *Peccata Mundi* for chorus, orchestra, speaker and four tapes, other orchestral and choral pieces, instrumental music and songs, some with tapes, and pure electronic scores including a nonet for computer.

CARYLL, Ivan

12 May 1861 – 29 Nov. 1921

A larger-than-life character, Felix Tilkin came to London in 1882 and adopted the name Ivan Caryll. He was born in Liège, Belgium, and studied there at the Conservatory. After his first stage work, *The Lily of Leoville*, was produced, Caryll was appointed conductor at the Lyric Theatre, where *Little Christopher Columbus* had much more success. Moving to the Gaiety Theatre he wrote several more musical comedies and in 1899 formed his own light orchestra, for which Elgar composed *Sérénade Lyrique*. Caryll toured widely in Europe and in the USA, where his music was most successful. He died in the USA during rehearsals for the newly written *Little Miss Raffles*. Overall Caryll composed forty operettas and musical comedies, together with many songs, dances and other salon pieces.

CELLIER, Alfred

1 Dec. 1844 – 28 Dec. 1891

An organist and conductor, Alfred Cellier composed operas both grand and comic (*Dorothy* had a longer run than *The Mikado*), operettas, a suite for orchestra, songs, incidental music and piano pieces. His setting of Gray's *Elegy* was performed at the Leeds Festival in 1883. Cellier was born of French parents in Hackney, London, and at the age of eleven he joined the choir of the Chapel Royal, St James. He spent some time in Australia and the United States before settling in England, conducting at the Prince's Theatre, Manchester, then the Opera Comique theatres in Manchester and London. He was also conductor of the Savoy Opera Company for D'Oyly Carte. Cellier died in London.

CENTER, Ronald

1 Apr. 1913 – 18 April 1973

Center first became known as a piano recitalist in Scotland and as accompanist to his wife, the soprano Evelyn Center, with whom he gave many broadcasts on the BBC Home Service. He was born at Aberdeen and studied music with Julian Rosetti and Willan Swainson, developing his musical talents at an early age. In 1943 he was appointed music teacher at the Gordon Schools at Huntly, Scotland, and became conductor of the Huntly Choral Society. In his later years he devoted himself to composition and private tuition. Mainly self-taught as a composer, he wrote a symphony, three string quartets, several works for string orchestra, a cantata (*Dona Nobis Pacem*) and other choral works, motets, songs and part-songs, church music and other instrumental pieces. He died at Huntly.

CHACKSFIELD, 'Frank' (Charles Francis)
9 May 1914 – 9 Jun. 1995
Renowned for his long career of light music recordings, Frank Chacksfield was born at Battle in Sussex. He had piano and organ lessons from the age of seven and passed his Trinity College exams, expressing a particular interest in the theory of music. By his mid-teens he was appearing at Hastings Music Festivals and was a deputy organist at Salehurst Parish Church, East Sussex. He began work in a solicitor's office then, disillusioned, formed his first band in 1936 before volunteering for the army at the outbreak of World War Two. After a bout of illness Chacksfield was posted to the Royal Army Service Corps' Entertainments Division, when he met Sergeant Charlie Chester. He soon became staff arranger for 'Stars in Battledress'.

Many engagements on radio shows followed after the war, with many television contracts following, both in Britain and the USA, and Frank toured extensively abroad with light orchestras playing mush in the Mantovani vein. Frank's own successes as a composer, sometimes under the pseudonyms of Martino Paticano and Roger Senicourt, included *Evening in Paris*, *Broadway Melody*, *Mediterranean Moonlight*, *Lovely Lady* and a host of others. Chacksfield died in Kent after a prolonged struggle against Parkinson's disease.

CHAGRIN, Francis
15 Nov. 1905 – 10 Nov. 1972
Chagrin settled in England just before World War Two and joined the Overseas Service of the BBC. An energetic committee man, he worked hard to promote the interests of British composers and founded the Committee for the Promotion of New Music (later the Society for the Promotion of New Music) in 1943. Chagrin was born in Bucharest, his apparently French name being a pseudonym. Alexander Paucker, to give him his real name, originally studied engineering at Zürich, at the same time taking piano lessons at the Conservatoire. Returning to Bucharest he studied composition with Mihail Jura then went to l'École Normale in Paris as a pupil of Dukas and Nadia Boulanger. Chagrin composed two symphonies (he was working on a third when he died), a piano concerto, many chamber works, music for the theatre and radio, and over 200 film scores, including cartoons. He also founded and conducted the Francis Chagrin Ensemble. Francis Chagrin died in Hampstead, London.

CHAPLIN, 'Charlie' (Charles Spencer)
16 Apr. 1889 – 28 Dec. 1977
Legend of the silent film and beyond, both as star and director, Charles Chaplin is less well known as a composer, though he invariably wrote the music for his films. His popular songs *Smile* and *Eternally* were drawn respectively from Modern Times (1936) and Limelight (1952) with words by English lyricists Geoffrey Parsons and John Turner.

CHEVALIER, Albert Onesime Britannicus Gwathveoyd Louis
21 Mar. 1862 – 11 Jul. 1923
A thoroughbred Londoner from start to finish (born in Notting Hill), this well-known music hall comedian began his stage career as a straight actor with George Alexander and others. Known as the 'Coster's Laureate', he wrote his own sketches and songs, many of the latter becoming long-standing favourites, such as *Wot cher* (*Knocked 'em in the Old Kent Road*) and *My old Dutch*.

CHIGNELL, Robert
8 May 1882 – 27 Feb. 1939
A native of Romsey in Hampshire, Chignell studied singing with Gustave Garcia and composition with Stanford at the Royal College of Music. He was also a pupil of Charles W. Clark. As a performer his most notable achievement was as a soloist on a world tour with the Sheffield Choir. Composer of over 250 songs, he also wrote three operas and two symphonic poems. *The Jackdaw of Reims* acquired a modest following. He also wrote music for radio. Chignell died in London.

CHIPP, Edmund Thomas
25 Dec. 1823 – 17 Dec. 1886
Born in London, son of a harpist and timpanist, Edmund Chipp studied the violin and played in Queen Victoria's private band as well as for the Royal Italian Opera. He gained his Mus.Doc. in 1860 and he held posts as organist in London, Belfast, Edinburgh and at Ely Cathedral, composing an oratorio (*Job*), much church music, songs, part-songs and organ pieces. He died in Nice, France.

CHISHOLM, Erik
4 Jan. 1904 – 7 Jun. 1965
A man whose life was driven by considerable energies, Chisholm was born at Cathcart near Glasgow. Some of his boyhood keyboard pieces were published before he became a student at the Scottish National Academy of Music and at Edinburgh University, where he gained his doctorate. Chisholm studied piano with Lev Pouishnov, composition with Sir Donald Tovey and organ with Herbert Walton. In 1924 he went to Canada as organist and choirmaster at a Presbyterian church in Nova Scotia and as Director of Music at the Pictov Academy.

Returning to England in 1928 he held various conducting posts in Glasgow, wrote as a music critic and toured abroad with an opera company. In 1929 he founded the Active Society for the Propagation of Contemporary Music. During World War Two Chisholm worked tirelessly for ENSA organising concerts for the troops in Singapore and touring with ballet and opera. In 1946 he settled in Cape Town as Professor of Music at the University and Principal of the South African College of Music.

Chisholm's compositions include two symphonies, two piano concertos, eight ballets, other orchestral works and twelve operas. He wrote the libretto for his *Isle of Youth* himself, and based another on Oscar Wilde's *The Importance of being Ernest*. An ardent Scottish Nationalist, he arranged many Scottish folk-songs. At the other end of the musical spectrum, Chisholm championed the music of his long-standing friend Kaikhosru Sorabji. Eric Chisholm died in Rondebosch in South Africa.

CHRISTOPHER, Cyril Stanley
23 Jun. 1897 – 1979
Cyril Christopher was born at Oldbury near Birmingham and studied with Bairstow, Kitson, Hollins and Cunningham. He followed a career as an organist, adjudicator, lecturer and conductor and eventually became senior tutor in the Adult Education Department of Birmingham University. Christopher composed works for voice, chorus and orchestra, cantatas and other choral works, a piano quartet, other chamber compositions, pieces for organ and for piano, songs and part-songs, and church anthems.

CLARIBEL. See **BARNARD**, Charlotte Alington

CLARK, Rev. Frederick Scotson
16 Nov. 1840 – 5 Jul. 1893
A composer of over 500 pieces for the organ and a few for the piano, Scotson Clark's music once provided popular organ voluntaries. They were easy to play and suitably pompous or reverential. He was born in London and studied at the Royal Academy of Music under Sterndale Bennett and John Goss, and in Leipzig and Stuttgart. He wrote a harmonium tutor, though sadly the world has now stopped pedalling. In 1865 he founded the London Organ School. He later became Headmaster of a school in Brighton and a curate in Lewes, Sussex. Scotson Clark died in London.

CLARKE, James Hamilton Siree
25 Jan. 1840 – 9 Jul. 1912
 James Hamilton Clarke was a prolific composer, having over 400 published works to his credit. He was born in Birmingham, played organ in local churches at the age of twelve, trained as an analytical chemist, but started his musical career as an organist in Ireland. He later became organist at Llandaff, then at Queen's College, Oxford, where he graduated with a Mus.Bac. in 1867. Clarke conducted at various West End theatres and toured as an operatic conductor. After some time in Australia he returned to England to the Carl Rosa Opera Company. His works include two symphonies (1873 and 1879) which were much admired by Gounod, six overtures, incidental music, cantatas, operettas, string quartets, anthems and services, songs and part-songs, and pieces for organ.

CLARKE, Rebecca
27 Aug. 1886 – 13 Oct. 1979
Rebecca Clarke was well-known in the 1920s and '30s as the viola player in the English Ensemble, an all-women piano quartet which she formed in 1913, her fellow string players being Marjorie Hayward and May Mukle, with pianist Kathleen Long. Her abilities as a composer, though well attested by her achievement of having two of her works gain second prize in the Elizabeth Coolidge competitions in 1919 and 1921 (in the earlier competition her Viola Sonata tied with Bloch's Suite for viola and piano and, as all entries were anonymous, the judges were somewhat aghast to find a woman composer represented among the winners), were generally ignored until

recently. She was born in Harrow, daughter of a German mother and an idiosyncratic and difficult American father, of whom she reminisces entertainingly in her memoirs. Rebecca began her violin studies at the Royal Academy of Music with Hans Wesseley. Stanford, having seen some of her songs, took her in as the first female composition student at the Royal College of Music in 1908. It was at his suggestion that she changed her allegiance from the violin to the viola, at which point she became a student of Lionel Tertis. Counterpoint and fugue were instilled in her by Frederick Bridge.

Rebecca Clarke's works met with some success in the 1920s, and a concert at the Wigmore Hall in 1925 was devoted entirely to her compositions. But by 1930 she was finishing fewer scores and her popularity waned. When World War Two broke out she was in the United States, visiting relatives. She was forced to remain there and, in 1944, met the pianist and composer James Friskin, who had been with her at the RCM. They married and lived the rest of their lives in New York (where she died), having toured the world with him giving recitals of piano and viola works. From 1945 she lectured at the Chautauqua Institute in New York. Rebecca Clarke's total output comprised fifty-eight songs and part-songs (in a style peculiarly ahead of its time), a vocal and a choral psalm setting, a piano piece, and twenty-four instrumental chamber pieces, of which the Viola Sonata has recently been cited as one of the finest ever written for the instrument. Some of her works, such as *Morpheus* for viola and piano of 1918, were written under the pseudonym of Anthony Trent.

CLARKE, Robert Coningsby
17 Mar. 1879 – 5 Jan. 1934
A pupil of Sir Frederick Bridge at Westminster Abbey, Clarke held several positions as organist in the Oxford area. He was born at Old Charlton in Kent and went to Marlborough College. He composed numerous popular ballads, and piano and organ works. His cycle *Songs of a Rover* includes the songs *The Vagabond* and *Sea Fever*. Clarke died at Walmer in Kent.

CLAY, Frederic Emes
3 Aug. 1838 – 24 Nov. 1889
Frederick Clay, son of the MP for Hull, was born in Paris and studied with Molique and Hauptmann in Leipzig. He taught in London and was, for a time, on the staff of the Treasury Department. Clay's first works were operettas, written for amateur groups; but in 1862 a performance of *Court and Cottage* at Covent Garden Theatre provided a springboard for further, more ambitious works. Thus followed many more light operas, including *The Pirates' Isle*, *Princess Toto*, *Don Quixote*, *Out of Sight*, and *Gentleman in Black*. He also wrote incidental music for plays, songs and two cantatas (a song from the cantata *Lalla Rookh*, '*I'll sing thee songs of Araby*', may still be heard occasionally).

CLEEVE, Stewart Montagu
20 October 1894 – 5 January 1993
While a Second Lieutenant of the 36th Siege Artillery Battery, Montagu Cleeve helped to design the highly effective World War One heavy artillery piece that became known as H.M. gun 'Boche-Buster'. While following a successful career in

the army, rising to become Lieutenant Colonel, he pursued a second career as a musician. His chosen instrument was the viola d'amore, and he designed and built a modernised version that could perform in concert with a bigger sound than the older instruments.

'Monty' Cleeve was born at Southsea in Hampshire. His father was in the Royal Engineers and came from a long line of military men. Mother was a talented painter and amateur pianist, who encouraged her son of six years old to learn piano and later the violin. Boarding school in Cheltenham interrupted his musical education for a time, as did his cadet days at the Royal Academy, Woolwich, where he developed an interest in science. As a young officer he had violin lessons with Editha Knocker and Emil Telmanyi and, when posted to India, gave the first ever violin recital broadcast on Radio Delhi.

In 1946 Cleeve retired from the army and turned full-time to music. He taught violin at Cheltenham College for Boys, then Emmanuel School in Wandsworth, and at a couple of grammar and preparatory schools. His increasing interest in the viola d'amore led him to develop the new design. His instrument differed from its precursors in having a rounded back, no strengthening piece, reduction from seven to six playing strings, a separate bridge for the sympathetic strings and a lengthening of the fingerboard. He founded the Viola d'Amore Society, arranged many pieces for the new instrument and composed several original works: *Whitgift Suite* for strings; *Prelude and Fugue in E* for violin, viola (or viola d'amore) and cello; four sonatas, a fantasy and a Barcarolle – all for the viola d'amore; other works for the instrument, some church anthems, an *Ecumenical Mass* and a trumpet fantasia. He continued teaching violin into his mid nineties.

CLIFFE, Frederic
2 May 1857 – 19 Nov. 1931
Better known as an organist and pianist than a composer, Cliffe was born at Low Moor near Bradford and was appointed organist to the Bradford Festival Choral Society at the age of sixteen. He studied with Stainer, Sullivan, Prout and Franklin Taylor and became a professor of piano at the Royal College of Music in 1884 (where he taught John Ireland), and at the Royal Academy of Music in 1901. He composed two symphonies, a violin concerto, other orchestral works, songs, choral works and church music. His first Symphony, Op. 1, first performed at the Crystal Palace, was hailed as a masterpiece. His second, *A Summer Night,* a programmatic work in five movements, was written for the Leeds Festival in 1892. Frederic Cliffe died in London.

CLIFFORD, Hubert J.
31 May 1904 – 4 Sep. 1959
Australian born Hubert Clifford read chemistry before taking up music as a pupil of Fritz Hart at the Melbourne Conservatorium. In England he studied at the Royal College of Music with C.H. Kitson and Vaughan Williams, winning the friendships of Mátyás Seiber and Benjamin Frankel. In the early 1940s he worked for the BBC as Empire Music Supervisor, soon becoming a professor at the Royal Academy of Music. He composed a symphony, a *Serenade for Strings* and some light orchestral music including *Five Nursery Tunes, Cowes Suite, Kentish Suite* and *Greenwich: Pageant of the River.*

CLIFTON, Henry Robert
1852 – 15 Jul. 1872
'Harry' Clifton, though born in Hoddesdon, Hertfordshire, spent most of his life in Glasgow. He was orphaned at the age of three, yet managed to earn a living as a singer at various supper rooms and in the music hall. He wrote and composed many songs, and several albums of his songs were published in his lifetime. They included the still memorable *Polly Perkins of Paddington Green*, *Shelling green peas* and *The weepin' willer*. Clifton died in London.

CLUTSAM, George Howard
26 Oct. 1866 – 17 Nov. 1951
George Clutsam started his musical career as a self-taught musical prodigy, touring New Zealand as a pianist. He was born in Sydney but settled in England in 1890 after touring the Far East. In Britain he was soon in demand as an accompanist and at popular concerts. In 1908 he became music critic for the *Observer*. He composed over 150 songs and pseudo-Negro ballads (of which *Ma curly-headed baby* was best known), many piano pieces, cantatas, a symphonic idyll and several operas (*The Damask Rose*, *A Summer Night*, etc.), the most successful of which was *Lilac Time*, produced in London in 1923. His opera *Konig Harlekin* had a long run in Berlin. George Clutsam died in London.

COATES, Albert
23 Apr. 1882 – 11 Dec. 1953
Though he was born in St Petersburg in Russia, trained at Leipzig, conducted in Germany and the United States and died in Cape Town, South Africa, Coates can nevertheless make some claim to inclusion among British composers. His father was a Yorkshire merchant who married a Russian. Their son, born in St Petersburg, was sent to school in England and had music lessons with an elder brother, who was an organist in Liverpool. For four years he studied sciences at Liverpool under Sir Oliver Lodge. He returned briefly to Russia, and received lessons from Rimsky-Korsakov, then entered the Leipzig Conservatoire to study cello, piano and conducting (the latter with Nikisch). His career began as an opera conductor in Germany, then Russia, but he fled from the Revolution in 1919 (or, possibly, illness forced him to move – the Bolsheviks had approved his presidency of the Opera House in 1917) and settled in England, becoming conductor of the LSO and the Royal Philharmonic Society. He championed the music of Scriabin. The last seven years of his life were spent in South Africa. Coates' compositions include some orchestral works and piano pieces, but the bulk of his output was opera (*Assurbanipal*, *Samuel Pepys*, *Pickwick*, *Gainsborough's Mistress*, etc.). *Pickwick* was the first opera ever to be televised.

COATES, Eric
27 Aug. 1886 – 21 Sep. 1957
Born at Hucknall in Nottinghamshire, Eric Coates took violin lessons from the age of six. In 1906 he entered the Royal Academy of Music to study with Lionel Tertis, Frederick Corder and Hartley Braithwaite. Changing from violin to viola, Coates played in various theatre orchestras before deputising for Tertis in the Hambourg String quartet for a tour of South Africa. He also played in the Cathie and Walenn

Quartets. Coates was a founder member and, later, Director of the Performing Right Society. As a composer of light music he saw early success when his song *Stonecracker John* (written while on tour in South Africa) sold over half a million copies.

Fame was assured when *Knightsbridge* from the *London Suite* was chosen by the BBC as the signature tune for the long-running series 'In Town Tonight'. Just as well known is *Sleepy Lagoon* as the introductory music for 'Desert Island Discs'. Eric Coates also wrote other orchestral and ballet suites, marches, film scores (including *The Dam Busters*), some songs and two ballets. Often appearing as a guest conductor of his own works, his conducting tour of the Americas after World War Two was a huge success.

For many years Coates had a retreat near Selsey, West Sussex, where he spent his final years. After suffering a stroke, he died in the Royal West Sussex Hospital in Chichester and was cremated at Golders Green Crematorium.

Blue plaque on the sea wall at Selsey, Sussex.

COBB, Gerard Francis
15 Oct. 1838 – 31 Mar. 1904
Gerard F. Cobb was a Fellow of Trinity College, Cambridge, and President of the University Board of Musical Studies and the University Musical Society. He was born at Nettlestead, near Maidstone, and was a prolific composer of chamber music, solo piano works, songs and part-songs, and church music.

COCKSHOTT, Gerald Wilfred
14 Nov. 1915 – 3 Feb. 1979
For several years Lecturer in English at the Froebel Institute College of Education in Roehampton, Gerald Cockshott published many essays and articles on music and was for a time chairman of the Peter Warlock Society. He was born in Bristol and graduated from Bristol University before studying composition with Vaughan Williams. He composed a symphony, three one-act operas, orchestral suites and a divertimento for flute and orchestra, a string quartet, 130 songs, and instrumental and choral music. He also arranged folk-songs. Cockshott died in London.

COKE, Roger Sacheverell
1912 – 1972
Coke, born in Alfreton, Derbyshire, came from an affluent family background. After leaving school, having heard a record of Moiseiwitsch, he struck up a friendship with the pianist, who in turn was to nurture a desire in Coke to become a concert pianist. His debut came in 1932, when he performed one of his own works. His tutors were Mabel Lander (piano) and Dr Frederick Staton (organ), and later Alan Bush for composition. It was composition which eventually dominated his life. He lived for many years as a semi-recluse at his family mansion near Alfreton. He founded the Brookhill Symphony Orchestra which played a number of his own works as well as neglected works by others. He was the pianist in the broadcast premiere of his own

Third Piano Concerto with the Bournemouth Municipal Orchestra in 1939. His most ambitious work was the two hour opera on Shelley's *The Cenci*, performed at the Scala Theatre, London. After this, he was afflicted with a mental disorder and retired from the public gaze. His other works include three symphonies, six piano concertos, two vocal concertos for soprano and orchestra, symphonic poems and numerous songs and piano solos. His music is preserved in Chesterfield Public Library.

COLAHAN, Arthur
12 Aug. 1884 – 15 Sep. 1952
Born in Galway, it must be inevitable that Colahan composed the song *Galway Bay*. He also wrote several Irish songs, such as *Cade Ring* and *Macushla Mine*. He practised as a medical doctor, serving in the British Army's Medical Corps in India in World War One, then worked as a psychiatrist and consultant neurologist, primarily in Leicester prison. A quiet, reserved man, Colahan died in Leicester, but his remains are buried with his family in his birthplace.

COLBORNE, Langdon
15 Sep. 1837 – 16 Dec. 1889
Born in Hackney, Colborne was organist of St Michael's Tenbury. After various short appointments as organist he settled as organist at Hereford Cathedral in 1877, conducting the Three Choirs festivals there. He composed one oratorio, *Samuel*, a quantity of church music and a few part-songs. Contemporary sources suggest that he was a diffident and insecure conductor.

COLERIDGE-TAYLOR, Avril Gwendolen
8 Mar. 1903 – 21 Dec. 1996
Daughter of Samuel (below), Avril studied composition in the United States at the Tanglewood and Juilliard Schools after an early start at Trinity College of Music, where one of her tutors was Gordon Jacob. Her first published work dates from 1915. She founded and conducted the Coleridge-Taylor Orchestra, a pioneering enterprise for women at the time. During World War Two she served in the WRAF. In her later years she taught at various Chicago public schools. Avril Coleridge-Taylor composed over 200 works, some under the soubriquet of 'Peter Riley'. They include orchestral suites, a piano concerto, works for chorus and orchestra, chamber music, songs and piano works. But her most lasting legacy may be her Ghanaian National Anthem. Born in Upper Norwood, London, she died at Seaford , East Sussex.

COLERIDGE-TAYLOR, Samuel
15 Aug.1875 – 1 Sep.1912

In 1874 a West African medical graduate married an English girl, Alice Holmans. Their son Samuel was born a year later in Holborn. The father soon returned to Africa, leaving Alice to bring up the child on her own. She moved to Croydon, where a local musician, Joseph Beckwith, perceived and nurtured Samuel's musical talents. Beckwith gave him free violin tuition and Col. H.A. Walters, a local choirmaster, approached Sir George Grove and arranged that Coleridge-Taylor should enter the Royal College of Music to study with Stanford and Charles Wood. Among his fellow pupils were Vaughan Williams, Holst and Hurlstone. The latter was to remain a lifelong friend and supporter.

A clarinet quintet made the first big impression on the public, but acclaim was assured by the choral/orchestral *Hiawatha's Wedding Feast* of 1898. Coleridge-Taylor was greatly respected as a conductor, and in 1901 became conductor of the Westmorland Festival. Two years later he was appointed a professor of composition at Trinity College of Music. In 1904 he took up the baton for the Handel Society, and in 1910 began to teach composition at the Guildhall School. Inevitably and constantly reminded of his colour by the critics, he devoted himself to restoring the dignity of those with whom he identified, making much use of African song in his music. Three tours of the United States made Coleridge-Taylor an idol of the American black population, and he had thoughts of emigrating until he died of pneumonia in Croydon. His compositions include a symphony, an opera (*Thelma*), violin concerto, various orchestral works, five choral ballads and some large-scale choral/orchestral settings, incidental music, oratorios, cantatas, chamber music, piano pieces, anthems and songs.

COLES, Cecil Frederick
7 October 1888 – 26 Apr. 1918
Cecil Coles died of wounds from a sniper's bullet received at the Battle of the Somme whilst rescuing casualties, and is buried at Crouy, near Amiens, where his grave bears the epitaph, 'He was a genius before anything else, and a hero of the first water'. He was born in Kirkudbright and went to Edinburgh University before entering the London College of Music, studying later at Stuttgart, where he was appointed assistant conductor of the Royal Opera House. He joined the Morley College orchestra in 1907 and his association there with Holst, then the college's Director, led to a scholarship and studies in Stuttgart. He was appointed assistant to Max von Schillings at the Stuttgart Royal Opera and worked with Richard Strauss. Some of his works were performed there. Two years after a walking tour with Holst in the Swiss Alps in 1911, Coles returned to London to become chorusmaster with the Beecham Opera Company and to teach harmony at Morley College.

He enlisted in 1915 and joined the Queen Victoria Rifles, later becoming the regiment's bandmaster. Had he survived active service in France, his music would surely be better known today. Coles composed a *Comedy of Errors* overture and scherzo, a *Suite from the Scottish Highlands*, *Behind the Lines* (a cortège), *Four Verlaine Songs* for soprano and orchestra, and his largest work, the scena *Fra Giacomo* for baritone and orchestra. His output also included several piano works, songs and two pieces for organ. Many of his works may not have survived had he not sent many of his mss to Gustav Holst during the war.

COLLINGWOOD, Lawrance Arthur
14 Mar. 1887 – 19 Dec. 1982
Born in London, Collingwood was educated at Westminster Abbey Choir School, the Guildhall School of Music, Exeter College, Oxford, and St Petersburg Conservatoire in Russia (due to his early love of Russian music), where he was a pupil of Glazunov,

Tcherepnin and Albert Coates. From 1931 to 1946 he was musical director of Sadler's Wells Opera and held several organist's posts in London. From the 1930s to 1972 he was musical adviser and a producer at EMI. One of his operas, *Macbeth*, was first performed in 1927. He also composed another opera (*The Death of Tintagiles*), some orchestral music, a piano concerto, piano quintet, two piano sonatas, a violin rhapsody, preludes for piano and several songs. Collingwood died at Killin in Perthshire.

COLLINS, Anthony
3 Sep. 1893 – 11 Dec. 1963
Anthony Collins was born at Hastings and studied at the Royal College of Music with Holst and Boult. He started his career as a viola player, mainly with the Scottish Orchestra, LSO and Covent Garden Orchestra, then made his name as a conductor, especially on tours for ENSA and with Carl Rosa Opera Company, the LSO and Sadlers Wells Orchestra. He spent some time in the United States in the 1930s and died in Los Angeles. Collins' film music (most notably for *Victoria the Great*, *Odette*, *The Lady with the Lamp* and many Anna Neagle films) and light orchestral works became well-known, though he also wrote four operas, two symphonies, two violin concertos and some chamber music. One of his most successful works was *Romney Marsh* for viola and orchestra, though most of his large-scale works have so far remained unperformed, many of which are lost.

COLLISSON, Rev. William Alexander Houston
1865 – 1920
Collisson was born in Dublin and studied there at Trinity College. He settled in London in 1901 and took up various appointments as an organist after obtaining his Mus.Doc. in Dublin. He composed comic operas, cantatas, an *Irish Suite* and songs.

CONNELLY, Reg
1895 – 23 Sep. 1963
Born at Buckhurst Hill in Essex, Reg Connelly will surely be remembered as the composer and sometimes lyricist of songs like *Show me the way to go home*, *Goodnight sweetheart* and *Try a little tenderness*. Connelly worked in collaboration with Jimmy Campbell as a publisher in Charing Cross Road, London, and became one of Britain's leading popular music publishers. He died in Bournemouth.

COOKE, Arnold Atkinson
4 November 1906 – 13 August 2005
The Seamew for baritone, oboe, string quartet and flute must be one of the most beautiful vocal settings by any British composer, yet its composer, Arnold Cooke, has never received popular acclaim. He did receive commissions and his works were performed, but their indebtedness to his teacher Hindemith, with their largely unfamiliar harmonic idiom, may not have moved the public at large. Cooke was born at Gomersal in Yorkshire and went to Repton School before studying for a B.Mus. degree with Edward J. Dent at Gonville and Caius College, Cambridge. The next three years were spent with Hindemith at the Hochschule für Musik in Berlin, after which he took over from Walter Leigh as musical director at the Cambridge Festival Theatre. From 1933–38 he taught composition at the Royal Manchester College of

Music (later the Royal Northern College). During World War Two Cooke served as an officer with the Royal Navy, and his Piano Trio of 1944 may have been written off the coast of Normandy during the invasion of Europe. In 1947 he was appointed professor of composition and harmony at Trinity College of Music, and soon gained his Mus.D. at Cambridge.

Arnold Cooke composed six symphonies (the last never performed), two operas (*Mary Barton* and *The Invisible Duke*), a ballet (*Jabez and the Devil*), a Concerto for Orchestra and concertos for violin, piano, cello, and two for clarinet. He also produced a wealth of chamber and instrumental works, including five string quartets, an oboe quartet, two organ sonatas, song cycles, and part-songs, but ceased composing in 1987. He was a founder member of the Composers' Guild of Great Britain. He died in in a nursing home near Five Oak Green, Kent.

COOPER, Walter Thomas Gaze
11 Jun. 1895 – 25 Mar. 1981
Gaze Cooper was born at Long Eaton in Derbyshire and studied with Frederick Moore and Benjamin Dale. At the Royal Academy of Music he was a pupil of Eaglefield-Hull and Frederick Dawson. He founded and conducted for twenty-six years the orchestra which eventually became the Nottingham Symphony Orchestra. From 1925 he taught at the Midland Conservatory of Music. Gaze Cooper composed eight symphonies, four piano concertos, concertos for violin, oboe, horn, double bass, bassoon and viola, two ballets, overtures and other orchestral works, an opera, chamber music and songs. He was a keen collector of Chinese, Greek and Egyptian works of art.

CORDER, Frederick
26 Jan. 1852 – 21 Aug. 1932

A Londoner, who was born in Hackney and died in St John's Wood, Frederick Corder studied at the Royal Academy of Music and with Hiller at Cologne. He held conducting posts at Brighton and was a professor of composition at the RAM from 1888 until 1923, being one of the most influential teachers of the time. Many of his pupils achieved recognition as composers, e.g. Bantock, Bax and Holbrooke. Corder was a Romantic and a Wagnerian, and his works include operas (*Nordisa,* 1887), operettas, oratorios and cantatas, orchestral and chamber works, songs and anthems, including a motet in fifty parts for female voices. He wrote the English versions of Wagner's opera libretti, founded the Society of British Composers in 1905 and the publishing firm of Charles Avison in 1906. He also wrote 'A History of the Royal Academy of Music, 1822–1922'.

CORDER, Paul Walford
14 Dec. 1879 – 6 Aug. 1942
Son of Frederick Corder above, Paul Walford was one of his father's leading students at the Royal Academy of Music and of the same generation as York Bowen, Benjamin Dale, Joseph Holbrooke and Arnold Bax. In 1907 he joined the staff of the RAM as a professor of harmony and composition. Many of his compositions remain unpublished and unknown. He had a close association with Arnold Bax, who

dedicated his song *Aspiration* and his fourth symphony to Paul Corder. His works include the operas *Rapunzel* and *Grettir the Strong*, choral works with orchestra *Sunset, Sunrise, Pelleas and Melisande*, a violin concerto, *Five Orchestral Tone Pictures*, a string quartet and various piano solos.

COSTA, Sir Michael Andrew Agnus
4 Feb. 1808 – 29 Apr. 1884

Born in Naples, Costa moved to England in 1829, where he Anglicised his names. By 1833 he had established his reputedly dictatorial style of conducting in London opera. He then directed the Philharmonic Society's concerts from 1846 until 1854. His contribution as a conductor of oratorio is well known, but his composing efforts – three symphonies, two oratorios, ballèt music and some sacred music – are less so. His compositions were regarded by critics of the time as somewhat second-rate. Costa was knighted in 1869 and died at Hove.

COULDERY, Claudius Herbert
17 Aug. 1842 – 8 Mar. 1930
Couldery's father was a landscape painter. His son, born at Lewisham, only took to music later in life, studying at the Royal Academy of Music under Sternale Bennett and John Goss. He subsequently taught at the Guildhall School of Music. Couldery has composed a number of works, some of a patriotic nature, such as the overture *To the Memory of a Hero* and the cantata *For Valour*, as well as a number of other works for orchestra (some of which were performed at the Crystal Palace), violin, and piano.

COWARD, Henry
26 Nov. 1849 – 1944
A famous choral conductor, Coward started his musical career as an amateur, being apprenticed to the cutlery business in his home city of Liverpool. At the age of 22 he became a school teacher and choir trainer and it was not until he was 40 that he decided to devote himself full time to music. After a doctorate at Oxford he was given a lectureship at Sheffield University. As a choral conductor he travelled all over the world and was knighted in 1926. Coward composed several cantatas (*Magna Charta* was once popular), concert overtures, anthems, songs, glees and hymns.

COWARD, Noël Pierce
16 Dec. 1899 – 26 Mar. 1973
An actor and dramatist whose 1920s plays in particular engaged an enormous public with their wit and sophistication, Noel Coward was also a successful composer of musical revues, a ballet, operetta and many songs. Of the plays, *Hay Fever, Private Lives* and *Blithe Spirit* gained the most popular acclaim, while the operetta *Bitter Sweet* had long runs in London and New York. After World War Two he became a nightclub and cabaret entertainer. Noel Coward was born at Teddington in Middlesex and studied at the Guildhall School of Music. He published short stories, verse and two volumes of autobiography. He was knighted in 1970 and died at Port Maria in Jamaica.

COWEN, Frederick Hymen
28 Jan. 1852 – 6 Oct. 1935

 A child prodigy who had published an operetta (*Garibaldi, or The Rival Patriots*) when he was only eight years old, Frederick Cowen was born in Kingston, Jamaica. He came to Britain at the age of four and studied with Sir Julius Benedict and Sir John Goss until 1865. The next three years he spent in Berlin and Leipzig as a pupil of Moscheles, Hauptmann and Reinecke. Cowen succeeded Sullivan as conductor of the Philharmonic Society in 1888 and a few years later took the baton of the Hallé Orchestra. Of his six symphonies, his first, along with his piano concerto (which he performed himself at the age of seventeen), won him recognition, and his third, the *Scandinavian*, established his reputation as a symphonist. He also composed operas (including *Thorgrim, Signa, Pauline* and *Harold*), oratorios, cantatas, chamber music and songs. He conducted at all the major festivals and from 1918 taught at the Guildhall School of Music. He was knighted in 1911 and received honorary doctorates from Cambridge and Edinburgh universities. Cowen died in London.

COX, Desmond
1903 – 14 Nov. 1966
A director of the music publishing firm of Box-Cox Ltd, Desmond Cox collaborated with his business partner, Harold Elton Box, in writing many popular songs. *In the quartermaster's stores* (1940) still resounds whenever the beer flows, while *Horsey, horsey* (1937) and *I've got sixpence* still achieve an occasional vernacular rendering. Cox was born in London.

CREITH, Guirne
21 Feb. 1907 – 29 Apr. 1996
Gladys Mary Cohen was born in London, yet she entered the Royal Academy of Music under the name of Guirne Creith, studying under Benjamin Dale and Adam Carse, and winning prizes for composition. She was an able concert pianist until an injury to her right hand in 1962 forced her to give up performing. Works include a violin concerto (dedicated to Albert Sammons and broadcast in 1936), a ballet suite, a tone poem *Rapunzel*, a string quartet, violin sonata and a number of songs, much of which are lost. As Guirne van Zuylen, she left to live in France in 1964, then Germany, where she wrote books on gourmet cooking and wine. She returned permanently to England in 1976, and remarried.

CRESER, William
9 Sep. 1844 – 13 Mar. 1933
William Creser was born at York, where he was a chorister at the Minster. A pupil of G.A. Macfarren, he then graduated in music at Oxford, and later gained a doctorate. Creser held several posts as organist in the North of England until he was appointed organist and composer to the Chapels Royal. He is known to have conducted the Bach Passions in the 1880s. He composed several oratorios, an orchestral suite, operetta, a string quartet and other chamber works, and pieces for organ. Creser died in London.

CRIPPS, Alfred Redgrave
1882 – 1950
Remembered now for a setting of Housman's *A Shropshire Lad* and for some other songs, of which *There be none of beauty's daughters* and *O mistress mine* are best known, Alfred Cripps was born in Worthing, where he spent most of his life. He studied at the Royal College of Music and contributed articles to various musical magazines and journals. He was also a playwright.

CROOK, John
1852 – 10 Nov. 1922
Born in Manchester, John Crook's early career was spent there as a conductor before he was persuaded by Harry B. Farnie to try his hand in London. Augustus Harris appointed him as musical director at Drury Lane and he later took up similar posts at the Adelphi, Vaudeville and the Duke of York theatres. He wrote scores for many musicals and incidental music for several plays, including that for *Peter Pan* in 1904. Crook's best known works remain *The Recruit* and *Lancelot the Lovely*. Among his many songs *The Coster's Serenade* and *Jerusalem's Dead* may still be remembered. Crook spent his last days in London.

CROUCH, Frederick Nicholls
13 Jul. 1808 – 18 Aug. 1896
Frederick Crouch was born at Warren Street, St Pancras in London, and studied cello at the Royal Academy of Music. He worked as a cellist in London, then, in 1849, settled in the United States (fighting on the Confederate side in the American Civil War) and held appointments in Boston, Baltimore, New York and Portland, where he composed several operas (*Sir Roger de Coverley*, *The Fifth of November*), songs (one of the most successful, *Kathleen Mavourneen* of 1835, is still sung). He died in Portland. Crouch also invented the printing process of zincography.

CRUFT, Adrian
10 Feb. 1921 – 20 Feb. 1987
Adrian Cruft was born at Mitcham in Surrey to a distinguished family. His father Eugene taught him the double bass and Adrian played the instrument in several orchestras. In his youth he was head chorister at Westminster Abbey and won a Boulting Conducting Scholarship to the Royal College of Music. He studied composition with Gordon Jacob and Edmund Rubbra and became a professor of theory and composition at the RCM in 1961. He was a member of the Composers' Guild of Great Britain and helped establish the British Music Information Centre.

Adrian Cruft's music is diatonic, though distinctive, and is largely choral. He composed orchestral overtures and suites, a *Divertimento* for strings (a lighter, exuberant work that deserves more frequent performance), several cantatas (the dramatic chamber cantata *Alma Redemptoris Mater* shows Cruft in more austere vein), other orchestral and choral works, a great deal of church music, including masses, canticle settings and anthems, some chamber music, works for brass and military bands, songs, and pieces for organ, piano, and double bass.

CRUIKSHANK, William Alexander Campbell
1 Jun. 1854 – 1934

William Cruikshank was born in Greenlaw Barracks near Edinburgh, the son of a military surgeon. He was educated at Epsom and held various posts in Scotland as an organist, before settling in Burnley, where he occupied the organ stool at the Parish Church. Cruikshank was a founder member of the Incorporated Society of Musicians and served on the General Council for twenty years. He composed songs and part-songs, piano and organ works and much church music.

CUMMINGS, William Hayman
22 Aug. 1831 – 6 Jun. 1915

W.H. Cummings was born at Sidbury in Devon. From the age of seven he sang in various London church choirs, receiving musical tuition from William Hawes at St Paul's Cathedral and E.J. Hopkins and J.W. Hobbs at the Temple. Cummings became a successful professional singer, professor of singing at the Royal Academy of Music and Principal at the Guildhall School of Music. He was also an organist, an officiating member of several musical societies and a respected musical antiquarian. He composed a cantata, glees, songs, anthems and services, and wrote a primer on the rudiments of music. He died in London and was buried at West Norwood cemetery.

CUNDELL, Edric
29 Jan. 1893 – 19 Mar. 1961

Edric Cundell was born in London and went to Haberdashers' Aske's School and Trinity College of Music, where he later became a professor of composition. He was also Principal at the Guildhall School of Music and Drama, and toured extensively as a conductor. He played the horn and the piano. Cundell's compositions include a symphony, a piano concerto, symphonic poems, string quartets, other chamber works, choral music and songs. He died in Ashwell, Hertfordshire.

CURZON, Frederic Ernest
4 Sep. 1899 – 6 Dec. 1973

Frederic Curzon, President of the Light Music Society and Head of the Light Music Department at Boosey and Hawkes, was a successful and captivating composer of light orchestral overtures (*Bouffe, Punchinello*, etc.) and orchestral suites (*In Malaga, Charm of Youth, Salon Suite*). He also wrote works for piano and orchestra, violin and orchestra, many scores for documentary films, songs and much educational music, especially for cello, flute, oboe, clarinet, and piano. He was born in London and studied privately, learning violin, cello, piano and organ as a boy. He had begun composing by the time he was twelve and was pianist in a London theatre orchestra at sixteen. Four years later he was composing and playing accompaniments to silent films. He was also organist at the Shepherd's Bush Pavilion. Frederic Curzon died in Bournemouth.

CUSINS, William George
14 Oct. 1833 – 31 Aug. 1893
Sir William Cusins was a violinist, pianist and organist, and a conductor of the Philharmonic Society. He taught at the Royal Academy of Music and was appointed Master of the Queen's Musick in 1870. Born in London, Cusins studied with Fétis at the Brussels Conservatoire, and with Charles Lucas, Cipriani Potter, Sterndale Bennett and Prosper Sainton at the RAM. He composed an oratorio (*Gideon*), a *Te Deum* and other church music, orchestral overtures, a piano concerto and a violin concerto, marches and songs. Cusins died in Remonchamp, Belgium.

DACRE, Henry ('Harry')
1860 – 1923
Harry Dacre was born and died in London, though he emigrated to the United States, where his songs were eminently successful in vaudeville. On his return to England Dacre founded the Frank Dean publishers and wrote a large number of songs. *Daisy Bell* and *I'll be your sweetheart* may still be sung at social gatherings.

DALE, Benjamin James
17 Jul. 1885 – 30 Jul. 1943

Benjamin Dale was born in Crouch Hill, London and studied at the Royal Academy of Music with Harold Lake and Evlyn Howard-Jones for piano, H.W. Richards for organ, and Frederick Corder for composition. He later became a professor there. His wife, Kathleen, was also a composer. Dale's works include overtures, a *Fantasia* for organ and orchestra, a cantata (*Before the Paling of the Stars*), other choral works, songs, chamber music, an *Introduction and Andante* for the unusual medium of six violas, and piano music. His Piano Sonata and Violin Sonata are particularly fine works. Benjamin Dale died a few hours after conducting a rehearsal of his large-scale symphonic tone poem, *The Flowing Tide*, the evening before it was due to be performed at a Promenade Concert.

DANN, Horace
20 Nov. 1896 – 18 Dec. 1958
Horace Dann may be remembered mostly as a Director of Light Music at the BBC from the early 1930s. His early skills as a musician were honed as accompanist to his father, a popular tenor soloist, and in 1912 he entered the Guildhall School of Music. The war interrupted his studies and he served with the Middlesex Regiment before gaining a commission in the Royal Fusiliers. After demobilisation Dann entered the Royal College of Music, where he composed a prelude, *Aurora*, based on his impressions of the battlefield on the eve of Armistice. Subsequently *Aurora* received several performances. By this stage he was in some demand as a concert pianist.

In 1921 Dann accepted a professorship at Stellenbosch University in South Africa, lecturing, performing, and working as Music Director of the African Theatre Group in Johannesburg. On his return to England he worked in various capacities for the BBC until he died after heart surgery. Dann's compositions were few and mostly light. As well as *Aurora*, they include a valse intermezzo for small orchestra, the march *Worcester Beacon*, some other light orchestral works, piano solos and several songs.

DARE, Margaret Marie
1902 – 1976
Marie Dare was for some time principal cellist with the Reid Orchestra in Edinburgh. She taught cello and played in the Scottish Trio. Born at Newport on Tay in Fifeshire, she studied at the Guildhall School of Music. Her compositions include three ballets, a string quartet, several works for cello (including an *Elegy* for four cellos) and some for double bass, music for string orchestra, and other chamber works.

DARKE, Harold Edwin
29 Oct. 1858 – 28 Nov. 1977
Known mainly as an organist and composer of organ music, Harold Darke was born at Highbury. He trained at the Royal College of Music, taking organ with Walter Parratt and composition with Stanford. After gaining a doctorate at Oxford he became a teacher and examiner (a professor at the Royal College of Music for fifty years) and held a post at King's College, Cambridge, where he died. He was organist at the Temple church, then at St Michael's, Cornhill. Founder and director of the St Michael's Singers, he conducted many British choral works. In addition to his organ and choral works Darke composed a symphony, two fantasies for strings, songs and piano music. He was awarded the CBE in l966.

DARNTON, Philip Christian
30 Oct. 1905 – 14 Apr. 1981
Christian Darnton was born near Leeds into a wealthy family that originated from the Spanish Netherlands, his father having renounced the title of Baron von Schunk prior to World War One. Christian began piano lessons at the age of four and was composing by the time he was nine. He took lessons at the Brighton School of Music, later studying at the Matthay School in London with Harold Craxton. He studied composition with Benjamin Dale and Harry Farjeon, and while at Gonville and Caius, Cambridge, in the early 1920s, became a private pupil of Charles Wood and Cyril Rootham. In 1928 he went to Berlin as a pupil of Max Butting. Darnton was a prolific composer between 1930 and 1939, producing avant-garde works which were widely performed. During World War Two he received spinal injuries while in the Fire Service and suffered from them for the rest of his life. After a long and gradual change of political awareness he became a member of the Communist Party and his music tended to be written more for mass appeal, becoming simpler and more diatonic.

During his later years Darnton travelled extensively and taught English in Italy and Greece. His music regained some of its radicalism as he grew disillusioned with left-wing politics. From this period date the fourth symphony, fourth string quartet and a *Concerto for Orchestra*. Earlier compositions include concertos for piano (two), violin (two), viola, and harp and wind; other orchestral and string works, a ballet, an opera (*Fantasy Fair*) and a mime for puppet theatre; choral and vocal works, songs, piano and chamber pieces, film scores and incidental music. He wrote poetry and his 'You and Music' was published by Pelican in 1939 (2nd ed. 1945).

DAVENPORT, Francis William
9 Apr. 1847 – 1 Apr. 1925

Davenport was born at Wilderslowe near Derby and went to University College, Oxford. He studied music with Sir George Macfarren, whose daughter he married. In 1879 he joined the staff of the Royal Academy of Music as a professor of harmony and composition, and in 1902 was appointed a professor at the Guildhall School of Music. Davenport's compositions are varied, including two symphonies (the first in D minor winning first prize at the Alexandra Palace competition in 1876 – Macfarren being one of the judges!), some chamber music, works for violin, for cello and for piano, and songs. He also wrote texts on music theory and became Hon. Secretary to the Musical Association in 1883. Davenport died in Scarborough.

DAVIDSON, Malcolm
1891 – 1947

Malcolm Davidson was born at Harrow and studied at the Royal College of Music, where he later taught, and at Cambridge. He composed a suite for violin and piano, other chamber works, songs and part-songs, and made several arrangements of Scottish folk music.

DAVIE, Cedric Thorpe
13 May 1913 – 18 Jan. 1983

Davie, though born at Blackheath in London, was of Scottish descent and spent most of his life in Scotland. He studied at the Scottish National Academy of Music in Glasgow, the Royal Academy of Music, and the Royal College of Music under R.O. Morris, Vaughan Williams and Gordon Jacob. He studied piano with Petri in Germany and composition with Kodaly in Budapest and Kilpinen in Helsinki. Davie was appointed to the staff of the Royal Scottish Academy of Music and became a church organist in Glasgow. In 1948 he accepted the music chair at the University of St Andrews. Much of Davie's music is based on Scottish themes and includes a symphony, an opera (*Gammer Gurton's Needle*), chamber music, songs and anthems, incidental and film music (including scores for *Rockets Galore* and *Rob Roy*; earnings from the latter enabled him to buy a car, which he named 'Rob Roy'), a concerto for piano and strings, and various instrumental works.

DAVIES, Evan Thomas
1878 – 25 Dec. 1969

Evan Davies was born at Merthyr Tydfil and studied music privately. He toured abroad as a pianist and organist and was active as an examiner, adjudicator, broadcaster and conductor, eventually becoming director of music at the University College of North Wales. He edited and arranged folk-songs, wrote articles on Welsh music, and composed songs and part-songs, piano works and some chamber music.

DAVIES, Henry Walford
6 Sep. 1869 – 11 Mar. 1941

Walford Davies came from a musical family in Oswestry, Shropshire. As a child he was sent to St George's Chapel, Windsor, to sing under Sir George Elvey and Sir Walter Parratt, later becoming organist there himself. He studied at the Royal College

of Music with Parry, Stanford and Rockstro and gained a doctorate from Cambridge. His name as a composer was first assured by the cantata *Everyman*, written for the Leeds Festival of 1904. In 1898 he began a twenty year career as organist at the Temple Church in London. He was also organist at several other London churches, a professor of counterpoint at the RCM, conductor of the London Bach Choir, Professor of Music at Aberystwyth and director of music at the University of Wales. During World War One Davies was director of music for the RAF. In 1934 he succeeded Elgar as Master of the King's Musick and was knighted in 1922. Walford Davies contributed enormously to musical education and was a gifted and popular broadcaster, being appointed musical adviser to the BBC in 1927.

With the exceptions of *Solemn Melody*, the *RAF March Past* and the church music, little of his extensive output is now performed. He composed several cantatas, oratorios and other works for chorus, voice and orchestra, a symphony (and a *Children's Symphony*), overtures and orchestral suites, string quartets and other chamber works, pieces for military and brass bands, part-songs and organ pieces. He wrote several large-scale works for children and arranged many songs, both Welsh and English. His editions of hymnals and psalters, song collections and carol books are still in use and his didactic works are of lasting value.

DAVIES, Hubert
24 May 1893 – 27 Oct. 1965
Hubert Davies played the violin in several orchestras including the Welsh Symphony Orchestra, London Symphony Orchestra, Queen's Hall Orchestra and Covent Garden Orchestra. He also played the viola in a string quartet and taught violin and composition at the Cardiff College of Music and Drama. His compositions include works for orchestra and for strings, chamber music (often in variation form), string quartets, songs and part-songs, church music, and pieces for violin and piano.

DAVIES, Hugh Seymour
23 April 1943 – 1 January 2005
It is said that Dame Ethel Smyth conducted with a toothbrush. Hugh Davies composed with an egg slicer! He was a renowned exponent in the performance of electronic, electro-acoustic and experimental music and was an innovator in the creation of musical instruments from discarded household items, using contact microphones to record them as a prelude to electronic tapes. As a teenager he had found a recording of Stockhausen's *Gesang der Jünglinge*, a work which determined his musical career, though parental pressure guided him first to a formal musical education.

Davies was born in Exmouth, Devon, and went to Westminster School before completing a music degree at Worcester College, Oxford, studying with Frank Harrison and Edmund Rubbra. Soon afterwards he went to Cologne to be Stockhausen's personal assistant, scoring and documenting his early mentor's works. Returning to England he furthered his development of home-made instruments and the use of Stockhausen's contact microphone methods. By the late 60s he was playing with Gentle Fire, a septet specialising in live electronic music, and with Music Improvisation Company. From 1966-68 he did research at the Groupe de Recherches Musicales, and published his definitive International Music Catalog. In 1968 he founded the Electronic Music Studio at Goldsmith's College, London, directing it until 1986. His enthusiasm found vent in the many workshops he gave for children, his researches at Middlesex University from 1999, and his membership of the Artist Placement Group.

DAVIS, John David
22 Oct. 1867 – 20 Nov. 1942
Born at Edgbaston near Birmingham, John Davis studied at the Raff Conservatorium, Frankfurt and the Brussels Conservatoire. He taught at the Midlands Institute and was a professor of harmony and composition at the Guildhall School of Music. Davis composed a symphonic poem, cello concerto and other orchestral music, sonatas for violin and piano, two string quartets, a string quintet and other chamber works, an opera (*The Zaporogues*), songs and part-songs, piano and other instrumental pieces. John Davis died in Estoril, Portugal.

DAVISON, James William
5 Oct. 1813 – 24 Mar. 1885
James Davison was born in London and trained to enter the Bar. He studied music with W.H. Holmes and G.A. Macfarren and was a friend of Mendelssohn and Sterndale Bennett. He married the concert pianist Arabella Goddard, a former pupil. Before giving up composition to be a critic for The Graphic, The Times and Musical World, he wrote orchestral pieces, a piano sonata, smaller piano solos and songs to words by Keats and Shelley. He died at Margate.

DE LARA, Isidore
9 Aug. 1858 – 2 Sep. 1935
Isidore de Lara, born to an English father and a Portugese mother, and whose real patronym was Cohen, was born in London and studied with Emanuel Aguilar. At fifteen he went to Milan, where he took composition with Mizzucato and singing with Lamperti. He won the Grand Prix for composition, then returned to England and settled in London as a singer and conductor, gaining renown as a recitalist and composer of salon ballads. As a conductor he championed many premieres of British works. De Lara composed songs, best-known of which is *The Garden of Sleep*, and several operas, including *The Light of Asia, Amy Robsart, Messaline, Les Trois Masques* and *The Three Musketeers*.

DELIUS, Frederick
29 Jan. 1862 – 10 Jun. 1934
Born Fritz Theodore Albert, one of fourteen children of German parents in Bradford, Yorkshire, Frederick Delius started a career in his father's wool business, using his supposedly commercial trips to Germany, Scandinavia and France to further his musical education. After a period in Florida as an orange grower Delius, aided by Grieg, persuaded his father to send him to Leipzig, where he studied with Isett and Reinecke. He settled in France, first at Paris then at Grez-sur-Loing, where he

remained for the rest of his life, cut off from the English musical world except for his close friendships with younger admirers such as Philip Heseltine and Percy Grainger, who is said to have taken Delius to the summit of Mont Blanc in his bathchair.

Delius's music belongs to no particular school and, although accepted in Germany, was not received well in this country until it was adopted enthusiastically by Sir Thomas Beecham, who championed it for the rest of his life. Among his compositions are operas (*Koanga, A Village Romeo and Juliet, Fennimore and Gerda, Irmelin, The Magic Fountain* and *Margot la Rouge*), symphonic poems, concertos for piano, cello, violin and violin and cello, works for voice and orchestra, chorus and orchestra and orchestral pieces, songs, instrumental works and the *Mass of Life*, claimed by many to be his finest work. Delius's last few years were spent blind and bedridden, a result of syphilis contracted during his time in Paris. His last compositions were effected solely through the patient dedication of his friend and amanuensis, Eric Fenby. Delius is buried at Limpsfield in Surrey with Jelka, the German painter whom he had married in 1903.

DEL MAR, Norman René
31 Jul. 1919 – 6 Feb. 1993
An orchestral conductor of some renown, Norman Del Mar scored chiefly as an interpreter of the music of Strauss, Mahler and Elgar, though he gave excellent accounts of many complex twentieth-century works. A pupil at Marlborough College, he later went to the Royal College of Music to study piano with Cyril Smith, composition with R.O. Morris and Vaughan Williams, conducting with Constant Lambert, and horn with Frank Probyn. His studies were interrupted by World War Two, but he joined the Central Band of the RAF and then the RAF Symphony Orchestra. After the war he assisted Walter Goehr at Morley College, and in 1944 founded the Chelsea Symphony Orchestra. As a guest conductor of leading orchestras he was in constant demand. Del Mar composed two symphonies, a string quartet, a flute concerto and some works for horn. He also wrote a three-volume, definitive study of the works of Richard Strauss. He died in London.

DEMUTH, Norman
15 Jul. 1898 – 21 Apr. 1958
Norman Demuth was born at South Croydon and was educated at St George's Chapel, Windsor, and at the Royal College of Music. He became a professor of composition at the Royal Academy of Music and wrote books on Franck, Ravel and Roussel, and on music theory. He also produced army training manuals in combat techniques, and served in both world wars (in the London Rifle Brigade and the Pioneer Corps). His compositions include five symphonies, several concertos (for piano, violin, viola, saxophone, Ondes Martenot, etc.), ballets (*Conte Vénitien, Le Flambeau* and *Volpone*), other orchestral works film scores, chamber music, instrumental music (much for organ) and songs. He was also a popular broadcaster for the BBC. Norman Demuth died in Chichester.

DERBYSHIRE, Delia
5 May 1937 – 3 Jul. 2001

While not generally recognised by the public as a name, Delia Derbyshire has left an indelible public record in her electronic realisation (1963) of Ron Grainer's theme music for 'Doctor Who'. She was born in Coventry and went to Coventry Grammar School before taking a degree in music and maths at Girton College, Cambridge. After a brief stint at the United Nations she was given a job as studio manager in the BBC. Two years later in 1962 she joined the BBC Radiophonic Workshop. Delia's work in this department realised some outstanding scores, particularly in collaboration with the poet Barry Bermange (*The Dreams, Amor Dei*). Delia's sources were the most mundane: a resonant lampshade, subjected to acoustic analysis and every form of electronic manipulation conceivable, showed an extraordinary creativity as well as an aesthetic sensitivity. At various times she worked with Peter Maxwell Davies, Luciano Berio, Roberto Gerhard and other twentieth-century composers.

In the mid-1960s Delia and her colleagues worked with Peter Zinovieff, pioneer of electronic music. She also became involved with sound backdrops for light projections and magnetic sculptures. In 1968 she was responsible, but not credited for, the album *Electric Storm*. Theatre work and concerts of electronic music followed and she produced over 200 programmes over eleven years; but she left in 1973 to join Brian Hodgson at Electrophon. She left there soon afterwards and took on a variety of jobs unrelated to music, finding a life partner in 1980. She died in Northampton.

D'ERLANGER, Baron Frédéric Emile
29 May 1868 – 23 Apr. 1945

Son of a German father and an American mother, Frederic D'Erlanger was born in Paris, where he pursued his literary and musical studies (the latter with Anselm Ehmant) before settling in London for the rest of his life. A banker by profession, D'Erlanger was also a director of the Royal Academy of Music and, for many years of Covent Garden Opera. He composed four operas (*Jehan de Saintré* of 1893; *Inès Mendo* of 1897; *Tess*, based on Hardy's novel, which received its London premiere in 1909 after performances in Naples and Milan; *Noel*, also 1909), a *Requiem Mass*, symphonic works, two ballets (incl. *Les Cent Baisers*), concertos for violin and piano, a string quartet, piano quintet and other chamber works, piano pieces, music for violin and for cello, and songs.

DIEREN, Bernard van
27 Dec. 1887 – 24 Apr. 1936

Though born at Rotterdam in Holland, Bernard van Dieren spent most of his life in London; he died in Golders Green. He came to England in 1909 as a musical correspondent but sadly, at about the same time, contracted an illness which would frustrate his work for the rest of his life. His early compositions possess an originality equal to that of any of his contemporaries, and although never popular, his music gained many highly enthusiastic admirers. His later works were conservative in idiom. Constant Lambert and Philip Heseltine considered van

Dieren to be one of the greatest musicians of his generation and he was acknowledged as their mentor. His ideals were unique and his artistry beyond question.

In the early 1930s the BBC broadcast several of his works and revival seemed imminent. But the composer died in 1936 and war prevented further progress. He is now almost entirely forgotten. His works include a Choral (*Chinese*) symphony, an uncompleted *Symphony in Three Movements,* a comic opera (*The Tailor*), overtures and settings for voice, chorus and orchestra, six string quartets (the first is reputed to be the most difficult ever written), instrumental pieces for violin, violin and piano, cello, harp, and piano solo. His many songs were once highly regarded. Van Dieren wrote a book on Epstein the sculptor, and a collection of musical essays entitled *Down among the Dead Men* (1935), said to be one of the finest collections on the subject ever published and certainly one of the most vitriolic. Bernard van Dieren studied sciences until he decided to devote himself to music at about the age of twenty. His musical education was completed in Germany.

DOLMETSCH, Rudolph
8 Nov. 1906 – 7 Dec. 1942

Rudolph Dolmetsch was born in Cambridge, Massachusetts, and received his early musical training from his father, Arnold Dolmetsch, pioneer of early music performed on period instruments. He became a harpsichordist and viola da gamba player. In 1929 he married one of his pupils, Millicent Wheaton, and toured with her, giving recitals on the harpsichord and viola da gamba. Eventually he broke away from the family traditions in early music and studied conducting at the Royal College of Music, establishing his own orchestra, led by Olive Zorian. He later published a tutor on Orchestral Conducting.

When war broke out, Dolmetsch was called up to serve in the Artillery. In 1942 he was aboard The Ceramic when it was torpedoed in mid-Atlantic, and was lost at sea. His compositions (which are in ms. in the RCM Library) include two symphonies, a sinfonietta, concertos for violin, clarinet and harp, and shorter orchestral pieces. His *Two Movements of a Symphony* were written as a conclusion to Borodin's unfinished Symphony No. 3 in A minor. This and *Spring Tidings* have been broadcast by the BBC.

DRING, Madeleine
7 Sep. 1923 – 26 Mar. 1977

A violinist, pianist and singer as well as a composer, Madeleine Dring was born at Hornsey in London. At the age of nine she won a violin scholarship at the junior department of the Royal College of Music, where she later studied with Herbert Howells and, occasionally, with Vaughan Williams. While at the RCM her talents were recognised and she was soon writing music for children's plays. Her later works included an opera (*Cupboard Love*), the orchestral *Dansa Gaya*, incidental music for radio, television and West End revues, several trios and other chamber works, songs and instrumental music, especially for piano (including a *Fantasy Sonata in B flat*) and for oboe (her husband was the oboist and composer, Roger Lord). Madeleine Dring's music never displayed influences of contemporary developments, but it was distinctive, entertaining and suffused with vivacity and wit, as may best be seen in the *Three Fantastic Variations on 'Lilliburlero'* for two pianos (1948). She died in London.

DRYSDALE, F. Learmont
3 Oct. 1866 – 18 Jun. 1909
Born in Edinburgh, Drysdale studied architecture before deciding to devote his life to music. At the Royal Academy of Music under Frederick Corder he won several prizes for composition and had some of his works performed. He was an organist in Edinburgh and Kensington, and did some conducting. Little of his music was published, though he wrote several orchestral overtures, eleven operas (*Fionn and Tera* was published; the others included *Red Spider, The Plague* and *Hippolytus*), the overture *Tam O'Shanter* (awarded a prize in 1891), cantatas, songs and part-songs, choral works and piano pieces. Many of his more important manuscripts have, sadly, been lost. Drysdale died at Lasswade in Midlothian.

DUARTE, John William
2 Oct. 1919 – 23 Dec. 2004
John Duarte was one of the most prolific composers for the classical guitar, having published nearly 200 works, both original and arrangements. Duarte was born in Sheffield, but soon moved to Manchester, where he trained in chemistry at the University. Although he had lessons in jazz guitar, he worked during the war as a chief industrial chemist in the Ministry of Supply. From the age of thirty he concentrated his efforts on classical guitar and moved to London to teach at the Spanish Guitar Centre. Although he never considered himself to be a performer, he met some of the leading players of the time, including Segovia, who became a lifelong friend. By 1973 he had taken up composing and teaching full time, and his works were being recorded internationally. His output consists not only of numerous works for solo guitar, but also guitar ensembles, flute and guitar, voice and guitar, guitar and string quartet, etc. His style is eclectic, ranging from folk-song to the aleatoric, exploring the vast range of sonorities and techniques of the instrument.

DUNCAN, William Edmonstoune
22 Apr. 1866 – 26 Jun. 1920
W.E. Duncan was born at Sale in Cheshire. He studied with G.A. Macfarren, and with Parry and Stanford at the Royal College of Music. Although known primarily as a critic, Duncan composed operas, orchestral works, pieces for chorus and orchestra (*Ye Mariners of England* being written for the Glasgow Choral Union in 1890), chamber music, church services, and organ pieces. He also wrote a history of music, a biography of Schubert and a comprehensive dictionary of musical terms.

DUNHILL, Thomas Frederick
1 Feb. 1877 – 13 Mar. 1946
Thomas Dunhill, born at Hampstead in London, studied piano with Franklin Taylor and composition with Stanford at the Royal College of Music. For nine years he taught music at Eton and was a professor at the RCM from 1905. His main interest lay in Sullivan's light operas, a subject on which he wrote copiously. His own light opera of 1931, *Tantivy Towers*, to words by A.P. Herbert, achieved some success. He also composed other operas (*The Enchanted Garden* and *Happy Families*), a symphony and other orchestral works, a great deal of music, including three

children's cantatas, and instrumental works (many piano pieces for children). He penned a biography of Sir Edward Elgar. Dunhill died at Scunthorpe.

DUNLOP, Isobel Violet Skelton
4 Mar. 1901 – 12 Mar. 1975
Isobel Dunlop is best remembered for her commissioning of works by young composers and for the awards which she instituted. She studied with Donald Tovey and Hans Gal at Edinburgh University, in the city where she was born, before moving to London to become a pupil of George Dyson. She taught music for a few years, then took up an appointment as Concert Organiser for the Arts Council of Scotland. With Hans Oppenheim she co-founded the Saltire Music Group and the Saltire Singers. Her compositions include incidental music and tone poems, a one-act opera (*The Silhouettes*), a children's opera (*The Stephenson Triptych*), four cantatas, choruses and works for voice and orchestra, songs, part-songs and anthems, some chamber music including a suite for cello, and piano pieces. She died in Edinburgh.

DYKES, Rev. John Bacchus
10 Mar. 1823 – 22 Jan. 1876

Father of John St Oswald Dykes, a concert pianist and composer of light music, John Bacchus was born at Kingston upon Hull. He studied music with Walmisley and was ordained in 1848. After a period as precentor at Durham Cathedral he became vicar of the Parish Church of St Oswald in Durham. Dykes was a renowned theologian and possessed a wide knowledge of music. While at St Catherine's, Cambridge, he established the Cambridge University Orchestra. Dykes composed church services, anthems, and many well-known hymn-tunes, such as *Nicaea* (Holy, holy, holy! Lord God almighty), *Hollinside* (Jesu, lover of my soul), *Melita* (Eternal Father, strong to save) *Dominus regit me* (The King of Love my shepherd is) and *Horbury* (Nearer my God to thee). He died at St Leonards-on-Sea in Sussex.

DYSON, George
28 May 1883 – 28 Sep. 1964

George Dyson was born at Halifax, the son of a blacksmith. He became an FRCO at the age of sixteen, gained scholarship to the Royal College of Music, and travelled in Italy and Germany on a Mendelssohn Scholarship. He served in the Royal Fusiliers and wrote an official booklet on grenade technique. He taught at several public schools (Marlborough, Rugby, Winchester College) and then taught at the RCM, becoming its Director in 1937 – a post he retained until 1952. Dyson was knighted in 1941 and was awarded the KCVO in 1953. He died in Winchester.

As a pupil of Stanford, his music is conservative in idiom, yet has depth and charm; his large-scale choral and orchestral work *The Canterbury Pilgrims* well deserves a revival. Dyson also composed a symphony, several other vocal and choral works, a violin concerto, orchestral pieces, chamber music, much effective church music, songs, part-songs, and piano solos.

EASDALE, Brian
10 Aug. 1909 – 30 Oct. 1995

Born in Manchester, Easdale went to Westminster Abbey Choir School and the Royal College of Music, studying with Armstrong Gibbs and Gordon Jacob. His operas received performances, as did his orchestral compositions (a piano concerto, *Five Pieces for Orchestra* and some tone poems.) His most noted work was *Missa Coventriensis* of 1962, written for the consecration of Coventry Cathedral; but it was for film music that he was most noted, particularly for Powell and Pressburger's *The Red Shoes*.

EDMUNDS, Christopher
1899 – 1990

Dr Christopher Edmunds lived and worked in Birmingham all his life. Edmunds was teacher of harmony and composition at the Birmingham School of Music from 1929 and Principal from 1945-56. He was one of a circle of pupils surrounding Sir Granville Bantock during his time as Principal of the School. His music is preserved at Birmingham University. He will be best known for his widely played Sonatina for recorder and piano. Edmunds wrote three symphonies in quick succession – the first for strings in 1937; the third has never been performed. The turbulent wartime Second Symphony was first broadcast in 1944. In addition he wrote four operas, a number of choral and chamber works, and numerous shorter pieces. He died at Whixley, Yorks.

EDWARDS, Henry John
24 Feb. 1854 – 8 Apr. 1933

H.J. Edwards was born at Barnstaple, Devon and was a pupil first of his father John Edwards, then of Sterndale Bennett, G.A. Macfarren, H.C. Banister and George Cooper, completing a doctorate at Oxford. He became an organist at Barnstaple and was appointed conductor of the Exeter Oratorio Society. His compositions include oratorios, cantatas, motets, songs and part-songs, and a triumphal March for orchestra.

ELGAR, Edward William
2 Jun. 1857 – 23 Feb. 1934

Although the foundations of the English Musical Renaissance may be attributed to Stanford and Parry, it was Elgar who put England on the musical map. *The Dream of Gerontius* and the *Violin Concerto* were widely acclaimed in Europe and gained for Elgar the accolade of being the 'first great English composer since Purcell'. At home Elgar's music was assimilated only slowly because of his provincial background – 'a local talent' – and it was the local festivals that gave him his chance. Some minor works – *Salut d'amour*, the overture *Froissart*, and especially the *March Imperial* for Queen Victoria's Diamond Jubilee in 1897 – brought Elgar to the public's notice, but it was the Variations for Orchestra (*Enigma Variations*) of 1899, premiered by Hans Richter in London, that finally set the scene and Elgar's reputation was secured.

He was born at Broadheath near Worcester into a musical family. His father was an organist and kept a music shop. The young Elgar taught himself much by avidly perusing his father's stock of scores and by playing various instruments in local amateur groups. He also conducted locally and his gifts as an orchestrator must have benefited from the arrangements he had to make for the unusual instrumental combinations at his disposal. He received some violin tuition from Adolf Pollitzer and made a living for some time as a solicitor's clerk and by teaching violin.

In 1898 the Worcestershire Philharmonic Orchestra was formed in recognition of his achievements, and for six years he conducted it in performances in Birmingham of mainly contemporary British music. During this period his oratorio *The Dream of Gerontius* to words by Cardinal Newman, was performed in Birmingham on 3 October 1900. The premiere was technically severely flawed but, by the time the oratorio had been performed all over Europe, it returned to England to great acclaim.

In 1904 Elgar was knighted. In 1911 he received the Order of Merit, and in 1924 became Master of the King's Musick. A baronetcy followed in 1931. By 1933 his health had been failing for some time, but he flew to France and met Delius, who was by then bedridden. A few months later he died at Worcester and is buried in St Wulstan's Church, Little Malvern.

Elgar composed two symphonies (his sketches of a third have been completed by Anthony Payne), oratorios (*The Apostles* and *The Kingdom*) and cantatas, concertos for violin and for cello (the latter being one of his finest works), a ballet, an incomplete opera (*The Spanish Lady*), orchestral suites, incidental music (that for *The Starlight Express* is the most extended), marches and overtures, a string quartet, piano quintet, wind quintets, violin sonata and other chamber works. He also wrote pieces for the organ and piano, songs part-songs and anthems.

ELKINGTON, Lilian
15 Sep. 1900 – 13 Aug. 1969

Born in Birmingham, Lilian Elkington studied piano and composition at the Birmingham Midland Institute School of Music under Granville Bantock, where she gained her LRAM and later ARCO. She also played piano concertos in various public concerts. On her marriage she moved to Bookham and East Horsley, Surrey. She died while on holiday in Austria. Bantock conducted the first performance of her atmospheric tone poem *Out of the Mist* (1921), recorded much later. The only other known works are a *Romance* and *Rhapsodie*, both for violin and piano, and a song *Little Hands*, all of which manuscripts were found in a secondhand bookshop in Worthing in the late 1970s.

ELLERTON, John Lodge
17 Jan. 1801 – 3 Jan. 1873

This prolific amateur composer and poet was born near Chester. Born John Lodge (he later adopted his surname), he was educated at Rugby and Brasenose College, Oxford, and studied music in Rome with Terziani. Among his many works, many of which were self-published, were seven Italian operas, two German operas, an English opera, six symphonies, fifty string quartets, much church music and a plethora of songs. Lodge Ellerton died in London.

ELLICOTT, Rosalind Frances
14 Nov. 1857 – 5 Apr. 1924

Daughter of a Bishop of Bristol and Gloucester and of a mother who was a keen singer who helped found the Handel Society, Rosalind Ellicott was born in Cambridge.

It is said that she began to compose at the age of six. She studied piano with Frederick Westlake and composition with Thomas Wingham at the Royal Academy of Music. Her works, often heard during her life at the Three Choirs festivals, include cantatas (*Elysium* and *The Birth of Song*), a choral ballad (*King Henry of Navarre*), orchestral overtures (her *Dramatic Overture* was premiered at the Crystal Palace in 1891 and appeared at the opening of the Women's Building at the Chicago World's Columbian Exposition later that year), a fantasia for piano and orchestra, and much chamber music including two string quartets and two piano trios. Few of her works have survived, despite their success during her lifetime. Rosalind Ellicott died in Kent.

ELVEY, George Job
27 Mar. 1816 – 9 Dec. 1893
Sir George Elvey was organist of St George's Chapel, Windsor, for fifty years, serving both William IV and Queen Victoria, who knighted him in 1871. He was born in Canterbury and studied with Highmore Skeats at the Cathedral, then with Potter and Crotch at the Royal Academy of Music. He composed a Fantasy on Rossini's *Moses in Egypt*, which Thalberg played when he visited Elvey at Windsor, oratorios (*The Resurrection and Ascension* and *Mount Carmel*), odes, anthems and other church music, all of which – like many church compositions of his time – are conventional and conservative in style. Elvey died at Windlesham in Surrey and is entombed in St George's Chapel.

FANING, Eaton Joseph
20 May 1850 – 28 Oct. 1927

Faning was born at Helston in Cornwall. His first music lessons were with his father, before he entered the Royal Academy of Music to study with Sterndale Bennett, Charles Steggall, Ciabatta and Sullivan, carrying off several prizes and playing cello, timpani and organ, as well as singing. In 1878 he was appointed a professor of piano at the RAM. He held numerous other appointments – at the National Training School for Music, the Guildhall School of Music and as an examiner for various boards – and became director of music at Harrow School in 1885. He composed a symphony, operettas, string quartets, church music and songs (many of which, such as *The Song of the Vikings*, were very popular). Faning died in Brighton.

FANSHAWE, David Arthur
19 April 1942 – 5 July 2010
With its backing tracks of, among other things, African rainfall accompanying choir and orchestra, David Fanshawe's *African Sanctus* made a huge splash when its first recording was released in 1975. The work is, in many ways, an apt summary of the composer's ground-breaking life and work, fusing ethnic music, sounds of nature, Western musical genres and multicultural spirituality. It deserved its success, but was never rivalled by any other work.

Fanshawe was born in Paignton, Devon, and went to St George's choir school, Windsor, and Stowe before working for the Film Producers Guild in London. At the same time he was taking piano lessons with Guirne Creith. In 1965, to his own considerable surprise, he won a Foundation scholarship to the Royal College of Music, where he studied with John Lambert.

Travelling widely in the holidays he developed a keen interest in the music of the middle east and, after his studies were completed in 1969, travelled again, recording whatever he could of the music of the Mediterranean and northern and eastern Africa. This would lead to his *African Sanctus* but, more importantly, to a lifetime spent recording and documenting music all over the world, especially in the Pacific and south-east Asia. He amassed several thousand hours of recordings of world music, much of which, together with 60,000 images, form the basis of the Fanshawe Collection, and his enthusiasm probably saved much indigenous music from total extinction. In recognition he was awarded an honorary Doctorate in Music by the University of the West of England in 2007. Three years later he died from a stroke.

David Fanshawe composed scores for over fifty films and television documentaries (*When the Boat Comes In*, *Tarka the Otter*, *Mountains of the Moon*, *Seven Years in Tibet*, and *The Feathered Serpent* among them). Other significant works include *Requiem for the Children of Aberfan*, *Arabian Fantasy*, *The Awakening* for cello and piano (written for Stephen Isserlis), and *Pacific Song*, all that was completed of a choral *Pacific Odyssey* drawing on the experiences of his Pacific travels.

FARJEON, Harry Herbert
6 May 1878 – 29 Dec. 1948
Harry Farjeon was born of English parents at Hohokus, New Jersey, but returned to Britain at an early age. He studied music privately with Landon Ronald and John Storer, then in 1895 went to the Royal Academy of Music under Battison Haynes, Frederick Corder, and Septimus Webbe. After leaving the RAM as a student, Farjeon returned there to teach harmony and composition. He was also on the staff of the Blackheath Conservatoire. His opera *Floretta* was performed while he was a student. His other works include several more operettas (including *The Registry Office* and *Gentleman of the Road*), orchestral suites and tone poems, a piano concerto and a *Phantasy Concerto* for piano and chamber orchestra, a ballet, string quartets, three violin sonatas, a mass and other choral works (the best of these for young voices), two ballads for female chorus, piano and other instrumental works, songs, and an *Idyll* for oboe and orchestra. Farjeon wrote regularly for Musical Times and The Telegraph. He died in London.

FARMER, John
16 Aug. 1836 – 17 Jul. 1901
John Farmer was born at Nottingham and studied music at Leipzig. He taught at Zürich and at Harrow and became organist at Balliol College, Oxford, in 1885. Farmer composed an oratorio (*Christ and his Soldiers*), a requiem, an opera (*Cinderella*), music for chorus and orchestra, some chamber music and songs. He died at Oxford.

FARRAR, Ernest Bristow
7 Jul. 1885 – 18 Sep. 1918
Ernest Farrar's life was tragically short. He was born at Blackheath, London, and was killed in action on the Somme at the end of the World War One. During this brief span

he composed orchestral rhapsodies, a symphony and other orchestral works, *The Blessed Damozel* for solo, chorus and orchestra, other cantatas or works for chorus/voice and orchestra, string quartet music and pieces for violin, piano and organ, as well as some very fine songs. Farrar studied at the Royal College of Music with Stanford, winning the Arthur Sullivan Prize. He was organist of an English church in Dresden, and at South Shields and Harrogate.

FAWCETT, John Jnr
17 Oct. 1824 – 1 Jul. 1857
John Fawcett was born in Bolton and lived in Manchester, where he died. He became organist at St John's Church, Farnworth before studying at the Royal Academy of Music under Sterndale Bennett. He conducted the Bolton Philharmonic Society and composed a cantata, church music, organ and piano pieces.

FELLOWES, Rev. Edmund Horace
11 Nov. 1870 – 20 Dec. 1951
A renowned authority on old English music and editor of many editions of the English Madrigal Society, Edmund Fellowes was born in London. He studied at Winchester College, then Oriel College, Oxford, his teachers being Percy Buck and Percy Fletcher. Ordained in 1894, he spent four years as precentor at Bristol Cathedral before becoming organist and conductor at St George's Chapel, Windsor. He served as a minor canon there for 51 years, under five sovereigns. Fellowes composed some competent, but hardly inspired, church music and organ works.

FENNEY, William
21 May 1891 – 25 Jun. 1957
William Fenney was born in Birmingham and was self-taught as a composer until he entered the Midland Institute to study with Granville Bantock. His style was influenced by Elgar, and he gave up composition in his later years rather than conform to the developing contemporary idioms. He died at Epsom. Fenney wrote several orchestral pieces, two string quartets and a piano trio, works for violin and piano, piano solos and songs.

FERGUSON, Howard
21 Oct. 1908 – 31 Oct. 1999
Howard Ferguson was born in Belfast, where at the age of thirteen he was heard playing piano in the Belfast Musical Competition by Harold Samuel. Samuel was sufficiently impressed to persuade the boy's parents to allow Howard to study with him in London, where he also enrolled in Westminster School. Two years later the young man entered the Royal College of Music, where he studied composition with R.O. Morris (and, later, Vaughan Williams), conducting with Malcolm Sargent, and piano with Samuel. At the RCM he met Gerald Finzi, who was to become a lifelong friend. On leaving college Ferguson played piano in chamber groups and began to compose. His first Violin Sonata appeared in 1931 and his Octet two years later. Originally scored for clarinet and strings, the octet was later rewritten, at R.O. Morris's suggestion, for the same forces as Schubert's Octet – for clarinet, bassoon,

horn and strings. Ferguson eventually abandoned performance except for recitals of his own music. He toured the USA to this end in 1953.

During World War Two Ferguson and Dame Myra Hess organised lunchtime chamber concerts at the National Gallery. Ferguson also joined the RAF, entertaining troops in concert with the Griller String Quartet. From 1948 to 1963 he taught composition at the Royal Academy of Music. In the early '60s Ferguson gave up composition, having reached his Opus 19, and devoted himself to editing early keyboard music. Among the nineteen original works are the Piano Sonata of 1940, two violin sonatas, the Octet, the song-cycle *Discovery*, two choral works (*Amore Langueo* and *The Dream of the Rood*), an orchestral Partita and the Concerto for piano and strings. There were other piano and chamber works (a ballet was later disowned). Howard Ferguson died in Cambridge.

FINCK, Herman
4 Nov. 1872 – 21 Apr. 1939
Herman Finck was born in London of Dutch parents. His father, Louis von der Finck, was conductor at Drury Lane and the Gaiety Theatre. Herman started his musical career as a violinist at the age of fourteen, later studying at the Guildhall School of Music with Edward Solomon and Henry Gadsby. For thirty years musical director at the Palace Theatre and later at Drury Lane, he conducted the premiere of the operetta *Rose Marie*, which ran for over two years. He was also a founder member of the Performing Right Society. Finck composed a great deal of light orchestral music, two operettas (*Hiawatha* and *Moonshine*), a comic opera (*The Palace Revue*), ballets, piano pieces and songs. His *In the Shadows* sold more than a million copies.

FINZI, Gerald Raphael
14 Jul. 1901 – 27 Sep. 1956
Gerald Finzi is considered by many to be one of the finest song composers of his time. He was born in London to an Italian-Jewish family and after the death of his father and three elder brothers while he was still a young schoolboy, suffered a lonely and unhappy childhood. In 1913 he was removed from boarding school and sent abroad in the hope that it would cure his frequent illnesses. Returning to England he began studying music with Ernest Farrar. When Farrar was killed in action on the Somme in 1918, Finzi was deeply affected, but resumed studies with Sir Edward Bairstow at York and with R.O. Morris in London. In 1930 he accepted a post as professor of composition at the Royal Academy of Music, but stayed there for only three years before retiring to the country with his wife Joyce Black, to devote himself to composition. He remained in rural Berkshire for the rest of his life – except for the war years, when he worked for the Ministry of War Transport, despite being a committed pacifist – and is buried at Ashmansworth, Hampshire. He died in Oxford as a result of exposure to chicken pox, his immune system already weakened by leukaemia.

Finzi identified himself closely with the English countryside, as can be seen in much of his music and in his collection of Old English apple trees. With amateur string orchestras he performed works by many neglected English composers. Finzi's music shows little of the sadness of his early life. He was essentially a miniaturist until the last few years of his life, when he composed a clarinet concerto, cello concerto, and the Wordsworth setting *Intimations of Immortality*. These works, together with other orchestral pieces, the songs (many reflecting a respectful affection for the poetry of Thomas Hardy), six cantatas, and instrumental and chamber music, place Finzi in the nationalist English Pastoral tradition. He also edited for publication some eighteenth-century works for strings by John Garth, Richard Mudge, John Stanley and Charles Wesley. The collection of English poetry that inspired so much of Finzi's work is now held in the Reading University Library.

FISKE, Roger
10 Sep. 1910 – 22 Jul. 1987
Born in Surbiton, Fiske was an English musicologist, music educationist, broadcaster and composer. After taking a BA in English at Wadham College, Oxford in 1932, he studied composition with Herbert Howells at the Royal College of Music, and criticism with H.C. Colles until 1937, when he was awarded an Oxford D.Mus. In 1939 he joined the BBC, where he remained for twenty years, producing educational programmes for the armed forces (1948-53) and music talks for the Third Programme (1953-59). From 1968 to 1975 he was general editor of Eulenberg (London) miniature scores, notably editing Handel's *Water Music* and *Fireworks Music* suites. Fiske wrote several books on music, including *English Theatre Music in the Eighteenth Century* (1973) and *Scotland in Music* (1983), as well as many more popular and educational works (particularly on Beethoven). Among his original mss. held at the Bodleian Library are a string quartet (*Midsummer Hill*), piano trio, piano sonata, a sonata and sonatina for clarinet and piano, and ten songs.

FITZWILLIAM, Edward Francis
1 Aug. 1824 – 20 Jan. 1857
Fitzwilliam, whose parents were actors and singers, was born at Deal. He studied with Sir Henry Bishop and John Barnett and became musical director at the Lyceum and, for a short time, the Haymarket theatres. He wrote much music for the stage, including operetta and a comic opera (*Queen of a day*). Although these genres constituted the bulk of his writing, he also composed a *Stabat Mater* (performed in 1845), a *Te Deum*, four books of dramatic songs and piano pieces. His promising career was ended when he died in London of tuberculosis.

FLETCHER, Percy Eastman
12 Dec. 1879 – 10 Dec. 1932
Fletcher is now remembered only by the brass and military band fraternities, who still perform his *Labour and Love* and *Epic Symphony*. In his day he was a popular composer of light orchestral music and musical comedy (*Cairo*, which had 267 performances in 1921, and *The Good Old Days*). He was born at Derby and studied violin, piano and organ before devoting himself to theatrical conducting. He held positions at the Prince of Wales, Savoy and His Majesty's theatres. In addition to his brass and military band music, Fletcher composed ballads and choral music (including a sacred *Passion*), light orchestral suites, marches and other short pieces, a string quartet, part-songs, organ pieces and piano music (mostly comprising reductions of his orchestral scores). He re-orchestrated *Chu Chin Chow* and some of Coleridge-Taylor's and Delius's music. Fletcher died in London.

FLOOD, William Henry Grattan
1 Nov. 1859 – 6 Aug. 1928
Born at Lismore in Ireland, Flood was self-taught as a musician. He became organist at the cathedrals of Thurles, Monaghan and Enniscorthy, and composed masses, motets, songs and part-songs. He also did some valuable research into the history of Irish and early English music. He died at Enniscorthy, County Wexford.

FOGG, Charles William Eric
21 Feb. 1903 – 19 Dec. 1939
Eric Fogg was born in Manchester, where he was a chorister at the Cathedral and later, organist at St John's Church. His first music lessons were with his father, but he became a pupil of Granville Bantock in 1920. He started composing as a young boy and developed an idiom showing some influence of Stravinsky, though this idiom was tempered in later years. His *Phantasy* for cello and piano, composed before he was fifteen, was published; and his ballet of around the same time, *Hansel and Gretel*, was received with success. Much of his orchetral music,however, is lost. Fogg became musical director of the BBC Northern Region, then of the Empire Services. He wrote several orchestral works, two ballets, choral/orchestral music, a bassoon concerto, string quartet, instrumental music, songs and part-songs.

FORBES, Henry
1804 – 24 Nov. 1859
A piano recitalist, organist of the Parish Church of St Luke's in Chelsea, and conductor of the Societa Armonica, Henry Forbes was born in London. He studied with Smart, Hummel, Moscheles and Herz and composed songs, psalm-tunes (he published *National Psalmody*), an opera (*The Fairy Oak*, 1845), an oratorio (*Ruth*), other choral works, songs, organ works and pieces for piano.

FORD, Ernest
17 Feb. 1858 – 2 Jun. 1919
Ernest Ford was born at Warminster in Wiltshire. His father was organist at the Minster, and Ernest was a chorister at Salisbury Cathedral before studying at the Royal Academy of Music with Sullivan, Charles Steggall and Harold Thomas, and in Paris with the composer Edouard Lalo. He held various posts as an operatic conductor and accompanist, and was a professor of singing at the Guildhall School of Music. Ford died in London. His compositions include an *Elegy* for violin and orchestra, a string quartet and other chamber works, operas (*Nydia, Daniel O'Rourke, Joan*) and operettas (*Jane Annie* was to a libretto by J.M. Barrie and Conan Doyle), ballets, cantatas, songs and church music. He also published an encyclopaedic 'History of Music in England'. Ford died in London.

FORRESTER, James Cliffe
1860 – 25 Feb. 1940
James Forrester was born at Burslem in Staffordshire and studied at the National Training School for Music with Arthur O'Leary and Frederick Bridge. He taught piano and organ and conducted the Ealing Musical Society for many years. He composed cantatas, anthems and choruses, part-songs and song cycles, chamber works and pieces for violin and for piano. He died in Bournemouth.

FOSS, Hubert James
2 May 1899 – 27 May 1953
A man of diverse talents, Hubert Foss was born at Croydon and was a Classics scholar at Bradfield College in Berkshire. He began a career as a journalist, and in 1924 was appointed musical editor for Oxford University Press, where he did much valuable work in fostering the music of new composers such as William Walton. Foss was a lecturer and adjudicator, conductor and founder of the Bach Cantata Club, author of a study of Vaughan Williams and *Music in My Time*, and editor of the two-volume *Heritage of Music*. He accompanied his wife Dora Stevens in recitals. Foss composed several songs and *Seven Poems by Thomas Hardy* for baritone, male chorus and chamber orchestra. He died in London.

FOSTER, Arnold Wilfred Allen
6 Dec. 1896 – 30 Sep. 1963
Born at Sheffield, Arnold Foster studied at the Royal College of Music with Vaughan Williams. He taught at Morley College (succeeding Holst), Westminster School and London University Institute of Education, and conducted the English Madrigal Choir, which he founded in 1928. In 1945 he founded and conducted his own orchestra, introducing many new works to this country. His compositions include a piano concerto (on English folk tunes), music for strings, chamber works, a ballet, piano pieces and songs. He also arranged English and Manx folk music.

FOSTER, Myles Birket
29 Nov. 1851 – 18 Dec. 1922
Son of the famous water colourist of the same name, Myles Birket Foster was born in Staines and died at Acton in London, where he spent most of his life. Son of a Quaker family, he started a career in a stockbroker's office but soon became a music pupil of Hamilton Clarke, later studying at the Royal Academy of Music with Sullivan, Prout and Frederick Westlake. Primarily an organist and choirmaster (in Marylebone and at the Foundling Hospital Chapel), he was also musical director at Boosey and Hawkes. He composed  symphonies, overtures, children's cantatas, a string quartet, trios and church music.

FOULDS, John Herbert
2 Nov. 1880 – 24 Apr. 1939
John Foulds was the son of a member of the Hallé Orchestra and was born in Manchester. He started to learn the piano at the age of four and was a competent cellist at ten. He ran away from home when he was fourteen, escaping from his parents' strict religious fundamentalism, and made a living by playing in local bands before himself joining the Hallé. He greatly admired the music of Busoni and Bartók and wrote a stimulating book 'Music Today'. Foulds married Maud MacCarthy, a well-known violinist and authority on Indian music. From 1917-26 he was musical director for various London societies such as Ciro's Club, Mansion House, London University Musical Society, and the London Central YMCA. He spent many years in Paris and the last part of his life in India, where he collected traditional Indian folk music, using it to great effect in his own compositions. He founded an orchestra of

traditional instruments and composed much music especially for them. His wife Maud began to write poetry under a Hindu pseudonym and established a fabric factory in Kashmir. As Head of European Music for All India Radio he built up a symphony orchestra from nothing, and when he died in Calcutta from cholera, he was in the process of composing *Symphony of East and West*, unifying the two musical cultures. Sadly only sketches of this work remain.

Foulds composed a *World Requiem* requiring enormous orchestral forces, a cello concerto, *Dynamic Triptych* (effectively a piano concerto, the slow movement of which makes eloquent use of quarter-tones), much incidental music, a concert opera (*The Vision of Dante,* in which the soloist uses microtones); an opera (*Avatara*), many other works for orchestra (including the ambitious symphonic poem *Mirage*, and *Lyra Celtica* for voice and orchestra, using microtonal scales of Indian music), ten string quartets, other chamber works, songs and instrumental music, including the masterly *The Twelve Essays in the Modes* for piano and the empathic *April-England* for the same medium. Of the light music, the *Keltic Lament* achieved much popularity.

FRANKEL, Benjamin
31 Jan. 1906 – 12 Feb. 1973
Benjamin Frankel was born in London to parents of Polish-Jewish origin and displayed his talents as a pianist and viola player at a very early age. He relinquished his apprenticeship to a watch maker in order to study music, encouraged by the American pianist Victor Benham, who tutored him without fees and took the young pupil to Germany for six months. On his return to England Frankel paid his way at the Guildhall School of Music by playing piano in cafes (and on ocean liners) and jazz violin. He then won a composition scholarship and studied with Orlando Morgan.

Between the wars Frankel emerged into the public view as a jazz musician and composer of film music (among many titles were the notable *The Night of the Iguana*, *The Seventh Veil*, *The Man in the White Suit*, *Curse of the Werewolf* and *Battle of the Bulge*), also orchestrating and conducting West End musical revues and comedies. His considerable success in these fields enabled him to devote much of his life to serious music, and he became a respected symphonist.

After 1959, when he had his first heart attack, his health progressively deteriorated. Frankel composed eight symphonies, the sixth composed entirely in hospital (a ninth remained uncompleted), five string quartets, an opera, a ballet, concertos for violin (dedicated to the six million Jews who died in the Holocaust) and for viola, other orchestral and chamber works, piano and violin music, songs and choral works. Frankel died in London.

FRICKER, Peter Racine
5 Sep. 1920 – 1 Feb. 1990
In 1958 the Leeds Festival heard Fricker's large-scale commissioned choral and orchestral work with two brass bands, *The Vision of Judgment*, based on words by the eighth-century Cynewulf, which was very well received. The work had several more performances before its London appearance; but response there was lukewarm and *The Vision* fell into obscurity, except for a 1980 revival in Ripon. Fricker's early works reflected a rejection of the then current pastoral nationalism of British music,

and he turned more towards composers such as Bartók, Hindemith and Schoenberg. Surprisingly, his early works – the First Symphony, the Wind Quintet and the first Violin Concerto (all of which won awards) – were very successful. But fashions changed and momentum was lost, though Cheltenham continued to support his music. So, later, did his adopted country, the USA.

Peter Racine (after the French tragedian, on his grandmother's lineage) Fricker was born in London and went to St. Paul's School before being accepted by the Royal College of Music, studying composition with R.O. Morris and organ with Ernest Bullock. He also had some lessons at Morley College. Soon after the outbreak of war Fricker joined the RAF, working in signals and intelligence. He learned Japanese and was posted to India.

After demobilisation, Fricker resumed his classes at Morley College, where Michael Tippett recommended him to study with Mátyás Seiber. When his course finished he stayed as assistant to Seiber, helping with film scores. In 1952 he succeeded Tippett as Director, later becoming a professor of composition at the RCM. He was also heavily involved in the Composers' Guild of Great Britain, the Arts Council, the BBC and the Royal Philharmonic Society. In 1964 he was invited to be visiting professor for a year in the music department of the University of California, when he was offered a permanent post there.

Fricker wrote five symphonies (the fourth dedicated to Seiber), a *Litany* for string orchestra, a *Comedy Overture,* several concertante works (cor anglais and strings; three pianos, strings and timpani; piano; viola; violin), *O Longs Désirs* for soprano and orchestra, choral works, a cantata for tenor and chamber ensemble, chamber music, piano and organ music, and much more. Given that he received the highest honour that the University of California could bestow (Faculty Research Lecturer), the Order of Merit from the Federal Government of West Germany, the Freedom of the City of London, an Honorary Doctorate from Leeds University and Honorary Membership of the Royal Academy of Music, it is hard to believe that Fricker's music is not more frequently heard in the UK. He died in Los Angeles.

FRISKIN, James
3 Mar. 1886 – 16 Mar. 1967
Although he spent most of his life and died in the United States, where he was a piano recitalist and teacher at the Juilliard School, James Friskin was born in Glasgow. He studied there with Alfred Heap, then entered the Royal College of Music under Dannreuther, Hartvigson and Stanford. He settled in New York in 1914 and married Rebecca Clarke in 1944. Most of Friskin's works are for chamber groups, but he also composed an orchestral suite, motets, and instrumental pieces, notably for piano and cello.

FROST, Mary. See **PLUMSTEAD**, Mary

FULTON, Norman Robert
22 Jan. 1909 – 1980
Norman Fulton was widely known in his various positions on the staff of the BBC. He was born in London and studied at the RAM, where he was appointed Professor of Harmony in 1966. He composed three symphonies, concertos for piano and for violin, some chamber works, piano pieces, and over fifty songs with various accompaniments. He died at Bromley in Kent.

Gabriel, Mary Ann Virginia
7 Feb. 1825 – 7 Aug. 1877

Virginia Gabriel was born at Banstead in Surrey into a military family and studied piano with J.P. Pixis, Theodor Dohler and Sigismond Thalberg, and composition with Bernhard Molique. By the time she was in her fifties her songs and ballads (over 300 in total) had become best-sellers. *Ruby* and *When Sparrows Build* were particularly successful. In addition to the songs and ballads Gabriel composed cantatas (*Dreamland*, *Evangeline* and *Graziella*), and seven operettas, including *Widows Bewitched*, *The Lion's Mouth*, *Lost and Found*, *The Shepherd of Cornouailles*, and *Who's the Heir?*. Her later operettas were to libretti by her husband, George March. Gabriel died in London as a result of a road accident.

GADSBY, Henry Robert
15 Dec. 1842 – 11 Nov. 1907

Born in London the same year as Arthur Sullivan, Henry Gadsby was largely self-taught. He succeeded John Hullah at Queen's College, London in 1884, and was one of the original professors at the Guildhall School of Music. He was an organist and composed a concerto for the instrument. He also wrote three symphonies, overtures such as *Andromeda* and *The Witches Frolic*, incidental music, string quartets, cantatas and anthems, services and songs, as well as writing some educational publications.

GARDINER, Henry Balfour
7 Nov. 1877 – 28 June 1950

Balfour Gardiner was born in London, the son of a wealthy businessman. He went to Charterhouse and Oxford, then to Frankfurt, where he studied with Iwan Knorr. Gardiner and his circle of friends (Percy Grainger, Cyril Scott, Roger Quilter and Norman O'Neill) later became known as the 'Frankfurt Group'. His music won him the respect and admiration of his friends, and his warm personality their affection. He is now best remembered for the selfless generosity he displayed in promoting the music of young British composers and in helping his friends whenever they were in difficulties. He did little, on the other hand, to promote his own works, and before he was fifty he gave up composition, complaining that his muse had left him. He devoted the rest of his life to the restoration and afforestation of the Dorset Downs.

Before his retirement Balfour Gardiner wrote two symphonies (both withdrawn and destroyed), overtures, and other orchestral works (the enormous popularity of *Shepherd Fennel's Dance* may have eclipsed the rest of Gardiner's music), a string quintet and string quartet, many impressive songs, choral works and instrumental pieces. The church anthem, *Te lucis ante terminum* (*Evening Hymn*), is regarded as one of the finest pieces of church choral writing. After Gardiner died in Salisbury, Percy Grainger set about publicising his friend and benefactor's music, but Grainger's own death in 1961 left the task unfulfilled.

GARRATT, Percival Maurice
21 May 1877 – 16 Apr. 1953

Percival Garratt, born at Little Tew Grange in Oxfordshire, studied in Vienna with Ree, in Berlin with Klindworth and in England with Egon Petri. Garratt was a professor at the Guildhall School of Music and toured Europe and the Far East as a piano recitalist and accompanist. His compositions include short pieces for orchestra, incidental music, a pantomime (*A Cartload of Villains*) and a musical play for children (*Cherry-stones*), two song albums, and pieces for violin and for piano. He also wrote books on piano technique. Garratt died in London.

GARRETT, George Mursell
8 Jun. 1834 – 8 Apr. 1897
Garrett was organist of Madras Cathedral, then of St John's College, Cambridge. He succeeded J.L. Hopkins as organist to Cambridge University in 1873, obtaining his Mus.D. in 1857. He was born in Winchester and studied with Sir George Elvey and S.S. Wesley. Garrett composed church services, five cantatas, anthems, songs and part-songs, and organ pieces. His oratorio *The Shunamite*, received at the Hereford Festival in 1882 with little success, was his only work of any note. He died in Cambridge.

GATTY, Nicholas Comyn
13 Sep. 1874 – 10 Nov. 1946
Born at Bradfield, near Sheffield, Gatty studied at Cambridge and at the Royal College of Music with Stanford and Charles Wood. He was an organist and a music critic for the Pall Mall Gazette and The Times. As a composer Gatty specialised in operas (*Greysteel, Duke or Devil, Prince Ferelon, Macbeth, The Tempest*, etc.), but he also wrote orchestral works, pieces for chorus and orchestra, instrumental music and songs. He died in London.

GAUL, Alfred Robert
30 Apr. 1837 – 13 Sep. 1913
Born at Norwich, A.R. Gaul was a pupil at the cathedral with Dr Zechariah Buck (the assistant organist) before becoming an organist at Fakenham Church. After graduating at Cambridge he moved to Birmingham, where he held appointments at various churches in and around the city, and where he died. He taught at the Midland Institute and conducted the Walsall Philharmonic Society. His compositions include an oratorio *Hezekiah*, sacred cantatas – the best known of which is *The Holy City* (sales of which numbered 162,000 at his death), anthems, hymns and chants, part-songs and piano pieces, including a piano sonata.

GAUNTLETT, Henry John
9 July 1805 – 21 Feb. 1876
The son of a parson, born in Wellington, Shropshire, Gauntlett devoted himself to writing church music. Articled to a firm of solicitors, he soon gave up the law and took various organists' posts in London, where he died. During his lifetime he was knowledgeable in organ design and was a writer, critic and lecturer, besides being recognised as one of the most important authorities on psalmody. He compiled several hymnals and psalters, and composed a number of anthems, as well as a few part-songs and glees. Some of his many hymns are still sung today, 'Once in Royal David's City', set to the tune *Irby*, being the most famous.

GEEHL, Henry Ernest
28 Sep. 1881 – 14 Jan. 1961
Henry Geehl was one of the first English composers to write specifically for brass and military bands and did much to further the cause of these media. He was born in

London and studied with his father and in Vienna (where he met Brahms) with Benno Schönberger. A pianist and conductor of theatre orchestras, he was on the staff of Trinity College of Music for thirty years and edited music for Edwin Ashdown and Enoch. Geehl composed a symphony, piano concerto and other orchestral works, military and brass band music (also arranging a great deal), piano pieces (especially teaching pieces) and songs (*For you alone* was one of the few sung in English by Caruso). In his later years, when he gained a reputation as something of an eccentric, he began to write in the twelve-tone system so as to gain 'a more immediate knowledge of the technique'.

GERHARD, Roberto
25 Sep. 1896 – 5 Jan. 1970

Born at Valls, near Tarragona in Spain, of French and Swiss parents, Roberto Gerhard studied piano with Granados until his teacher drowned attempting to save his wife after being torpedoed on HMS Sussex by the Germans in 1915. Gerhard continued to study with Pedrell and, when he died, turned to Schoenberg, adopting the latter's twelve-tone technique in his own music. In 1938 he was invited to adjudicate in an ISCM (International Society for Contemporary Music) competition. While he was away, the city of Barcelona, where he was a teacher and librarian, fell to Franco. Rather than return to Barcelona Gerhard settled in England with his wife, remaining there for the last thirty-one years of his life.

Gerhard's compositions include four symphonies, concertos for piano, harpsichord and violin, a concerto for orchestra, a ballet, opera (*The Duenna*), a dramatic cantata, two string quartets and many other chamber works, guitar pieces, choral music and songs. Several lighter pieces were written for financial reasons and Gerhard acknowledged some, like *Alegrias*, as part of his catalogue of works. Towards the end of his life he became interested in electronic music, using it in his third symphony.

Though entering England as a research student at King's College, Cambridge through the good offices of E.J. Dent, a friend and colleague in the ISCM, he did little teaching at Cambridge, but accepted a visiting professorship to an American University for a brief period. Gerhard died in Cambridge.

GERMAN, Edward
17 Feb. 1862 – 11 Nov. 1936

German Edward Jones – who later dropped his surname – was born at Whitchurch in Shropshire and died in London. He studied at the Royal Academy of Music with Charles Steggall, Thomas H. Weist-Hill and Alfred Burnett. Here he became briefly engaged to Ethel Boyce, a fellow student and composer; both remained single thereafter. As a composer of light opera he succeeded Sullivan and was commissioned to complete Sullivan's last opera, *The Emerald Isle*. German's operas, including *Merrie England* and *Tom Jones*, were once enormously popular, as were his dances for Shakespeare's *Henry VIII*. In addition to the light operas German  wrote two symphonies, other orchestral works, instrumental music and songs. His second symphony (the *Norwich*) and *Theme and Six Diversions* are held to be his best works. German conducted at the Globe Theatre from 1888 and was knighted in 1928.

In old age he was afflicted with blindness, though he still ardently followed his cricket team.

GIBBS, Cecil Armstrong
10 Aug. 1889 – 12 May 1960
Born at Great Baddow near Chelmsford in Essex, Armstrong Gibbs went to Wick Preparatory School near Brighton, then Winchester College, before studying at Trinity College, Cambridge with E.J. Dent and Charles Wood, and at the Royal College of Music under Boult and Vaughan Williams, the former paying all his fees for a year. Gibbs later taught at the RCM. He composed two orchestral symphonies, a choral symphony (*Odysseus*), a Shakespeare opera (*Twelfth Night*), a comic opera (*The Blue Peter*), incidental music and other works for the stage, cantatas, an oboe concerto, concertino for piano and orchestra, five string quartets and other chamber works, instrumental music, church anthems, one hundred songs and even more part-songs. Armstrong Gibbs died in hospital at Chelmsford.

GIBSON, Henry
1882 – 2 Jul. 1954
London born Henry Gibson studied at the Guildhall School of Music and the Royal College of Music, and his teachers included Sir Charles Stanford and Sir Walter Parratt. Thereafter he taught at Francis Holland School and was organist and choirmaster at Holy Innocents Church, Hammersmith. He served in World War One, and subsequently seems to have become particularly involved in music for the theatre: he was sometime Musical Director in various London theatres, and was Music Secretary to Sir Thomas Beecham from 1927-32. He was co-arranger with Beecham of music by Handel for the production of *A Woman's Privilege* in 1931.

Gibson composed at least one musical theatre piece, *Sir Roger de Coverley* (c. 1932). For orchestra he wrote a *Neil Gow* overture and a three-movement Japanese Suite *Kakemonos*. The latter work appears to have existed also as a song cycle, and there was another song cycle, *Songs of the Desert*.

GILBERT, Alfred
21 Oct. 1828 – 1902
Gilbert was born in Salisbury and studied with Charles Corfe and Alexander Lucas. He was an organist, a learned musician, lecturer and concert organiser, later becoming secretary to and a leading figure in the Musical Artists' Society. He was also a director and orchestral manager of the Philharmonic Society. A concert of his music was given in Rome in 1884. He wrote cantatas, operettas and some chamber music. His son, also Alfred Gilbert, was well-known as a sculptor.

GIPPS, Ruth Dorothea Louisa
20 Feb. 1921 – 23 Feb. 1999
Born in Bexhill-on-Sea, Sussex, Ruth Gipps began studies with her mother. At the age of sixteen she played Beethoven's 'Emperor' concerto at the 1936 Hastings Festival. She entered the Royal College of Music as an oboist, studying under Leon Goossens, and also studied composition under R.O. Morris and Gordon Jacob. She obtained a B.Mus. at Durham University and in 1948 was only the second woman to receive a doctorate in composition from that university.

As an oboist in the City of Birmingham Orchestra, she not only had the opportunity to have some of her compositions performed (including her first symphony) but also to study conducting. Her performing career, however, was ended owing to a hand injury and in 1953 she returned to London to concentrate on composition and conducting. Meeting some resistance from the male profession, she formed the London Repertoire Orchestra of mainly good amateur players, and later the Chanticleer Orchestra, performing works by Alwyn, Bliss and Arnold, who later wrote *Variations on a Theme of Ruth Gipps* for her. She lectured in composition for a time at Trinity College of Music, eventually becoming Senior Lecturer at Kingston Polytechnic. In 1981 she received an MBE, and later retired to Sussex, where she worked with amateur groups and continued her composition.

Her list of works is extensive: five symphonies, several concertos, a concertante (*Leviathan*) for contra-bassoon and orchestra, much chamber music for differing combinations, and a number of choral works for both large and small groups. Determined not to espouse those new ideas emerging from Europe that so much influenced composers like Searle and Fricker, Gipps developed her own distinctive and often robust style of English pastoralism. Perhaps this is why interest in her music declined in the 1950s, though there has been a recent revival of her work. Ruth Gipps died of a stroke after a period of illness.

GLADSTONE, Francis Edward
2 Mar. 1845 – 6 Sep. 1928
Dr Gladstone, cousin of the Prime Minister of the same name, was organist successively at the cathedrals of Llandaff, Chichester and Norwich, and was a professor at the Royal College of Music for twenty-seven years. He was born at Summertown near Oxford, and studied music with S.S. Wesley, then at Winchester Cathedral. He composed a symphony, cantatas, masses, anthems and services, songs, and an orchestral overture. He also wrote a successful text on counterpoint.

GODFREY, Arthur Eugene
28 Sep. 1868 – 23 Feb. 1939
The cousin of the conductor Sir Dan Godfrey, Arthur was born in London. He was a chorister at St Paul's Cathedral School before studying at the Royal Academy of Music. He became a successful theatrical conductor and was musical director of the Alhambra Theatre in Glasgow. Godfrey wrote incidental music, string quartets, a musical comedy, and songs.

GODIN, Felix. See **BROWN**, Henry Albert

GOLDSCHMIDT, Otto
21 Aug. 1829 – 24 Feb. 1907
Though born in Hamburg, Goldschmidt spent most of his life in London, settling there at the age of twenty, having studied with Mendelssohn in Leipzig. His career began as an accompanist to the singer Jenny Lind, a relationship that eventually led to their marriage. He founded the Bach Choir in 1875, giving the first complete performance in the UK of Bach's *Mass in B Minor* in the following year. His interest in choral music led to the composition of an oratorio (*Ruth*) and a cantata (*Music*) for soprano

and female chorus. He also wrote a piano concerto, piano trio, piano duets and solos. Goldschmidt died in South Kensington, London.

GOLDSCHMIDT, Berthold
18 Jan. 1903 – 17 Oct. 1996
Born and educated in Hamburg, where he had a promising career as a conductor and composer, his work was condemned by the Nazi regime and he fled to England in 1935, where he worked for the BBC while continuing his composition. His opera *Beatrice Cenci* was one of four winning works in the Arts Council competition for operas for the 1951 Festival of Britain, though it was never performed. His works continued to be neglected until the 1980s, when they had a modest revival. Goldschmidt continued composing up until 1993. His output includes a number of shorter orchestral works, concertos for violin, cello and clarinet, four string quartets, songs with orchestral accompaniment, and a number of piano works dating from his earlier time in Germany.

GOODWIN, Ronald Alfred
17 Feb. 1925 – 8 Jan. 2003
Ron Goodwin will be remembered for his light orchestral recordings, and backings for singers such as Max Bygraves and for several Peter Sellers sketches. He was musical director and arranger of many film scores, including *I'm All Right, Jack* (1959), *The Trials of Oscar Wilde*, *Village of the Damned* (from the 1960s), *The Cracksman* (with Charlie Drake, 1963), *Children of the Damned* (1964), *633 Squadron* (1964), *Those Magnificent Men in their Flying Machines* (1965), *The Early Bird* (Norman Wisdom, 1965), *The Magnificent Two* (Morecambe and Wise, 1967), and *Where Eagles Dare* (1969). He also produced documentary scores for the Petroleum Film Board and for the British Tourist Authority, as well as several memorable jingles for TV advertisements.

Goodwin was born in Plymouth and attended Pinner County School. He had some early piano lessons, then studied trumpet, composition and orchestration at the Guildhall School of Music. He worked briefly with Henry Gould's band and, at eighteen, joined Campbell Connelly as an arranger for Geraldo and Ted Heath among others. A contract followed with Polygon, which was later subsumed into EMI. In the 1970s Goodwin was effectively composer in residence for Walt Disney's productions in Britain.

GOOSSENS, Aynsley Eugene
26 May 1893 – 18 Jun. 1962
The name Eugene Goossens spans three generations. Eugène the grandfather came to England from Belgium and became a successful conductor, as did his son, Eugène II. Eugene III was born in London, and at the age of six, by which time his family had moved to Liverpool, he was sent to study at the Bruges Conservatoire. Returning to Liverpool he attended the Liverpool College of Music and then proceeded to the RCM, where he was a pupil of Stanford, Charles Wood, and Achille Rivarde (violin). He played the violin at the Haymarket Theatre, in the Queen's Hall Orchestra under Sir Henry Wood, and in the Philharmonic String Quartet, founding his own orchestra in 1921. As a young conductor Goossens gave a sense of direction to modern English music, and his achievements in this field (British National and Carl Rosa opera

companies, London Symphony Orchestra, Rochester Symphony Orchestra, Cincinnati and Sydney Symphony orchestras, etc.) seem to have overshadowed those as a composer.

In 1947 Goossens went to Sydney to conduct the orchestra and to be director of the New South Wales State Conservatorium. While in Australia he did more than anyone to put Australia on the musical map. His works include two symphonies and other orchestral works, a large-scale oratorio (*The Apocalypse* – said to be his finest work), two operas to words of Arnold Bennett (*Judith* and *Don Juan de Mañara*), a ballet (*L'Ecole en Crinoline*), phantasy concertos for piano and violin, and an oboe concerto, choral music, two string quartets and other chamber works, instrumental pieces and songs. Some of these works adopted a neo-Classical idiom. Eugene Goossens was knighted in 1955.

GOSS, John
27 Dec. 1800 – 10 May 1880
Born at Fareham in Hampshire, where his father was the parish organist, John Goss entered the Chapel Royal under John Stafford Smith in 1811, and then studied with Thomas Attwood. At the age of seventeen he sang tenor in the first English production of *Don Giovanni*, subsequently gaining a name as a singer. (A further interesting Mozart connection is that Goss inherited Mozart's student exercises from Attwood on his death). Goss became organist at St Luke's, Chelsea, then at St Paul's Cathedral. He was a professor of harmony at the Royal Academy of Music and composer to the Chapels Royal from 1856 to 1872. Goss composed orchestral overtures, an operetta (*The Sergeant's Wife*), services, anthems and chants, glees and songs, and organ pieces. Two of his hymn-tunes to the words, 'Praise my soul the King of Heaven' and 'See amid the winter's snow' are still popular. He wrote didactic works and edited hymnals. His services to music were rewarded with a knighthood in 1872. Sir John Goss died at Brixton and was buried at Kensal Green cemetery.

GOW, David Godfrey
6 Apr. 1924 – 23 Feb. 1993

Although from a Scottish family, David Gow was born in London and studied at the Royal College of Music with Frank Merrick for piano and Gordon Jacob for composition, and later privately with Alan Bush. At the RCM he soon established himself as a composer by winning two composition prizes. His teaching work was mainly in adult education, with the WEA and the Open University, where he was one of the first music tutors and a much respected lecturer at the University's summer schools. He moved to Swindon in 1970, where he lectured at the local Further Education college for sixteen years.

Following his retirement from full-time teaching, David Gow concentrated on composition. His style is loosely serial, and his list of works is extensive: three symphonies (no. 3, *Wessex Heights*, celebrated the 150th anniversary of Thomas Hardy's birth), overtures and incidental pieces for orchestra; concertos for clarinet, trombone, basset horn, violin, piano; nine string quartets, as well as a quantity of choral music, songs, piano and organ music. One of his most successful and accessible works is his *Mini Symphony* (1968), lasting just nine minutes.

GOW, Dorothy
1893 – 1 Nov. 1982

Born in London to a Scottish family, Dorothy Gow began serious musical studies when she was thirty-one years old, entering the Royal College of Music and studying composition with R.O. Morris and Vaughan Williams. The latter championed her music throughout his life, despite his pupil's acute shyness and modesty. At the RCM she won several scholarships, one of which took her to Vienna to study with Wellesz.

Some of Gow's early works were performed at the Macnaghten-Lemare concerts to good but cautious reviews. In 1978 Dorothy Gow had a stroke and destroyed much of her music. The critics had dubbed it 'intellectual', perhaps rightly so, but it had stalwart champions in Malcolm Williamson and Elisabeth Lutyens, among others. Gow wrote a *Prelude and Fugue* for orchestra, string quartets and other chamber works, and songs (one set for tenor and string quartet). Her *String Quartet in One Movement* was published by OUP and has been broadcast and recorded several times. She died in London.

GRAINGER, Percy Aldridge
8 Jul. 1882 – 26 Feb. 1961

Percy Grainger spent only a brief portion of his life in this country but his contribution to the English folk-song revival was invaluable. He was born near Melbourne, Australia, where he studied music with his mother and with Louis Pabst. In Melbourne he gave his first piano recital at the age of eleven. While still a child, Grainger was sent to Frankfurt to be taught by Kwast and Busoni. There he met the other young students who, with him, were to become known as 'The Frankfurt Group' (Cyril Scott, Norman O'Neill, Roger Quilter and Balfour Gardiner).

Grainger pioneered the use of the phonograph as a means of collecting folk-song. His approach to everything – music, language, life itself – was different. The proceeds of a concert tour in 1935 were used to found the Grainger Museum in Melbourne, to which he also bequeathed his skeleton. From 1914 he lived mainly in the United States, dying of cancer at White Plains, New York.

Percy Grainger completed over 600 works, one-third being settings of folk music, one-third arrangements of music ranging from the tenth to the twentieth centuries, and one-third original compositions. The last category included shorter works for chorus, for wind band, tuned percussion, voice and piano, and piano solo or ensemble. Longer works include *Hill Songs* (1 and 2), *Lincolnshire Posy*, *The Power of Rome and the Christian Heart* and *The Warriors* – music to an imaginary ballet. In his last years Grainger experimented with machine generated music. Among his most popular works were occasional piano pieces such as *Handel in the Strand*, *Molly on the Shore* and *Country Gardens*, the last, according to Grainger being 'more to do with turnips than flowers'.

GRAY, Alan
23 Dec. 1855 – 27 Sep. 1935

Dr Alan Gray is mostly known for his church music and four organ sonatas, but he also composed cantatas, choruses, songs and part-songs, a string quartet, a piano quartet and a violin sonata. Born in York, he studied music with Dr E.G. Monk, organist at the Minster, and law at Cambridge, before turning fully to music and gaining a doctorate. Gray became director of music at Wellington College and succeeded Stanford as organist at Trinity College, Cambridge, where he also conducted the University Music Society, and where he eventually died. He was one of the editors of the Purcell Society and did much to further the music of that composer, as well as Bach's cantatas. His compositions include several sacred and secular cantatas, church music with orchestra, services, anthems, an overture, chamber music and organ music. Gray died in Cambridge.

GRAY, Cecil
19 May 1895 – 9 Sep. 1951
Cecil Gray is remembered as a musical critic, essayist and biographer, especially of Peter Warlock. He was born in Edinburgh and studied privately. Gray co-edited 'The Sackbut' with Philip Heseltine (Peter Warlock), wrote two studies of Sibelius, a history of music, and composed operas – *Deirdre, The Temptation of St Anthony* and *The Trojan Women* to his own texts – a Symphonic Prelude and an orchestral piece *Syllogism*. After the First World War he promoted the New Music Concerts. Gray died at Worthing, Sussex.

GREATHEED, Samuel Stephenson
22 Feb. 1813 – 19 Jan. 1887
Greatheed was born at Weston-super-Mare. He studied at Cambridge and was ordained in 1838. In the same year he went to Berlin to study music with G.W. Schwarz. On his return he became rector at Corringham, Essex. From 1844 onwards he produced many works for the church, including an oratorio (*Enoch's Prophecy*, to words by James Montgomery), a setting of Coxe's *Hymn of Boyhood*, many anthems, chants and hymns, and some organ pieces. He also wrote a text on the history of church music and one on the science of music.

GREEN, Russell
10 Apr. 1908 – 6 Feb. 1975
Russell Green was born at Norwich and studied music at Lichfield Cathedral and the Birmingham and Midland Institute. He was also a pupil of Herbert Howells. A schoolteacher, organist and conductor of the Birmingham Festival Chorus Society, Green later founded his own choir. He composed anthems, songs and part-songs, pieces for orchestra, choral works, and music for military band.

GREENBAUM, Hyam
12 May 1901 – 13 May 1942
Born at Brighton, Hyam Greenbaum studied at the local School of Music and at the Royal College of Music. He played the violin in the Queen's Hall Orchestra and the Brosa Quartet. In 1936 he was appointed musical director for BBC TV. He formed the Revue Orchestra and conducted the BBC Symphony Orchestra. Greenbaum's compositions were few, but his *Sea Poem* for orchestra and *Parfums de la Nuit* for oboe and orchestra are said to have some merit. Greenbaum was the first husband of Sidonie Goossens.

GREENWOOD, John Darnforth Herman
26 Jun. 1889 – 16 Apr. 1975
John Greenwood was born in London and studied with Stanford at the Royal College of Music, winning the Arthur Sullivan Prize and the Grove Scholarship. He conducted at the Queen's Hall and in the provinces, introducing some of his own works. He composed two symphonies, a setting of Psalm 150 for chorus and orchestra, a ballet, other works for orchestra or strings, a viola concerto, incidental music, two string quartets and other chamber works, piano sonatas and instrumental music, songs and scores for over fifty British films. He later lived and died in Ditchling, Sussex.

GRIMSHAW, Arthur Edmund
1864 – 5 Aug. 1913
Arthur Grimshaw spent most of his life as an organist in Leeds, where he was born and educated. He composed two operettas, songs and part-songs, a Romance for violin and orchestra, works for string orchestra and much church music. He died while walking on Hawkshead Moors in the Lake District, his body being found only several weeks after he had been reported missing.

GUNDRY, Inglis
8 May 1905 – 13 Apr. 2000
Although born in Wimbledon, London, the name Gundry is indicative of his Cornish ancestry. His father expected Inglis to train in law and he was sent to Mill Hill School and later to Oxford to read classics and law, a profession which he followed for some years. It was not until he was thirty that Gundry decided to follow a course in music at the Royal College of Music, under Vaughan Williams, Gordon Jacob and R.O. Morris. In 1952 he, like Sir Malcolm Arnold some seventeen years later, was made a Bard of the Cornish Gorsedd (for which ceremony he composed a Fanfare), although he never lived in Cornwall. His love of the county, however, is recognised in the work he did in preserving and publishing Cornish folk-songs and carols.

Notable amongst his thirteen operas are *The Logan Rock*, produced at the open-air Minack Theatre in Cornwall in 1956, *The Prince of Coxcombs*, *The Partisans*, and his last opera *Galileo* (1996). His works also include a number for orchestra, such as the overture *Per Mare, Per Terram* and, for chorus and orchestra *Five Bells* (1942), both of which were inspired by his time in the Royal Navy. Gundry also wrote two books: *Opera in a Nutshell*, and *Composers, by the Grace of God*, as well as an autobiography.

GURNEY, Ivor Bertie
28 Aug. 1890 – 26 Dec. 1937

Ivor Gurney is remembered as a composer of songs, though he also wrote some orchestral pieces, string quartets and instrumental music. Gurney also wrote poetry (his first collection, *Severn and Somme*, was published in 1917), which is at present as underrated as his music, though his output in both disciplines was not consistent. Son of a tailor, he was born at Gloucester and served at the cathedral as a choirboy before winning a scholarship in 1911 to the Royal College of Music, where he studied with Stanford. Here he was regarded as one of the most promising but most unteachable students. During his war service with the Gloucester

Regiment he was exposed to mustard gas at Passchendaele. Gurney's later life was spent tragically in a struggle against poverty and coping with periods of depression caused by bipolar disorder, which resulted eventually in a complete nervous breakdown. He was helped by Marion Scott in his final years in the City of London Mental Hospital at Dartford, Kent, where he died of tuberculosis. He is buried at Twigworth Church near Gloucester.

Hadley, Patrick Arthur Sheldon
5 Mar. 1899 – 31 Dec. 1973

Patrick Hadley was the son of a Master of Pembroke College, Cambridge. He studied there with Wood and Rootham, then at the Royal College of Music with Vaughan Williams and R.O. Morris. As a gunner in the First World War he lost a leg. In 1925 Hadley joined the staff of the RCM, later becoming Professor of Music at Cambridge and Fellow of Gonville and Caius College. He composed a symphonic poem and a sketch for orchestra, several cantatas and other large-scale works for voice, chorus and orchestra (including *The Hills* and *The Trees So High*, both of which have been issued on record), eight works for solo voice and ensemble, songs and choruses, a string quartet and some incidental music. His music shows the influence of Delius. Hadley also arranged several folk-songs. He died at King's Lynn.

HADOW, William Henry
27 Dec. 1859 – 9 Apr. 1937

Sir Henry Hadow's greatest contributions to music were undoubtedly his essays and criticism, which set a new and liberal standard in music literature. From 1901 he edited the Oxford History of Music, writing the section on the Viennese period himself, and he published many literary works unconnected with music. He was born at Ebrington in Gloucestershire and read classics at Worcester College, Oxford, where he later became a lecturer and tutor. He also studied music at Darmstadt and with C.H. Lloyd (organist at Gloucester Cathedral). In 1909 Hadow was appointed Principal of Armstrong College, Newcastle upon Tyne, and in 1919 accepted the Vice-Chancellorship of Sheffield University. He was knighted in 1918. He composed a cantata, anthems, a string quartet, violin sonatas and pieces, piano sonatas, a viola sonata and songs. Hadow died in London.

HALL, Richard
16 Sep. 1903 – 24 May 1982

As a professor of composition at the Royal Manchester College of Music from 1938 to 1956, Richard Hall helped in the musical development of a celebrated generation of musicians that included John Ogdon, Maxwell Davies, Harrison Birtwistle and Alexander Goehr. His interest in and sympathy with contemporary developments – Scriabin, Hindemith, Tippett, Messiaen, Webern, etc. – is evident in the work of his pupils, though it was frowned upon at the time by the establishment. Richard Hall was born in York and went to Loretto School in Edinburgh. In 1922 he became organist at Dorchester Abbey and a year later won an organ scholarship to Peterhouse, Cambridge, though financial difficulties forced him to give this up after only one year. After an organists's appointment in Leeds, in 1926 he was ordained, becoming

Precentor at Leeds Parish Church. Ten years later Hall left the Church, moved by an increasingly liberal and pantheistic theology. By the end of his life he had become minister of a Unitarian church at Horsham in Sussex, where he died.

Hall's work with the Lancashire County Council from 1936-40, during which he encouraged practical music making among the unemployed, was invaluable: he became closely associated with the Pipers' Guild, which made simple pipes for amateur musicians, and composed several pieces for the medium. He lectured at the Cheshire County Training College (1940-45), in the extra-mural department of Manchester University (1940-56), and examined for the Associated Board. Richard Hall composed four symphonies, concertos for violin, piano and cello, a *Rhapsody* for organ and strings, three fugal overtures and other orchestral works, seven string quartets, sonatas for several instruments (viola, violin, cello, flute, etc.) with piano, other chamber works, solo piano music (including over twenty piano sonatas), organ works, choral pieces, songs and incidental music.

HAMILTON, Iain Ellis
6 Jun. 1922 – 21 Jul. 2000
Though he left his native Glasgow for London at the age of seven and spent twenty years in the United States, Iain Hamilton always remained a Scot. During his seven years in engineering he won a scholarship to the Royal Academy of Music, studying composition with William Alwyn and piano with Harold Craxton. At the same time he took a B.Mus. at London University. While still at the RAM he won several prizes and finally graduated in 1951 with the Academy's highest award. For the following ten years he composed prolifically, was an inspiring teacher at Morley College and London University, broadcast on radio and television, and played active roles in the Composers' Guild, the Society for the Promotion of New Music, and other organisations. In the late 1950s Hamilton espoused the European avant-garde movement and produced works such as the *Sonata for Chamber Orchestra.*

In 1961 Iain Hamilton moved to New York, commuting to Duke University in North Carolina as Professor of Music. Within a year he was resident composer at Tanglewood, then visiting composer to the University of Alabama. Twenty years in the USA were fruitful and his interest in opera came to the fore with *The Royal Hunt of the Sun, The Cataline Conspiracy, Raleigh's Dream* and *Anna Karenina.* Back in England from 1981 he wrote further operas and stage works, but his music was heard less frequently and he largely withdrew from society. He left a legacy of four symphonies, two piano and two violin concertos, a jazz trumpet concerto, other concertante and chamber orchestral pieces, four string quartets and many other chamber works and instrumental sonatas. His many choral works include the wonderful *Epitaph for this World and Time* for three choruses and two organs, works for organ and for piano, several scores for voice and orchestra or piano, and some film scores.

HAMILTON, Janet Christina Monteith
5 Aug. 1898 – 6 May 1979
Janet Hamilton, daughter of artist Vereker Hamilton, was born in St John's Wood, London. She had lessons from Cecil Forsyth and John Ireland. Although she composed mostly songs – there are several settings of Housman – between 1913 and 1926, other works were a string quartet and an Elegy for cello (or viola) and piano, a symphonic

poem for tenor and small orchestra, and variations on an original theme for piano. She married Allen Leeper in 1921, though she continued to write a few works under her maiden name. After the death of her husband in 1935, she ceased composition but continued as a writer, publishing books on ballet and the theatre.

HARKER, Clifford Arthur
5 Feb. 1912 – 2 Nov. 1999
Clifford Harker was organist and director of music at Bristol Cathedral for thirty-four years, during which time he also conducted the Bristol Madrigal Society, the Bristol Choral Society and the Bath Choral Society, introducing many new twentieth-century works. He was born in Newcastle upon Tyne, attending Dame Alleyn's School before studying at the Royal College of Music with Marmaduke Barton, Dr Henry Ley, Dr Malcolm Sargent and Vaughan Williams. He volunteered for service with the RAF in World War Two and was posted to Egypt. There he was relieved from duties as a radio operator to entertain the troops as Director of Lady Dorothea Russell's 'Music for All'. He found time to study for an external B.Mus. from Durham University. After the war he became organist at Rugby Parish Church and founded the Rugby Singers, travelling to London to teach piano at Trinity College. Harker was the highly respected conductor of several choirs, but enjoyed success too as an orchestral conductor. His music included many sacred and secular choral works, organ pieces, songs and part-songs.

HARRIS, Clement Hugh Gilbert
8 July 1871 – 23 Apr. 1897
Clement Harris was born at Wimbledon and died at the age of twenty-six, killed in action at the battle of Pente Pigadia, having enlisted in the Greek army when war broke out with Turkey. He studied at Frankfurt with Clara Schumann and gained a reputation as a virtuoso pianist. He was also a skilled painter and accompanied Richard Wagner's son Siegfried on a painting tour to Asia in 1892. Harris composed a tone poem for orchestra (*Paradise Lost*), songs, piano pieces, and some chamber works.

HARRIS, William Henry
8 Mar. 1883 – 6 Sep. 1973
W.H. Harris was born in London and studied with Herbert Morris at St David's Cathedral, at New College, Oxford, and at the Royal College of Music with Walter Parratt. He held various posts as organist and conducted several choirs (Christ Church Cathedral, Oxford; St George's Chapel, Windsor; Windsor and Eton Choral Society, etc.). Harris composed works for solo, chorus and orchestra (*The Hound of Heaven* and *Michael Angelo's Confession of Faith* are notable examples of his work), other choral works, church and organ music. He died in Petersfield, Hampshire.

HARRISON, Annie Fortescue. See **HILL**, Lady Arthur

HARRISON, Julius Allan Greenaway
28 Mar. 1885 – 5 Apr. 1963
Julius Harrison was born at Stourport in Worcestershire. He studied with Granville Bantock at the Midland Institute and followed a successful career as a conductor until deafness brought about his retirement in 1940. He had by then conducted a great variety of orchestras, including the Sir Thomas Beecham Opera Company, British National

Opera Company, Covent Garden, London and Liverpool
Philharmonics, the Hallé, and the Hastings Municipal Orchestra.
He was also a professor of composition at the Royal College of
Music and published works on Brahms as a symphonist. His
compositions include orchestral pieces, a dramatic cantata and
church cantatas, string quartets and other important chamber works,
a cello concerto, three masses, songs and part-songs, church and
organ music, and pieces for solo piano. His best work is perhaps the *Requiem for
Archangels* of 1919 while the *Bredon Hill Rhapsody* for violin and orchestra has
achieved modest popularity. There are two ambitious Three Choirs works: *Mass* and
Requiem. Julius Harrison died in Harpenden, Hertfordshire.

HART, Fritz Bennicke
11 Feb. 1874 – 9 July 1949
Fritz Hart was a close friend of Gustav Holst, William Hurlstone and Samuel
Coleridge-Taylor, all fellow students at the Royal College of Music. He was born at
Bromley in Kent and sang as a boy at Westminster Abbey, attending the choir school
before entering the RCM. He followed a career as a conductor of theatre orchestras
until 1915, when he emigrated to take charge of the Melbourne Conservatorium of
Music. After twenty-seven years in Australia, Hart moved to Hawaii to become
Professor of Music at the University and conductor of the Honolulu Symphony
Orchestra. He stayed in Honolulu until his death.

     His compositions include a symphony and other orchestral works, twenty-three
operas (many to his own libretti, but others to words by Shakespeare, Yeats, Synge
and others); also a biblical opera (*Ruth*), choral works, chamber music, violin sonatas,
piano pieces and songs. The elements of English folk-song can be identified in Hart's
music, while his wide English literary interests are displayed in his choral and song
settings.

HARTY, Herbert Hamilton
4 Dec. 1879 – 19 Feb. 1941
Born at Hillsborough in County Down, Hamilton Harty came to England in 1900. He
was taught music by his father and became a church organist at the age of twelve. In
England he gained a reputation as a piano accompanist, then as a conductor, in which
latter capacity he was renowned as an interpreter of the music of Berlioz. In 1920 he
was appointed conductor of the Hallé Orchestra and was knighted five years later. His
wife was the singer Agnes Nicholls, who sang in the premiere of the soaring *Ode to
a Nightingale* and *The Children of Lir*. Harty composed an *Irish Symphony*, orchestral
overtures, a violin concerto (first performed by Szigeti), piano concerto, a quintet,
instrumental music for oboe, cello, violin, piano, harp, etc., a cantata (*The Mystic
Trumpeter*), and songs. His best known work is the tone-poem *With the Wild Geese*,
written for the Cardiff Festival of 1910. Harty died at Hove in Sussex.

HARWOOD, Basil
11 Apr. 1859 – 3 Apr. 1949
Basil Harwood was born at Olveston, Gloucestershire, and was educated at
Charterhouse and Trinity College, Oxford, where he studied with Dr Corfe. He was
also a pupil of Reinecke and Jadassohn at Leipzig. Organist successively at St Barnabas

(Pimlico), Ely Cathedral and Christ Church Cathedral, Oxford, he was also a choral conductor and composed anthems, services, a psalm-setting for soli, chorus and orchestra, an organ concerto, many organ works, a cantata, vocal trios and songs. Some of his hymn-tunes are still popular: *Luckington* ('Let all the world in every corner sing') and *Thornbury* ('Thy hand, O God, has guided') are perhaps the best.

HATTON, John Liptrot
12 Oct. 1809 – 20 Sep. 1886
John Hatton was born in Liverpool, but followed his musical career in London, teaching and playing the piano. In 1832 he was appointed to the Drury Lane Theatre and later became musical director of the Princess's Theatre. Hatton was mainly self-taught as a composer and his output included several operettas, incidental music, an overture, opera, cantatas, two fantasias for piano and orchestra, anthems and services, drawing-room songs and part-songs, and piano pieces. His best known work is perhaps the song *Simon the Cellarer*. A few of his works were published under the pseudonym of 'Czapek'. Hatton died at Margate, where he had spent the last part of his life.

HAWLEY, Stanley
17 May 1867 – 13 Jun. 1916
Stanley Hawley was born at Ilkeston in Derbyshire and studied at the Royal Academy of Music. As a pianist he performed Grieg's Piano Concerto at the age of 19, and later toured as accompanist to Adelina Patti. He was also a London organist and secretary to the Royal Philharmonic Society. He wrote historical biographies and was an active member of various musical societies. His editions of Romantic piano music were notable for their simplicity, achieved by changing key signatures so as to eliminate accidentals. Hawley composed melodramas (recitations with piano or orchestral accompaniment) to Poe's *The Bells* and *The Raven*, Hood's *The Song of the Shirt*, as well as *Elizabethan Love Lyrics* and other songs.

HAY, Edward Norman
19 Apr. 1889 – 10 Sep. 1943
Edward Hay spent most of his life in Ireland, where he was organist of Coleraine Church and Bangor Abbey Church. He was born at Faversham in Kent and studied with Eaglefield Hull, Brennan and Chaundy, graduating with a B.Mus. from Oxford. Hay composed orchestral pieces, a madrigal, cello sonata, string quartets and other chamber works, some instrumental pieces, songs and a musical comedy. He died in Belfast.

HAYNES, Walter Battison
21 Nov. 1859 – 4 Feb. 1900
Born at Kempsey in Worcestershire, Battison Haynes attended Hanley Castle Grammar School, He studied with Ebenezer Prout and Franklin Taylor in London, then with Reinecke and Jadassohn at the Leipzig Conservatory, where he won the Mozart Scholarship. He was an organist and professor of harmony and composition at the Royal Academy of Music, and organist at the Savoy Chapel Royal from 1891 to 1899. His works include a symphony, overture, *Idyll* for violin and orchestra, two cantatas for female voices (*The Fairies' Isle* and *Sea Dream*), chamber music, organ pieces and church music. He was also an inveterate orchestrator, having been responsible for adding additional instrumentation to some of Handel's choral music. He died in London.

HEAD, Michael Dewar
28 Jan. 1900 – 24 Feb. 1976
Michael Head made his name as a pianist and singer, giving one-man recitals of his own songs. He was born at Eastbourne and began to study mechanical engineering until he gave it up to devote himself to music. He was a pupil of Frederick Corder, T.B. Knott and Reginald Steggall at the Royal Academy of Music, where he won nine awards and later became a professor of piano. His travels as a recitalist and adjudicator took him all over the world. In addition to over eighty songs Head composed choral works, several light operas (*Key Money*, *The Bidder's Opera*, *Day Return*, *After the Wedding*, a school opera *Through Train* and the children's opera *The Bachelor Mouse*), a piano concerto, chamber works (including *Contrasts* for twelve cellos and percussion) and instrumental music. He died in Cape Town, South Africa.

HEAP, Charles Swinnerton
10 Apr. 1847 – 11 Jun. 1900
Heap enjoyed considerable status in his time. Born in Birmingham, he was taught by E.G. Monk, organist of York Minster, and was awarded the Mendelssohn Scholarship to study in Leipzig. On his return to Birmingham he studied the organ with W.T. Best and obtained his Mus.Doc. in 1872. He was appointed conductor of various choral societies in the area, the Birmingham Philharmonic Union and later the Birmingham Festival Choral Society.

His oeuvre consists of an oratorio *The Nativity*, several cantatas for chorus and orchestra, sacred works with orchestra, concert overtures, a quintet for piano and winds, a piano trio, a violin sonata, a clarinet sonata dedicated to Henry Lazarus (available in Lazarus Editions), as well as organ and piano works. His cantata *The Maid of Astolat* was performed on the visit of the Prince of Wales to Hanley in 1897. He died suddenly during preparations for the 1900 Birmingham Festival. His obituary recorded that 'Birmingham has lost the most distinguished musician she could claim for her own'.

HEATH, John Rippiner
1887 – 23 Dec. 1950
A medical practitioner by profession and a fine violinist, John Heath was born in Birmingham and educated at Clifton College before going to Trinity College, Cambridge. He spent most of his life in Barmouth, Wales as a highly respected and popular GP who in his spare time conducted the Barmouth Choral Union as well as helping with the Harlech Festival. While at Cambridge he led many string quartets for the University Musical Club. During World War One he served with the RAMC at Salonika. Dr Heath was self-taught as a composer but wrote prolifically, with originality and no small sense of humour. Most of his works were for chamber groups: a great deal for violin and piano – *Three Macedonian Sketches* and *A Serbian Quartet* (published by Chester) were both influenced by his service in the war. He also composed a cello concerto, triple concerto and other orchestral pieces, a choreographic drama (*In the Valley of White Poppies*) and a symbolic drama (*The Lamp*) for actors, dancers, chorus and a wind quintet, as well as over a hundred songs and many piano pieces.

HELY-HUTCHINSON, Christian Victor
26 Dec. 1901 – 11 Mar. 1947
Son of the Governor of Cape Colony and born at Cape Town, Victor Hely-Hutchinson came to England to study at Eton, Balliol College, Oxford, and the Royal College of Music. After gaining a doctorate he lectured for four years at Cape Town University, then returned to England to join the staff of the BBC, eventually becoming a regional director. In 1934 he succeeded Granville Bantock at Birmingham University and in 1944 returned to the BBC as Director of Music. He died in London.

Hely-Hutchinson is remembered mainly for his light music, of which the *Carol Symphony* is a thoroughly delightful example. He also wrote orchestral suites and dances for string orchestra, a piano quintet, string quartet and other chamber works, an operetta (*Hearts are Trumps*), film scores, choral music, a piano sonata and songs (including some settings of Edward Lear).

HEMING, Michael Savage
14 Jan. 1920 – 3 Nov. 1942
Michael Heming was a son of the singer Percy Heming. He was born in London and studied at the Sorbonne and at the Royal Academy of Music, with the intention of conducting. When war broke out, he was called up and became an intelligence officer in the King's Royal Rifles. He was killed in action at El Alamein at the age of twenty-two. Very few of his works are known, but the symphonic poem *Tamburlane* has been highly spoken of. Heming's unfinished *Threnody* for orchestra was completed by Anthony Collins as *Threnody for a Soldier Killed in Action*.

HENLEY, William
1876 – 1957
'Henley', to many musicians, is the familiar name for *A Universal Dictionary of Violin and Bow Makers*, a standard reference on the subject, though it was completed and published posthumously by Cyril Woodcock. Less well known is the William Henley who composed a large number of works for the violin, including three concertos and seven string quartets as well as solo pieces. He also composed some songs and wrote extensively on violin technique. Born in West Bromwich, Henley had lessons as a boy with August Wilhemj, and began to perform on European tours at the age of twelve. He was later a professor of composition and a violin teacher at The Academy, Kew.

HENRY, Leigh Vaughan
23 Sep. 1889- 8 Mar. 1958
L.V. Henry, born in Liverpool, showed an early interest in music from the age of eleven when he began studying the piano. He later pursued studies towards qualifying as an architect in parallel with music. At the age of sixteen some of his work attracted the attention of Granville Bantock. He was later appointed Director of Music at Gordon Craig's School for the Art of the Theatre in Florence. Here he lectured and gave recitals at the Fenzi Palace, and conducted the Anglo-Italian Choral Society. He was invited to Germany just before the start of the Great War, and was interned for the duration at Ruhleben Camp. On his return to England he began contributing to various music journals and founded and became editor of 'Fanfare', a music review of advanced tendencies which ran for just six months. He wrote a number of books on music

appreciation. His works include the ballet *The Rogueries of Corvielo*, *Cymric Poem* for small orchestra, *Sheen of Waters* for piano and orchestra, *A Celtic Poem* for male chorus, and works for flute, clarinet, bassoon and solo piano.

HENSCHEL, Isidor Georg(e)
18 Feb. 1850 – 10 Sep. 1934
This great baritone singer of Polish-Jewish descent was born at Breslau in Germany, but became a British citizen in 1890, having settled here in 1884 after three years of conducting the Boston Symphony Orchestra. He studied at Leipzig, but made his debut as a pianist at the age of twelve, first appearing as a singer four years later. He founded the London Symphony Concerts in 1886 and was the first conductor of the Royal Scottish National Orchestra. Henschel's many recitals in Britain and the United States with his first wife, the soprano Lillian Bailey, were enormously successful, as were his solo stage appearances as a baritone. He was knighted in 1914. After his first wife's death he retired to Scotland for a while before remarrying. Henschel composed operas (*A Sea Change*, *Frederick the Fair* and *Nubia*), a *Requiem Mass*, *Stabat Mater* and other large-scale choral works, orchestral pieces, string quartet, piano music, songs and part-songs. His paintings were exhibited in London just before he died at his home Tullochgrue, Aviemore in Scotland.

HERVEY, Arthur
26 Jan. 1855 – 10 Mar. 1922
Born in Paris of an Irish father and an English mother, Arthur Hervey studied with Berthold Tours and Edouard Marlois. He became music critic of Vanity Fair and was on the staff of the Morning Post. In addition to writing several books on French music and contributing to 'Encyclopaedia Britannica', Hervey composed tone-poems and overtures for orchestra, an opera (*The Fairy's Post Box*), an operetta, *The Gates of Night* for voice and orchestra, songs, and pieces for piano, violin, and for cello. Hervey's best known work must be the variations for orchestra, *Life Moods* (1912), first performed at the Brighton Festival, and popular in its time. Hervey died in London.

HESELTINE, Philip.   See **WARLOCK**, Peter

HEWARD, Leslie
8 Dec. 1897 – 3 May 1943
A well-known conductor with several recordings to his credit, Leslie Heward has not been recognised as a composer and, in fact, destroyed most of his own scores. He was born at Liversedge in Yorkshire and joined the choir of Manchester Cathedral, where he was taken under the wing of Sir Sydney Nicholson. He became an organist at Ancoats, then at Holy Trinity, Windsor. He later went to the Royal College of Music to study with Stanford and Boult, supporting himself by teaching at Eton College, then Westminster School. He conducted the British National Opera Company for a time before succeeding Boult in 1930 as conductor of the City of Birmingham Orchestra. Heward also spent some time in South Africa as director of the Cape Town Municipal Orchestra, but died in Birmingham. He composed an opera (*Peer Gynt*; another, *Hamlet*, from his sixteenth year was never completed), several works for orchestra and for

strings, music for voice and orchestra, choral music, songs, piano works, a string quartet, organ pieces and a film score (*The Loves of Robert Burns*).

HILES, Henry
31 Dec. 1826 – 20 Oct. 1904
Like his brother John (see below), Henry Hiles was born at Shrewsbury. He played the organ, holding organ appointments at the age of thirteen, and conducted several musical societies in the North of England (including Preston and Warrington) before graduating with his Mus.Doc. in 1867 at Oxford. He taught at Owen's College and at the Victoria University, and in 1893 became professor of harmony at the Royal Manchester College of Music, as well as an examiner and lecturer. He was instrumental in helping the formation of the Incorporated Society of Musicians. Hiles died at Worthing. Henry Hiles's compositions were considerable: they include two oratorios, cantatas, anthems and glees, organ music, operettas, an orchestral overture, songs and piano pieces, as well as several textbooks on harmony etc., and technical exercises for the piano.

HILES, John
1810 – 4 Feb. 1882
John Hiles, brother of Henry (above), was likewise born at Shrewsbury and became an organist there, but soon moved south to take up organist's appointments in Portsmouth, Brighton and London. He wrote books on music theory, including a *Dictionary of 12,500 Musical Terms*, as well as finding time to compose piano and organ pieces, arrangements and transcriptions, and some songs.

HILL, Lady Arthur
1851 – 12 Feb. 1944
Annie Fortescue Harrison, born in Sussex, was the second wife of Lord Arthur William Hill. He himself composed in his spare time – he was Comptroller of Her Majesty's Household until 1892. His wife wrote and had published several patriotic songs and ballads, the most well-known of which, *In the Gloaming* (1876), was popular in its day and for some while afterwards. She composed two operettas (*The Ferry Girl* and *The Lost Husband*), both of which were produced in London. She died in Easthampton, Berkshire.

HINTON, Arthur
20 Nov. 1869 – 11 Aug. 1941
Arthur Hinton was born at Beckenham in Kent and went to Shrewsbury School. He began a commercial career but gave this up to study music. He entered the Royal Academy of Music, where he studied violin with Prosper Sainton and composition with F.W. Davenport. After three years as a sub-professor at the RAM he went to Munich as a pupil of Rheinberger, then proceeded to Vienna and finally, Italy. Returning to England he conducted at various London theatres. His wife was the pianist Katharine Goodson. He died at Rottingdean in East Sussex. Hinton composed two symphonies, a piano concerto and other orchestral works, an opera (*Tamara*), children's operettas (*The Disagreeable Princess* and *St Elizabeth's Roses*), chamber works, piano pieces, songs and part-songs.

HODDINOTT, Alun
11 Aug. 1929 – 12 Mar. 2008
A prolific and internationally prominent Welsh composer, Alun Hoddinott founded, with John Ogdon, the Cardiff Festival of Twentieth Century Music and commissioned over 200 works. He was born at Bargoed in Glamorgan and went to Gowerton Grammar School, winning a scholarship at the age of sixteen and going to University College, Cardiff. As a viola player he was a founder member of the National Youth Orchestra of Wales. After university he studied with Arthur Benjamin. From 1951-59 he was lecturer in music at the Welsh College of Music and Drama, moving to University College, Cardiff as Lecturer, then Reader, and finally as Professor of Music and Head of Department. In 1957 Hoddinott was awarded the Arnold Bax Medal for composers, and in 1983 was made a CBE. He accumulated awards and honorary doctorates galore.

Among Hoddinott's vast output are ten symphonies plus a choral symphony and other orchestral works (including concertos for clarinet, harp, piano, violin, organ, horn, piano trio, orchestra, euphonium), six operas, five string quartets, thirteen piano sonatas, six violin sonatas and a large number of other chamber and instrumental works. He produced songs and several works for solo voice and orchestra, church anthems, two oratorios and music for brass. His portfolio ranges stylistically from serial and aleatoric to traditional, and to jazz- and dance-influenced oeuvres, all conceived with consummate skill.

HOLBROOKE, Josef Charles
5 July 1878 – 5 Aug. 1958
Josef Holbrooke's music seems nowadays to provoke critics into extremes both of enthusiasm and condemnation; and certainly his output varied in quality from the clichéed Piano Concerto to the brilliant *Queen Mab* for chorus and orchestra. In his time Holbrooke's work was neglected and, in his later years, he responded with embittered panegyrics to his own music. Throughout his life he had been a fierce protagonist in support of the works of many other British composers.

Holbrooke was born at Croydon, where his father taught violin and piano. His mother, a professional singer, died when Josef was only two years old. He studied at the Royal Academy of Music with Frederick Westlake and Frederick Corder and became a music hall pianist and conductor, writing books and articles on contemporary music.

His early struggle to make a living was relieved by the patronage of Lord Howard de Walden who, under the name T.E. Ellis, wrote the libretti to his opera trilogy, *The Cauldron of Annwn* (*The Children of Don, Dylan* and *Bronwen*), and he became a fairly successful concert pianist and conductor. Holbrooke composed other operas, eight symphonies, a violin concerto, a saxophone concerto, tone-poems (many inspired by the writings of Edgar Allan Poe and often brilliantly orchestrated), choral works, six string quartets and many other chamber works (including some of his finest music), instrumental pieces and songs. He died in London.

HOLD, Trevor James
21 Sep. 1939 – 28 Jan. 2004
Like Malcolm Arnold, William Alwyn and Edmund Rubbra, Trevor Hold was born in Northampton, where he grew to love the countryside and the poetry of John Clare. Despite a damaging onset of polio at the age of six and missed schooling, he gained a place at Northampton Grammar School and became a competent pianist. Will Yeomans taught the young musician before he won a scholarship to read English at Nottingham University. A year later he opted instead for a B.Mus., graduating with a first class Honours degree, then an MA. Hold became Head of Music at Market Harborough Grammar School, then Assistant Lecturer in Music at Aberystwyth. His following lectureship at Liverpool University (1965-70) provided a vehicle for many of his own works, as did a post in Leicester University's adult education department. His contribution to local schools and choirs was enormous. By 1989 he was sufficiently secure as a composer to retire from teaching.

Trevor Hold's finest work lay in his many songs and song-cycles, one of the highlights of the latter being the 1974 cycle *For John Clare* for tenor and eleven instruments. He also composed a symphony, a piano concerto, a *Keele Overture*, several operas (some for children), and four piano sonatas. His own poetry was published in four collections and he wrote two books: *The Walled-in Garden – The Songs of Roger Quilter*, and *Parry to Finzi*, a study of twenty English song composers.

HOLLAND, Theodore Samuel
25 April 1878 – 29 Oct. 1947
T.S. Holland was born at Wimbledon and studied with Frederick Corder at the Royal Academy of Music, then in Berlin with Joachim, Kahn and Stillman-Kelley. In 1927 he joined the staff of the RAM where he was a much respected teacher. As a result of Holland's efforts to further the music of other composers, his own was neglected. His compositions, light in mood but by no means uninteresting, include some orchestral pieces (*Ellingham Marshes* for viola and orchestra being a particularly good and once popular example), a concerto in one movement for violin and orchestra, two string quartets and other chamber works, choral music, piano and instrumental pieces, and songs. He died in Wimbledon.

HOLLANDER, Benno (Benoit)
1853 – 1942
Benno Hollander was born in Amsterdam, but settled in London at the age of twenty-three. He studied violin with Lambert Massart and with Saint-Saëns in Paris. He played viola in Leopold Auer's quartet and went on to lead several important orchestras, later establishing his own. He taught violin for a while at the Guildhall School of Music. Hollander composed a symphony, symphonic poem and other orchestral works, an opera (*Mietje*), two violin concertos and a *Pastoral Fantasy* for violin and orchestra. He also wrote several chamber works, songs and piano pieces.

HOLLINS, Alfred
11 Sep. 1865 – 17 May 1942
Though blind from birth, Alfred Hollins followed a successful career as a concert pianist (at the age of thirteen playing Beethoven's 'Emperor' Concerto under August

Manns) and organist, touring in the UK, Germany and in America extensively in his youth, and settling down as organist at West St George's Church in Edinburgh, where he died. He was born in Hull and studied with E.J. Hopkins, Hans von Bülow and Joachim Raff. For a time he was a professor at the Royal Normal College for the Blind. His compositions include a concert overture, organ overtures and other pieces, anthems, a *Romance* for violin and piano, vocal trios and piano pieces.

HOLMES, Alfred
9 Nov. 1837 – 4 Mar. 1876
Brother of Henry Holmes (see below), Alfred was mainly self-taught as a musician. Having studied violin with his father, he became a famous violinist and toured Europe playing duets with his brother. He was born in London but settled in Paris in 1864, where he died. He composed an opera (*Inez de Castro*), a choral symphony *Jeanne D'Arc*, further programmatic symphonies including *The Siege of Paris*, *Robin Hood* and three others, several orchestral overtures and some piano music and songs.

HOLMES, Henry
7 Nov. 1839 – 9 Dec. 1905
Henry Holmes was born in London. He followed a career as a violinist, touring with his brother Alfred, before the latter moved to Paris. Henry gave chamber concerts in London and was one of the first professors of violin at the Royal College of Music. He retired to California, where he died. Henry Holmes composed five symphonies (the last two titled *Fraternity* and *Cumberland*), two cantatas, two string quartets, a piano quintet, an octet for strings and wind, a violin concerto, and songs. He died in San Francisco.

HOLMES, William Henry
8 Jan. 1812 – 23 Apr. 1885
W.H. Holmes was born at Sudbury in Derbyshire and studied at the Royal Academy of Music, where he later became principal professor of piano, teaching, among others, Sterndale Bennett and both George and Walter Macfarren. He composed symphonies, concertos including a 'Jubilee' piano concerto, a cantata, sonatas, piano pieces, songs, and an opera *The Elfin of the Lake*. Holmes died in London.

HOLST, Gustav (Gustavus Theodor von)
21 Sep. 1874 – 25 May 1934
Holst's music has been subjected to a puzzling variety of criticism, ranging from Cecil Gray's disparaging dismissal to enthusiastic assertions of originality and orchestrational brilliance. That his music, admirably exemplified by the orchestral suite *The Planets* (itself a brilliant essay in orchestration), has remained highly popular demonstrates the falseness of Gray's assessment. Gustav Holst was born at Cheltenham (his Swedish great-grandfather came to England from Russia in 1807) and began his musical career as a village organist and as a conductor of village choral societies. At the age of nineteen he went to the Royal College of Music, where he studied with Stanford and William Rockstro. Although frail in health, he played the trombone in theatre orchestras and in the Scottish Orchestra until 1906, when he became director of music at St Paul's School for Girls. This post, together with another at Morley College, he held for thirty

years, and for four years he taught at the RCM. The influence of William Morris, Walt Whitman and Sanskrit mythology helped to shape some of his music, as did his interest in English folk-song.

Holst composed operas (*Sita, The Idea, The Wandering Scholar, Savitri, The Perfect Fool* and *At the Boar's Head*), ballets, orchestral suites, the *St Paul's* and *Brook Green* suites for strings, several large-scale works for chorus and orchestra (*Hymns from the Rig Veda* and *The Hymn of Jesus* are splendid examples), a somewhat

neglected *First Choral Symphony* on poems by Keats (there was no second one), *A Fugal Concerto* for flute, oboe and strings, and a double concerto for two violins. In addition he wrote music for military band, chamber and instrumental works, piano solos, hymns, anthems and songs, and edited some choral and orchestral works. Holst's ashes are interred in Chichester Cathedral beneath a commemorative stone.

HOLST, Imogen
12 Apr. 1907 – 9 Mar. 1984

Daughter of Gustav Holst, Imogen was born in Richmond, Surrey. She was educated at St Paul's School for Girls and at the Royal College of Music, where she studied piano with Kathleen Long and composition with George Dyson and Gordon Jacob. In 1928 she won the Cobbett prize for her *Phantasy* String Quartet. A year later she won the Arthur Sullivan prize. Her varied and active career began as a schoolteacher (Roedean, near Brighton, among others). She became lecturer and conductor to the English Folk Dance Society, worked for CEMA (Council for the Encouragement of Music and the Arts) during the World War Two, was

amanuensis to Benjamin Britten and from 1952 to 1964 helped run the Aldeburgh Festival, becoming its Artistic Director in 1956.

Director of Music at Dartington (where she was affectionately known as 'Imo') and founder and conductor of the Purcell Singers, she was awarded the CBE in 1975. Her work for English folk music won her much acclaim and she published much on the subject, as well as two biographical studies of her father. She also published guides to the music of Britten, J.S. Bach, Henry Purcell and William Byrd. Her compositions include a *Persephone* Overture for orchestra, a brass band suite (*The Unfortunate Traveller*), a suite for strings, *Three Psalms* for chorus and strings, a cantata (*The Sun's Journey*), a demanding string quartet, a string quintet, other chamber works and piano pieces. She produced many valuable arrangements of folk dances and songs. Imogen Holst died at Aldeburgh in Suffolk and is buried next to Benjamin Britten and Peter Pears.

HOPEKIRK, Helen
20 May 1856 – 19 Nov. 1945

Helen Hopekirk was born near Edinburgh, where she studied with Lichtenstein and Alexander Mackenzie. After a period in Vienna with Leschetizky she made her debut as a pianist at Leipzig, returning to Britain and a recital tour. In 1883 she emigrated to the United States, where her career as a pianist was assured. After several international tours she settled in Boston and became a successful teacher. Her works include some orchestral music, a piano concerto, a *Konzertstück* for piano and orchestra, two sonatas for violin and piano, piano solos and over one-hundred songs, many to Scottish texts. Her 1905 edition of *Seventy Scottish Songs* sold very well. She died in Boston, Massachusetts.

HOPKINS, Edward John
30 Jun. 1818 – 4 Feb. 1901
One of a large family of organists, E.J. Hopkins was born at Westminster and studied with William Hawes and Thomas F. Walmisley. For over fifty years he was organist at the Temple Church in London and was a respected authority on organ construction. Hopkins was one of the founders of the Royal College of Organists and a professor of organ at the Royal Normal College for the Blind. He composed anthems and church services, songs and art-songs, hymn tunes and many works for the organ. He died at Camden Town in London.

HOPKINS, John
1822 – 27 Aug. 1900
A brother of E.J. Hopkins (above), John was also born at Westminster. As a boy he was a chorister at St Paul's Cathedral. He was an organist in London and Jersey, and then accepted an appointment at Rochester Cathedral, which he held for the rest of his life. His compositions include services and anthems, chants and hymn-tunes, songs and part-songs, and pieces for organ and piano. John Hopkins died at Rochester in Kent.

HORDER, Thomas Mervyn
8 Dec. 1919 – 3 Jul. 1977
Mervyn Horder was chairman of Gerald Duckworth publishing company (1948–70) following an earlier career as an intelligence officer in the RAF. He was born in London, son of a royal physician, and was educated at Winchester before gaining a BA from Trinity College, Cambridge. In 1955 he succeeded to the title of (2nd) Baron Horder of Ashford. Horder composed several song collections – *Six Betjeman Songs*, *A Shropshire Lad*, *Seven Shakespeare Songs*, *Black Diamonds* (six Dorothy Parker songs) among them – and edited two carol books as well as publishing a biography of his father and a memoir and critique of Ronald Firbank.

HORROCKS, Amy Elsie
23 Feb. 1867 – after 1915
Born of British parents in Brazil, Amy Horrocks studied composition at the Royal Academy of Music with F.W. Davenport. Continuing to teach and run chamber music concerts in London, she composed extensively, though her output was mainly concerned with chamber music and songs. She eventually returned to Brazil where she died.

HORSLEY, Charles Edward
16 Dec. 1822 – 2 May 1876
Horsley was born in London and had early music lessons from his father, William Horsley, his grandfather John Wall Callcott, and Ignaz Moscheles. Like many others of his generation he studied abroad: in Kassel with Hauptmann and later in Leipzig

(1841-46), where he was greatly influenced by Mendelssohn, a friend of the family. By 1850 Horsley was in Liverpool, where two oratorios (*David* and *Joseph*) were commissioned. Another, *Gideon*, was written for the first Glasgow Festival. Several church anthems also date from this period. He returned to London as organist of St John's Notting Hill. In 1866 Horsley moved to Melbourne, Australia . His ode *Euterpe* was commissioned for the opening of Melbourne Town Hall. Six years later saw him in New York, where he died. His works include, beside the three oratorios mentioned above, a symphony, a piano concerto, two concert overtures, some chamber works, madrigals and songs, as well as a quantity of piano music.

HOWELL, Dorothy Gertrude
25 Feb. 1898 – 12 Jan. 1982

Born in Handsworth in Birmingham into a musical family, Dorothy Howell was a pupil at St Anne's Convent in Birmingham, then in convents in Bonn and Belgium before entering the Royal Academy of Music at the age of fifteen to study piano with Tobias Matthay and Percy Waller, composition with John McEwen and violin with Gladys Chester. She became a professor of harmony and composition there in 1924. A symphonic poem, *Lamia*, written when she was only twenty-one, caused a sensation and was premiered by Sir Henry Wood at the Proms in 1919. Five further performances rapidly followed, but it was not heard again at the Proms until 2010. *Lamia* was harmonically daring at the time and was followed by many others, including a ballet (*Koong Shee*) and a piano concerto, which Howell herself premiered in 1923. Other works include sketches of an undated symphony (probably written in the 1930s), an orchestral overture and other orchestral pieces, a string quartet, a prize-winning *Phantasy* for violin and piano, piano and other instrumental pieces, some excellent church masses, anthems, and songs.

Dorothy Howell worked in the Women's Land Army during World War Two, a conflict which prevented the proposed premiere of her *Three Divertissements* for orchestra when the Queen's Hall was bombed in May 1941. Although she continued composing towards the end of her life, little was published. She died at Malvern and, having tended Sir Edward Elgar's grave for several years, is buried next to Elgar, at St Wulstan's Church, Little Malvern.

HOWELLS, Herbert Norman
17 Oct. 1892 – 24 Feb. 1983

Herbert Howells, whose sympathetic teaching at the Royal College of Music spanned six decades, was born at Lydney in Gloucestershire. He was a pupil of Herbert Brewer before winning an open scholarship to the RCM, where he studied composition with Stanford, organ with Walter Parratt, and other subjects under Parry, Walford Davies and Charles Wood. In addition to his professorship at the RCM, Howells was sub-organist at Salisbury Cathedral, John Collard Fellow of the Worshipful Company of Musicians from 1932 onwards, Director of Music (following Holst) at St Paul's School for Girls from 1936-52, and in 1954 King Edward VII Professor of Music at the University of London. In 1937 he received a Mus.Doc. from Oxford.

Herbert Howells admired Vaughan Williams and Elgar and his music reflected the current musical trends of his youth, the church choral tradition, the re-discovery of English folk music, and the revival of Elizabethan music. His own works tended to be contrapuntal and his most inspired work was the *Hymnus Paradisi*, written in 1938 in memory of his son who died at the age of nine. Other large-scale works are *Missa Sabrinensis* and the *Stabat Mater*. Though his most performed works are those for the organ and the church, he also wrote chamber and instrumental music (in 1916 his piano quartet became the first work to be published by the Carnegie Trust), as well as keyboard music (*Lambert's Clavichord* was composed with that instrument in mind), secular choral music and songs, two piano concertos, a concerto for strings, a fantasia for cello and orchestra and several other orchestral works. Howells was awarded a CBE in 1953 and made a Companion of Honour in 1972. He died in London and his ashes are interred in the north aisle of Westminster Abbey.

HUGHES, Edward John
1888 – 1967
Schoolmaster, organist, choir trainer and conductor, E.J. Hughes was born at Trefor in Caernarvonshire. He studied with Drs. R. Rogers, C. Harris and A.W. Pollitt and composed anthems, songs and part-songs, choral music, and pieces for piano and organ.

HUGHES, Richard Samuel
14 Jul. 1855 – 5 Mar. 1893
Hughes, the 'Sullivan of Wales', was born at Aberystwyth, sone of an ironmonger. At the tender age of seven years he won a solo piano competition at the Caernarvon Eisteddfod. He gained a place at the RAM, where he remained for eighteen months before becoming assistant organist at Bangor Cathedral. For three years he taught in London before returning to his native Bethesda to play the organ in the Congregational Chapel. He was much in demand as an accompanist at eisteddfodau, and some of his many songs are still popular in Wales (*The Inchcape Bell*, *Y Dymestl*, *Arafa Don*, *Elen Fwyn* etc.). He also wrote a cantata, a string quartet, part-songs and several church anthems. Hughes died at Bethesda in Gwynedd.

HULLAH, John Pyke
27 Jun. 1812 – 11 Feb. 1884
Famous for his system of teaching sight-singing, John Hullah was a native of Worcester. A pupil at the Royal Academy of Music, he studied composition with Charles Horsley and singing with Gaetano Crivelli, and became an organist at Croydon and at Charterhouse. Most of his life was spent promoting his controversial 'fixed-doh' system, to which end he had built St Martin's Hall at Long Acre in London with the help of many admirers. The hall was burnt down (together with much of his music) and his system eventually superseded by that of John Curwen. Hullah was appointed a government inspector of music to training colleges; he had already been a professor of voice at King's, Queen's and Bedford Colleges in London. He wrote on musical history and composed operas (*The Village Coquettes*, written when he was twenty-four to a libretto by Charles Dickens, *The Outpost* and *The Barbers of Barsora*), madrigals and songs (notably *The Three Fishers* and *O that we two were a-maying*). Hullah died at Westminster.

HUME, James Ord
14 Sep. 1864 – 27 May 1932
A native of Edinburgh, Ord Hume pursued a military career and played cornet in the Royal Scots Greys from 1880–87. He was appointed organist at the Military Presbyterian Church, Aldershot, and was bandmaster of the Aldershot Town and Farnham Institute bands before settling in Sunderland as bandmaster of the 3rd V.B. Durham Light Infantry. Hume was a respected teacher and adjudicator, and many of his 500 works for brass band are still played world-wide: *Hollywood*, *Brilliant* and *Tranquillity* are particularly popular. He sometimes used the pseudonyms 'William German' and 'Lilian Raymond'. Ord Hume died in London.

HURD, Michael
19 Dec. 1928 – 8 Aug. 2006

Jonah Man Jazz and *Swingin' Samson* are two of Michael Hurd's seven jazz cantatas which will be remembered by generations of schoolchildren. Born in Gloucester, Michael Hurd did not formally begin musical studies until 1950, having been called up for National Service to work in the Army Intelligence Corps, where a posting to Vienna encouraged his growing interest in opera. He then went to Pembroke College, Oxford to study under Thomas Armstrong and Bernard Rose. Following graduation he became Professor of Theory at the Royal Marines School of Music in Deal, and for several years was a pupil of Lennox Berkeley. After the deaths of his parents Hurd bought a property in Liss, Hampshire, where he lived alone, remaining there for the rest of his life. He was a champion of the music of Ivor Gurney, Rutland Boughton and Gerald Finzi, and his campaigning for Boughton's music was widely influential.

As well as his interest in writing for young people, Michael Hurd's best music is to be found among his many choral and vocal works such as *Shepherd's Calendar* (to words by John Clare) and *The Phoenix and the Turtle*, both for baritone, chorus and orchestra. He wrote operas (*The Widow of Ephesus*, *The Aspern Papers* and *The Night of the Wedding*), two operas for children and some orchestral pieces (among the latter *Overture to an Unwritten Comedy*, *Concerto da Camera* and the *Sinfonia Concertante*). His operas *The Widow of Ephesus*, *The Aspern Papers* and *The Night of the Wedding* are noteworthy. Other vocal works with orchestra include a song cycle (*Shore Leave*) and *Missa Brevis*. Many of his works were the result of commissions, and much of his music was published by Novello and Co. He died in Petersfield after a battle against cancer, leaving a generous bequest to the British Music Society.

HURLSTONE, William Yeates
7 Jan. 1876 – 30 May 1906
William Hurlstone was born at Richmond Gardens in London. Both his parents were amateur musicians and he himself showed considerable talent at an early age, starting to compose when he was only seven. In spite of chronic bronchial asthma he was an active child and even produced a weekly periodical, 'The Boys' Half-Holiday', written and illustrated almost completely by himself. At fifteen he wrote a trio for violin, cello and piano.

At eighteen Hurlstone won a scholarship to the Royal College of Music, where he studied with Stanford, Algernon Ashton and Edward Dannreuther. On his departure from the RCM he took to the baton and conducted various musical societies in the Croydon area. Later he was appointed a professor at the Croydon Conservatoire of Music and accompanist to the Bach Choir. Just before his untimely death he became a professor of harmony and composition at the RCM. Hurlstone composed a great many chamber works, a piano concerto, a ballad (*Alfred the Great*) for chorus and orchestra, other orchestral and choral works, instrumental pieces and songs. He died of bronchial asthma aged thirty, with only a few fragments of a symphony completed. He is buried in Croydon Cemetery.

ILIFFE, Frederick
21 Feb. 1847 – 2 Feb. 1928

Frederick Iliffe was born at Smeeton-Westerby in Leicestershire. After studying music privately he held several posts as an organist, finally accepting that at St John's College, Oxford. He conducted the Queen's College Music Society (for which he commissioned a number of works by several composers of the time), and gained his doctorate in 1879. Iliffe composed an oratorio (*The Visions of St John the Divine*), cantatas (notably *Lara*, written for the college Music Society) and other works for chorus and orchestra, orchestral overtures, a *Serenade in C* for strings, much church music, and pieces for organ and piano. He also published a critical analysis of Bach's *Well-Tempered Clavier*, which remained a standard textbook for some years. Iliffe died in Oxford.

IRELAND, John Nicholson
13 Aug. 1879 – 12 Jun. 1962

John Ireland was born at Bowdon in Cheshire. At the age of fourteen he went to the Royal College of Music to study with Stanford, two of his fellow pupils being Vaughan Williams and Holst. Both his parents died very shortly afterwards, and so the young Ireland had to make his own way in London. While still a student he held various posts as an organist in London. In 1904 he moved to Chelsea and soon afterwards became organist of St Luke's there. For a time he taught composition at the RCM. When war broke out in 1939, Ireland moved with his close friend John Longmire to Guernsey, where he had already spent many a holiday. Several months later they were joined by Percy Turnbull and the three composers only just managed to escape when the Nazis invaded the Channel Islands. Ireland spent the last few years of his life at Rock Mill, a converted windmill, in Washington, West Sussex. Here his eyesight became poor and the ageing composer was tended by his life-long friend and companion, Norah Kirby.

Ireland's piano works are outstanding, and include the widely acclaimed Piano Sonata, the three-movement suite *Sarnia*, and many shorter piano pieces. He also composed about ninety songs, of which several became household favourites, such as *Sea Fever*. His choice of words for his vocal and choral settings reflects the fine literary upbringing he must have received from his parents in his early years – his father was an author and journalist and his mother an author and literary critic. The larger part of his output is for chamber groups, but he also wrote many orchestral pieces, a piano concerto (considered to be one of his finest works), choral works and incidental music. His second violin sonata first won him public recognition in 1917, though he had expressed doubts before the premiere, believing the work to be too avant-garde.

One year after Ireland died, the fine memorial window in the Musicians' Chapel of the Holy Sepulchre-without-Newgate in the City of London was dedicated to him, publicly opened by Mrs Kirby. The John Ireland Memorial House was, until 1982, located in the High Street in Steyning, near Washington, Sussex. After Norah Kirby's death in that year, the Ireland Trust (which was established in 1968) moved to London. Ireland is buried opposite the south door of Shipley Church, near his West Sussex home.

IRVING, Kelville Ernest
6 Nov. 1878 – 24 Oct. 1953
Born at Godalming in Surrey, Ernest Irving was a musical director of most London theatres, and also conducted in Paris and Madrid. As Musical Director of the Ealing Film Studios he was responsible for the music of nearly 100 films, including that for *Whisky Galore* and *The Great Mr. Handel* (the latter for GHW Productions). In addition he composed incidental music for about fifty plays, many of them commissions from the Shakespeare Memorial theatre at Stratford-upon-Avon, and several operettas, including *The Two Bouquets*, *An Elephant in Arcady*, and *Tom Thumb the Great*. Irving was chess editor of the Illustrated London News. He died in London.

ISAACS, Edward
14 Jul. 1881 – 31 Jul. 1953
Born and deceased at Fallowfield near Manchester, Edward Isaacs was a pupil at Manchester Grammar School before entering the Royal Manchester College of Music. He later studied in Vienna, Berlin, Hamburg and Leipzig. He established himself as a piano recitalist, and in 1923 was appointed Musical Director of the Manchester Tuesday Mid-day Concerts, a position he held until his death. Though totally blind from 1924, Isaacs still appeared as a concert pianist with a repertoire as wide as any, and he broadcast frequently as a recitalist and lecturer. He composed a piano concerto, a trio for violin, cello and piano, a violin sonata, piano pieces and instrumental music, and also published 'The Blind Piano Teacher'.

IVIMEY, John William
12 Sep. 1868 – 16 Apr. 1961
John Ivimey was born at Stratford in Essex. He was educated at Herne Bay College and the Guildhall School of Music, gaining a doctorate from Oxford University. He was Assistant Director of Music at Wellington College, then Harrow School, before becoming Director of Music at Chelsea Polytechnic, Cheltenham and Marlborough Colleges, and organist of several churches including St Peter's, Norbiton, St Paul's, Onslow Square, and All Souls, Langham Place. His final appointment was at Llandaff Cathedral. Ivimey wrote a book, *Boys and Music*, and edited the Marlborough hymn and song books as well as contributing articles to several magazines. He composed one grand opera (*Rose of Lancaster*), about twenty comic operas, cantatas, a symphony, trios, organ music and songs.

JACKSON, William John
9 Jan. 1815 – 15 Apr. 1866

'Jackson of Masham', as he was known (to distinguish him from the more famous William Jackson, 'Jackson of Exeter', organist of Exeter Cathedral) became well-known outside the Yorkshire Dales town where he was organist. Son of a miller in Masham, William, self-taught in music, worked as a tallow chandler, but enjoyed fame not only as an organist but as a 'jack of all trades', claiming to play on clarinet, all manner of brass instruments and the full range of strings, as well as being an expert in the repair of barrel organs in the North of England, which were in use in some of the village churches of the time. He later moved to Bradford as a music seller and organist of churches in Bradford, and conductor of the Bradford Choral Union. He composed two oratorios: *Israel from Babylon* (1845), and *Isaiah* (1847) which Alfred Novello heard by chance on a visit to Leeds, and which he later published; the work also received performances in London. Jackson also wrote cantatas, a mass, services and anthems. He died in Bradford, a memorial fund for his widow reaching £2,000.

JACOB, Gordon Percival Septimus
5 Jul. 1895 – 8 Jun. 1984

Gordon Jacob is best remembered for his brilliant orchestration, so apparent in his own prolific and varied output, as well as his textbook on the subject. He was born at Upper Norwood in London and went to Dulwich College, leaving to volunteer with his brother for army service in 1914. His brother died at the Somme, while Gordon was taken prisoner in 1917, to be moved around several prisoner-of-war camps. After the war he entered the Royal College of Music, where he was a pupil of Stanford, Parry and Wood, Howells and Vaughan Williams. He taught for a time at Birkbeck and Morley Colleges, then returned to the RCM, joining the staff in 1924 and remaining for forty years as a teacher of theory and composition before retiring. He was an examiner for several universities and for the Associated Board, edited the Penguin series of scores and received several honours for his services to music, culminating in 1968 with a CBE.

Jacob's compositions are traditionally diatonic but exhibit a dignity and charm that entertain the listener. They include two symphonies, two ballets, a host of concertos (e.g. for piano, violin, oboe, bassoon, trombone, viola, horn, flute, cello, harmonica), orchestral suites, string quartets, saxophone quartet and many more chamber works. He has also written solo pieces for harmonica, tuba, saxophone, virginal, recorder, organ etc., works for military and brass bands, and songs. Gordon Jacob died at Saffron Walden in Essex.

JACOBSON, Maurice
1 Jan. 1896 – 2 Feb. 1977

Maurice Jacobson was born in London and studied at the RCM with Stanford and Holst. He was a successful pianist in the 1920s, an adjudicator and broadcaster, and was managing director of the music publishers Curwen. He composed much incidental music for Shakespeare plays at the Old Vic, a ballet suite, other pieces for orchestra or strings, two cantatas including the remarkable *The Hound of Heaven*, instrumental sonatas, piano music and songs. Jacobson died at Brighton.

JEFFREYS, John
4 Dec. 1927 – 3 Sep. 2010

In 1983 John Jeffreys found four old reel-to-reel tapes of some of his songs. He had destroyed much of his music years before, disheartened with the then prevailing attitudes towards fairly traditional styles of composition. But this discovery prompted him to rework the songs, mainly with piano accompaniment rather than the original string quartet, and Kenneth Roberton published them together with other songs in three hefty volumes. Jeffreys began to compose again. He was born in Thanet, Kent, and the inspiration for many of his works came from the poetry in his father's collection (father was a Congregational minister) and his mother's singing of Welsh folksongs. Jeffreys had piano lessons as a child and was a chorister. After National Service with the RAF he studied piano, theory and musical philosophy at Trinity College, London, and studied recorder with Edgar Hunt. Sadly his symphony, a cello concerto, two of three violin concertos, a string quartet and piano sonata were destroyed. Only one violin concerto, some other orchestral works and the songs remained. Jeffreys began working as a garden designer for Tottenham Council, publishing two books on gardening. A final work, written for Ian Parrott's ninetieth birthday, was a setting for recorder and string quartet of the Welsh song *Watching the wild wheat.*

JEKYLL, Charles Sherwood
29 Nov. 1842 – 1929

As a chorister at Westminster Abbey, Jekyll studied under James Coward and G.A. Macfarren before being appointed Assistant Organist at the Abbey. He then moved to other organists' posts in the city, as well as being Organist and Composer to the Chapels Royal, a post he held from 1876-91. He was a distinguished musician of his time and received a Silver Jubilee medal presented by Queen Victoria. His works include several services composed for St Paul's Cathedral, anthems, part-songs and organ pieces for special occasions. He died in Leeds.

JENKINS, Cyril
9 Oct. 1889 – 15 Mar. 1978

Cyril Jenkins was born at Swansea. He studied music with Harry Evans, then with Alcock, Sharpe and Stanford, later taking some classes with Ravel. His first large-scale work, *Young Lochinvar* (for tenor, chorus and orchestra), was produced in 1911 for the Welsh National Eisteddfod and was received with enthusiasm. Jenkins was appointed Director of Music for the London County Council and spent the last few years of his life in Australia. He composed a symphony, an oboe concerto and other orchestral works, choral and orchestral music, pieces for brass band, varied chamber works, organ pieces and part-songs. Cyril Jenkins died at Hove in East Sussex.

JENKINS, David
30 Dec. 1848 – 10 Dec. 1915

David Jenkins was born at Trecastle, Brecon, and studied with Parry at Cambridge. He became Professor of Music at Aberystwyth and played an active role in promoting Welsh national music, helping to organise eisteddfodau and editing the journal 'Y Cerddor' (The Musician). He composed an opera, operetta, oratorios, hymns and other liturgical works. Jenkins died at his home in Aberystwyth but is buried at Trecastle.

JESSETT, Michael
1932 – 1979
Michael Jessett is remembered as a broadcaster on the BBC schools' music programmes. He was born at Christchurch in New Zealand but attended Haberdashers' Aske's School in London. A singer and guitarist, he pioneered the modern guitar teaching methods and was a professor of guitar at the Royal College of Music. In 1963 he was appointed Music and Art Director at the Elizabethan Rooms, London. He composed an oratorio for school choir and orchestra, four cantatas, TV film music, over seventy settings for voice and guitar, songs, and solo guitar and lute pieces.

JEWSON, Frederick Bowen
26 Jul. 1823 – 28 May 1891
Frederick Jewson was born in Edinburgh. He studied with Cipriani Potter at the Royal Academy of Music, where he later became a professor of piano, then a director on the Board of the RAM. In 1866 he was appointed Musician in Ordinary to the Queen. His compositions include five orchestral overtures, two piano concertos, a piano trio, songs and piano pieces. Jewson died in London.

JOHNSON, Bernard
1868 – 16 May 1935
Bernard Johnson was famous for his organ recitals at the Albert Hall. He was born in Norfolk and went to Selwyn College. He taught at Framlingham College and Leeds Grammar School, and was City Organist at Nottingham and organist at Bridlington Priory. He was Director of the Music Department of University College and President of the Incorporated Society of Musicians in 1931-32. Johnson composed a cantata (*Ecce Homo*) and church music, pieces for organ and for piano, songs and part-songs.

JOHNSTONE, Maurice
28 Jul. 1900 – 1976
Maurice Johnstone was born in Manchester and studied at the Royal Manchester College of Music and at the RCM. He worked as a retailer and freelance journalist, then, from 1932-35, was secretary to Sir Thomas Beecham. From 1938 he worked on the staff of the BBC. He was well known as an arranger under the pseudonym David Bowden. Johnstone composed a *Cumbrian Rhapsody* (*Tarn Hows*), *Dover Beach* for baritone and orchestra, a *Ballad* for saxophone and orchestra, several sterling works for brass band, and songs. He died at Harpenden in Hertfordshire.

JONES, Sidney
17 Jun. 1861 – 29 Jan. 1946
Sidney Jones, together with the unrelated German Edward Jones (known as Edward German), inherited the mantle of Sullivan's light operas. His *The Geisha* sold over a million copies and has probably been one of the most successful British operettas. He was born in Leeds, and followed in his father's footsteps by becoming a military bandmaster at an early age. He played the clarinet for a while before touring as conductor with several opera companies. Eventually he settled at the Prince of Wales Theatre in London, where his first two musical comedies were produced (*A Gaiety Girl* and *An Artist's Model*). In addition to the operettas, Jones composed several ballets and some incidental music. None of his works achieved anything like the

success of *The Geisha*, and he retired in 1916, composing very little after that date. He died at Kew in London.

JORDAN, Charles Warwick
28 Dec. 1840 –
Jordan, born in Bristol, became organist at various churches in London before gaining his Mus.Doc. in 1886. He was an examiner for the Royal College of Organists and Trinity College, London, and taught organ and composition at the Guildhall School of Music. He wrote some large-scale sacred works for soli, chorus and orchestra which were performed (with a chorus of 4,000 voices) at the Crystal Palace in the 1890s. Other compositions include works for organ and brass – an unusual instrumental combination at that time.

JOSEPHS, Wilfred
24 Jul. 1927 – 18 Nov. 1997
The fourth son of a wealthy Jewish family in Newcastle upon Tyne, Wilfred Josephs' childhood interest in music matured despite the active discouragement of his family. At the age of sixteen he began composition lessons with Arthur Milner, but his parents guided him into dental surgery, which he practised for two years while doing his National Service in the army. In 1954 he won a scholarship to the Guildhall School of Music, where he studied with the composer Alfred Nieman. Four years later he further developed his compositional skills with the serialist Max Deutsch in Paris. An early choral work, *Requiem*, earned Josephs some acclaim in 1963, winning the International Competition of La Scala, and was probably decisive in his final move from dentistry to music. He went on to write twelve symphonies, five operas (one of them based on Du Maurier's *Rebecca*), four ballets (including *Cyrano* and *Equus*), twenty-two concertos including one for brass band, an oratorio (*Mortales*), songs and song-cycles and a great deal of chamber and instrumental music. But he will be remembered mainly for his highly tuneful music for films and television (including that for *The Great War*, *I Claudius*, *A Voyage Round my Father*, *Cider with Rosie*, *Grasshopper Island* and many more). Josephs died at home in London.

KEAL, Minna
22 Mar. 1909 – 14 Nov. 1999
Mina Nerenstein was born in East London, the daughter of a Jewish prayer book publisher and seller. As a pupil of William Alwyn at the RAM, where she studied for a year, she had several early works performed. On the death of her father she helped her mother continue the family business, at the same time as composing. Following her first marriage to a lawyer she renounced her Jewish origins and turned towards Stalinism. After the war she lived with William Keal, whom she eventually married, sharing a life devoted to the communist party. In 1969 Minna Keal took up composition again, studying with Justin Connolly and Oliver Knussen. Her compositions were strongly influenced by Bartók and Schoenberg, resulting in a performance in 1989 at the Proms of her Symphony, a work combining free use of the twelve-tone system and the Golden Section principle. Another important work was *Cantillation* for violin and orchestra. Her cello concerto was performed at the Aldeburgh Festival in 1994.

KELLY, Frederick Septimus
29 May 1881 – 13 Nov. 1916
Kelly was born in Australia but was sent to England to school at Eton. At Balliol College, Oxford, he became a first class rower and eventually competed in the Olympic Games of 1908. Following his studies in Frankfurt with Iwan Knorr, he became friends during his war years with the composer Denis Browne. Like Browne, killed on active service in World War One, Lt-Cdr Kelly, DSO, was killed in the Battle of the Somme. Works include an Elegy for strings (*In Memoriam Rupert Brooke*), written at Gallipoli, and a serenade for flute, harp and strings. There is a memorial to him in Bisham Church, Buckinghamshire.

KENNEDY-FRASER, Marjory
1 Oct. 1857 – 22 Nov. 1930
Daughter of the famous Scottish singer David Kennedy, Marjory was born at Perth. She studied music with her father, a well-known singer, and also in Milan and Paris under Mathilde Marchesi. At the age of twelve she toured with her father as accompanist, soon after embarking with him on a four-and-a-half year tour. After her husband's death she settled as a teacher and lecturer in Edinburgh, devoting much of her life to the collection, arrangement and publication of Scottish folk-songs, especially those of the Hebrides. The *Eriskay Love Lilt* and *Road to the Isles* still retain considerable charm. She gave many recitals of such songs. She also wrote the libretto for Granville Bantock's opera *The Seal Woman* and sang the title role in Birmingham in 1924 under Adrian Boult's baton. Kennedy-Fraser composed a *Hebridean Suite* for cello, and several piano pieces.

KETÈLBEY, Albert William
4 Aug. 1875 – 26 Nov. 1959
Albert Ketèlbey was born at Aston Manor in Birmingham and studied locally with A.R. Gaul and the Birmingham organist Herbert Wareing. At the age of thirteen he won the Queen Victoria Scholarship to Trinity College, London, where he studied piano with Bainbridge and composition with Dr G. Saunders. Before the age of sixteen he had already composed several orchestral and chamber works, a piano and  wind quintet which won the Costa Prize. In addition to playing the cello, piano and organ (at St John's Church, Wimbledon) he became a theatre conductor and was Music Director of the Columbia Graphaphone Co. and a music editor for Chappell's. Ketèlbey composed a comic opera (*The Wonder Worker*), an overture, a piano concerto, a quintet for piano and woodwind, and other chamber works. But he is best remembered for lighter pieces such as *In a Monastery Garden* and *In a Persian Market*. He sometimes composed under the pseudonym of Anton Vodorinsky, probably to differentiate between his lighter and more serious work. Ketèlbey died at Cowes on the Isle of Wight.

KETTLE, Charles Edward
28 Mar. 1833 – 2 Mar. 1895
Charles Kettle was born at Bury St Edmunds and held various posts as organist in London, Woolwich and Brighton, where his life ended. He composed church music, songs, piano and organ works, and three operas, *Amelie*, *Hermina* and *The Water Cure*.

KLEAN, Bluebell
1875 – Dec. 1950
Born Isabel Maud Klean in London to a German-born father, a wealthy watch manufacturer, and an English mother, she changed her name to Bluebell (the middle name of an aunt) while still a teenager. She studied with Samuel Coleridge-Taylor at Trinity College, and privately. She was an able pianist, appearing regularly at London venues around the turn of the century. Her works include a piano quintet in C Minor, a piano concerto (performed by the Bournemouth Municipal Orchestra under Sir Dan Godfrey in 1917), other chamber music and several songs. She appears to have dropped out of sight as a composer and pianist after World War One and eventually settled in Hastings where, according to a relative, she became a champion competition angler.

KLEIN, Ivy Frances
23 Dec. 1895 – 25 Mar. 1972
Ivy Salaman was born in Maida Vale, London, grand-daughter of composer Charles Kensington Salaman. She was exposed to music of a high standard in her childhood home, and studied harmony and composition with A. Pollitt in Liverpool (the family had moved to Cheshire for a time). She had singing lessons from 1912-15. Ivy's first songs were published under her maiden name in 1921 and two years later she had composition lessons with Benjamin Dale at the Royal Academy of Music and singing lessons with Anne Thursfield. After her marriage in 1924 to Daryl Klein, she wrote and published many more songs, as well as broadcasting, lecturing, and giving piano and singing lessons. Ivy was a founder member of the Crowborough Music Club. Her song *She Walked in Beauty* (for women's choir and organ), written for the Coronation of Elizabeth II, was performed at St Martin-in-the-Fields in 1953. Altogether Ivy Frances Klein composed over sixty songs (including an unadopted Nigerian National Anthem!).

KNIGHT, Rev. Joseph Philip
26 Jul. 1812 – 2 Jun. 1887
Born at the vicarage of Bradford-on-Avon in Wiltshire, Knight studied with John Davies Corfe, organist at Bristol Cathedral. He began composing at the age of twenty, at first under the pseudonym of Philip Mortimer, and his songs gained popularity not only in Britain but in the United States (which he visited in 1839, and where he wrote his most famous song *Rocked in the cradle of the deep*) and in Germany. He wrote over 200 songs, duets and trios. Knight was known as an able extemporiser on the organ. After taking holy orders, he served as vicar and organist for a period on the Isle of St Agnes in the Scillies. He died at Great Yarmouth.

LAHEE, Henry
11 Apr. 1826 – 29 Apr. 1912
Henry Lahee, born at Chelsea, was a pupil of Sterndale Bennett, John Goss and Cipriani Potter. He became organist of Holy Trinity, Brompton, in 1847 and remained there for twenty-seven years. Lahee composed several cantatas which were performed in his time (*The building of the ship* was once popular), anthems, madrigals, glees, songs and instrumental pieces. His hymn-tune *Nativity* is still used to the words 'Come, let us join our cheerful songs'. Lahee died in London.

LAKE, Ian Thomson
26 Jan. 1935 – 12 Aug. 2004
Born in Quorn, Leicestershire, Lake gained a scholarship to the Royal College of Music where he later became a professor, a post he held for twenty-nine years. He studied piano under Kendall Taylor, and his work as a concert pianist was renowned. Composition was very much a sideline, but his intimate works for piano, such as *Prelude and Scherzo Impetuoso*, the berceuses written for his children, and *Rumplestiltskin* and *Cinderella* for speaker and piano, as well as his piano sonatas are little known today.

LAMBERT, Leonard Constant
23 Aug. 1905 – 21 Aug. 1951
Constant Lambert is best remembered as a conductor and as Director of Music at Sadlers Wells. His compositions are little known (with the exception of *The Rio Grande* of 1929, a choral/orchestral *quasi* piano concerto showing the influence of jazz), though he was one of only two Englishmen from whom Diaghilev commissioned ballets. Lambert was only twenty at the time, and was still a pupil at the Royal College of Music where he studied with Herbert Fryer, Malcolm Sargent, R.O. Morris, George Dyson and Vaughan Williams. Unfortunately his ballet *Romeo and Juliet* was not a success, though a later one, *Horoscope*, achieved some popularity.

Born in London, the son of a painter and sculptor, Lambert was left lame by a succession of childhood illnesses. But he had a brilliant intellect and a wide knowledge of art and literature, as witnessed by his witty and impassioned book 'Music Ho!', an eminently readable criticism of the music of his time. Among his closest friends were Alan Rawsthorne, the novelist Anthony Powell, Tom Driberg, Philip Heseltine, William Walton and the Sitwells. (Lambert and Edith Sitwell were the reciters in the first performance of Walton's scandalous *Façade*.) Lambert composed several ballets, two piano concertos, a splendid choral *Summer's Last Will and Testament*, other chamber and orchestral works including the striking *Music for Orchestra*, songs and piano pieces. He also wrote incidental and film music and arranged and edited the symphonies and other works of William Boyce. Ill-health, alcohol, over-work and multiple disappointments brought his life to a premature close, and he died in the London Clinic of broncho-pneumonia and diabetes mellitus, his ashes being interred at Brompton Cemetery.

LAMBETH, Henry Albert
16 Jan. 1822 – 27 Jun. 1895
Henry Lambeth was born at Hardway near Gosport, Hampshire, and studied organ with Thomas Adams and Henry Smart. He became City Organist in Glasgow, where he died, and conductor of the Choral Union. He composed piano pieces, songs and psalm settings.

LAMOND, Frederic Archibald
28 Jan. 1868 – 21 Feb. 1948
Frederic Lamond was born in Glasgow. He studied at the Raff Conservatory in Frankfurt, taking piano with Schwartz, violin with Hermann and composition with Anton Urspruch. He later studied composition with Hans von Bülow and Liszt. He

became a concert pianist, renowned for his interpretations of Beethoven, and toured extensively. He was professor of piano at the Hague Conservatory from 1917, but returned to London during World War Two, teaching and playing. Lamond composed a symphony, overture, piano trio and several solo piano pieces. He died at Stirling.

LANCHBERY, John
15 May 1923 – 27 Feb. 2003
John Lanchbery dedicated over half a century to raising musical standards in the world of ballet. He was born in London and went to Alleyn's School, Dulwich, before winning a scholarship to the Royal Academy of Music. His studies there were interrupted by war service in the Royal Armoured Corps. Soon after leaving the RAM Lanchbery was appointed conductor of the Metropolitan Ballet, but funding problems led to the company's collapse two years later. He began to arrange and orchestrate works for the ballet and soon commanded considerable respect. From 1950 he spent ten years as musical director of Sadler's Wells Theatre Ballet, then a further twelve as principal conductor of the Royal Ballet. In 1972 he moved to the Australian Ballet, then in 1978 to the American Ballet Theatre in New York. Lanchbery often included his own original work into arrangements of other composers' music; his *Clog Dance* became a popular BBC Radio theme tune. He also wrote incidental music for radio, television and films, notably *The Tales of Beatrix Potter* and *The Turning Point*. John Lanchbery received many international awards and an OBE in 1990.

LANG, Craig Sellar
1891 – 26 Nov. 1972
C.S. Lang was born at Hastings in New Zealand, but settled in Britain after studying at Clifton College and the Royal College of Music. He followed a career as an organist and teacher and for sixteen years was Director of Music at Christ's Hospital in Sussex. He composed cantatas, church services and anthems, works for piano, violin and organ. His books of exercises in score-reading and keyboard harmony became standard textbooks for music students for many years.

LAZARUS, Henry
1 Jan. 1815 – 6 Mar. 1895
Henry Lazarus was celebrated as the greatest clarinettist of his day. He was born in London and studied with Charles Godfrey Sr. He played with various orchestras (being principal clarinettist and soloist with the Philharmonic Society on several occasions), and taught at the Royal Academy of Music, the Royal College of Music, Trinity College and Kneller Hall. He retired from playing in 1891. His tutor for the Albert and Boehm systems ran to several editions. Lazarus composed several fantasias for the clarinet.

LEE, George Alexander
1802 – 8 Oct. 1851
George Lee was conductor at the Olympic Theatre in London and pianist at the 'Poses Plastiques' in Bow Street. He was born in London and began his professional career as a tenor singer in Dublin before moving in 1826 to the Haymarket in London, where he managed various music shops. Lee composed operettas and incidental music to several plays (*Invincibles*, *Sublime and Beautiful*, *Love in a Cottage*, *Fairy Lake*, etc.). He also was a prolific writer of songs and ballads, duets and part-songs.

LE FLEMING, Christopher Kaye
26 Feb. 1908 – 13 Jun. 1985
Christopher Le Fleming spent most of his life as a schoolteacher and many of his compositions were conceived with children in mind. He studied music at the Brighton School of Music and the Royal School of Church Music, and had lessons with Howard Jones and George Reeves, but he was self-taught as a composer. Le Fleming's first teaching post was at St Mary's School, Calne (1943-46), after which he was appointed assistant director of the Rural Schools Music Association. In 1955 he joined the staff of Sutton Valence School and two years later became Director of Sussex Rural Music School. He was also honorary advisor to the Religious Drama Society. Le Fleming composed an orchestral suite *London River*, *The Singing Friar* for tenor, chorus and orchestra, incidental music for plays, *Five Psalms*, the *Peter Rabbit Music Books* piano pieces and songs. Born at Wimborne Minster in Dorset, Christopher Le Fleming was a student of the paranormal and a keen railway enthusiast. His autobiography *Journey into Music: (by the slow train)* was written in 1982.

LEHMANN, Elizabeth Nina Mary Frederika
11 Jul. 1862 – 19 Sep. 1918
Liza Lehmann first made her name as a singer, appearing professionally for the first time when she was twenty-three. She researched and championed songs by early British composers such as Purcell and Arne, and often included her own songs in performance. After her marriage in 1894 to Herbert Bedford, the composer and painter, she gave up singing for composition. She was born at Westbourne Terrace in Paddington, London, though she spent the first five years of her life in Italy. Her maternal grandfather was the Edinburgh publisher Robert Chambers, anonymous author of 'Vestiges of the Natural History of Creation' that so scandalised Victorian society.

Liza Lehmann studied singing with her mother, Amelia Lehmann, and with Randegger. For composition she was a pupil of Hamish MacCunn, Raunkilde in Rome and Freudenberg in Weishaden. Her lighter works, such as the song-cycle *In a Persian Garden*, to words by Omar Khayyám, were highly successful, but she was often disappointed by the public and critical coolness towards her more serious works, like the opera *Everyman*. Her works include some song cycles, musical comedy (*Sergeant Brue*, the first to be commissioned from a woman composer), a light opera (*The Vicar of Wakefield*), incidental music, ballads for voice and orchestra (*Endymion* and *Young Lochinvar*), a few chamber works, and piano pieces. She died at Pinner, where she had lived for many years, having just finished writing her memoirs.

LEIGH, Walter
22 Jun. 1905 – 12 Jun. 1942
The death of Walter Leigh, killed in action near Tobruk in Libya in 1942, deprived England of a gifted and promising young composer. He was born in Wimbledon and studied at University College School and Christ's College, Cambridge, where he was taught by E.J. Dent. He went also to Berlin for lessons with Hindemith, whose influence can be seen in Leigh's many works for amateur groups. Walter Leigh wrote much light music, often cleverly bridging the gap between serious and popular styles. His two operettas, *Jolly Roger* and *The Pride of the Regiment*, had successful runs and he was commissioned to write the music for several revues, stage productions and

films. In addition he composed chamber works, a splendid concertino for harpsichord and strings, piano pieces and songs.

LEIGHTON, Kenneth
2 Oct. 1929 – 24 Aug. 1988

The music of Kenneth Leighton is becoming increasingly popular. It bears a highly distinctive hallmark, though one may have to look beneath the surface to find it: often deeply religious, always sincere, it is never sombre; it can exhibit a wildness of spirit or express exuberance and merriment without ever losing dignity; it can be passionate, austere, granitic or gentle, but displays an unerringly faultless craftsmanship; it is musicians' music and has won many international awards.

Kenneth Leighton was born at Wakefield in Yorkshire, where he was a pupil at Queen Elizabeth Grammar School and a Cathedral choirboy. He read Classics at Queen's College, Oxford, before going to Rome to study composition with Petrassi. His professional life was devoted to composition and teaching, and he began his career as an instructor to the Royal Marines at Deal. After three years at the Music Department of Leeds University (1953–56) he moved to Edinburgh as Senior Lecturer and Reader in Composition. In 1968 he followed Rubbra as Fellow of Worcester College, Oxford, then succeeded to Edinburgh University's Reid Professorship in 1970, a post which he held until his death. Kenneth Leighton's music, which he claims has been described as having such typical Yorkshire characteristics as 'vigour, forthrightness and emotionalism tempered by common sense', is harmonically, rhythmically and, in its dependence on counterpoint, reminiscent of Hindemith; even so, it is indisputably Leighton.

He composed three symphonies, an opera (*Columba*), ten concertos – three of which are for piano, and one each for viola and harp, cello, organ with timpani and strings, etc. – and other orchestral works, a great deal of chamber and instrumental music, vocal and choral/orchestral music, church anthems and services. Leighton was a first-rate keyboard player, as the quality of his works for piano and organ, and his own performances, testify. His *Fantasia Contrappuntistica* of 1956 won the Busoni prize and was premiered by Maurizio Pollini at Bolzano. Leighton died in Edinburgh.

LEMARE, Edwin Henry
9 Sep. 1865 – 21 Sep. 1934

Born at Ventnor on the Isle of Wight, Edwin Lemare studied at the Royal Academy of Music. He held various posts as a church organist before becoming a full-time virtuoso concert pianist and organist, settling in the United States. He died in Los Angeles. Lemare's output included two organ symphonies and many other original organ works and transcriptions, usually with a Romantic orchestral flavour. Of particular note are the Concert Fantasia on *Hanover* and the *March Héroïque*, but his Andantino in D flat, originally for organ and later more commonly known as as *Moonlight and Roses,* became his most well-known work. Lemare's conductor daughter, Iris, was co-founder of the Macnaghten Concerts.

LESLIE, Henry David
18 Jun. 1822 – 4 Feb. 1894
Remembered now only for his part-songs, Leslie also composed operas, an oratorio, cantatas, symphonies, orchestral overtures, chamber music, church anthems, songs (*Annabel Lee* can still be heard) and piano pieces. He was born in London and studied with Charles Lucas, becoming a cellist and later a renowned choral conductor. The Henry Leslie Choir was formed in 1856 and was renowned for singing an eclectic range of 'a cappella' music from Elizabethan madrigals to Victorian part-songs. The choir won first prize in the Paris International Contest of 1878. Leslie died at Llansantfraid-ym-Mechain in Powys.

LEVEY, William Charles
25 Apr. 1837 – 18 Aug. 1894
W.C. Levey was born in Dublin. He studied with his father, the composer Richard Michael Levey, and later with Auber, Thalberg and Prudent in Paris. He conducted at Drury Lane, Covent Garden and several other theatres, and composed two operettas, incidental music to plays, a cantata, piano pieces and songs. Levey died in London.

LEWIS, Idris
1889 – 14 May 1952
Born at Birchgrove in Swansea, Idris Lewis studied at the Royal College of Music with Hartvigson, Frederick Bridge and Charles Wood. He toured India and the Far East as a pianist then settled in London, becoming a theatre conductor and musical director. He played the organ and conducted the London Welsh Choral Society and the BBC Welsh Orchestra. Lewis composed a ballad-opera, orchestral and choral/orchestral works, songs (Bryn Terfel described him as 'The Welsh Schubert') and part-songs. He also wrote on the history of Welsh music and, for sixteen years, was Director of Music for BBC Wales.

LEY, Henry George
30 Dec. 1887 – 24 Aug. 1962
Born at Chagford in Devon, Henry Ley was a choirboy at St George's, Windsor, and a student at Keble College, Oxford, of which he was later an Honorary Fellow. He studied music at the Royal College of Music with Walter Parratt and later became organist of Christ Church Cathedral, Oxford. His other appointments included those of professor at the RCM, Precentor at Radley and Eton Colleges and an examiner for the Royal College of Organists. He composed *Variations on a Theme of Handel* for orchestra, choral and church music, and organ works. Ley died at Ottery St Mary in Devon.

LITOLFF, Henry Charles
6 Feb. 1818 – 6 Aug. 1891
Litolff, whose family came from Alsace, was born in London and studied with Moscheles. He made his name as a virtuoso pianist, touring all over the world, and established the publishing firm which bore his name. He eloped to the Continent at the age of seventeen with the first of a succession of brides, the last being seventeen years old, only thirty-eight years younger than her rampant spouse. Most of the rest of his life he spent across the Channel, serving at one time as Kapellmeister to the

Duke of Saxe-Coburg-Gotha. Many of Litolff's compositions were published, including seven operas, orchestral overtures, four symphonic concertos for piano and orchestra, a violin concerto, oratorio, and chamber and piano music. Litolff died in a Paris suburb, Bois-les-Combes.

LLOYD, Charles Harford
16 Oct. 1849 – 16 Oct. 1919
C.H. Lloyd was born at Thornbury in Gloucestershire. He went to Hertford College, Oxford, and, with his friend Hubert Parry founded the Oxford University Music Club in 1872, and was its first President. He was organist at Gloucester Cathedral from 1876 to 1882, succeeding S.S. Wesley, when he moved to Christ Church, Oxford. Whilst at Gloucester he conducted the Three Choirs Festival. Lloyd taught organ and composition at the Royal College of Music before moving to Eton to succeed Barnby as Precentor. After his retirement in 1914 he became Organist at the Chapel Royal, St James. He composed cantatas (including *Hero and Leander*, 1884), an ode to Queen Victoria, anthems and church services, madrigals, an organ concerto and other organ works. He died at Slough.

LLOYD, David John de
30 Apr. 1883 – 20 Aug. 1948
David Lloyd was born at Skewen in Glamorganshire and studied at Leipzig (under Zollner, Schreef and Hoffmann) and at Aberystwyth University. He taught at the County School in Llanelli and was an organist and conductor of local choral societies. He was given a lectureship at Aberystwyth, and then became Professor of Music from 1926 to 1948, succeeding Walford Davies. Lloyd was a keen promoter of the Welsh language and wrote some 400 arrangements of Welsh tunes. He also composed two operas, choral works, songs, a *Welsh Requiem*, and edited a Welsh hymnal.

LLOYD, George Walter Selwyn
28 Jun. 1913 – 3 Jul. 1998

At the end of a pre-concert talk George Lloyd was asked a technical question about one of the items in the programme. His reply was, 'Don't ask me about my music; just listen to it', an answer that is explicit in his music. It is approachable and without pretension; it is not afraid of a 'big tune' yet still manages subtlety; it is expertly crafted and distinctive within its late romantic idiom. Lloyd was born at St. Ives in Cornwall and decided at an early age to be a composer. Rheumatic fever interrupted his schooling, but he recovered and studied with Harry Farjeon and Albert Sammons. When he was nineteen his first symphony was performed by the Bournemouth Municipal Orchestra under Sir Dan Godfrey. Two other symphonies soon followed, as well as the operas *Iernin* and *The Serf*. In World War Two Lloyd was a bandsman and gunner with the Royal Marines, escorting Arctic convoys in HMS Trinidad. When a torpedo hit the ship below the waterline, seventeen of his comrades died. Only Lloyd and three others survived. He was badly shell-shocked and suffered a total collapse. For the next few years he found composing difficult, but with his wife's help managed his third and fourth symphonies and a third opera, *John Socman*.

With Lloyd's health further deteriorating he and his wife moved to Dorset, growing mushrooms and carnations in their market garden. He tried composing again but with little success. In the 1960s John Ogdon, Charles Groves and Edward Downes championed his music and he experienced a revival that lasted until he died. He composed twelve symphonies, four piano concertos, a *Symphonic Mass* and the large-scale choral work *The Vigil of Venus*, other choral and orchestral works, some brass band music and many instrumental pieces. He survived heart problems just long enough to finish his *Requiem*.

LLOYD, John Morgan
19 Aug. 1880 – 30 Jun. 1960
J.M. Lloyd was born at Pentre in the Rhondda valley, Glamorganshire. He studied at University College, Cardiff, where he later became a lecturer, then in 1939 Professor of Music. Amongst his pupils were Grace Williams and Alun Hoddinott. He was also an examiner and adjudicator. His compositions include a cantata, a *Te Deum* for choir and orchestra, madrigals, songs, part-songs and piano pieces.

LLOYD WEBBER, William Southcombe
11 Mar. 1914 – 29 Oct. 1982
For the last eighteen years of his life Dr William Lloyd Webber was Director of the London College of Music. He was born in Chelsea of musical parents and showed musical talents at an early age, playing his own organ works with Sir Walford Davies at St George's Chapel, Windsor. He went to Mercer's School, then to the Royal College of Music, obtaining his FRCO at the age of nineteen, a London B.Mus. shortly afterwards, and proceeded to his Doctorate in 1948. Lloyd Webber was a first-class organist, serving at Christ Church, Newgate Street, St Cyprian's, Clarence Gate and at All Saints', Margaret Street. In 1946 he was appointed professor and examiner in theory and composition at the RCM and in 1958, Musical Director of the Central Hall, Westminster. He was also Master of the Worshipful Company of Musicians 1973–74. His sons Julian and Andrew are well known respectively as cellist and highly successful composer of light stage music. William Lloyd Webber composed orchestral music, large-scale choral works (such as the oratorio *St Francis of Assisi*) and instrumental pieces. He died in London.

LODER, Edward James
1813 – 5 Apr. 1865
Born at Bath, Edward Loder went to Frankfurt at the age of thirteen to study with Ferdinand Ries. He became conductor at the Princess Theatre in London, and then moved to Manchester. He composed several operas, which were once extremely popular: *The Night Dancers* of 1846 is said to be his finest work. His songs, in an old-fashioned ballad style, were greatly admired and *The Brave Old Oak*, *The Diver* and *The Brooklet* were among the finest of the period. Loder also composed some sacred songs, a cantata and string quartets. He died in London.

LODER, Kate Fanny
21 Aug. 1825 – 30 Aug. 1904
Like her cousin Edward, Kate Loder was born at Bath. She studied piano with Henry Field and at the Royal Academy of Music with her aunt, Lucy Anderson. Her harmony and composition tutor was Charles Lucas. Soon after leaving the RAM, at the age of eighteen she played the solo part in Mendelssohn's G minor piano concerto in the composer's presence. In 1844 she was appointed as the first woman professor of harmony and composition at the RAM, where one of her pupils was the pianist and composer Landon Ronald. She composed an opera, *L'Elisir d'Amore*, an overture, two string quartets, two piano sonatas, a sonata for violin and piano and a piano trio. After her husband Henry Thompson, an eminent surgeon, was knighted she turned to writing songs and piano pieces, which were published under the name of Lady Thompson. It was at the family home in London that Brahms's *Requiem* was first heard in Britain in 1871, when she and Cipriani Potter played the accompaniment as a piano duet. In her last twenty years she became increasingly paralysed, and died at Headley in Surrey.

LONGHURST, William Henry
6 Oct. 1819 – 17 Jun. 1904
Born at Lambeth in London, from the age of two Longhurst moved to Canterbury and began his career there, becoming a chorister at Canterbury Cathedral, then assistant organist, master of the choristers and a lay clerk, and finally (succeeding Thomas Jones) organist from 1873-98 – a span of seventy-one years devoted to the Cathedral! He composed anthems and services, songs and an oratorio, *David and Absolom*.

LONGMIRE, John Basil Hugh
19 Jan. 1902 – 6 Apr. 1986
A lifelong friend of John Ireland, with whom he spent two years in Guernsey before fleeing from the Nazi invasion of 1940, John Longmire was born at Gainsborough in Lincolnshire. He was a pupil at Benjamin Adlard's School and a chorister under Dr Alan Stephenson at the parish church. At the Royal College of Music he studied with Arthur Alexander and John Ireland. His career began as a schoolteacher, first at Tonbridge, then at Sevenoaks Schools. Other teaching posts followed in England (Bromsgrove County High and Epsom College), Guernsey and New Zealand, and in 1958 he joined the staff of Trinity College of Music. From 1936 onwards he devoted much of his time to composition, especially of an educational nature. Longmire conducted various choral societies, founding an operatic society in London and the Guernsey Choral Society. He and Reginald Jevons established the Surrey College of Music. His compositions were mainly for piano, but he wrote three operettas (*The Bells of Bruges*, *Pedro the Gipsy Boy* and *The Stammering Princess*), some chamber music, choral works and a few orchestral pieces. Longmire composed special music for Queen Elizabeth II for three ceremonial occasions. He contributed to various musical journals and wrote *John Ireland:Portrait of a Friend.*

LUCAS, Charles
28 Jul. 1808 – 23 Mar. 1869
Charles Lucas was born at Salisbury and was a chorister at the cathedral there under Corfe. At the Royal Academy of Music he studied composition with William Crotch

and cello with Robert Lindley, He become Principal of the RAM in 1859, succeeding Cipriani Potter. He retired through ill health seven years later, handing over to William Sterndale Bennett. He was a cellist, organist and conductor and became a partner in a firm of music publishers. His compositions include an opera (*The Regicide*), three symphonies, a cello concertino, orchestral overtures, string quartets, anthems and songs. Lucas died at Wandsworth in London.

LUCAS, Leighton
5 Jan. 1903 – 1 Nov. 1982
A native of London, Leighton Lucas taught himself music while employed as a dancer with Diaghilev's 'Ballets Russes'. At the age of nineteen he was appointed conductor at the Birmingham Repertory Theatre, receiving accolades for his direction of Rutland Boughton's opera *The Immortal Hour*. By 1934 he was an established ballet conductor. He was also on the staff of the Royal Academy of Music. Lucas composed ballets, *Missa pro Defunctis* (in memory of Delius, Elgar and Holst), various concertante works (e.g. for piano, viola d'amore, viola da gamba, violin, clarinet) and other orchestral pieces, vocal and choral/orchestral works, chamber and instrumental music, songs and film music (*Ice Cold in Alex* being most memorable). Lucas died in London.

LUCAS, Mary Anderson
24 May 1882 – 14 Jan. 1952
Mary Lucas, born in London, studied at the Dresden Conservatoire with Albanesi, and in London with R.O. Morris, Herbert Howells and Maurice Jacobson. She served on the committee of the original British Music Society (founded 1918 by Eaglefield Hull) and composed some orchestral pieces, a ballet (*Sawdust*), a Concertino for flute and orchestra and other orchestral works, string quartets and other chamber works, instrumental music and songs. She died in London.

LUTYENS, Elisabeth Agnes
9 Jul. 1906 – 14 Apr. 1983

Daughter of the architect Sir Edward Lutyens, Elisabeth became a composer despite opposition from her family, and throughout her life fought energetically for the acceptance of women in a male-dominated vocation. Her own works were slow to gain recognition.

The most radical British composer of her generation, she abandoned late Romanticism in the 1930s and adopted the twelve-tone techniques of Webern long before serialism became well-known, though she always claimed to have arrived at the idea independently as a result of listening to Purcell's Fantasias. Her uncompromisingly progressive work contrasted sharply with the prevailing milieu of English pastoralism.

She was born in Bloomsbury Square, London and studied in Paris, where she cultivated an interest in theosophy. This interest was strengthened when she had lessons in London with John Foulds before he settled in India. Returning to Britain in 1926 Lutyens entered the Royal College of Music, studying composition with Harold Darke, and viola as a second study. She survived in her youth by music copying, arranging and orchestrating, later writing scores for radio and films. Her interest in films continued to her death, and nearly one hundred scores, including many Hammer

Horror productions, remain as testimony to her craftsmanship. In the 1930s she co-founded with Iris Lemare the Macnaghten-Lemare concerts; in the 1950s she formed the Composers' Concourse.

Although Elisabeth Lutyens composed several large-scale works for the stage, including opera (*The Numbered*, the charade to her own libretto *Time off? Not a Ghost of a Chance* and the ballad opera *The Goldfish Bowl*), her best works were in miniature form (especially *O Saisons, O Chateaux!*) and often inspired by poetry. Her wide choice of texts, from Ovid to Paolozzi and Stevie Smith, and taking in Wittgenstein's *Tractatus Logico Philosophicus* on the way, is matched by the eclecticism of her musical sources, deriving from pop music, pre-recorded tapes and dance. Her output includes a viola concerto and other orchestral pieces, five chamber concertos, cantatas and other vocal and choral/orchestral works, much chamber music (including six string quartets), instrumental pieces and songs. Her autobiography, *The Goldfish Bowl*, was published in 1972. Lutyens rejected all of her earlier music. She was honoured with the CBE in 1969, after which some of her finest works were written. She died at Hampstead in London.

LUTZ, Wilhelm Meyer
1822 – 31 Jan. 1903
Born and trained in Germany, Lutz came to England in 1848. After holding organist's posts in Birmingham and Leeds, and at a Catholic church (for which he composed several masses), Lutz changed his career to become an operatic conductor at the Surrey Theatre in Guildford, where he composed five operettas, then the Gaiety Theatre in London, for which he wrote the music for many burlesques. Lutz died in London.

LYDIATE, Frederick
1906 – 1978
Frederick Lydiate was born at Salford and studied music with Dr F.H. Wood, Claude Biggs and Dora Gilson. After the war, during which he was an artist manager with ENSA, he spent his time teaching in schools in Lincolnshire, London and, since 1957, Coventry. He also played the piano as accompanist. He composed mainly chamber music – two string quartets, various quintets, etc. – sonatas for violin and for piano, other instrumental works and several song cycles. Lydiate's aim was to introduce modern compositional techniques gently into his works so as not to 'bewilder' the public ear. The critic Alan Blyth wrote of him in the *Daily Telegraph*, 'Lydiate certainly seems to have had a musical mind of his own and his neglect is unwarranted.'

LYON, James
25 Oct. 1872 – 25 Sep. 1949
Born in Manchester, James Lyon was almost entirely self-taught as a musician. He held various teaching posts – at St Michael's College in Tenbury, King Edward's School at Warwick, as a professor at the Birmingham and Midland Institute and at Trinity College – and toured as a lecturer and examiner. Lyon composed a symphony, orchestral suites, several operas (including *The Palace of Cards* and *Stormwrack*) and cantatas, string quartets and solo pieces for organ, violin and piano. He also wrote songs, anthems and services, and various educational works. His *Coronation March* and *The Miracle of the Roses* were once popular. James Lyon died in Australia.

Macbeth, Allan
13 Mar. 1856 – 25 Aug. 1910

Allan Macbeth was born at Greenock and studied at Edinburgh with Robert Davidson and Otto Schweizer, and at Leipzig with Richter, Reinecke and Jadassohn. He held posts as organist at churches in Edinburgh and Glasgow, conducted the Glasgow Choral Union from 1880-87, and was appointed as the first Director of the Music School of the Glasgow Athenaeum in 1890. He died in Glasgow. Macbeth composed an operetta (*The Duke's Doctor*), cantatas, incidental music and orchestral music, chamber works, songs and part-songs and pieces for piano solo.

MACCUNN, Hamish
22 Mar. 1868 – 2 Aug. 1916

Hamish MacCunn achieved recognition at the age of nineteen with an orchestral overture, *Land of the Mountain and the Flood*. During the following seven years three more overtures and an opera (*Jeanie Deans*, commissioned by the Carl Rosa Opera Co.) consolidated this success, but his star waned after the turn of the century and his music fell out of favour. He was born at Greenock, son of a shipowner, and studied with Stanford and Parry at the Royal College of Music where, at the age of twenty, he became a professor of harmony. In 1898 he joined the Carl Rosa Company as conductor, later working for a succession of opera and theatre companies. In 1912 he joined the staff of the Guildhall School of Music. MacCunn's works were almost entirely based on Scottish literature or folk-music. They included another opera (*Diarmid*), several light operas and dramatic works (e.g. *The Wreck of the Hesperus*, a ballad for chorus and orchestra), cantatas, songs, and pieces for violin, piano and cello.

MACFARREN, George Alexander
2 Mar. 1813 – 31 Oct. 1887

G.A. Macfarren was born at 24 Villiers St in London, son of a dancing master. He studied with Charles Lucas and at the Royal Academy of Music, where he later became a professor, then Principal in 1876. He was knighted in 1883. For the last twelve years of his life he was Professor of Music at Cambridge, succeeding Sterndale Bennett. By the end of his life he was totally blind. For most of his time he lived in Hamilton Terrace, St John's Wood, where his former composition pupil Oliveria Prescott was his amanuensis until 1887. Macfarren played a very active part in the Purcell Society and wrote books on harmony and counterpoint that were standard texts for many years.

He composed twenty operas (*The Devil's Opera*, *The Adventures of Don Quixote*, *Robin Hood*, *She Stoops to Conquer*, etc.), cantatas, nine symphonies, overtures (*Chevy Chase* is occasionally heard today), string quartets and quintets, piano sonatas, five concertos, church anthems and over 250 secular vocal works. Many of these were popular in his life time and he was knighted by Queen Victoria. As well as a prolific composer and workaholic, he was perhaps the most influential teacher of composition in his time, as can be seen from the many references to him in these Profiles. His wife, Clarina Thalia Andrae (who as Natalia Macfarren was a noted contralto), was Schumann's god-daughter. He died in London.

MACFARREN, Walter Cecil
28 Aug. 1826 – 2 Sep. 1905

Like his brother, George Alexander, Walter Macfarren was born in London. A choirboy at Westminster Abbey, he studied piano with W.H. Holmes and composition with Cipriani Potter. He became a professor of piano at the Royal Academy of Music, conducting many concerts there, and was appointed a director of the Philharmonic Society. His compositions include seven orchestral overtures on Shakespearean subjects, a symphony, a piano concerto and sonatas, church music and part-songs. Walter Macfarren also edited many classical keyboard works including the Beethoven piano sonatas. He died at Vaterstetten near Munich.

MACFARREN, Emma Marie
19 Jun. 1824 – 9 Nov. 1895
Married to John Macfarren, G.A.'s other brother, Mrs John Macfarren (née Emma Marie Bennett), after three years in New York, returned to London. She was an able concert pianist, giving lectures and recitals and holding musical matinées for many years. She was most famous for her translations of German and Italian operas into English, but under the name of 'Jules Brissac' she also produced many light-weight piano pieces, including fantasias on operatic themes. She died in London.

MACIRONE, Clara Angela
20 Jan. 1821 – 19 Aug. 1895
Of Italian parentage, Clara MacIrone was born in London and was a pupil of Cipriani Potter and W.H. Holmes for piano, Negri for singing and Charles Lucas for composition. She became a professor of piano at the Royal Academy of Music, followed by positions in two London girls' schools. She wrote church anthems and services (her *Te Deum and Jubilate* was possibly the first canticle by a woman to be performed), songs and piano pieces. Her songs were popularised by Clara Novello, Charlotte Sainton-Dolby and others.

MACKENZIE, Alexander Campbell
22 Aug. 1847 – 28 Apr. 1935
Like his predecessor at the helm of the Royal Academy of Music, Sir George A. Macfarren, Alexander Mackenzie was a man of unparalleled energy. He found time to conduct, write voluminously on musical topics, teach, compose prolifically, give concert performances on the violin, and to lead the Royal Academy of Music to greater heights, being one of its longest serving Principals  (from 1888 to 1924). Mackenzie was noted for introducing new works to English audiences, notably Tchaikovsky's *Pathétique* Symphony. His efforts over his many years of service were rewarded with seven honorary doctorates and two knighthoods.

Mackenzie, who came from a musical family spanning several generations, was born at Nelson near Edinburgh. At the age of ten he was sent to Germany to study with Ulrich and Stein. In 1862 he returned to study at the RAM with Prosper Sainton for violin and Charles Lucas for composition. He composed several oratorios, operas (e.g. *The Troubadour, Colomba, The Cricket on the Hearth, Coriolanus, Manfred*, etc.), cantatas, two violin concertos, a viola concerto, orchestral overtures, rhapsodies and other works, instrumental music, church music and songs. Mackenzie died in Bloomsbury, London.

MACLEAN, Alexander Morvaren
20 Jul. 1872 – 18 Apr. 1936
Son of Charles Donald Maclean, 'Alick' was born at Eton, where he studied music with Barnby. He was best known as a conductor of theatre and light music, being associated with the Scarborough Spa Orchestra, various Music Festivals and the New Queen's Hall Light Orchestra in his later years. He composed several operas (*Petruccio, Die Liebesgeige, Maitre Seiler, Quentin Durward, The Hunchback of Cremona*, etc.), an oratorio, incidental music, choruses, orchestral suites and songs. Maclean died in London.

MACLEAN, Charles Donald
27 Mar. 1843 – 23 Jun. 1916
Charles Maclean was born at Cambridge. He studied at Exeter College, Oxford, where he was also organist and, after reading Classics, he went to Cologne to study composition with Ferdinand Hiller. He later gained a music doctorate at Oxford and achieved fame as a concert organist. For four years Maclean was Director of Music at Eton College. In addition to his vice-presidency of the Orchestral Association, Musical Association and the Royal College of Organists he was an active member of many other musical societies. In between these duties he spent twenty-two years in India as a civil servant. His later years were devoted to composition in London, where he died, and he was one of the first British organists to identify himself with orchestral music. His works include symphonic poems, oratorios, a cantata, a symphony, a piano concerto and some chamber music.

MACONCHY, Elizabeth
19 Mar. 1907 – 11 Nov. 1994
'You'll get married and won't write another note' was the reason given for refusing the Mendelssohn Scholarship to a great talent at the Royal College of Music. Elizabeth Maconchy did get married within the year, but she certainly didn't give up composing. She was born at Broxbourne in Hertfordshire but spent her childhood in rural County Dublin. When she was sixteen, her father died of tuberculosis and, as the young girl had already showed considerable musical ability, her mother took her back to England to enter the Royal College of Music. She studied piano with Arthur Alexander and composition with Charles Wood. Later she was to study with Vaughan Williams, who eventually admitted that he could teach her no more.

Maconchy developed an interest in European composers – Debussy, Ravel, Janáček, Bartók and Stravinsky – before their work became recognised in England and spent some time in Prague as a pupil of K.B. Jirák. Her music rapidly won over performers, conductors and critics after performances in Prague and at the 1930 Proms. Soon after her marriage in 1930 she was diagnosed with tuberculosis, like her father. She refused to follow medical advice and move to Switzerland, but moved with her husband, William LeFanu, to Kent, living mainly outdoors. She gradually recovered and her works won acclaim again. During this recovery she managed to raise funds for the Republicans in the Spanish Civil War and helped publish left-wing books. As war was declared, William, as librarian of the Royal College of Surgeons, was evacuated to Downton Castle in Shropshire and Elizabeth was able to contribute actively to the music at Leasowes Bank in the village of Ratlinghope. It was here in Shropshire that she first adopted serial technique in her compositions, but she was later to disown these works. When the war ended the couple moved to Essex, where their daughter, Nicola LeFanu, was born. Like her mother, Nicola would become a successful composer.

Elizabeth Maconchy left a great deal of splendid music in most genres. Her early suite for orchestra, *The Land*, premiered by Henry Wood, started her career. She composed other orchestral works, among which the *Symphony for Double String Orchestra* and the *Sinfonietta* stand out, as well as works for soloists with orchestra (soprano, clarinet, bassoon, piano, oboe, violin, etc.). Also notable are *Epyllion* for cello and strings and other ensemble pieces, many songs, *Music for Woodwind and Brass*, *Notebook* for harpsichord, works for chorus and orchestra, and instrumental pieces. Perhaps the thirteen remarkable string quartets form the pinnacle of her output, while the stage works – *The Sofa*, *The Departure* and *The Three Strangers* – should certainly not go unmentioned.

MACPHERSON, Charles
10 May 1870 – 28 May 1927
Charles Macpherson was born in Edinburgh. He became a chorister at St Paul's Cathedral and studied organ with Sir George Martin. He entered the Royal Academy of Music, where he later became a professor of harmony and counterpoint. He succeeded Martin as organist of St Paul's Cathedral in 1916 and became conductor of the London Church Choirs Association in 1913. Macpherson composed orchestral suites, an overture on Scottish themes, quartets, a sextet, glees, anthems church music, glees, songs and organ pieces.

MACPHERSON, Charles Stewart
29 Mar. 1865 – 27 Mar. 1941
Born in Liverpool, Stewart Macpherson attended the City of London School and the Royal Academy of Music, where he became a distinguished pupil of both G.A. and W.C. Macfarren, and where he was later appointed professor of harmony and composition. For several years Macpherson conducted the Westminster Orchestral Society. He devoted himself to musical education and wrote valuable texts on harmony (*Melody and Harmony* was for many years a standard textbook), counterpoint, musical appreciation and interpretation. He was also instrumental in founding the Music Teachers' Association in 1908. Macpherson's compositions include a symphony, violin concerto (*Concerto alla fantasia*), overtures, a mass, church music, piano pieces and songs. He died in London.

MADDISON, Katherine Mary Adela
15 Dec. 1866 – 12 Jun. 1929

Ever the socialite, Adela Maddison was the daughter of vice-admiral Louis Tindal of Irish descent. After some early successes with piano and song publications she married one of the directors of the German motor cycle manufacturer Metzler. The Maddisons frequented Paris, Bayreuth, St Moritz, Berlin, Brittany and, on home ground, Hyde Park Corner. In the 1890s the Maddisons became involved with Gabriel Fauré and rumours were heard that Adela and Gabriel were lovers. Adela certainly went to live in Paris for a time without her husband, but rejoined him before he died.

In addition to many highly original songs, Adela Maddison composed an *Irische Ballade* for orchestra, an opera (*Der Talisman*, which achieved eight performances in Leipzig and was described as the first real success for an English opera in Germany), and a piano quintet. She also became involved in Rutland Boughton's Glastonbury Festivals. Her incidental music for Malleson's *Paddly Pools* was performed at Glastonbury in 1917. Three years later her ballet *The Children of Lir* was produced at The Old Vic. Adela Maddison died at Ealing in London.

MANN, Arthur Henry
16 May 1850 – 19 Oct. 1929

Arthur Mann was born at Norwich, where he was a chorister under Zechariah Buck. He held posts as organist at Wolverhampton, Tettenhall, Beverley Minster and King's College, Cambridge, and, together with Ebenezer Prout, attempted to restore Handel's *Messiah* to its original state, without the additional wind parts that had been used in performances by Costa and others. He also edited Tallis's 40-part motet *Spem in alium*. Mann composed an oratorio (*Ecce Homo*), anthems, church services and hymn-tunes. He died at Cambridge.

MARK, Jeffrey
1898 – Dec. 1965

Jeffrey Mark, born in Cumberland, enlisted at the age of seventeen and was badly gassed as a gunnery officer in World War One. Returning to England he took a degree in Music and English at Exeter College, Oxford, then went on to the Royal College of Music. In 1924 he accepted the position of Chief of the Music Department at New York Public Library, but returned to England after a nervous breakdown. Mark studied the folk-songs of Cumberland, Northumberland and the Border Counties and arranged them, also contributing on the subject in various journals. In the 1960s he was a professor of composition at the RCM. Jeffrey Mark composed a piano concerto and choral and orchestral music, often based on or around the poetry of Robert Burns. His ballad-opera *Mossgiel* was based on the same source.

MARTIN, Frederick John Easthope
1882 – 1925

Martin was born in Stourport and studied piano, organ, harmony and composition with Coleridge-Taylor at Trinity College, London. His *Evensong*, variously arranged for piano, organ and orchestra, became very popular but – apart from *An Old Time Tune* which also appeared in various versions, the posthumously published *Souvenirs* for piano and a few other piano solos, the bolero *Castanets* for violin and piano, and *Two*

Eastern Dances for orchestra premiered by Sir Henry Wood at the Proms – his output was primarily for the voice: anthems, sacred songs, and songs grouped into sets. So popular was he as a song writer that a selection of his songs was arranged by Henry Geehl. He died young: he was always troubled with his lungs and as a result spent part of each year latterly in Monte Carlo, though he died in Hampstead.

MARTIN, George Clement
11 Sep. 1844 – 23 Feb. 1916
George Martin was born at Lambourn in Berkshire, and studied with John Stainer and J. Pearson. He held honorary doctorates from Canterbury and Oxford. He succeeded Stainer at St Paul's Cathedral and taught organ at the Royal College of Music and at the Royal Academy of Music. For two years he was private organist to the Duke of Buccleuch. Having conducted the Diamond Jubilee at St Paul's, for which he composed a *Te Deum*, performed on the cathedral steps, he was knighted by Queen Victoria. He composed anthems, church services (sometimes with orchestra) and songs. He died in London and is buried in St. Paul's Cathedral.

MARTIN, George William
8 Mar. 1828 – 16 Apr. 1881
G.W. Martin was born in London and was a chorister at St Paul's Cathedral under William Hawes. He became organist at Battersea and music master at St John's College. He composed madrigals, glees and part-songs. He died in Wandsworth, London.

MATTHAY, Tobias Augustus
19 Feb. 1858 – 14 Dec. 1945
 Though his youthful ambition was to become a composer, Tobias Matthay is remembered as a highly influential and successful teacher of piano technique and as founder of the school which bore his name. His parents were both German, but his father settled in England to teach languages and Tobias was born at Clapham in London. He studied at the Royal Academy of Music with Sullivan, Sterndale Bennett and Prout, and was the first Sterndale Bennett Scholar in 1872, winning several prizes as a student. Matthay composed two symphonic movements, four concert overtures, a piano concerto, works for voices and orchestra, a string quartet, choral works, songs and part-songs, instrumental sonatas and much piano music. His periods of composition were interrupted by many years devoted to the writing of articles on music in general, and larger didactic works on piano technique and interpretation. Matthay died at Camelsdale in West Sussex.

MATHIAS, William James
1 Nov. 1934 – 29 Jul. 1992
William Mathias was born at Whitland in Carmarthenshire (Dyfed). He began composing at the age of five, giving him plenty of time to become one of Wales's most prolific composers. Unlike the music of many of his contemporaries who embraced a conservative idiom, his received lasting popular acclaim, and he was commissioned to write for several royal occasions (Investiture of the Prince of Wales,

Queen's Silver Jubilee, wedding of the Prince and Princess of Wales, etc.). Mathias studied at the University College of Wales, Aberystwyth, gaining first class honours, then won an open scholarship to the Royal Academy of Music in 1965, studying composition with Lennox Berkeley (he was later made an FRAM). A year later Mathias was awarded a D.Mus. from the University of Wales. Several prizes ensued and from 1970-88 he was professor of music and head of department at the University of Bangor. He was active as a pianist and conductor, and in 1972 founded the North Wales Music Festival at St. Asaph, remaining its Director until 1992. Appropriately, he is buried outside St Asaph Cathedral. For nine years he served on the British Council's music advisory committee.

Mathias's music is approachable but distinctive, making much of intervals of the third and fourth and often excitingly rhythmic. He was not afraid to re-use good ideas in different works. He wrote three symphonies, three piano concertos, concertos for other instruments (including one for harpsichord), and other orchestral pieces. His opera *The Servant* was written to a libretto by Iris Murdoch. A profusion of choral works includes many for church use (*Sir Christemas* and *Lift up your heads* are typical, and fun to perform). His chamber works include three string quartets and pieces for brass quintet, and he also composed solo pieces for harp, piano and organ.

MAUNDER, John Henry
21 Feb. 1858 – 25 Jan. 1920

J.H. Maunder is still remembered as composer of the oratorio *Olivet to Calvary*, which continues to be performed with some regularity, though another cantata, *Penitence, Pardon and Peace*, was once also enormously popular. In addition he composed other cantatas, comic operettas (*Daisy Dingle* and *The Superior Sex*), part-songs, church services and many anthems and other choral works. Maunder was born in Chelsea, London, and studied at the Royal Academy of Music. Apart from posts as organist at various churches in and around London, he conducted the Civil Service Vocal Union choir and was also choir trainer at the Lyceum Theatre and accompanist to Sims Reeves. He died in London.

MAW, John Nicholas
5 Nov. 1935 – 19 May 2009

Nicholas Maw was born in Grantham and, after his parents contracted tuberculosis, he and his sister were sent to live with relatives. Their mother died. Nicholas went to a Quaker boarding school in Wetherby, where he was introduced to the music of Bartók, Stravinsky and Ravel and where he took up the clarinet. In 1955 he entered the Royal Academy of Music to study with Lennox Berkeley and Paul Steinitz. Three years later he won a French Government scholarship and studied privately in Paris with Nadia Boulanger and Max Deutsch. It was inevitable at that time that Maw would experiment with post-Webernian modernism and two of his early works, *Eight Chinese Lyrics* and the *Flute Sonatina*, were products of this venture. But on his return to England Maw gave freer rein to his instinctive harmonic and melodic post-Romantic feelings and, in 1962, produced his *Scenes and Arias* for orchestra and three female voices. It received a mixed reception, (as did his last opera *Sophie's Choice*). Maw's music was not sufficiently modernist for the critics, but neither was it populist enough for the masses. To generate a living income he turned to freelance journalism and teaching part-time at the RAM and later at the University of Exeter. In 1964 his first opera, *One Man Show*, was performed, and two years later he was appointed artist-in-residence at Trinity College, Cambridge. During his four years there his second opera, *The Rising of the Moon*, was completed. In 1984 Maw settled in the United States, living in Washington DC and teaching variously at Boston University, Bard College and Yale University. From 1998-2008 he taught at the Peabody Institute at Johns Hopkins University.

During his time in the USA interest in his music declined in the UK, though a few commissions arrived. Greater enthusiasm was shown on the Continent, and in the States and he won several major prizes and awards. Interest only recovered in the UK when modernism began to be forgotten, though his opera *Sophie's Choice* was slammed by the critics. Nicholas Maw's finest works are regarded as *Life Studies* for fifteen strings (1976 revn.), *Scenes and Arias*, and the 90-minute, non-stop *Odyssey* for orchestra. He also composed a violin concerto and other orchestral pieces, works for choir and orchestra and voice and orchestra, three string quartets and other chamber works, songs and solo works for guitar and piano. Among the piano pieces are *Personae I* to *VI*, a series finished in 1986 and retaining some of his earlier atonalism.

MAY, Oliver
27 Jan. 1814 – 12 Apr. 1894
Oliver May was primarily a pianist, who studied at the Royal Academy of Music at the same time as Sterndale Bennett, and was a highly praised teacher. Born in Greenwich, he held organists' appointments, including St Martin-in-the-Fields. His compositions were few but considered worthy at the time: a piano quartet (performed in 1862), an overture *Don Sebastian*, and some songs, madrigals and piano pieces.

His niece, **Florence May**, was also a skilled pianist who composed a few piano pieces and songs.

MAYBRICK, Michael. See **ADAMS**, Stephen

MAYER, John
28 Oct. 1930 – 9 Mar. 2004
John Mayer was an original and inspired composer whose work was highly influential among both jazz and classical musicians in Britain. He was the fourth child of a Roman Catholic family, born into poverty in Calcutta. Showing promise at an early age he was fortunate enough at the age of seven to receive free lessons in violin and western music from Phillipe Sandre at the Calcutta School of Music. He studied Indian music with Sanathan Mukerjee. While still at school he earned pocket money playing in cinemas and at various churches. Later, in Bombay, he studied with Mehli Mehta, who persuaded him to study abroad. In 1950 Mayer won an All-India government scholarship enabling him to come to London and to enrol at the Royal Academy of Music. Private lessons in composition from Mátyás Seiber convinced him that the way forward was through a synthesis of Indian and western music, and this is where Mayer found his true medium.

When funds were low, Mayer played as an orchestral violinist, firstly with the London Philharmonic, then the Royal Liverpool Philharmonic and finally with the

Royal Philharmonic. At the RLPO Sir Charles Groves commissioned a *Dance Suite* for sitar, flute, tabla, tambura and symphony orchestra. Several more commissions followed, and by 1965 Mayer felt he could earn enough from composition alone. In 1967 his exquisitely beautiful *Shanta Quintet* for sitar and string quartet was recorded. Shortly before this, Mayer's work had been brought to the notice of Ahmed Artegun in the United States. The result was the release of a succession of successful recordings by Indo-Jazz Fusions, whose music was partly notated and partly improvised.

John Mayer was appointed Composer in Residence at Birmingham University, where he introduced the first B.Mus. course in Indian music. He died at the age of seventy-three following a road accident.

McALPIN, Colin
1870 – 1942
Colin McAlpin was born at Leicester. He was organist at three London Presbyterian churches (Kensington, Clapham and Ealing) and composed organ and church music, songs, a cantata (*The Prince of Peace*, a work which deserves a revival) and four operas (*Robin Hood*, *King Arthur*, *The Vow* and *The Cross and the Crescent*).

McEWEN, John Blackwood
13 Apr. 1868 – 14 Jun. 1948
John McEwen was born at Hawick in Scotland, and studied at the Royal Academy of Music, where he later became a professor of harmony and composition. In 1924 he succeeded Mackenzie as Principal, retiring in 1936. McEwen founded the Society of British Composers in 1905, which continued until 1918. (The society published contemporary British music under the name of 'Avison Edition'). His works have a characteristic charm, and include the *Solway* Symphony, overtures, a viola concerto, string quartets, choral works, *Highland Dances* for strings, piano pieces and part-songs. These latter songs were considered adventurously modern for their time. McEwen also wrote didactic works on musical theory and aesthetics, and was awarded a knighthood.

MELLON, Alfred
7 Apr. 1820 – 27 Mar. 1867
Mellon was a violinist in the Royal Italian Opera and conductor at the Haymarket Theatre and of the Musical Society of London (from 1863 until it folded in 1867), and of other concerts. There are stories of his ability to start but not finish a work, leaving much to the orchestra! Born in London, he died there after a relatively short life. F.E. Bache lived for a time with Mellon, his teacher. His output comprises three operas (*Victorine* was produced at Covent Garden in 1849), songs, glees and piano pieces.

MERRICK, Frank
30 Apr. 1886 – 19 Feb. 1981
Frank Merrick will be remembered as a gifted teacher and concert pianist, in which capacity he championed much modern music, especially that of Bax, Ireland, Rawsthorne, as well as Ravel and Debussy. He was born at Clifton in Bristol, and studied with his parents (his father was Dr Frank Merrick) and with Leschetizky in Vienna. He toured Australia in 1907 and won a prize in St Petersburg in 1910. One year later he accepted a post as professor of piano at the Royal Manchester College

of Music, and in 1929 at the Royal College of Music. During World War One he was imprisoned as a conscientious objector, and he became a fluent speaker in Esperanto. Merrick's wife was the pianist Hope Squire, with whom he researched and performed many little-known works for two pianos. His own compositions, rather more dated than one might expect and often quite Brahmsian, included a symphony, two piano concertos and several other orchestral works, choral music, some chamber works, several piano sonatas and many piano pieces. He championed the music of John Field, producing an edition of Field's piano concertos for Musica Britannica. Frank Merrick died in London.

MERRITT, Thomas
26 Oct. 1863 – 17 Apr. 1908
The son of a copper miner, Merritt was born near Redruth. His father died when he was eleven, and he was sent to work in the tin mines. At the age of eighteen he had received just six months' formal music tuition, but he was eventually able to scratch a living by teaching, conducting the local church choir and playing the organ at the local chapel. Lost works are an oratorio and a sacred cantata, but his anthems and carols were published, many of which continue to be sung to this day by Cornish choirs. Their worth was recognised by Malcolm Arnold in his *Salute to Thomas Merritt* for orchestra and two brass bands, performed in Truro Cathedral in 1968. Arnold also discovered and orchestrated Merritt's *Coronation March* for King Edward VII.

MILES, Philip Napier
21 Jan.1865 – 19 Jul. 1935
Philip Miles was born at Shirehampton in Gloucestershire. He studied in Germany with Draeseke, Schreyer and Roth, and with Parry and Dannreuther in England. As a wealthy citizen, he devoted himself to the encouragement of new music, and was responsible for the first performances of many new works in Bristol and at his own country estate at King's Weston, Gloucs., where he died. He composed operas (*Westward Ho!*, *Queen Rosamund*, *Markheim* and *Fireflies*), various orchestral works, choruses with orchestra (including a setting of Coleridge's *Hymn before Sunrise*), songs and part-songs.

MILFORD, Robin Humphrey
22 Jan. 1903 – 29 Dec. 1959
Born in Oxford, Robin Milford went to Rugby School and the Royal College of Music, where he was a pupil of Holst, Vaughan Williams and R.O. Morris, and was influenced as a composer by Balfour Gardiner. Having suffered a breakdown during his service in World War Two, Milford returned to continue his profession as a schoolteacher at Badminton School, near Bristol. Milford was a prolific composer, whose music included an opera, two ballets, a *Double Fugue* for orchestra, violin concerto, concertinos for harpsichord and for piano, two oratorios, cantatas and many other choral works, chamber and instrumental music, songs and several short orchestral works. Milford was particularly interested in organ and church music. Affected deeply by the earlier death of his five-year-old son in a road accident, and in the later 1950s by the deaths of Gerald Finzi and Vaughan Williams, he died by his own hand at Lyme Regis, Dorset.

MILNER, Anthony Francis Dominic
13 May 1925 – 22 Sep. 2002
Anthony Milner was born in Bristol to a devout Roman Catholic family based in London. He went to Douai School in Berkshire, where he won a piano scholarship to the Royal College of Music, benefiting from the disciplines of counterpoint instilled by the teaching of R.O. Morris. Milner later had private lessons with Mátyás Seiber. His own outstanding teaching career began in 1947 as tutor in music theory and history at Morley College, London. Here Tippett's friendship and advice had a great influence on him. In 1954 he joined the staff of the then embryonic adult extra-mural department of London University. There followed posts at King's College, London (1965), Goldsmith's six years later, then at the RCM. At times he played with the London Cantata Ensemble and wrote about music. In 1965-66 he was Composer–in–Residence at Loyola University, New Orleans, and in 1976 presented a postgraduate course in twentieth-century music at the University of Western Ontario.

Much of Anthony Milner's music was inspired by the liturgy of the Roman church, from his Op. 1 *Salutatio Angelica* (a cantata in praise of the Virgin Mary) and *Variations for Orchestra* (a meditation through the Stations of the Cross) to the mass he wrote in 1982 for Pope John Paul's service at Wembley Stadium. In recognition Pope Paul II made him a Knight of St Gregory. Milner's music included three symphonies and a chamber symphony, several cantatas and masses, an oratorio (*The water and the fire*), a string quartet, wind quintet, songs and organ pieces. His music was tonal, and made much use of plainchant and counterpoint, but had a singular freshness and vitality. Milner's achievements in teaching and composing are all the more remarkable considering that he had a speech impediment from childhood and also suffered multiple sclerosis for the last thirty-odd years of his life.

MILNER, Arthur Frederick
22 Oct. 1894 – 11 Sep. 1971
Arthur Milner spent most of his life in the North-East of England, where he taught at the Royal Grammar School at Newcastle upon Tyne. He also lectured for the extra-mural departments of Durham University, conducted the Hartlepool Symphony and Northumberland Orchestras, played the organ at various local churches and founded the Newcastle Oriana Choir. Milner was born at Manchester and studied music notably with Oscar Beringer and Edgar Bainton. His compositions include a symphony, other works for full orchestra and for strings, choral/orchestral music, chamber works, church music and pieces for organ and for piano. Severely self-critical, he destroyed many of his works.

MOERAN, Ernest John
31 Dec. 1894 – 1 Dec. 1950
'Jack' Moeran has been described as one of the finest English composers to follow the nationalist school. Certainly his symphony and his cello concerto (the latter written for cellist Peers Coetmore the year before they were married) testify to this, and the latter work has been ranked with Elgar's concerto for the same instrument. Moeran was a keen collector of folk-songs, mainly from East Anglia and Ireland, a country he loved. Son of a

clergyman, he was born at Heston in Middlesex and went to Uppingham School before entering the Royal College of Music. The war interrupted his studies but, after active service, during which he was wounded, he returned to take lessons with John Ireland. He was further influenced by his more cosmopolitan, less conventional group of friends which included Peter Warlock, Bernard van Dieren and Constant Lambert.

Moeran became known as a composer of chamber and instrumental music, and it was only towards the end of his life that he felt able to tackle the larger-scale works. In addition to the genres already mentioned he wrote a sinfonietta, violin concerto, rhapsody for piano and orchestra and an overture. Songs and part-songs formed an important part of his output. Moeran died tragically, his body being found in the River Kenmare in County Kerry, showing evidence of a heart attack.

MONCKTON, John Lionel Alexander
18 Dec. 1861 – 15 Feb. 1924
Lionel Monckton's light opera, *The Quaker Girl* of 1910, was a great success in his time. Apart from *A Country Girl* it was the only opera to come entirely from his pen. Most of his music was written in collaboration with other composers: *Our Miss Gibbs* with Ivan Caryll; *The Arcadians* with Howard Talbot, etc. He contributed popular songs to light operas by Sidney Jones and others. Monckton was born in London. He attended Charterhouse School and graduated from Oriel College, Oxford, where he was an enthusiastic participant in dramatic productions. He began a legal practice in 1885 and for the next few years wrote many theatrical and musical reviews for various London papers. His wife was Gertie Miller, the glamorous 'Gaiety Girl'. Monckton died in London.

MONK, Edwin George
13 Dec. 1819 – 3 Jan. 1900
Monk was born at Frome in Somerset and studied piano with Henry Field, singing with the baritone Henry Phillips, and composition with G.A. Macfarren. Having obtained his Mus.Bac. and Mus.Doc. at Oxford University, he took up an appointment as organist and music master at Radley College, Oxfordshire, then organist at York Minster from 1859 to 1883. On his resignation he returned to Radley, where he died. Monk composed anthems, church services and some secular works, edited hymnals and chant books, and was a keen amateur astronomer, rewarded with an FRAS in 1871.

MOORE, Timothy
19 Feb. 1922 – 1 Feb. 2003
For thirty-two years (1950-82) Timothy Moore was Director of Music at Dartington Hall School in Devon, succeeding Imogen Holst. A son of the radical analytical philosopher G.E. Moore, Timothy was born in Cambridge and attended Dragon School in Oxford before going to Dartington Hall as a pupil. There he began to compose and to cultivate a life-long interest in jazz. A scholarship enabled him to read moral sciences at Trinity College, Cambridge, and after the interruption of the war (during which he became a conscientious objector) he gained a 'double first' in Philosophy and Music. At the Royal College of Music, where he studied for a year, his composition tutors were Herbert Howells and Edmund Rubbra, followed by private lessons with Tippett, who was then at Morley College.

Moore was an inspiring teacher, and wrote several musicals for children. He also wrote a Symphony in E flat, other orchestral pieces, a comic opera (*Cannibal Island*), concertos for clarinet and strings and for trumpet and strings, a cantata (*The Scrapyard*), other choral works, songs and instrumental and chamber works – in most of which could be detected the influences of Hindemith, the English madrigalists and jazz. Moore spent much time and effort arranging visits to Britain for members of the Soviet Composers' Union and for pupils from the Gnesin Music School. Consequently his music received frequent airings in the Soviet Union.

MORELLE, Max. See **TATE**, Phyllis

MORI, Frank
21 Mar. 1821 – 2 Aug. 1873
Son of a violinist, Mori was born in London and established himself as a conductor. He was the first to conduct the choir which was eventually taken over by Henry Leslie and which became known as 'Mr Leslie's Choir'. He also founded the short-lived London Orchestra, and conducted some concerts for the Musical Society of London. He died at Chaumont in France. Works include the cantata *Fridolin* and an operetta *The River Sprite*, and songs, published in groups of six and twelve.

MORRIS, Haydn
18 Feb. 1891 – Dec. 1965
Born at Cross Hands in Camarthenshire, Haydn Morris worked in the local coal mine from the age of twelve, before gaining financial assistance to study at the Royal Academy of Music with Frederick Corder, Ernest Read, W.G. Kipps, Wood and Stanley Marchant. Here he was awarded the Oliviera Prescott Prize for composition and received a commendation from Edward Elgar. He taught piano privately, was an organist and choirmaster in various South Wales churches, and was greatly in demand as an adjudicator at eisteddfodau and festivals. Morris composed an opera, operettas, cantatas, a piano concerto, orchestral suites and overtures, other orchestral works, sacred and secular choruses, songs and part-songs, music for brass band and pieces for violin, piano, harp and organ. He also arranged Welsh folk-songs.

MORRIS, Reginald Owen
3 Mar. 1886 – 14 Dec. 1948
R.O. Morris was born at York. He went to Harrow, then New College in Oxford, and the Royal College of Music. He became an authority on sixteenth-century polyphony, writing extensively on the subject, and taught composition at Oxford and the RCM. After a period lecturing in Philadelphia, USA, he returned to a professorship at the RCM, where he remained until his death. Though Morris's compositions are nowadays never heard, those of his pupils (a list that includes Rubbra, Tippett, Finzi, Lambert and Fricker) bear testimony to his teaching. Among his works are a symphony, a suite for cello and orchestra, a violin concerto, *Concerto Piccolo* for two violins and strings, string quartets, *Corinnna's Maying* for chorus and orchestra, and instrumental pieces. His hymn-tune, *Hermitage*, to 'Love came down at Christmas' is still used. Many musicians were brought up on his didactic works on sixteenth-century counterpoint, harmony and counterpoint, figured bass and score-reading. R.O. Morris died in London.

MOUNSEY, Ann Sheppard
17 Apr. 1811 – 24 Jun. 1891

Ann Mounsey, sister of Elizabeth, was born in London and studied with J.B. Logier, later with Samuel Wesley and Thomas Attwood. She was organist at various London churches, notably St Vedast in Foster Lane, which post she held for nearly fifty years (an innings only exceeded by John Stainer's sister Ann). Mounsey composed over 140 songs and part-songs (the first of which was published when she was twenty-one), an oratorio (*The Nativity* – her most well-known work), a cantata, and pieces for organ and piano. Several of her songs were set to words by William Bartholomew, whose name she eventually adopted in 1853 through the expediency of marriage. One of the founder members of the Royal Society of Female Musicians, she also established a series of charity concerts at Crosby Hall, for which her friend Mendelssohn composed *Hear my prayer*. Ann Mounsey Bartholomew died in London after several years of ill-health.

MOUNSEY, Elizabeth
8 Oct. 1819 – 3 Oct. 1905

Elizabeth Mounsey, like her sister Ann, was born in London. At the age of fifteen she became organist at St Peter's, Cornhill, where Mendelssohn frequently played, and continued there for forty-eight years. She composed a few pieces for organ, guitar and piano. Elizabeth Mounsey, like her sister, died in London.

MUDIE, Thomas Molleson
30 Nov. 1809 – 24 Jul. 1876

Thomas Mudie was born in Chelsea and studied at the Royal Academy of Music with William Crotch and Cipriani Potter. He was an organist and teacher, and became a professor of piano at the RAM. He moved to Scotland and taught in Edinburgh from 1844 to 1863, returning to London on his retirement. Mudie composed five symphonies; several quintets, quartets and trios for strings; piano pieces, anthems and songs.

MURRILL, Herbert Henry John
11 May 1909 – 24 Jul. 1952

Born at Brackley in S.E. London, Herbert Murrill attended Aske's School, Hatcham, before going to the Royal Academy of Music to study with York Bowen, Stanley Marchant and Alan Bush. He went to Worcester College, Oxford, and then held various posts as organist and choirmaster. In 1936 he joined the staff of the BBC, becoming Head of Music in 1950. He was also a professor of composition at the RAM. Most of his output was in a lighter vein – film scores and incidental music for plays – but he also composed an opera (*Man in Cage*), a ballet, a string quartet, two cello concertos, choral and church music, other chamber works, songs, and pieces for organ and for piano. Murrill died in London.

NAYLOR, Bernard
22 Nov. 1907 – 19 May 1986

Naylor's considerable output, most of it choral and sacred, displayed effective use of English Romanticism. He composed an opera, a symphonic poem, a 'scena' for tenor and orchestra, several cantatas and motets (notably *King Solomon's Prayer*), and the

Nine Motets (depicting the major celebrations of the Christian year), some chamber works, songs and other choral works, and a 'modern mystery' for three characters and string quartet. Bernard Naylor was born at Cambridge. He was a pupil of Vaughan Williams, Holst and Ireland at the RCM and entered Exeter College, Oxford, as an organ scholar. His long career as conductor and teacher began in Canada, and he returned to Britain to teach at Oxford (1950-52) and Reading (1953-59), after which he settled in Canada for the rest of his life.

NAYLOR, Edward Woodall
9 Feb. 1867 – 7 May 1934
Edward Naylor, born at Scarborough, took his first music lessons with his father John, the organist at York Minster (see below), before entering Emanuel College, Cambridge, as an organ scholar. He also studied at the Royal College of Music. Naylor held various posts as organist at London churches (including St Mary's, Kilburn), returning to Cambridge in 1897 to become organist and a lecturer in music at his old college. He composed an opera (*The Angelus*, performed ten times by the Carl Rosa Opera Company), a requiem, cantatas, motets and other choral works, a couple of orchestral works and some chamber music. He also wrote extensively on the subject of music in Shakespeare's works. His hymn-tune for 'Soldiers of Christ, arise' is still widely used. Edward Naylor died in Cambridge.

NAYLOR, John
8 Jun. 1838 – 14 May 1897
John Naylor was born at Stanningly in Leeds, and was a choirboy at Leeds Parish Church and later assistant organist. He became organist and choirmaster at York Minster in 1883 (following the retirement of Dr E.G. Monk) where he is said to have raised the standard of performance, and conducted the York Musical Society. He composed anthems, some anthems with military band accompaniment, church services and cantatas (*Jeremiah*, *The Brazen Serpent*, *Manna*, etc.) composed especially for festivals held in the Minster, as well as a few songs and part-songs. John Naylor died at sea while on a voyage to Australia.

NICHOLAS, John Morgan
1895 – 1963
John Nicholas was born at Port Talbot in Glamorganshire. He studied at Eton College Choir School and at the Royal College of Music. His various appointments included those of organist at Windsor Royal Chapel, music master at Shrewsbury and Oswestry Schools, organist at Oswestry Parish Church, Director of Music for Montgomeryshire and Chief Officer of the University of Wales Council of Music. He was well-known as a pianist and speaker on the radio and as a conductor at many of the important Welsh festivals. He composed works for soloists, chorus and orchestra, songs to Welsh words and pieces for oboe with piano.

NICHOLL, Horace Wadham
17 Mar. 1848 – 10 Mar. 1922
Horace Nicholl was born at Tipton in West Bromwich. He studied with Samuel Prince, and held posts as organist at Dudley and Stoke on Trent before settling in New York

in 1878, remaining there as organist and teacher until his death. He composed four oratorios, two symphonies and other orchestral works, a mass, chamber music, a great deal of highly rated organ music, anthems, songs and works for solo piano.

NICHOLSON, Sydney Hugo
9 Feb. 1875 – 30 May 1947
Sir Sydney Nicholson is remembered as the founder of the Royal School of Church Music and St Nicholas College, both established to maintain and improve (which they certainly have done) the standards of British church music. He was born in London, attended Rugby School, and studied at New College, Oxford, at the Royal College of Music under Walter Parratt and Stanford, and at Frankfurt with Iwan Knorr. His chief appointments as organist were at Carlisle and Manchester Cathedrals and at Westminster Abbey. In addition to church services and anthems, he composed a choral ballad, *Ivry*, and *The Luck of Edenhall* for female voices. He was knighted in 1938. Nicholson died at Woodchurch in Kent and is buried in Westminster Abbey. A memorial plaque is displayed in the chapel of St Sepulchre at the Old Bailey.

NIXON, Henry Cotter
1842 – 25 Dec. 1907
Henry Cotter Nixon's claim to fame is to have composed the first British symphonic poem, or tone poem, *Palamon and Arcite* (completed in 1882 and first performed in 1888), pre-dating the much cited first, William Wallace's *Passing of Beatrice* of 1892. He was born in Southwark, and in his teens was sent to Hull to study with a family friend, Dr Harry Deval, earning a little as organist at St Mary's Catholic church. Returning to London, he studied with Henry Smart, Charles Steggall and G.A. Macfarren and was made a Fellow of the Royal College of Organists. He occupied the organ lofts in several churches,and in 1864 made his debut as a concert pianist with the Apollo Glee Society, though the viola was his favourite instrument. In 1976 he obtained a Mus.B. at Cambridge and accepted an appointment as conductor of Hastings and St. Leonard's Orchestral Society.

Other conductorships, piano performances, and organist's and teaching posts followed, where he provided private tuition in singing and composition. Among Nixon's compositions were several concert overtures, a *Concertstück* for piano and orchestra, other orchestral works, an opera (*Osmond*) and operatic farce (*The Gay Typewriters*), cantatas and other choral works, a piano trio, pieces for violin, a cello sonata and songs.

NOBLE, Thomas Tertius
5 May 1867 – 4 May 1953
A native of Bath, Thomas Noble was educated at Colchester and the Royal College of Music, where he studied with Walter Parratt, Stanford and Frederick Bridge. He held various posts as organist, assisting Stanford at Trinity College, Cambridge, later moving to Ely Cathedral, then York Minster. While at the latter he founded the York Symphony Orchestra and revived the York Festival. In 1912 he settled in New York. His compositions include church music, motets, chamber music, pieces for violin, piano solos, a comic opera (*Killibegs*), music to Aristophanes' *Wasps* and the *York Pageant*. Noble died at Rockport in Massachusetts.

NORTON, Caroline Elizabeth Sarah
22 Mar. 1808 – 15 Jun. 1877

The marriage at the age of nineteen to a violent and malicious barrister and MP and their separation after five years, led Caroline Norton to campaign vociferously for the rights of women who, like herself, were denied access to their children and who were legally excluded from property ownership. Her efforts earned her some vilification, but helped bring about the Matrimonial Causes (Divorce) Act of 1857. Her husband died in 1877. Two years later she married an old friend, just four months before her own death.

Despite such a sad life, Caroline Norton managed to publish some volumes of poetry and to contribute to several magazines before having some of her songs published. As a contralto she was much in demand as a performer of her own songs, which eventually ran to several volumes. Best known of these were perhaps *Juanita* and *Maraquita: a Portugese love song*. Norton's paternal grandparents were the playwright Sheridan and the singer Elizabeth Linley. She was born in London and brought up at Hampton Court, courtesy of the Duke of York.

NOVELLO, Ivor
5 Jan. 1893 – 6 Mar. 1951

Born in Cardiff, David Ivor Davies took his professional name from his mother, the singer Clara Novello-Davies. He studied organ and piano and was a choirboy in Magdalen College, Oxford. He began his career as a songwriter in his early teens, and at twenty-one wrote the enormously successful World War One song *Keep the home fires burning*. He contributed to some musicals and acted in plays and films. Then followed a series of highly successful operettas and musicals: *Careless Rapture, Crest of the Wave, Perchance to Dream,* and *King's Rhapsody*. His *The Dancing Years* ran right through World War Two. Ivor Novello died in London, and there is a memorial to him in St Paul's Cathedral.

OAKELEY, Herbert Stanley
22 Jul. 1830 – 27 Oct. 1903

Born in the vicarage at Ealing, London, Sir Herbert Oakeley was educated at Rugby and at Christ Church, Oxford. He studied with Stephen Elvey (brother of Sir George Elvey), Schneider at Dresden and with Breidenstein at Leipzig. He was appointed Professor of Music at Edinburgh University in 1865 and received a knighthood in 1876, as well as a number of honorary degrees. Oakeley's greatest talent was for improvisation at the organ, and he wrote much for the instrument. He also composed orchestral works, songs, anthems and piano pieces. Some of his anthems are still in use. Oakeley died at Eastbourne.

OBERTHÙR, Charles Karl
4 Mar. 1819 – 8 Nov. 1895

Charles Oberthur was born in Munich but came to Britain in 1844, remaining there until his death in London. He studied harp in Germany with Elisa Brauchle and G.V.

Röder. In England Oberthür took up teaching the harp and composed operas, a mass, cantatas (including *The Pilgrim Queen*, *Lady Jane Grey* and *Macbeth*), two overtures, *Loreley* for orchestra with obbligato harp, a concertino for harp and orchestra as well as a number of other works for harp, and some chamber music, including a quartet.

O'BRIEN, Charles
6 Sep. 1882 – 27 Jun. 1968
A pupil of Hamish MacCunn, Charles O'Brien was born in Edinburgh. He went into teaching and still had time to compose a symphony, three overtures, chamber music (including two piano trios), a piano sonata, many songs, and a respectable selection of piano pieces.

OLD, John
28 May 1827 – 4 Feb. 1892
Born at Totnes in Devon, John Old studied with John and Edwin Loder, then at the Royal Academy of Music with Sterndale Bennett and John Goss, as well as privately in London, and also with Sigismund Thalberg and Bernhard Molique. He taught and conducted at Torquay and settled in Reading, founding Layston College of Music. He composed an opera (*Herne the Hunter*), a sacred drama (*The Seventh Seal*), an orchestral overture, piano music, songs and part-songs. He died in Reading.

OLDHAM, Arthur William
6 Sep. 1926 – 4 May 2003
In 1965 Lord Harewood and Alexander Gibson asked Arthur Oldham to put together a choir capable of performing Mahler's Eighth symphony at the Edinburgh Festival. He was director of the resulting Edinburgh Festival Chorus for the next twelve years, often tackling other difficult works such as Schoenberg's *Moses und Aron*. Ten years later Oldham went on to found the Chorus of the Orchestre de Paris, then in 1979 the Concertgebouw Orchestra Chorus in Amsterdam. While juggling with these he also directed the Scottish Opera Chorus (1966-74) and the London Symphony Chorus.

Oldham was born in London but grew up in Wallington, Surrey. When he was fourteen, his mother committed suicide. A scholarship enabled him to enter the Royal College of Music to study composition with Herbert Howells, and while only nineteen he was appointed musical director of the Ballet Rambert. After private lessons with Benjamin Britten (he arranged several of Britten's works while a student with him) his opera *Love in a Village* was performed, but its reception was mixed. This and other disappointments led Oldham to a nervous breakdown, but a conversion to the Roman church and a move to Edinburgh as teacher at Scotus Academy and choirmaster at the Roman Catholic cathedral restored his confidence. When he moved to Paris, his farewell gift to his Festival Chorus was the splendid *Psalms in Time of War*. Oldham wrote many religious works for chorus, a ballet (*Mr Punch*), song-cycles, a musical for children (*The Land of Green Ginger*), and hymns for children.

OLDROYD, George
1 Dec. 1886 – 26 Feb. 1951
George Oldroyd was born near Batley in Yorkshire. He studied with Eaglefield-Hull, and also took violin lessons with Johann Rasch and Frank Arnold. In the 1920s he

taught at Trinity College, London, from 1944 was Dean of the Faculty of Music at London University and from 1933-48 Director of Music at Whitgift School. He was organist at St George's English Chapel in Paris, St Albans, Holborn and St Michael's, Croydon. Oldroyd composed a cantata, a mass, a *Spiritual Rhapsody* for choir and orchestra, songs and organ music. He also wrote books on plainchant, polyphony and fugue.

O'LEARY, Arthur
15 Mar. 1834 – 1919

Arthur O'Leary, born at Tralee in County Kerry, studied at Leipzig under Plaidy, Richter, Moscheles, Hauptmann and Rietz, then with Cipriani Potter and Sterndale Bennett at the Royal Academy of Music, where he later joined the staff. O'Leary also taught at the National Training School for Music. He composed a symphony (1865), a piano concerto and other orchestral pieces, songs and piano solos.

OLIVER, Stephen
10 Mar. 1950 – 29 Apr. 1992

Stephen Oliver wrote his first operatic work, *The Warden of the Tower*, at the age of thirteen while a pupil at St. Paul's Cathedral Choir School. Over forty more operas were to follow. He was born in Chester, and after St Paul's attended Ardingly College in Sussex before achieving a BA and B.Mus. at Worcester College, Oxford, where he studied composition with Kenneth Leighton and electronic music with Robert Sherlaw-Johnson. His ninth opera, *The Duchess of Malfi*, was a success during his degree course, and many commissions ensued. After college he was appointed lecturer in composition at Huddersfield Polytechnic, staying for two years before devoting himself full-time to composing.

Most remarkable of Oliver's operas must be the experimental *Perseverance* written to be performed in Liverpool Cathedral. It comprises two operas, *Dombey and Son* and *The Castell of Perseverance*, to be played simultaneously, with the audience seated between the transepts. Throughout, the themes of the two operas cleverly mirror each other. At the other extreme, *Three Instant Operas*, written for children, can be performed after one hour's rehearsal. As well as writing opera, sometimes to his own libretti, Oliver composed incidental music to a great many plays and TV and radio programmes (including Tolkien's *Lord of the Rings*), a considerable number of songs and other works for children. His output includes a symphony, a recorder concerto, music for wind, religious works, an organ duet and solo pieces for guitar and piano. In his will Stephen Oliver left a great deal of money to a trust that would support young people working in the field of opera and musical drama.

O'NEILL, Norman Houstoun
14 Mar. 1875 – 3 Mar. 1934

Son of a talented and successful Victorian painter, Norman O'Neill was born at Kensington in London. At fourteen he began music lessons with Arthur Somervell, and four years later, on the advice of Josef Joachim, was sent to Frankfurt to study with Iwan Knorr. There he met the rest of the 'Frankfurt Group' (Gardiner, Grainger, Quilter and Scott), as well as his wife-to-be Adine Ruckert. O'Neill taught for a time at Highgate Girls' School, and became a professor of harmony and composition at the Royal Academy of Music. But it was in the theatre that O'Neill made his mark. As a conductor and composer he did more than anyone of his time to raise the standard of theatre music. In addition to incidental music for over fifty plays (Shakespeare, Barrie, Maeterlinck, Ibsen, Scott, etc.), O'Neill wrote five ballets, chamber music, piano pieces, songs, choral works, overtures and other orchestral pieces. He died in Kensington, after a road accident, at the age of fifty-nine.

ORAM, Daphne Blake
31st Dec. 1925 – 5th Jan. 2003
A pioneering composer of electronic music and a keen billiards player, Daphne Oram was born at Devizes in Wiltshire. She went to Sherborne School for Girls and had private lessons for piano, organ and composition. Her musical career began in 1943, when she joined the BBC as a music balancer. She soon began to experiment with synthesised sound and in 1958 founded the BBC Radiophonic Workshop, only to leave a year later feeling that the BBC had undervalued her department's work. From then on she worked largely on her own, though she lectured at Morley College from 1959 and at Christ Church College, Canterbury from 1982 to 1989. Founding the Oramics Studio for Electronic Composition in 1959 in a converted Kent oast house, she designed and developed what was then the most sophisticated machine for converting a composer's graphic imaging into sound. This brainwave attracted Gulbenkian funding, but the Oramics system was rendered obsolete in the 1980s by developments in digital processing. She began to give open-air concerts (Out and Round About with Music) to elderly people, and played an active role in the Performing Right Society.

Oram composed *Pulse Persephone* for the Commonwealth Exhibition at Burlington House in 1965, *Episode Metallic* for tape and piano (in collaboration with Ivor Walsworth), two ballets, and a great deal of highly atmospheric incidental music for theatre, TV advertisements and films (notably for the 1961 Deborah Kerr film *The Innocents*). She also provided tapes for three of Thea Musgrave's works. Her book, *An Individual Note of Music, Sound and Electronics* (1972) testified to her independent spirit.

ORGER, Caroline.   See **REINAGLE** Caroline

ORR, Charles Wilfred
31 July 1893 – 24 Feb. 1977
C.W. Orr was born at Cheltenham. Like his contemporary Peter Warlock, he was a friend of Delius and composed songs in the Romantic tradition. Twenty-four of his thirty-six published songs were to words by A.E. Housman. Orr studied at the Guildhall School of Music with Orlando Morgan, and privately with Dent, but the dominating influence on his work was Hugo Wolf. In addition to the songs he composed *A Cotswold Tune* for strings. Orr died at Stroud in Gloucestershire.

ORR, Robert (Robin) Kemsley
2 Jun. 1909 – 9 Apr. 2006
Robin Orr will be remembered by many as a fierce campaigner, whether fighting for the survival of the BBC Scottish Orchestra, better facilities for undergraduates in Glasgow, or for many other worthy causes. He was born at Brechin in Angus and went to the strict Loretto School near Edinburgh. He was already showing considerable musical promise at the age of fourteen. At sixteen he went to the Royal College of

Music, studying with Herbert Howells (composition), Walter Alcock, Arthur Benjamin and Percy Buck. In 1929 he won an organ scholarship to Pembroke College, Cambridge, leaving with an MA and Mus.D. For three years he was musical director at Sidcot School in Winscombe, Somerset, then on the advice of E.J. Dent. went to Italy for lessons with Alfredo Casella, and Paris for some tuition from Nadia Boulanger. On his return to Britain he was appointed assistant lecturer in music at Leeds University, but in 1938 returned to Cambridge as Organist and Director of Studies in Music at St John's College. When war broke out Orr joined the RAF as a photographic intelligence officer, reaching the rank of flight lieutenant. After the war he taught again at Cambridge, and also at the RCM from 1956-65. He became Chairman of Scottish Opera in 1962. In 1965 he returned to Cambridge as Professor of Music, until his retirement in 1976. Robin Orr composed three symphonies (best known being the *Symphony in One Movement*), several religious and secular choral works, organ music and songs. In 1972 he was made a CBE.

OSBORNE, George Alexander
24 Sep. 1806 – 16 Nov. 1893
George Osborne, born at Limerick, was self-taught until he was eighteen, when he went to Paris to study with Pixis, Kalkbrenner and Fétis. In 1843 he settled in London, and earned a reputation as a teacher and composer of chamber music. Osborne was on the board of the Philharmonic Society, the Royal Academy of Music, and also read papers at the Musical Association. He wrote two operas, three overtures, piano pieces, duets for violin and piano, three piano trios and a sextet. Osborne was a close friend of Berlioz and Chopin.

OUSELEY, Rev. Frederick Arthur Gore
12 Aug. 1825 – 6 Apr. 1889
Sir Frederick Ouseley was Professor of Music at Oxford, where he had been a student. As vicar of St Michael's, Tenbury, he established the college of the same name and was warden there from about 1855 until he died. His library of music and valuable manuscripts can still be found there. Ouseley was born in London to a family with a distinguished history of travel and war service. He composed operas, two oratorios (considered rather uninspired at the time), over seventy anthems, church services, two string quartets, songs and part-songs, as well as treatises on harmony, etc.

OWEN, Morfydd
Oct. 1891 – 7 Sep. 1918
In her far too short twenty-six years of life Morfydd Owen achieved much, writing a tone poem (*Morfa Rhuddlan*), an orchestral suite (*Death Music: The Passing of Branwen*), works for voice and orchestra (*Ave Maria, Sea Drift, My Sorrow, Towards the Unknown Region*), a cantata (*Pro Patria*), songs and instrumental music. She was also a professional singer and co-publisher of volumes on Welsh folk music.

      Born in Trefforest near Cardiff, Owen had private lessons in piano and composition from David Evans before studying music at University College, Cardiff, where her works received many performances. In 1912 she moved to London and the Royal Academy of Music, taking composition with Frederick Corder. Here again her works were performed and she was awarded the Charles Lucas medal for composition. Later during the war she gave concerts for the troops and many other appearances, giving the first performance of Harry Farjeon's song cycle *A Lute of Jade*. Her own best songs are perhaps *To Our Lady of Sorrows* and *Slumber Song to the Madonna* (comprising *Two Madonna Songs*). Morfydd Owen died after a bungled anaesthesia for an appendectomy.

PAGE, Arthur James
3 Mar. 1846 – 1916

Born in Ipswich, Page had lessons from Zechariah Buck at Norwich Cathedral, where he was a chorister, and from Edward Bunnett. His main post was as organist of St Mary's, Nottingham, which he held for thirty-seven years. He was also one of the founder members, and Treasurer of, the Incorporated Society of Musicians. His compositions are almost entirely vocal, and include cantatas and operettas, church music, part-songs, rounds and some organ music.

PALLIS, Marco
19 Jun. 1895 – 5 June 1989

Of Greek parentage, Marco Pallis was born in Liverpool, and had an interesting and varied career, first in the army, serving as an interpreter in Macedonia, and then fighting in the trenches on the Western front. His mountaineering experience in the UK led him to climbing expeditions in the Alps and to the Himalayas, where he was strongly influenced by Tibetan Buddhism, and converted to that faith. Returning to England, he studied with Arnold Dolmetsch, and in London formed the English Consort of Viols. During the invasion of Tibet by the Chinese he was an adviser to the Government. At the same time he was writing (on mountaineering, Buddhism and music) and composing – his string quartet in F sharp and *Nocturne de L'Éphémère* for orchestra both received performances on the South Bank. Aged ninety-four, he was writing an opera on a Tibetan theme, which sadly was unfinished at his death.

PANUFNIK, Andrzej
24 Sep. 1914 – 27 Oct. 1991

In writing of his *Tragic Overture*, dedicated to his brother killed in the Warsaw Uprising of 1944, Panufnik describes it as 'the first work in which I began to achieve my artistic endeavour to find a balance between emotion and structure'. Such a balance is evident in all his music since then. He was born in Warsaw, his mother a violinist and his father a highly respected instrument maker. His mother taught him music before he began studies with Kazimierz Sikorski at the Warsaw Conservatoire, gaining a Distinction in half the normal time. Soon after graduation he conducted the Warsaw Philharmonic Orchestra in a performance of his *Symphonic Variations*; he then went to Vienna to hone his conducting skills under Felix Weingartner. After further lessons in Paris and London, Panufnik returned to Warsaw at the outbreak of World War Two. He survived in Nazi Poland by playing in cafés, often with Witold Lutosławski, and in illegal underground concerts. He cunningly recovered many of his father's instruments from the Gestapo, and used fluent German with a Viennese accent to avoid capture. In the Warsaw Uprising he lost all of his manuscripts, but managed to rework some of them, such as his *Tragic Overture*.

When the communists took over in Poland, Panufnik worked to restore Polish musical culture, becoming conductor of the Cracow Philharmonic, and then the Warsaw Philharmonic. His nationalistic *Sinfonia Rustica* won the Chopin Prize and the communist award, Standard of Labour Class 1. He was given several important positions on cultural bodies representing Poland internationally, but he found the stylistic restrictions imposed by the regime and its banning of performances of his own music soul-destroying. As a result he escaped while on a conducting visit to Zurich and fled to England. Here he was much in demand and for a time was far better known as a conductor than as a composer. From 1957 to 1959 he directed the City of Birmingham Symphony Orchestra, then retired to concentrate on composition. From then on his music was regularly heard and won several important prizes. He was knighted in 1990. It was only in 1977, twenty-three years after he had left the country, that his work was heard again in Poland, when *Universal Prayer* received a performance. Among Andrzej Panufnik's compositions are ten symphonies, concertos for piano, violin and bassoon, several other concertante and orchestral works, vocal and choral music, two string quartets, some piano pieces, music for children.

Most of Panufnik's music, including and after *Universal Prayer*, is highly structured, both mathematically and formally. He often created for performer and listener complex, geometric diagrams explaining that structure. As alluded to earlier, this formalism tempered the deep emotions prevalent in his work. In 1987 he wrote his autobiography, *Composing Myself*.

PÂQUE, Guillaume
24 Jul. 1825 – 2 Mar. 1876
Born in Brussels, Pâque studied the cello at the conservatoire there, coming to England in 1851 as a professional cellist and teacher. He played in many of the major London orchestras of the time, and led the cello section in the Philharmonic, also playing in the Philharmonic's chamber music concerts. He deputised for Piatti on several occasions. He was also in the Queen's Private Band (his brother also being Queen's trumpeter). He composed a number of drawing-room pieces for the cello, the most notable being *Souvenir de Curis* for four celli.

PARISH-ALVARS, Elias
28 Feb. 1808 – 25 Jan. 1849
Parish-Alvars was a celebrated virtuoso harpist in his time, and was the creator of many novel playing techniques. Born Eli Parish in Teignmouth, Devon, to a Jewish family that had come to England from Portugal during the Renaissance, he studied the harp with Bochsa, Dizi and Labarre. Demand for his skills must not have been great in these islands, for he escaped in 1831 to give concert  tours in Germany and Italy before finally settling in Vienna to teach. After a further series of tours in the Orient, and to Dresden, Naples and Leipzig, Parish-Alvars returned to Vienna and became harpist to the Emperor. After only two years of marriage to one of his pupils, he died in penury of pneumonia. He composed four harp concertos, several fantasias and many other works for the instrument.

PARRATT, Walter
10 Feb. 1841 – 27 Mar. 1924

Walter Parratt was born at Huddersfield, and studied with his father (organist at the Parish Church) and with G. Cooper. At the age of ten he memorised the entire forty-eight Preludes and Fugues of J.S. Bach. He was an organist at churches in Huddersfield and Wigan, and in 1868 was appointed to Magdalen College, Oxford, where he graduated with a Mus.Doc. In 1882 he moved to St George's Chapel, Windsor, and became a professor of organ at the Royal College of Music. Knighted in 1892 he was later created Master of the Queen's Musick (serving also to Edward VII and George V). Parratt contributed to Grove's dictionary and lectured on the organ and on ancient music. He composed for state occasions and wrote anthems, songs, dramatic works based on Greek mythology (*Agamemnon*), and organ pieces. For eleven years he was Professor of Music at Oxford. Parratt died in Windsor.

PARRY, Charles Hubert Hastings
27 Feb. 1848 – 7 Oct. 1918

Sir Hubert Parry and Charles Villiers Stanford together are said to have laid the foundations of the renaissance of English Music in the late nineteenth century. A man of considerable energy and wide interests, Parry exerted an enormous influence on the younger composers of his time by virtue of his academic position and by the example of his own music. He was born at Bournemouth and went to Eton, taking his Oxford Mus.Bac. while still at school. After completing an arts degree at Exeter College, Oxford, he visited Germany, where he was particularly influenced by the music of Henry Hugo Pierson. On his return he entered business with Lloyds of London, but continued to study music with G.A. Macfarren and the Wagnerian Edward
Dannreuther, who became his mentor. By 1883 he had given up his business pursuits to join the staff of the Royal College of Music where, in 1895, he was to become Director for twenty years, succeeding Sir George Grove. In 1900 he further added to his workload by accepting the Professorship at Oxford.

Parry was a prolific composer and a gifted writer on musical matters. His many compositions, which generally display a reassuring optimism, include an opera (*Guenever*), five symphonies, a piano concerto, several overtures, orchestral suites and incidental music to plays, oratorios (mostly written for festival commissions), quartets and other chamber and instrumental works (his *Shulbrede Tunes* for piano – Parry used Shulbrede Priory in Sussex as a family retreat in his later years – are worth a hearing). His most popular works need little mention: the anthem *I was glad* (written for the coronation of Edward VII and later revised for that of George V), the eight-part *Blest Pair of Sirens* (first conducted by Stanford), his hymns such as 'Repton' (*Dear Lord and Father of mankind*), which originated from a song in his oratorio *Judith*, and, of course, *Jerusalem*. He died at his home in Rustington in Sussex, and a memorial tablet to him is displayed in St Paul's Cathedral.

PARRY, Joseph
21 May 1841 – 17 Feb. 1903
Joseph Parry was born at Merthyr Tydfil. His family were too poor to provide music lessons, and Parry had to wait until he was nearly thirty before he entered the Royal Academy of Music with financial help from friends and acquaintances. At the RAM he studied with Sterndale Bennett, Manuel Garcia (singing) and Charles Steggall, and then went on to take his doctorate at Cambridge. He was appointed Professor of Music at Aberystwyth and lectured at Cardiff University. Composer of several well-known hymn-tunes such as *Aberystwyth*, Joseph Parry also wrote a string quartet, oratorios, a cantata and other choral works, orchestral overtures,operas (*Blodwen* – the first opera in Welsh, *King Arthur*, *Arianwen*, *Sylvia* and *Virginia*) and songs (*Myfanwy* is best known). He died at Penarth.

PARRY, Joseph Haydn
May 1864 – 29 Mar. 1894
Born while his parents were visiting Pennsylvania, USA, Joseph Haydn Parry studied with his father Joseph Parry (see above). In 1890 he became a professor at the Guildhall School of Music in London. He composed operas (*Cigarette*, *Miami*, *Marigold Farm*), a cantata, piano solos and some songs. He died at Hampstead in London.

PEACE, Albert Lister
26 Jan. 1844 – 14 Mar. 1912
The 'Last of the Summer Wine' village of Holmfirth was where the young Albert Peace became organist of the parish church at the age of nine. He was born in Huddersfield, and took his Mus.Bac. at Oxford in 1870 and his doctorate five years later. Peace was eventually appointed to Glasgow Cathedral and succeeded William Best at St George's Hall, Liverpool, in 1897. He composed a cantata, anthems and church services, organ music and a setting of *Psalm 138* for voices, chorus and orchestra. He died in Liverpool.

PEARCE, Charles William
5 Dec. 1856 – 1928
Pearce was born at Salisbury in Wiltshire, and studied music with T.E. Aylward, C.J. Read, C.G. Verrinder and E.J. Hopkins. At the age of fourteen he became a church organist and held several posts in London. After gaining a Mus.B. and then his Mus.D. at Cambridge in 1884, he was appointed a professor of organ and composition at Trinity College of Music. He was also professor of harmony at the Guildhall School of Music and an examiner for several universities and music colleges. He wrote church music and organ pieces and co-edited (with Dr Charles Vincent) 'The Organist and Choirmaster'.

PEARSON (Pierson), Henry Hugo
12 Apr. 1815 – 28 Jan. 1873
Henry Hugo Pearson, son of the Dean of Salisbury, was born at Oxford and went to Harrow and Trinity College, Cambridge. Despite parental opposition Pearson took music lessons with Attwood and Walmisley and began to compose. After leaving Cambridge he toured Europe, meeting Mendelssohn, Schumann and Spohr, and

changed his name in order to avoid embarrassing his parents (owing partly to his choice of career and partly to an unacceptable love affair). Pierson became Professor of Music at Edinburgh for one year before finally settling in Germany. He died in Leipzig. His music has never been popular in this country, though it was held in high esteem in Germany. He composed two oratorios, operas (*Der Elfensieg, Leila* and *Contarini*), orchestral overtures, church music (including a *Stabat Mater*), and instrumental pieces. His more 'modern' Germanic oratorio *Jerusalem* won a competition against William Bexfield's stylistically traditional *Israel Restored* in 1852.

PEEL, Gerald Graham
9 Aug. 1877 – 16 Oct. 1937
Graham Peel was born at Pendlebury near Manchester. He was educated at Harrow and Oxford and studied music with Ernest Walker. He composed the song-cycles *The Country Lover* and A *Shropshire Lad* and altogether over one hundred songs, many of them to words by A.E. Housman. *In summertime on Bredon* must surely be the finest ever setting of those words, and one of the loveliest of English songs. Peel died in Bournemouth.

PETERKIN, George Norman   .
1886 – 1983
Born in Birkenhead to parents of Scottish and Irish origin, Norman Peterkin was a self-taught composer, though he studied piano, organ and violin privately. While working for Rushworth's Music House in Liverpool, he travelled to Hong Kong, where his talents as a pianist were well exercised. On his return to England he was involved in the running of a contemporary music centre in Liverpool. In 1925 he joined the music department of Oxford University Press, becoming its Editor and Director from 1941-47. Peterkin composed ballets, orchestral works, chamber music, choral works, songs and piano pieces.

PHILLIPS, Montague Fawcett
13 Nov. 1885 – 4 Jan. 1969
Montague Phillips was born at Tottenham in London. He studied at the Royal Academy of Music with Frederick Corder and later became a professor of harmony and composition there. He was also a church organist for most of his life. His works include a symphony, two piano concertos, a string quartet and many other orchestral works, light operas (e.g. *The Rebel Maid*, from which comes his most successful song *The Fishermen of England*), a cantata, piano pieces and songs. His wife was Clara Butterworth, for whom he wrote *Fidelity* (a song with orchestra) and many other works. Phillips died at Esher in Surrey.

PHILLIPS, William Lovell
26 Dec. 1816 – 19 Mar. 1860
Phillips was conductor at the Olympic and Princess theatres and was organist at St Catherine's, Regents Park. He was born in Bristol and studied at the Royal Academy of Music with Cipriani Potter, and Robert Lindley for cello. He later became a professor of composition at the RAM. He composed a symphony, musical farce, a cantata, church music and songs, as well as writing a cello tutor. He died in London.

PHILP, Elizabeth
1827 – 26 Nov. 1885
Born at Falmouth, Elizabeth Philp studied singing with Manuel Garcia and composition with Ferdinand Hiller at Bristol. She followed a career as a singer and teacher ,and composed over one hundred songs and ballads, mainly to words by Arnold and Longfellow. She died in London.

PHILPOT, Stephen Rowland
12 Aug. 1872 – 12 Oct. 1950
Stephen Philpot is remembered for his operas (*Dante and Beatrice* ran for ten years with the Carl Rosa Company, and was the first English opera to be performed by that company in the twentieth century) and for his musical comedies. Of the latter his *The Algerian Girl* and *Bill Adams* also achieved long runs. Philpot was born in London and studied with Walter Macfarren at the Royal Academy of Music. In 1920 he emigrated to Monte Carlo, where many of his works were performed (his Mass in D minor was given several times in Monaco Cathedral). He returned to England in 1940, when Monaco was occupied by Italian forces, and became organist at St James's in Taunton. He composed seven operas, a cantata, some 200 songs, and pieces for violin and for piano. Philpot died at Ramsgate.

PIERSON, Henry Hugo. See **PEARSON**

PIGGOTT, Patrick
15 Jun. 1915 – 9 May 1990
As a student, Patrick Piggott passed through the Royal Academy of Music with flying colours, helped by receiving two scholarships and winning several prizes. He subsequently had lessons with Julius Isserlis, Nadia Boulanger and Benjamin Dale. During World War Two he was rejected for National Service on medical grounds, and worked as a pianist, teacher and lecturer to support an ailing brother and mother. He later became a lecturer in music at Cardiff University. In the early 1960s he joined the BBC as Head of Music for the Midland Region, and was in demand as a concert pianist. He specialised in the music of John Field and Rachmaninov, about both of whom he wrote impressive studies. He was also an expert on Jane Austen, publishing *The Innocent Diversion – Music in the life and writings of Jane Austen*. Piggott composed several orchestral and chamber works, piano music (including sonatas and preludes). His last major opus, *Rosanes Lieder* for soprano and orchestra, received its first performance two moths before his death.

PITFIELD, Thomas Baron
5 Apr. 1903 – 11 Nov. 1999

> There was a composer called Britten
> Sought play with a frolicsome kitten;
> The frolicsome kitten
> With Ben was not smitten,
> And Benjamin Britten got bitten.
>
> Here I am, still seemingly alive,
> And slowly coming up to seventy-five,
> That is, I think, three-quarters of a century
> (My skill with sums is only rudimentary).
> At this ripe age I find the problem difficult
> To sort out quickly from my birth certificult.

These rhymes from the pen of Tom Pitfield encapsulate the composer's sense of mischief, a quality which pervades much of his music. His works are diatonic but often quirky, as he likes to surprise with an unexpected harmony or rhythm. That said, there are also many works that thrill and delight rather than amuse, his piano concerto being a case in point.

Pitfield was born in Bolton, attending the local Church of England primary school and secondary school, which he left at the age of fourteen. Unwillingly, he spent over seven years as an engineering apprentice and managed to save enough money to buy a cello and enrol at the Royal Manchester College of Music. He had ensemble lessons from Frank Merrick and cello classes with Carl Fuchs. In 1930 he won a scholarship at Bolton Municipal School of Art where, he claimed, composition teaching was negligible. Funds ran out after a year and he took up teaching art and craft at schools in Lancashire and Shropshire as well as tutoring the unemployed in Wolverhampton. But his music began to be published and he was forging valuable friendships. During the war he was a conscientious objector and, as a teacher, was exempted. In 1947 he was offered and accepted a post at the RMCM teaching composition. Commissions from the famous flowed in and he was able to build himself a house in Bowdon, Cheshire. When the RMCM became the Royal Northern College of Music in 1972, he stayed on. Among his pupils were John Ogdon, John McCabe and Ronald Stevenson.

Throughout his life Pitfield used his artistic skills to the full. His watercolours were seen in several exhibitions, including the Royal Academy; his woodcuts, linocuts and sketches found a market; and he published several collections of poetry and three volumes of autobiography. He was also an accomplished furniture maker and calligrapher. When asked to provide a list of his compositions, he modestly claimed that he hadn't kept a record. A great many of his works were valued educational pieces, but there were also a piano concerto and other orchestral works, a striking xylophone (or marimba) sonata, a concerto for recorder, a concertino for percussion and orchestra, secular and religious choral works (including a trilogy of 'Sketchbooks'), chamber works, many songs and piano pieces. His music for amateur performers was supremely well judged, yet skilfully crafted. His *Household Symphony* had parts for sandpaper blocks, graters, jars and bottles, and incorporates a triple rhythm version of 'The Vicar of Bray'.

PITT, Percy
4 Jan. 1870 – 23 Nov. 1932
Born in London, Percy Pitt studied with Reinecke and Jadassohn at Leipzig and with Rheinberger at Munich. In 1893 he returned to England and shortly afterwards became chorus master of the Mottl concerts and organist at the Queen's Hall. In 1907 he was appointed Director of Music at Covent Garden, and held several other directorships of theatre companies, becoming Musical Director of the BBC in 1922. Among his compositions are suites, symphonies and other orchestral works, a clarinet concerto, a ballad for violin and orchestra, poems for voice and orchestra, incidental music and chamber works. He also wrote a ballet, two cantatas, piano pieces and songs. Pitt died in London.

PLUMSTEAD, Mary (née Frost)
1905 – 4 May 1980
Mary Plumstead is best known for her songs, written in the tradition of Butterworth and Quilter, and for her *Music for the Work of our Hands*, which was performed for the Festival of Britain in 1951. She was born at Warlingham in Surrey, went to Croydon High School, and studied at the School of Dalcroze Eurhythmics and for a term at the Royal Academy of Music – just long enough for her to gain her LRAM. This was followed by a career as accompanist and lecturer. Her songs were popular for a while, including *Ha'naker mill* and *A grateful heart*. Besides songs and part-songs she composed two orchestral pieces and some instrumental works. She retired to Devon with her husband, an estate agent, where she continued with her composition and her hobbies.

POLDOWSKI
18 May 1880 – 28 Jan. 1932
Irene Regine Wieniawska, as Poldowski could be known, was the daughter of the famous Polish violinist Henryk Wieniawski and his Irish wife Isobel Hampton. She was born in Brussels and her father died a year later. Irene studied at the Brussels Conservatoire, where her very early compositions impressed Gervase Elwes, before moving to London, where she studied piano with Michael Hambourg and took composition classes with Percy Pitt. In 1902-04 she studied in Paris with André Gédalge, then in 1907 with d'Indy at the Schola Cantorum. She found time during this period of study to have three children, though her first son died in 1902. Throughout the 1920s her music received many performances, though it was often too progressive and difficult for the critics. Much of it was written with a Gallic humour similar to that of Satie, or even his English rival Lord Berners.

Poldowski composed an orchestral *Nocturne* (which included an vast array of woodwind including heckelphone and basset horn), two symphonic sketches, *Pat Malone's Wake* for piano and orchestra, an operetta (*Laughter*), piano and other instrumental pieces, a string quartet and many songs, Verlaine being one of her most chosen wordsmiths. She died in London.

POLE, William
22 Apr. 1814 – 30 Dec. 1900
Dr William Pole, FRS is remembered best for his authoritive work 'The Philosophy of Music'. He was born in Birmingham and became Professor of Civil Engineering at University College, London. Having graduated at Oxford with his Mus.Doc. he became an organist in London and helped to initiate the first music degrees at London University. Pole composed anthems, motets and some organ music. He died in London.

POSTON, Elizabeth
24 Oct. 1905 – 18 Mar. 1987
Composer, pianist, writer and critic, Elizabeth Poston was born near Wallkern in Hertfordshire. She studied at the Royal Academy of Music (and on the continent), taking piano with Harold Samuel. She spent the 1930s abroad collecting folk-songs, and was senior administrator of the BBC European Service during World War Two. After the war she collected more songs in the USA and Canada,

returning in 1947 to advise the BBC on the development of the Third Programme. From 1955 to 1961 she was President of the Society of Women Composers. She edited the three Penguin collections of American folk-songs, two carol collections and the Cambridge Hymnal, and was a noted authority on Warlock. Her compositions include incidental music, songs and choral works, anthems, chamber music, a *Concertino* for recorder, oboe d'amore, bass viol and harpsichord, and a *Serenatina* for pipes. Elizabeth Poston was a close friend of Dylan Thomas and C.S. Lewis. She died in Stevenage.

PRAEGER, Ferdinand Christian Wilhelm
22 Jan. 1815 – 2 Sep. 1891
Born into a Dutch family of violinists in Leipzig, Praeger taught the violin at the Hague (where he may have had lessons from Hummel) before moving to London in 1834. He was a scholarly musician, being the English correspondent of 'Neue Zeitschrift für Musik' and contributing papers to the Musical Association. He was a friend of Wagner, who stayed with Praeger on his London visit in 1855. His compositions include a Symphonic Prelude *Manfred*, a symphonic poem *Leben und Lieben*, a cello sonata and a quantity of piano works.

PRENDERGAST, Arthur Hugh Dalrymple
28 Jun. 1833 – 1924
Born in London, Prendergast studied under James Turle, organist at Westminster Abbey. He was conductor of the Lombard Amateur Musical Association, (a group of singers from the City), and Secretary to the Bach Choir. Prendergast was a lawyer who worked in the Inner Temple. He composed sacred cantatas, anthems and madrigals.

PRENTICE, Thomas Ridley
6 Aug. 1842 – 15 Aug. 1895
Born at Ongar in Essex, Thomas Prentice studied at the Royal Academy of Music with both Walter and George Alexander Macfarren. He was a church organist, a professor of piano at the Guildhall School of Music and at Blackheath Conservatory. Prentice wrote books on piano technique and composed a cantata (*Linda*), anthems, part-songs and piano pieces. He died at Hampstead in London.

PRESCOTT, Oliveria Louisa
3 Sep. 1842 – 9 Sep. 1919
It is a pity that virtually all of Prescott's works have been lost, for she appears to have been one of the foremost women composers of her time. Born in London, she did not turn to music until the age of thirty, when she studied under G.A. Macfarren and various others at the Royal Academy of Music for at least seven years. She also acted as Macfarren's amanuensis until his death in 1887, before turning to teaching at a girls' school in Baker Street, London in 1879, where she remained for fourteen years. Prescott's book of 1880 'Form and Design in Music' became one of the standard textbooks for many years. She also penned 'About Music and what it is made of', a book for amateurs.

Oliveria Prescott, together with Alice Mary Smith, was one of the most prolific of the women in her time who wrote in large-scale forms rather than in genres more suited to the drawing room. After some early songs and anthems (one of which was sung in St Paul's Cathedral) she composed her first symphony, *Alkestis*, in 1876, which won a nominal third prize among the thirty-eight entries in the Alexandra Palace competition of that year. A further symphony was written in the early years of the twentieth century. Other orchestral works include *Bright October*, four concert overtures, a piano concerto (titled *Joy*) and two works for soprano and orchestra. In addition to two string quartets and other chamber music, there was a *Magnificat* for soloists, chorus and orchestra with organ, six secular works for chorus and orchestra and a published three-act musical comedy, *Carrigraphuga, the Castle of the Fairies*. Prescott died in Hambledon, Surrey. A composition prize in her name was established after her death at the Royal Academy of Music.

PRICE, Richard Maldwyn
16 Apr. 1890 – 11 Nov. 1952
R.M. Price was born at Welshpool in Montgomeryshire and studied at Aberystwyth, being the first student to be awarded a D.Mus. (Wales). He was an organist and choirmaster and taught at Redhill and Welshpool. He composed sacred choral works, orchestral suites and other pieces, part-songs, string quartets and trios, pieces for violin and for piano, and some music for brass band.

PROCTOR-GREGG, Humphrey
31 Jul. 1895 – 13 Apr. 1980
Born at Kirkby Lonsdale, Humphrey Proctor-Gregg was educated at King William's College, Isle of Man, and Peterhouse, Cambridge. He studied at the Royal College of Music with Stanford, Wood and Julius Harrison, later holding various appointments as stage manager, producer or manager to several opera companies (Covent Garden, Carl Rosa, Touring Opera, BBC, etc.). He was appointed Reader in Music at Manchester University, then Emeritus professor. In 1971 he was awarded the CBE. As well as writing twenty opera translations, Proctor-Gregg composed extensively: his works include a clarinet concerto, violin sonatas and several songs.

PROTHEROE, Daniel
24 Nov. 1866 – 24 Feb. 1934
Born at Ystradgynlais in South Wales, Daniel Protheroe studied with Joseph Parry. He lectured in the USA and was an adjudicator at several American musical competitions and at National Eisteddfodau in Wales. His compositions include orchestral tone poems, many cantatas, choral music and songs. Protheroe spent the last few years of his life in the United States, and died in Chicago.

PROUT, Ebenezer
1 Mar. 1835 – 5 Dec. 1909
Ebenezer Prout is best remembered for his theoretical works on harmony and counterpoint, renowned for their thoroughness, his editions of works of Handel (including *Messiah*), and by some for his mnemonic rhymes to Bach fugue subjects – the '48' and many organ fugues. He was born at Oundle in Northamptonshire and graduated from London University in 1854. He studied piano with C.K. Salaman and won several prizes, both for piano and for composition. Prout was a critic for several music journals and edited the Monthly Musical Record from 1871-74. He played the organ and taught harmony and composition at the Royal Academy of Music, the

Guildhall School of Music and the National Training School for Music. In 1894 he was appointed Professor of Music at Dublin (a non-resident appointment). He lived in Hackney, North London, where for fourteen years he ran the Borough of Hackney Choral Association (its logo having the notation BHCA, fortuitously an anagram of 'Bach'!). His compositions include four symphonies, cantatas (several written especially for his choral society), organ concertos, string quartets, a piano quartet and other chamber works, a clarinet sonata, and some somewhat academic choral pieces. Prout died in Hackney.

His son, embarrassingly named **Louis Beethoven Prout** (1864 – 1943), studied at the RAM and taught harmony and composition at the Guildhall School of Music. Besides lecturing and writing on both moths and music, he composed a few songs and sacred psalm settings.

PYE, Kellow John
9 Feb. 1812 – 22 Sep. 1901
K.J. Pye was born at Exeter and studied with Potter and Crotch at the Royal Academy of Music, taking his Mus.Bac. at Oxford in 1842. He was well known in the South-West of England as a conductor, but gave this up in 1853 to join a firm of wine merchants. However, he kept alive his interests in music, joining the directorate of the RAM and actively supporting the Madrigal Society. Pye composed anthems, madrigals and songs. He died at Exmouth, Devon.

Q UILTER, Roger
1 Nov. 1877 – 21 Sep. 1953
Roger Quilter was one of the Frankfurt Group, (with Balfour Gardiner, Cyril Scott, Percy Grainger and Norman O'Neill) who studied in Germany with Iwan Knorr. He was born into a wealthy family in Brighton and went to Eton. Songs and part-songs of considerable merit form the bulk of his output, but he also composed choruses, two ballets, a light operas (*Love at the Inn*, *The Blue Boar* and *Julia* are different versions of the same work), incidental music, anthems (his *Evening Hymn* is incomparably transcendental), piano pieces and several small-scale orchestral works, of which *A Children's Overture* is

a gem. Another work for children, the musical *Where the Rainbow Ends*, was once popular (an eleven year-old Noel Coward made his stage debut at its premiere). Quilter had a private income and lived quietly in London during his later years, when he was troubled by the aftermath of a stomach ailment, eventually suffering a mental breakdown after the death of a favourite nephew. He is buried in the family vault at St Mary's, Bawdsey in Suffolk. Quilter was generous and helpful towards younger singers and composers, and was a founder member of the Musicians Benevolent Fund.

Rainier, Priaulx

3 Feb. 1903 – 10 Oct. 1986

'Uncompromising', 'pointillistic', 'forceful' and 'dance-like' – all descriptive of Priaulx Rainier's music: distinctly modernist, yet flavoured with emotional intensity and biting rhythms that must have been influenced by her childhood in Howick, the Natal, South Africa. Her music was also informed by her friendships with artists like Barbara Hepworth, Henry Moore, Ben Nicholson and Lucien Freud, who instilled in her a feeling for movement and spatial transformation. Rainier began piano and violin lessons in early childhood before attending the Cape Town College of Music from 1913 to 1920, when her family moved to England and she won a scholarship to study violin with Hans Wessely and Rowsby Woof, and composition with John McEwen, at the Royal Academy of Music in London. She stayed in England for the rest of her life. Her first serious student piece was for string quartet, in $\frac{5}{8}$ time and ending on a discord: it foreshadowed what was to follow. After leaving the RAM, Rainier taught at Badminton School and played in cinemas. In 1937 she spent a few weeks in Paris, taking composition lessons from Nadia Boulanger. Six years later she became a professor of composition at the RAM.

Rainier's works include a *Sinfonia da Camera* for strings, an orchestral *Dance Concerto Phalaphala*, concertos for cello and for violin, *Ploermel* for wind and percussion, other orchestral pieces, incidental music for *Figures in a Landscape* (a film about Hepworth), a *Requiem*, vocal music, chamber works (including *Quanta* for oboe and string trio – based on concepts derived from the quantum theory), and pieces for piano, harpsichord and organ. Priaulx Rainier died at Besse-en-Chandesse while on holiday in the Auvergne.

RANKL, Karl

1 Aug. 1898 – 6 Sep. 1968

Karl Rankl was born near Vienna, but came to Britain after the German invasion of Czechoslovakia, where he was Musical Director of the German Theatre in Prague. He studied with Schoenberg and Webern, then held various theatre conductorships, including those of the Vienna Volksoper and the Kroll Opera in Berlin. In England he conducted the London Philharmonic, Liverpool Philharmonic and the BBC orchestras, becoming in 1946 the Musical Director of Covent Garden Opera Co. and staying there for five years before accepting the baton of the Scottish Orchestra. Rankl composed eight symphonies, an opera, choruses, songs and chamber music (including a string quartet).

RAWSTHORNE, Alan

2 May 1905 – 24 July 1971

Alan Rawsthorne was born at Haslingden in Lancashire, and studied dentistry until, in his early twenties, he decided to devote himself to composition. He entered the Royal Manchester College of Music to take piano, cello and composition, then went abroad to study piano with Egon Petri. Returning to England, he taught for two years at Dartington Hall before settling in London. His *Theme and Variations* for two violins, performed at the London ISCM Festival of 1938, first attracted attention, and the following Warsaw Festival introduced his *Symphonic Variations*, winning him a firm place in the orchestral repertoire. In 1941 Rawthorne was called up, and spent the war years writing scores for government documentaries.

Rawsthorne's style is chromatic, highly individual (though the influence of Hindemith is easily recognised) and consistent, most of his works being symphonic or for chamber ensembles. They include three symphonies; two piano concertos; concertos for strings, two pianos, violin, cello, oboe and clarinet; a ballet and other orchestral works. The chamber music includes several quartets and quintets, three string quartets, sonatas for various instruments, and piano pieces. His vocal and choral music is represented by *Carmen Vitale*, two cantatas, songs and part-songs. In 1935 Rawsthorne married the violinist Jessie Hinchliffe, for whom he wrote several works. In 1954 after the breakdown of his first marriage, Rawsthorne wed Constant Lambert's widow Isabel.

RAYNOR, John
5 June 1909 – 7 May 1970
John Raynor was a man to whom friends could always turn for reassurance in times of need. His fondness for repairing clocks and rearing moths and butterflies bore sharp contrast to his cycling, walking and swimming holidays in Cornwall. He was born at Westminster, son of the Master of the King's Scholars at Westminster School, and studied at the Royal College of Music and the School of English Church Music.

Raynor was hit by a car on his way home from playing at an Easter Vigil Service, and died on Ascension day. He left 680 songs, some of which were championed by Vaughan Williams and were enthusiastically received by the critics, but sadly are rarely heard today. His autobiographical 'A Westminster Childhood' is well worth reading.

REAY, Samuel
17 Mar. 1822 – 21 July 1905
Samuel Reay achieved fame in 1879 through his production of two secular cantatas by Bach – the 'Coffee' and 'Peasant' cantatas, with words of his own adaptation. He was born at Hexham in Northumberland, and studied organ with James Stimpson of Birmingham. He held a succession of organists' posts and composed church services, anthems, madrigals and part-songs. Reay died at Newark-on-Trent.

REDMAN, Reginald
17 Sep. 1892 – 1 Mar. 1972
Reginald Redman was born in London and studied at the Guildhall School of Music. He became an organist and conductor and joined the music staff of the BBC, eventually taking charge of music for the BBC Western Region. While at Bristol he founded the West Country Studio Orchestra and the West Country Singers. He composed a piano concerto (dedicated to his wife), cello concerto, three operas, two ballets, other orchestral works, incidental music to radio, choral and chamber music, songs and part-songs, and piano pieces.

REED, William Henry
29 July 1876 – 2 July 1942
A conductor, violinist and teacher, William Reed studied at the Royal Academy of Music with Emile Sauret, Ebenezer Prout and Frederick Corder. He was leader of the London Symphony Orchestra and a close friend of Elgar, whose biography he wrote.

He also taught violin at the Royal College of Music. His compositions include a symphony for strings, a violin concerto and a rhapsody for violin and orchestra, other orchestral works, a choral ballad (*Earl Haldan's Daughter*), five string quartets, violin pieces, songs and part-songs, piano solos and pieces for junior orchestra. He was born at Frome in Somerset and died in Dumfries.

REED, William Leonard
16 Oct. 1910 – 15 Apr. 2002
'Will' Reed was born in South London and went to Dulwich College before a Classics scholarship enabled him to go to Jesus College, Oxford. Following his degree he qualified with a teaching diploma. When his violin sonata won a composition prize, Hugh Allen recommended that he enter the Royal College of Music. During his two years there, studying composition with Herbert Howells and conducting with Constant Lambert, he won the first Cobbett Prize. As a result of receiving a travelling scholarship in 1936, Reed met Sibelius in the latter's home town. He returned to Scandinavia twice again to lecture for the British Council, before earning an Oxford Mus.Doc. in 1939. While at Oxford Reed was involved with the Oxford Group, which developed into the Moral Re-Armament campaign for spiritual and ethical renewal. He worked on its behalf for twenty years, composing choral works, songs and theatrical works (including *The Good Road* and *The Crowning Experience*) and during the war worked for the London Fire Auxiliary Service. In 1966 he was appointed Director of Music at the Westminster Theatre Arts Centre (the MRA's London venue). This work allowed Reed free rein, and he organised concerts and wrote further musicals for performance there – *Annie, High Diplomacy, Love All* and *The Vanishing Island.* As a gifted pianist he wrote many works for the instrument. He also contributed orchestral works and vocal music, edited books of carols, and co-edited a collection of national anthems of the world.

REINAGLE, Caroline
1818 – 11 Mar. 1892
Caroline Orger was trained as a pianist, giving her first concert at the Hanover Square Rooms, where, under her maiden name, she played her piano concerto. A piano trio, two piano quartets and a cello sonata soon followed. She, with Kate Loder, was one of the few women whose music was played at meetings of the Society of British Musicians, which folded in 1865. She married an Oxford organist, Alexander Reinagle (son of the cellist Joseph Reinagle), and remained in Oxford as a piano teacher for the rest of her life. Unable to get her instrumental works published, she found song writing to be more lucrative, publishing under her married name. Her songs were described by Nigel Burton as 'characterised by unremitting psychological power', and her Piano Sonata is a work of considerable technical mastery. She died in Tiverton, Devon.

REIZENSTEIN, Franz Theodor
7 Nov. 1911 – 15 Oct. 1968
Franz Reizenstein was born at Nuremberg in Germany, and studied piano with Leonid Kreutzer and composition with Hindemith at the Berlin Hochschule. He was a child prodigy, composing his first string quartet while in his early teens. Appalled by the rise of Nazism before World War Two, Reizenstein came to England to complete his studies. It was Vaughan Williams at the Royal College of Music who introduced him

to the English musical tradition, and Solomon who made him the fine pianist he was. Reizenstein remained in England for the rest of his life, though he was interned for a time during the war years. He toured as a concert pianist and taught piano at the Royal Academy of Music (from 1958) and the Royal Manchester College of Music. Though he never taught composition in Britain, except on an amateur basis, he was visiting professor of composition at Boston University, in the USA, for six months in 1966. He also broadcast frequently for the BBC.

Reizenstein's compositions were mainly chamber and piano works, which show strongly the influence of Hindemith, though their individuality is beyond doubt. Reizenstein's piano music is particularly suited to the instrument, and is written with great fluency and often wit. In addition he wrote two piano concertos, a violin concerto, cello concerto, an opera for radio, a concerto for strings, overtures, film music and songs. He also collaborated with Gerard Hoffnung on the spoofs *Concerto Popolare* and *Let's Fake an Opera*.

REYNOLDS, Alfred Charles
15 Aug. 1884 – 18 Oct. 1969
Alfred Reynolds was born in Liverpool, attended Merchant Taylors' School in Crosby, Liverpool, and studied at Paris and Berlin with Humperdinck. He remained in Berlin to become a répétiteur and conductor, and in 1910 took a German company on tour in Russia. Returning to England, he conducted for various theatre companies and, after war service, toured in the Far East as Musical Director of the Royal Opera Company. He continued to conduct theatre orchestras, and the pinnacle of his career was at the Lyric Theatre, Hammersmith, where he conducted his comic operas *Derby Day* and *The Policeman's Serenade*. Reynolds composed other operettas, songs and part-songs, and some short orchestral works. He died at Bognor Regis.

RHODES, Harold William
15 Sep. 1889 – 27 Feb. 1956
Born at Hanley in Staffordshire, Harold Rhodes went to the Royal College of Music before gaining a doctorate at London. He was assistant to Sir Walter Parratt at St George's Chapel, Windsor, becoming organist and choirmaster for the duration of 1909. After a short period teaching at Lancing College, he became successively organist at St John's, Torquay, Coventry Cathedral and Winchester Cathedral (1939-49). He was also a professor at the Royal Academy of Music. Rhodes composed services, anthems, songs and part-songs.

RICHARDS, Henry Brinley
13 Nov. 1817 – 1 May 1885
Brinley Richards is remembered as the composer of the song *God bless the Prince of Wales*. Born in Carmarthen, Richards turned away from medicine to study at the Royal Academy of Music, and was a pianist and lecturer on Welsh music. He composed a symphony, overtures and a piano concerto, but later turned away from larger-scale works to write piano pieces, songs and part-songs in a more popular vein. Richards died in London and is buried at Brompton Cemetery.

RICHARDSON, Alan
29 Feb. 1904 – 29 Nov. 1978
Alan Richardson was born in Edinburgh. He studied privately with Harold Craxton and at the Royal Academy of Music (where he later became a professor of composition) with Theodore Holland. He toured as a pianist and worked with Watson Forbes on a collection of classical music for viola and piano. His compositions include sonatas for piano, violin, viola, oboe, cor anglais and clarinet, other piano pieces and a *Junior Concerto* for piano and orchestra.

RICHARDSON, Arnold
6 Jan. 1914 – 26 Jun. 1973
As a recitalist at the organ Arnold Richardson performed frequently at the Proms and at the Royal Festival Hall. He was born at Ely, and studied at the Royal Academy of Music with G.D. Cunningham and Benjamin Dale. He joined the teaching staff there, later becoming an examiner. He was appointed organist at St Alban's, Holborn, where he invited Messiaen to give the British premiere of *La Nativité du Seigneur* in 1938. In the same year Richardson moved to Wolverhampton to become borough organist, then in 1955 accepted a post at the West London Synagogue. He composed a Mass in A, organ music, a three-part mass for women's voices, songs and piano pieces.

RIDOUT, Alan
9 Dec. 1934 – 19 Mar 1996
Few composers have achieved their one-hundredth opus before the age of thirteen, as did Ridout. History gives little indication of the worth of these early works, but his mature work is certainly impressive. Ridout was man of intense but not totally fulfilled Christian faith: he had ambitions to join the Greek Orthodox Church, but these never materialised. He did, however, write a large amount of music for liturgical use, as well as a series of music dramas with religious or moral themes. Of these, *Trial by Fire* is still topical in its exploration of Islamic-Christian relationships.

Ridout was born in West Wickham, went to the Guildhall School of Music at the age of fifteen, and graduated from the Royal College of Music five years later to have private lessons with Peter Racine Fricker and Michael Tippett. In 1957 a scholarship allowed him to travel to Amsterdam, leading to a period of tonal experimentation with Neo-Viennese compositional techniques. Returning to Britain, he taught composition at the RCM and in 1963 took up a post at Cambridge. He soon became composer-in-residence at Canterbury Cathedral's choir school, writing operas for the choirboys and works for the Canterbury Choral Society. A move to King's School, Canterbury, gave him further scope for choral and dramatic music writing. In 1993 Ridout moved to France and converted to the Roman faith. In addition to much successful children's music, he produced three symphonies, three cello concertos, a variety of other concertante works and orchestral pieces, cantatas and church services, four songs for countertenor and viola (*Whom time will not reprieve*), several organ works (*Seven Last Words* being the finest example), six string quartets and many other chamber works, piano and instrumental pieces. The year before he died his large-scale choral work, *Ode to Joy,* was written for and performed at the Three Choirs Festival. His autobiography, *A Composer's Life*, was published in 1995.

RING, Montague.   See **ALDRIDGE**, Amanda

ROBERTON, Hugh Stevenson
23 Feb. 1874 – 7 Oct. 1952
Hugh Roberton left his mark on music in Scotland as conductor of the Glasgow Orpheus Choir, which he founded in 1906. He was born in Glasgow, where he spent most of his life, and was self-taught as a composer. His works, numbering over 300, were nearly all for voice, and include solos, duets and part-songs. Roberton was a pacifist with strong convictions to the left of the political spectrum. He wrote the autobiographical *A Prelude to Orpheus*, and was knighted in 1931.

ROBERTS, Caradog
30 Oct. 1878 – 3 Mar. 1935
Caradog Roberts was born at Rhosllanercrugog, near Wrexham. He studied music with a local organist, but was apprenticed to a carpenter until his musical talents became obvious. By fourteen he was accompanying the Caradog Choir in London. He studied with Joseph Cox Bridge (organist at Chester Cathedral), then with Johannes Weingartner, gaining a B.Mus. and later a doctorate at Oxford. Roberts used his musical gifts locally, and in addition to collecting old Welsh and foreign hymn-tunes, he composed a cantata, oratorio, choral pieces, songs and part-songs, anthems, psalm chants and hymn-tunes.

ROBERTS, John Henry
31 Mar. 1848 – 30 July 1924
Born at Bethesda in North Wales, this young organist and choral conductor was brought to the attention of S.S. Wesley, who took him under his wing. In 1870 he went to the Royal Academy of Music to study with Sterndale Bennett. Roberts became an organist and teacher at Bethesda and Caernarvon, until he was appointed Principal of the Liverpool Cambrian School of Music. He composed orchestral pieces (including the overture *Caractacus*), choral music, piano pieces, part-songs and anthems, and adjudicated at festivals and eisteddfodau. Roberts died in Liverpool.

ROBERTS, John Varley
25 Sep. 1841 – 9 Feb. 1920
For nearly forty years Dr Roberts was organist at Magdalen College, Oxford, where he was an examiner and lecturer in music. He also held posts at Halifax and St Giles, Oxford, and in 1884 founded the University Glee and Madrigal Society, and also conducted the Oxford Choral and Philharmonic Society. He was born at Stanningly, near Leeds, and wrote cantatas, psalms for voices and orchestra, fifty anthems, church services, songs and organ pieces. He died in Oxford.

ROBINSON, Fanny
Sep. 1831 – 31 Oct. 1879
Fanny Arthur was born at Southampton, and studied with Sterndale Bennett and Sigismund Thalberg. She married the Irish baritone Joseph Robinson, with whom she helped revive the Irish Academy. She composed several piano pieces and a cantata, and was herself a talented performer at the piano.

ROCKSTRO, William Smyth
5 Jan. 1823 – 2 July 1895
William Rackstraw, to give him his real name, was born at East Cheam and studied with John Purkiss and Sterndale Bennett, and with Mendelssohn, Plaidy and Hauptmann at Leipzig. He was a pianist, and an editor for Boosey & Co.; he lectured at the Royal Academy of Music and at the Royal College of Music, and was an authority on Gregorian plainchant and other aspects of ancient church music. Rockstro composed a sacred cantata, a ballet, orchestral overtures, songs, and some light piano pieces. He also made several piano arrangements of operas, and wrote popular but influential books on Handel and Mendelssohn. Rockstro died in London.

RODWELL, George Herbert
15 Nov. 1800 – 22 Jan. 1852
Born in London, George Rodwell studied with Vincent Novello and Henry Bishop. In 1828 he was appointed professor of harmony and composition at the Royal Academy of Music and was also Musical Director at the Adelphi Theatre and, later, at Covent Garden. Rodwell composed forty operettas (e.g. *The Flying Dutchman*, *The Cornish Miners*, *The Devil's Elixir*, *The Lord of the Isles*) and other stage works, and some songs. He was also the author of several farces and novels. Rodwell died at Pimlico in London.

ROECKEL, Joseph Leopold
11 Apr. 1838 – 20 June 1923
Son of a singer and opera director J.A. Roeckel, Joseph was born in London. He studied with Eisenhofer in Wurzburg and Gotze in Weimar, and composed cantatas, a 'scena' for baritone and orchestra, songs and some orchestral music.

His wife, **Jane Jackson**, was a concert pianist who wrote piano pieces, songs and transcriptions of popular classical works under the name of 'Jules de Sivrai'. His brother **Edward** (b. 1816) also wrote piano pieces. Roeckel died at Vittel in France.

ROGERS, Roland
17 Nov. 1847 – 1927
Roland Rogers was born at West Bromwich, now in the West Midlands, and studied with S. Grosvenor. After gaining a doctorate at Oxford he held various posts as organist, including that at Bangor Cathedral, where he stayed for twenty years. He composed a symphony, cantatas, church music, songs and organ pieces.

RONALD, Landon
7 June 1873 – 14 Aug. 1938
Landon Ronald Russell was born in London, son of the song composer Henry Russell. He studied at the Royal College of Music with Parry, Franklin Taylor, W.H. Holmes, Frederick Bridge, Stanford and Walter Parratt. By the age of seventeen he had already had several works performed, and was playing the piano at theatres. He later toured with Nellie Melba as conductor and accompanist. Touring Europe as a conductor, he championed the music of his friend Elgar. In 1909 he succeeded Thomas Beecham as conductor of the New Symphony Orchestra (later known as the Royal Albert Hall Orchestra) and then the Scottish Orchestra. In 1910 Ronald became Principal of the Guildhall School of Music, and in 1922 received a knighthood for his services to music.

Ronald composed over 200 songs (many of which have deservedly been popular), orchestral music, ballets, incidental music to plays, and piano pieces. He was one of the pioneers of recorded music, and cut his first disc in 1900 – a piano transcription of Wagner's *Liebestod*. This was followed by many other recordings, including Grieg's piano concerto with Wilhelm Backhaus, in 1910. 'Variations on a Personal Theme' is a volume of Landon Ronald's reminiscences.

ROOPER, Jasper Bonfoy
1898 – 14 Aug. 1981
Jasper Rooper was born at Penkridge in Staffordshire and was educated at Lancing College, where he later became Director of Music. He studied music with Vaughan Williams, Thalben-Ball and Dr Alcock at the Royal College of Music, and spent many years as a lecturer in the Extra-Mural Department of Oxford University (1951-65) and at Sussex University. Rooper composed a puppet opera (*The Emperor's New Clothes*), an opera for schools (*The Musicians*), a *Christmas Rhapsody*, some church music, madrigals, part-songs and piano pieces.

ROOTHAM, Cyril Bradley
5 Oct. 1875 – 18 Mar. 1938
Born at Redland, Bristol, where his father was cathedral organist and professor of singing, Rootham went to Bristol Grammar School and Clifton College before entering the Royal College of Music to study with C.V. Stanford and Walter Parratt. He then went on to St John's College, Cambridge, to read classics and music. At the age of twenty-six he returned to Cambridge to teach with E. J. Dent, eventually becoming Music Director of his old college. In 1930 Rootham organised the first Cambridge Festival of British Music. He also introduced many contemporary European works to Britain. Rootham's compositions include various works for chorus and orchestra, pre-eminent among them being the *Ode on the Morning of Christ's Nativity* for soli, chorus and orchestra, two symphonies (the second completed by Patrick Hadley), three string quartets, a string quintet, orchestral suites and overtures, an opera (*The Two Sisters*, 1920), choral works, songs, part-songs and organ pieces.

ROSS, Colin Archibald Campbell
7 Dec. 1911 – 27 Feb. 1993
Colin Ross was born in Brecon, Wales and left Christ's College in Brecon to move to Hereford, to be articled to the Cathedral organist Dr Percy Hull, at the age of nineteen. Here, through the Three Choirs Festival, he came into contact with well-known musicians, including Sir Edward Elgar. After a time in the army, he went to the Royal College of Music to study organ, conducting and composition under R.O. Morris and Gordon Jacob. He was later appointed Director of Music at St Paul's Cathedral in Melbourne, Australia, teaching at the Melbourne Conservatorium. He returned to England in 1951 and soon moved to Crawley, where he conducted the Croydon Symphony Orchestra and other orchestras. He then moved north to be Master of the Music at Newcastle Cathedral for twelve years, before settling back south in Worthing, teaching piano and examining in his later years. His compositions include two cantatas, anthems, organ works, songs – (very much in the English tradition), and two string quartets and other works for strings which are strongly atonal. He died in Worthing.

ROSSE, Frederick
1867- 20 Jun. 1940
Born in Jersey, Rosse was educated at Harrow and abroad at Leipzig, Dresden, Brussels and Vienna. His first appointment was as chorus master in Daly's theatre, New York; he then moved to London as musical director in various theatres. As well as composing incidental music for various plays, Rosse wrote a number of orchestral suites (*The Three Musketeers, Petite Suite Moderne, Three Intermezzi, Merchant of Venice*) between 1910 and 1923, as well as a few songs.

ROWLEY, Alec
13 Mar. 1892 – 10 Jan. 1958
Alec Rowley was born in Kew, London, and studied at the Royal Academy of Music with Frederick Corder. He followed a career as a concert pianist, specialising in duets, and in 1920 joined the staff of Trinity College of Music as a teacher and examiner. His compositions include two piano concertos, an oboe concerto, a rhapsody for viola and orchestra, choral music, several chamber works, organ music, piano pieces and songs (*Sacramento* has been fairly well-known). *Three Idylls* for piano and orchestra was performed at the Proms in the 1940s. His not inconsiderable piano music in particular has some character and originality, yet much of it was written with the amateur pianist in mind. Rowley died at Weybridge.

RUBBRA, Edmund Charles
23 May 1901 – 14 Feb. 1986

One of the more prolific of British composers, Edmund Rubbra has at last earned the recognition of having many of his works commercially recorded. He was born in Northamptonshire to working class parents, and spent much of his youth in his uncle's music shop. At the age of fifteen he organised a local concert devoted entirely to the music of Cyril Scott who, having heard of it, offered the youth free lessons. Three years later Rubbra gained a scholarship to the University of Reading, where he studied with Evlyn Howard-Jones and Gustav Holst, who were to join R.O. Morris as his teachers at the Royal College of Music, when he won another scholarship in 1920. During World War Two Rubbra enlisted as an anti-aircraft gunner and, with two of his fellow soldiers, founded a piano trio which became the Rubbra-Gruenberg-Pleeth Trio, lasting until 1956. While at the RCM Rubbra was encouraged to study early English music, as is apparent in the polyphonic idiom of his own music.

Rubbra's compositions, though conservative, are highly individual and have paid no obeisance to fashion. They include an opera (*Bee Bee Bei*), eleven symphonies, concertos for piano, for violin and for viola, two overtures, five masses, a great deal of chamber music (including four string quartets), songs and choral music. That Rubbra was a devout communicant of the Roman faith is easily seen in the sincerity and admirable craftsmanship of his sacred music. His more mystical leanings are illustrated by his very fine Henry Vaughan setting, *The Morning Watch*. In 1947 Rubbra became a lecturer at Oxford University, and in 1961 was appointed a professor of composition at the Guildhall School of Music. He was awarded a CBE in 1960, an Honorary Ll.D. at Leicester in 1959, and a Fellowship of Worcester College, Oxford, in 1963. Rubbra died at Gerrards Cross.

RUBENS, Paul Alfred
29 Apr. 1876 – 5 Feb. 1917
Composer of several popular operettas (*Lady Madcap*, *Miss Hook of Holland*, *My Mimosa Maid*, *The Balkan Princess*, *The Sunshine Girl* etc), Rubens was also a librettist and contributed lyrics and music to many other comic operas. He composed songs and ballads. Rubens was born and died at Falmouth, and went to Winchester College and Oxford University, where he read Law.

RUSSELL, Henry
24 Dec. 1812 – 8 Dec. 1900
Henry Russell was the father of Landon Ronald, and was well known as a singer and composer of songs, over 800 in all, including *A life on the ocean wave* (the regimental march of the Royal Marines), *Woodman spare that tree*, *The Wreck of the Hesperus* and *Cheer, boys, cheer*. He performed in several entertainments with Charles MacKay. Henry Russell was born at Sheerness and studied music at Naples with Rossini. He emigrated to Canada in 1833, then became organist at the First Presbyterian Church of Rochester, New York. He returned to England in 1841 and died in London.

SAINTON, Philippe Catherine Prosper
5 Jun. 1813 – 17 Oct. 1890
Prosper Sainton was born in Toulouse and, after studying violin at the Paris Conservatoire, settled in London in 1845. He was leader of the Philharmonic Society (sometimes deputising for Costa as conductor) and the Covent Garden Orchestra. He taught at the Royal Academy of Music, A.C. Mackenzie being one of his distinguished pupils. He married Charlotte Dolby (see below) in 1860, his wife adopting the surname Sainton-Dolby. He composed two virtuosic violin concertos and a number of shorter works for violin and piano. Prosper Sainton died in London, and is buried with his wife in Highgate cemetery.

SAINTON, Philip Prosper
10 Nov. 1891 – 2 Sep. 1967
Grandson of the above, Philip Sainton was born in France, but the family moved to Godalming in Surrey, where Philip went to nearby Charterhouse School. Like his grandfather, he studied violin, later changing to viola during his course at the Royal Academy of Music, where he was a pupil of Frederick Corder. His military service was as a cipher officer in Cairo. As principal viola in the Queen's Hall Orchestra under Sir Henry Wood, and later in the RPO and BBCSO, he took an interest in composition. His output consists of impressionistic orchestral tone poems (*Sea Pictures*, *Nadir* and *The Island* were broadcast), *Serenade Fantastique* for viola and orchestra, film music for *Moby Dick* (1956) and some songs. He died in Petersfield, Hants.

SAINTON-DOLBY, Charlotte Helen
17 May 1821 – 18 Feb. 1885
Born at Bayswater in London, Charlotte Dolby was accepted into the Royal Academy of Music at the age of eleven. In 1837 she was elected a King's Scholar and she made her debut as a contralto with the Philharmonic Society in 1842. By 1947 she was already well known, and was invited to Leipzig by Mendelssohn to sing with Jenny Lind, appearing at the distinguished Gewandhaus Concerts in Leipzig. She was soon afterwards to win acclaim in France and Holland. Mendelssohn dedicated his Six Songs, Op. 57 to Charlotte and wrote the contralto part in his celebrated *Elijah* especially for her. In 1860 she married the French violinist Prosper Sainton. In 1870, after a successful career as a singer, she gave up performing to devote herself to teaching and composing. Within two years she had founded her Vocal Academy and had published a singing tutor. Many of her own songs and ballads – some sixty-five in number – were performed at the Academy. Sainton-Dolby composed four cantatas: *The Legend of Dorothea*, *The Story of the Faithful Soul*, *Thalassa, the Sea Maiden* (never published) and *Florimel* (for female voices, published posthumously). Charlotte Sainton-Dolby died in London.

SALAMAN, Charles Kensington
31 Mar. 1814 – 23 June 1901
This celebrated pianist was born in London and studied at the Royal Academy of Music and with Charles Neate, later going to Paris to have lessons with Heinrich Herz. After a period in Rome, he was awarded two honorary positions there. He was active in founding various chamber and musical groups, in lecturing and writing. His lectures included a private talk and demonstration on the history of the piano given to Queen Victoria and the royal family. He helped to establish the Musical Society of London, and also the Musical Association (later the Royal Musical Association) in 1874, of which he was the Hon. Secretary. His compositions include a *Rondo al Capriccio* for piano and orchestra, piano works, many anthems and Hebrew services, and some 200 songs in English and Hebrew. He also wrote a *Jubilee Ode for the Shakespeare Commemoration* at Stratford-upon-Avon in 1830.

SALZEDO, Leonard Lopès
24 Sep. 1921 – 6 May 2000
Few people will have heard of Leonard Salzedo but thousands would recognise the first six bars of his *Divertimento* for three trumpets and three trombones, the theme music for over twenty years of BBC's Open University broadcasts. Many too will have heard some of his eighteen film scores, largely for the Hammer horror films, such as *The Revenge of Frankenstein*. Of Spanish-Sephardic descent, Salzedo was born in London, and attended Madame Menges' School of Violin Playing before entering the RCM in 1940. There he studied composition with Herbert Howells and violin with Isolde Menges. His other tutors were Gordon Jacob, George Dyson and Ivor James, and he had also had lessons with William Lloyd Webber before entering the RCM. While still a student, in 1940 he won the Cobbett Prize with his first string quartet. The second such venture won the admiration of Marie Rambert, who commissioned him to write for the Ballet Rambert, the result being *The Fugitive*, the

first of his seventeen ballets (four of them written for the Ballets Nègres) and *The Witch Boy*, which had over 1,000 performances.

Salzedo was an accomplished violinist, playing with the London Philharmonic and the Royal Philharmonic orchestras. While a member of the latter, he assisted Sir Thomas Beecham, building a solid foundation as a conductor. He directed the Ballet Rambert, Scottish Ballet and London City Ballet consecutively until 1986, when he devoted himself full time to composing.

His portfolio includes two symphonies, *Requiem sine Voxibus* for very large orchestra (as yet unperformed, though the composer thought it his finest work), ten string quartets, concertos (for piano, harpsichord, bass viol, violin, viola, cello, double bass, percussion, trumpet), an oratorio, cantatas, songs, many chamber works, pieces for brass band and works for organ and for piano. Rhythm played a major role in Salzedo's work, and he had an ear for unusual instrumental combinations such as occur in his *Ballett Drei* for piano, harpsichord, woodwind, brass and piano, and the viola concerto with a large part for vibraphone as well as harp and strings. He published much of his own music under the name of Lopès. Leonard Salzedo died at Leighton Buzzard, Bedfordshire.

SAMUEL, Harold
23 May 1879 – 15 Jan. 1937

Harold Samuel was born in London and started his career by playing the piano in public houses for five shillings a week. He studied at the Royal Academy of Music under Edward Dannreuther and Stanford. He later joined the staff at the Royal College of Music and lectured at Yale. He began his career as an accompanist and chamber music pianist but, after a series of Bach recitals in 1921, was much in demand as an exponent of Bach's keyboard works, all of which he knew by heart. Samuel composed comic operas (e.g. *Hon'ble Phil*), incidental music to plays, piano and other instrumental pieces, and songs. Samuel died at Hampstead in London.

SANDERS, John Derek
26 Nov. 1933 – 23 Dec. 2003

The legacy that John Sanders left to church music and to the Three Choirs Festival was rewarded by an honorary doctorate from Lambeth, an honorary fellowship of the Royal School of Church Music, an OBE in 1994, and a special service in Westminster Cathedral organised by the Guild of Church Composers just before he died at the age of seventy.

He was born in Wanstead, Essex, and learned to play the organ while at Felsted School, before completing two years at the Royal College of Music. At Cambridge, where he was organ scholar at Gonville and Caius College, he was taught by Patrick Hadley. After graduation he undertook his national service with the Royal Artillery, then became assistant to Herbert Sumsion, organist of Gloucester Cathedral. He directed the St. Cecilia Singers and taught at Kings School, Gloucester. In the 1960s he spent four years at Chester Cathedral as organist and choirmaster (also reviving the Chester Music Festival) before returning to Gloucester in 1967 to replace Sumsion. His work at the Cathedral and for the Three Choirs Festival was supplemented with conductorships of the Gloucester Choral Society and the Gloucester Symphony Orchestra. He was also musical director of Cheltenham Ladies' College.

Sanders composed a great deal of church music (such as a *Requiem*, four cantatas – one for brass, double choir and soloists, *Urbs beata*), and some organ works. His secular music included four song cycles.

SANDERSON, Wilfrid Ernest
23 Dec. 1878 – 10 Dec. 1935
The son of a Wesleyan minister, Wilfrid Ernest Sanderson was born at Ipswich. After attending the City of London School he was articled to Frederick Bridge at Westminster Abbey, where one of his fellow pupils was Edward Bairstow. He gained a B.Mus. at Durham in 1900, and became a teacher and organist in London. In 1903 he moved north to Doncaster, where he was appointed organist of the parish church. He helped to found the Doncaster Amateur Operatic Society, conducting it for many years with great success. He also directed the Doncaster Musical Society and was an examiner for Trinity College of Music.

Sanderson composed church services, anthems and hymn-tunes, piano pieces, and over 170 songs. Of the latter, *My dear soul* sold 30,000 copies, but by no means all were in the same popular idiom; most display an easy fluency with the medium and some considerable charm. Best known are probably *Devonshire Cream and Cider*, *Shipmates o' mine*, *Drake goes west* and *Up from Somerset*. Sanderson sometimes used the pseudonym William Arnold. He died at Nutfield near Reigate.

SANTLEY, Charles
28 Feb. 1834 – 22 Sep. 1922

A renowned baritone and teacher of singing, Charles Santley was born in Liverpool, where he was a chorister in the cathedral. Having given a farewell concert in his home city, he went to Milan to study with Gaetano Nava for two years, before coming to London to study with Manuel Garcia. As one of the most renowned bass-baritones of his time, he sang at many of the big UK festivals, and toured America and Australia as well as singing many operatic roles. He composed a mass, anthems and church services for the Roman Catholic church, and several orchestral works – sometimes using the pseudonym Ralph Betterton. Santley was knighted in 1907. He died at Hove.

SAWYER, Frank Joseph
19 Jun. 1857 – 1908
Sawyer studied at the Leipzig Conservatoire under Ernst Friedrich Richter. A Brighton musician, he was a pupil of John Frederick Bridge. Having gained his Mus.Doc. at Oxford, he taught sight-singing for a while at the Royal College of Music. As well as being an organist, he lectured extensively on both music and dance, and is notable for reviving the organ works of the blind composer John Stanley. Sawyer became Hon. Secretary of the Royal College of Organists in 1907, a year before his death. His works include oratorios, sacred and dramatic cantatas, a *Concertstück* for organ and orchestra, and various pieces for violin, piano, part-songs and duets. He published a textbook on extemporisation, and a harmony course in conjunction with his former teacher Bridge.

SCOTT, Cyril Meir
27 Sep. 1879 – 31 Dec. 1970

Additionally a poet, philosopher, mystic, and an authority on alternative medicine, Cyril Scott won in his youth an international reputation as a composer. Though hailed as progressive in his earlier years, when he sometimes abandoned key signatures and bar-lines (dubbed by some as 'The English Debussy'), his later works grew more conventional and his music faded into obscurity, save for a few salon pieces that remained popular.

Scott was born at Oxton in Cheshire and, being a child prodigy at the piano, he was sent to Frankfurt at the age of twelve to study with Uzielli at the Hoch Conservatory, returning home after eighteen months to study in Liverpool. He returned a few years later to take composition lessons with Iwan Knorr, where he met the other British students of the Frankfurt Group (Gardiner, O'Neill, Grainger and Quilter). Scott was a prolific composer and his works include four symphonies (of which two early ones were withdrawn – though No.1 has been recorded), two ballets, two piano concertos, concertos for violin, cello, oboe and harpsichord, other orchestral pieces, choral works, songs, chamber and instrumental music, including four string quartets (by no means conventional), and many piano works. He also wrote four operas, of which *The Alchemist* of 1925 may have the greatest merit. Scott died in Eastbourne. Although his music tends to be neglected nowadays, he wrote some worthwhile music and some consider his piano sonatas to stand among the best.

SCOTT, Francis
25 Jan. 1880 –6 Nov. 1958

F.G. Scott has been described as one of the finest of British song composers, though his music is little known outside Scotland. He was born at Hawick, Borders, and studied music at Durham University and with Roger Ducasse in Paris. He taught English and was a lecturer in music at a Glasgow college. Scott composed works for full orchestra and for strings, a ballad for baritone and orchestra, and a great many songs and part-songs. He often drew inspiration from Scottish folk music, and many of his songs were skilful settings of poets such as MacDiarmid and Burns. He died in Glasgow.

SCOTT, Marion Margaret
16 Jul. 1877 – 24 Dec. 1953

Marion Scott, most noted as a critic, musicologist (she was an expert on Haydn and cataloguer of his music), biographer of Beethoven, violinist, music promoter, as well as Ivor Gurney's friend and guardian in his later years, has left us several songs and chamber music, all unpublished. The most important of these are songs with orchestra (*To Music* and *In Early Spring*) and with string quartet (*Rondel* and *The idle life I lead*); and in addition there are a substantial quantity of songs with piano, a violin sonata and a suite for piano trio. All are these in the RCM library.

Scott was born in Lewisham, and after early piano lessons took up the violin. She entered the Royal College of Music, where she studied composition with Walford Davies and Stanford – being (with Marie Wurm) one of Stanford's first female students – and violin with Arbos. After graduating, she remained with the RCM, working as director of the Student Union, which she co-founded, and later as editor of the College's magazine. As leader of the Marion Scott Quartet, she championed works by contemporary composers, giving first performances of chamber works by Stanford, Parry, Bridge and Hurlstone amongst others. She was instrumental in the founding of the Society of Women Musicians, guiding its direction and always seeking equal opportunities for women in music, and later turning to writing and lecturing. Scott met Ivor Gurney at the RCM in 1911, encouraged him in his work, and looked after his affairs when he was committed to the City of London Mental Hospital. She continued to be the driving force behind promoting Gurney's music and poetry after his death, until her own death from colon cancer some fifteen years later.

SEARLE, Humphrey
26 Aug. 1915 – 12 May 1982
Humphrey Searle was, with Elizabeth Lutyens, the first successful British composer to espouse the twelve-note system of composition. Despite this, his music has always been approachable, due to his flexible and undogmatic interpretation of twelve-note technique and to his music's rich vein of Romanticism, deriving in part from Liszt, on whom Searle was an authority. He was born in Oxford and graduated in Classics there. After a term at the Royal College of Music under Ireland, Jacob and R.O. Morris, he went to the New Vienna Conservatory, and while in Vienna studied privately with Webern. He returned to England as a programme producer with the BBC, but at the outbreak of World War Two he entered the Services. When hostilities ended, Searle was in Germany working with Hugh Trevor-Roper in sorting out the facts of Hitler's last moments. He spent two more years with the BBC before deciding to devote himself more to composition. For five years he was musical adviser to Sadler's Wells, and in 1964 served a year as composer-in-residence at Stanford University. From 1965 he taught at the RCM, but left in 1976 to return to Stanford, and from 1968 he was Guest Professor at the Badische Hochschule für Musik in Karlsruhe.

Humphrey Searle composed three operas (*The Diary of a Madman*, *The Photo of the Colonel* and *Hamlet*), six symphonies, three ballets, two piano concertos, other orchestral and string works, choral/orchestral music (two works based on poems by Edith Sitwell: *Gold Coast Customs* and *The Shadow of Cain*; the other on extracts from Joyce's *Finnegan's Wake: Riverrun*), songs and song-cycles, chamber music, a piano sonata, and incidental music to films, TV and radio. Searle died in London.

SEIBER, Mátyás Gyorgy
4 May 1905 – 24 Sep. 1960
Matyas Seiber was primarily a teacher, as witnessed by the success of so many of his pupils: Francis Chagrin, Racine Fricker, Hugh Wood, Don Banks, Anthony Milner, Anthony Gilbert and Francis Routh – to name but a few. He was born in Budapest and studied there with Kodály. After much travelling he joined the staff of the Frankfurt Conservatoire in 1927, organising a course in jazz, conducting, and playing the cello in the Lenzewski Quartet.

Seiber came to London in 1935 (where he remained for the rest of his life), and lectured at Morley College. In 1943 he co-founded the Society for New Music, and in 1945 founded the Dorian Singers. Seiber's music is varied and sometimes makes use of serial technique. It includes an opera and operettas, a cantata based on James

Joyce's *Ulysses* and *Three Fragments* (also based on Joyce), orchestral suites, concertante works for the violin, viola, horn, clarinet, flute and cello, string quartets, incidental music to films (his 'bread and butter' work, perhaps best of which was for an animated version of Orwell's *Animal Farm*), choruses and songs, and solo pieces for violin and for piano. His great interest in jazz may be seen in some of his works, and in *Improvisations* for Jazz Band and Orchestra (written in collaboration with John Dankworth). Seiber attempted to synthesise a 'third stream' type of music which eliminated the boundaries between jazz and classical music. He wrote articles on Bartók, jazz, and on music generally, and published manuals on accordion playing and jazz drumming techniques. Mátyás Seiber was killed in a car crash in Johannesburg at the age of fifty-five.

SELBY, Bertram Luard
12 Feb. 1853 – 26 Dec. 1919

Bertram Selby (later more commonly known as Luard-Selby) was born at Ightham in Kent. He was a pupil of Reinecke and Jadassohn at Leipzig. His first organist's post was at the age of thirteen, and he held a number of such posts, culminating as organist at Salisbury and Rochester Cathedrals, holding the latter position for sixteen years. He composed two operas (*The Ring* and *Adela*), a comic opera (*Weather or No*), incidental music, cantatas, church music, piano and organ pieces, songs, piano quintets, and a violin sonata. Selby died in Lincolnshire.

SEVERN, Thomas Henry
5 Nov. 1801 – 15 Apr. 1881

Little is known of his life. We know that he was born and died in London, was self-taught in music and was known as a teacher. He was primarily a song writer, although his cantata *The Spirit of the Shell* (1846) had some popularity in its time. One of his two brothers was a double bassist in the principal London orchestras, the other, Joseph, a painter.

SHAKESPEARE, William
16 Jun. 1849 – 1 Nov. 1931

William Shakespeare was born in Croydon and studied at the Royal Academy of Music with Sterndale Bennett. Having been awarded the Mendelssohn Scholarship he went to the Leipzig Conservatory, and to Milan where he was a singing pupil of Francesco Lamperti. From 1878 Shakespeare was a professor of singing at the RAM and conducted concerts there, sometimes singing in concerts and in oratorios. He composed a symphony, piano concertos, overtures and other orchestral pieces, string quartets and a variety of instrumental sonatas. He died in London.

SHARPE, Herbert Francis
1 Mar. 1861 – 14 Oct. 1925

Born in Halifax, Herbert Sharpe studied at the National Training School for Music. He began his musical career as a concert pianist and in 1884 became a professor of piano at the Royal College of Music, and in 1890 one of the original examiners for the Associated Board. He was the father of Cedric Sharpe, the noted cellist. He composed a comic opera, an orchestral overture, pieces for flute and for violin, piano solo and duets, songs, part-songs and vocal trios. Sharpe died in London.

SHAW, Geoffrey Turton
14 Nov. 1879 – 14 Apr. 1943
Geoffrey Shaw, brother of Martin Shaw, was born and died in London. He was a chorister at St Paul's Cathedral under Sir George Martin, until he won an organ scholarship to Caius College, Cambridge, where he studied with Stanford and Wood. He was appointed Inspector of Music for the Board of Education, and did much to raise the standards of music teaching in schools. He wrote several books on music, and was very active in reviving interest in the works of Henry Purcell. Shaw composed a ballad-opera (*All at Sea*), music for T.S. Eliot's play *The Rock*, choral settings of poems by Masefield, Binyon and others, songs and part-songs, church music and pieces for organ.

SHAW, Martin Edward Fallas
9 Mar. 1875 – 24 Oct. 1958
Elder brother of Geoffrey Shaw and son of a well-known organist, Martin Shaw was born in Kennington, London. He studied with Stanford at the Royal College of Music, and divided his career between conducting, composing and playing the organ. His works include a ballad-opera (*Mr Pepys*), light operas, musical dramas and incidental music, a fantasia for piano and orchestra, choral/orchestral works, chamber music, songs and church music. Martin Shaw edited, with Vaughan Williams, the well-known hymnal *Songs of Praise* and the *Oxford Book of Carols*, and set a new standard in promoting English church music that was free from much of the prevailing sentimentality of the previous generation. He died at Southwold in Suffolk.

SHERLAW-JOHNSON, Robert
21 May 1932 – 3 Nov. 2000
Robert Sherlaw-Johnson spent the final thirty years of his life as a highly respected teacher at Oxford University, first as lecturer, then reader and fellow of Worcester College. He was born in Sunderland, and attended Gosforth Grammar School in Newcastle upon Tyne before entering King's College there (a college of Durham University). After graduation he won a scholarship to the Royal Academy of Music. A Charles Black award allowed him to go to Paris to study composition with Nadia Boulanger and piano with Jacques Février. But the formative influences on his life's work were probably the classes in analysis that he took with Olivier Messiaen at the Conservatoire de Paris. He would later, in 1970, complete his doctoral thesis at Leeds University, a thesis that led to his still definitive book *Messiaen*, a study of the master's work (revised in 1989). For a time his own compositions showed the influence of the latter, and as a prodigious pianist he gained a reputation as an exponent of Messiaen's music.

Sherlaw-Johnson's first teaching post, from 1961 was at Leeds University. He became Director of Music at Bradford Girls' Grammar School in 1963 and two years later was recruited, together with other young composers who had absorbed European modernism, by Wilfred Mellers at York University. He spent five years there before moving to Oxford, where he founded the Electronic Music studio. In 1985 he was visiting professor of composition at the Eastman School of Music in Rochester (USA), and in 1988 he was awarded an Oxford doctorate in music. His conversion to Roman Catholicism led to his writing some liturgical works, and he was for many years musical director of the Spode Music Week, a course for musicians in the Roman faith. Sherlaw-Johnson wrote technically demanding works for the piano (*Asterogenesis* and three piano sonatas among them), and works for soprano, piano and tape, written for Noelle Barker (*Green Whispers of Gold* and *Praise of Heaven and Earth*). He never abandoned his north-eastern roots and wrote a *Northumbrian* symphony and an opera, *The Lambton Worm*, based on a folk-song about a giant worm ("with greet big heed and greet big gob and greet big goggly eyes") that terrorised the Lambton area of Durham.

He played the Northumbrian small pipes and was also a keen bell-ringer who took an interest in music that incorporated bell chimes. He died while ringing a peal in Appleton church tower, near Oxford. His last work, a mass, was premiered the year after he died.

SIMPSON, Robert Wilfred Levick
2 Mar. 1921 – 21 Nov. 1997
Few composers have deserved their own society of devotees as much as Robert Simpson. The Robert Simpson Society was formed in 1980 to promote his music, Simpson being very modest about his own highly impressive output. He was born in Royal Leamington Spa and went to Westminster School before studying medicine for two years in London, where music proved to be a greater motivation. It was here that took lessons with Herbert Howells. At the same time, as a staunch pacifist and conscientious objector, he served with an Air Raid Precautions mobile surgical unit throughout the London Blitz.

When the war finished, by which time Simpson was already lecturing in music and had founded the Exploratory Concerts Society, Howells persuaded him to take a Durham B.Mus. In 1951 he followed this with a doctorate and joined the staff of the BBC. A year later he published his pioneering and influential study of Carl Nielsen. For almost thirty years Simpson was a music producer and broadcaster with the Corporation, inaugurating the *Innocent Ear* series and, towards the end of his career, campaigning against the board's decision to do away with five of the eleven BBC orchestras. He eventually resigned in 1980, during the musicians' strike that brought about that year's cancellation of the BBC Prom concerts. His deep anxiety over the Corporation's music policies motivated him to publish a powerful critique, *The Proms and Natural Justice*. By 1986 his dislike of Thatcherism led to his emigration to Tralee Bay in County Kerry, where five years later a debilitating stroke left him in severe pain for the rest of his life.

Robert Simpson wrote significantly on Nielsen, Sibelius, Bruckner and Beethoven. His admiration for Beethoven's music informed much of his own work. He composed eleven symphonies (four early ones were discarded), concertos for violin, piano, cello and flute, fifteen string quartets and other chamber works, music for brass band, two motets and some piano pieces. For his contributions to astronomy he was rewarded with a Fellowship of the Royal Astronomical Association.

SIVRAI, Jules de   See **ROEKEL**, Mrs J.

SLATER, Gordon Archbold
1 Mar. 1896 – 1979
For the greater part of his career Gordon Slater was organist of Lincoln Cathedral, conductor of the Lincoln Music Society, and lecturer at Nottingham and Hull universities. He was born at Harrogate and studied music privately and at York Minster. His first appointment was at Boston Parish Church, then at Leicester Cathedral. Slater also adjudicated, and was a respected recitalist. He composed pieces for organ and for piano, songs and choral music, anthems and hymn-tunes (incl. *St Botolph*). In 1974 he was awarded an OBE.

SMART, Henry Thomas
26 Oct. 1813 – 6 Jul. 1879
Largely self-taught, though he had some tuition from W.H. Kearns, Henry Smart was renowned not only for his improvisation at the organ but was reputed also in his playing to have modulated a tone higher for each verse of the hymns he disliked, so that the congregation could eventually sing no more! He was born in London, and considered the Army and Law as careers before eventually devoting himself to music. His first post was as organist in Blackburn, but he settled in London in 1836, becoming an authority on organ design and editing works for the Handel Society. He composed operas (*Bertha, or The Gnome of Hartzburg* was produced in 1855; two others were unfinished), cantatas (*The Bride of Dunkerron* and *King René's Daughter* were once popular), anthems, organ works, songs (*Only a rose*; *The Lady of the Sea*) and part-songs, of which his six-part *Stars of the summer night* is notable. Several of his hymn-tunes are still used – among others, 'Light's abode, celestial Salem' and 'God of mercy, God of grace'. For the last fifteen years of his life Henry Smart was blind. He died at Hampstead in London, and is buried there.

SMITH, Alice Mary
19 May 1839 – 4 Dec. 1884
Alice Mary Smith was born in London into a relatively well-off family. She was a pupil first of Sterndale Bennett and then of G.A. Macfarren, and has until recently been remembered for a few published songs, the first of which appeared in 1857. Ten years later she married Frederick Meadows White, a lawyer, but continued to append her maiden name to her compositions. As a Female Professional Associate of the Philharmonic Society and Hon. RAM, she was in her time highly regarded as a composer of chamber music, orchestral music and cantatas, as well as songs, duets and part-songs, and many of her works received a number of performances. She was supported in her efforts at composition not only by her husband, but also by conductors  of the time such as Wilhelm Ganz, Sir Julius Benedict, August Manns and Ebenezer Prout.

Smith's oeuvre in larger-scale works was unusual for a woman at that time. She wrote two symphonies (published by A-R Editions), six concert overtures

(*Endymion* – 2 versions, *Lalla Rookh, Vivien, The Masque of Pandora* and *Jason, or the Argonauts and the Sirens*), a clarinet concerto (lost) – performed by Henry Lazarus at the Norwich Festival in 1871, the slow movement of which was later played on two subsequent occasions – an *Introduction and Allegro* for piano and orchestra, and other orchestral works. Her chamber music includes four piano quartets (the first of which was performed when she was only twenty-one), trios, three string quartets, a clarinet sonata, an operetta (*Gisela of Rüdesheim*), a setting of Longfellow's *The Masque of Pandora*, and four cantatas: *Ode to the North-East Wind, Ode to the Passions, Song of the Little Baltung* and *The Red King* – the last two for male voices. *Ode to The Passions*, a large-scale work for soloists, chorus and orchestra, was well received at the Hereford Festival in 1882, and was described by some critics at the time as being 'near to greatness'. Her last work, *The Valley of Remorse*, remained incomplete at her death. Of her forty songs and duets, *O that we two were maying* (words by Charles Kingsley) is one that has lasted. She also composed a few piano pieces, some early ones of which were published under the pseudonym of 'Emil Künstler'.

Alice Mary Smith was almost certainly the first female composer in the United Kingdom to have a symphony, written at the age of twenty-four, publicly performed (in 1863), and one of the very few women of her time who had any success in writing in large-scale forms. She died in London of typhoid fever.

SMITH, Edward Sydney
14 Jul. 1839 – 3 Mar. 1889

In addition to a great many transcriptions, Sydney Smith contributed some valuable piano pieces to the Victorian repertoire. His *La Harpe Éolienne* and various fantasias on operatic themes were once very popular. He was born at Dorchester and studied music first with his parents and later with S.S. Wesley before going to Leipzig as a pupil of Moscheles and Plaidy (for piano) and Grutzmacher (for cello). He settled in London in 1859, and gained a reputation as a piano teacher and recitalist. In his last years illness forced him to relinquish his career, and he suffered some financial hardship as a result. He died in London.

His brother, **Boynton Smith** (b. 23 Feb. 1837) was also a composer of church music and piano pieces in a popular vein.

SMITH, Joseph Leopold
26 Nov. 1881 – 18 Apr. 1952

Leo Smith was born in Birmingham. He went to Manchester University and the Royal Manchester College of Music, where he studied with Henry Hiles and Fuchs for cello. In 1910 he emigrated to Canada and joined the staff of the Royal Conservatory of Music in Toronto. He became principal cellist of the Toronto Philharmonic and Symphony orchestras, edited the Toronto Conservatory quarterly Review, and in 1928 was appointed Professor of Music at Toronto University. He composed some orchestral music, string quartets, songs and part-songs, and pieces for cello and for piano. In addition to books on the rudiments of music he wrote a valuable account of music in the seventeenth and eighteenth centuries.

SMITH, Ronald Bertram
3 Jan. 1922 – 27 May 2004

A distinguished champion and exponent of the music of Charles-Valentin Alkan, concert pianist Ronald Smith also wrote a definitive study of Alkan and his music. He was born in London, and first lessons at the piano with his mother led to early scholarships at the Brighton School of Music and to Lewes County Grammar School. In 1938 a further scholarship took him to the Royal Academy of Music, where he studied composition with Theodore Holland and piano with Percy Waller. Further piano classes in Paris completed and perfected Smith's technical grounding.

As well as being a highly regarded performer and teacher, Ronald Smith composed a violin concerto, other orchestral works, including a symphonic prelude (a student effort), and piano pieces, the most successful of which was his *Scherzetto* for piano.

SMITH BRINDLE, Reginald
5 Jan. 1917 – 9 Sep. 2003

Very little of Reginald Smith Brindle's music has ever been commercially recorded, though much of it is highly worthy of public airing. His many works for guitar are among the best by British composers, while his *Creation Epic* for orchestra (1964) and *Via Crucis* for cello and strings (1962) are particularly deserving. He was born in Bamber Bridge, Lancashire, to two amateur musicians. At Lostock Hall school he began to learn the piano, then the clarinet, playing in Hutton Grammar School's orchestra. Saxophone and guitar soon followed, and he won a prize for the latter in a 'Melody Maker' competition. His parents, however, insisted that he enter an architect's office and gain a qualification, and he found playing saxophone in a jazz group brought musical gratification – and some money. In 1937 he was inspired by a recital in Chester Cathedral to take up the organ, and he was later to write some impressive pieces for it.

War interrupted, and he spent seven years as captain in the Royal Engineers, serving in North Africa and Sicily. An exchange of cigarettes for a guitar, with an Italian prisoner of war, gave Smith Brindle the impetus to compose thirteen pieces for the instrument before demobilisation, one of them (arranged for strings) winning a composition prize in Rome. During an arts course in Florence he met his future wife, Giulia Borsi. After the war he began a B.Mus. course at University College of North Wales, Bangor, but gained the qualification from London University. He returned to Italy, studying at the Accademia Santa Cecilia in Rome with Pizzetti, meeting many of the Italian avant-garde community and steeping himself in their music. He also had some lessons with Dallapiccola. His eight years in Italy equipped him to write masterful texts on Italian modernism and avant-garde composition.

In 1957 he applied successfully for a lectureship at Bangor, eventually becoming Professor. From 1970-81 he was Professor of Music at Surrey University. Smith Brindle's own music was stylistically varied – he admired such diversity in Stravinsky's work – and among his compositions are two symphonies, a concerto for five instruments and percussion, a clarinet concerto and other orchestral pieces, choral and vocal works, a chamber opera (*The Death of Antigone*), a great many pieces for guitar and several for organ, works for percussion, and some electronic music. He found time to paint in oils and watercolours, and was a keen amateur astronomer. Smith Brindle died in Faversham.

SMYTH, Ethel Mary
22 Apr. 1858 – 8 May 1944

Dame Ethel Smyth

Daughter of General J.H. Smyth of the Bengali Royal Artillery, Ethel was born in Marylebone, London. Always headstrong and passionate, even when mountaineering or playing tennis, she spent much of her life fighting for women's rights and for acceptance of herself as a composer at a time when this was not considered a respectable career for a woman. In 1911 she was sentenced to two months in prison as a militant suffragette, having both fallen in love with Emmeline Pankhurst and thrown a stone through the Colonial Secretary's window. As it turned out she served only three weeks in Holloway prison. At the age of nineteen, after staging a rebellion against her reluctant family, Ethel Smyth went to study with Reinecke (composition), Jadassohn (harmony) and Maas (piano) at the Leipzig Conservatory, but very soon decided that she needed something a little less staid and so became a pupil of Heinrich von Herzogenberg. In 1884 her string quartet, Op. 1, was performed to wide acclaim, and from then on her success as a composer was assured.

Ethel Smyth composed an overture and a serenade, a *Solemn Mass* (first performed in 1893 to great interest, but not revived until 1924 by Adrian Boult), a double concerto for violin and horn, string quartets, a quintet and other chamber works, juvenile pieces for piano and for organ, songs and song cycles, a choral symphony (*The Prison*), other choral/orchestral works (*Hey, Nonny, No* and *Sleepless Dreams*) and six operas (*Fantasio, Der Wald, The Boatswain's Mate, Fête Galante*, a farce *Entente Cordiale*, and her greatest success *The Wreckers*, premiered by Beecham and performed also in Paris, Leipzig and Prague). Her works were championed not just by Beecham but by Mahler, Bruno Walter and Hermann Levi. In 1910 Ethel Smyth was awarded honorary doctorates from Durham, Oxford and St. Andrews universities and twelve years later became a Dame of the British Empire. Nine volumes of her memoirs have been published and offer entertaining and instructive reading. She also wrote a biography of Henry Brewster (her librettist for *The Prison*). Ethel Smyth died at Woking having just begun a fifth volume of autobiography entitled *A Fresh Start*.

SOMERVELL, Arthur
5 Jun. 1863 – 2 May 1937

Born in Windermere, Arthur Somervell went to Uppingham School and King's College, Cambridge, where studied music with Stanford. After two years at Berlin Hochschule für Musik with Kiel and Bargiel, he went to the Royal College of Music (where he later taught), and then took lessons privately with Parry. In 1901 he succeeded Sir John Stainer as Inspector of Music for England, Wales and Scotland, and was knighted in 1929 for his services to music.

Known nowadays for his more well-known works – the song cycle *Maud* (to poems by Tennyson), *The Passion of Christ* and his cantata *Christmas* – Somervell also composed a symphony (entitled *Thalassa*), a piano concerto and a violin concerto, suites and other orchestral works, music for chorus and orchestra, a mass, songs, and pieces for violin and for piano.

SOUSTER, Timothy Andrew James
29 Jan. 1943 – 1 Mar. 1994

Tim Souster was a founder member (with Roger Smalley, Robin Thompson and Andrew Powell) of Intermodulation – a live, electronics performing group, and was highly regarded as the composer of music for over forty television documentaries and dramas, among them *The Hitchhiker's Guide to the Galaxy*, *The Midas Touch*, *Great River Journeys* and *The Green Man* (which won a BAFTA award). Souster was born in Bletchley, Buckinghamshire, and went to Bedford Modern School before entering New College, Oxford, to study with Bernard Rose, David Lumsden and Egon Wellesz. He followed this with lessons at Darmstadt with Stockhausen, and with Richard Rodney Bennett. Within a year of leaving university he became a producer for the BBC's Third Programme, championing many avant-garde works.

He was already experimenting with electronic music, though not abandoning works for more conventional media, and in 1969 his *Titus Groan Music* for wind quintet, ring modulator, amplifiers and tape appeared. In 1969 he was appointed composer in residence at King's College, Cambridge, where Intermodulation was born. Souster never seemed to stand still; by 1971 he had moved to Cologne to assist Stockhausen, then to Berlin as a composer in residence. Back in England in 1975 he gained a Leverhulme Research Fellowship to Keele University, establishing an electronic music studio and founding another performing group, OdB, which had some affiliations to rock music. In 1978 six months at Stanford University in California allowed Souster to develop his electronic skills even further before he returned to Cambridge in 1979.

Many of Souster's works fall under no easily definable category, hybridising electronic and conventional resources in bewildering permutations and combinations. Notable are *Equalisation* (for Equale Brass) and *Echoes* (for Besses o'the Barn Band), *Waste Land Music* and *Triple Music II* for three orchestras (a Prom commission). He also wrote for piano and for percussion, more pieces for brass (*The Transistor Radio of St. Narcissus* for flugelhorn and electronic tape should be revived), vocal works, and some works for the children at Channing School in Highgate, where his wife was Director of Music. A brief scholarship in Siena elicited a massive choral-orchestral work that has never been performed. He died after contracting an undiagnosed infection during a holiday in Thailand.

SORABJI, Khaikosru Shapurji
14 Aug. 1892 – 15 Oct. 1988

A highly individualistic and independent composer, Sorabji forbade all performances of his works from 1940 until the mid 1970s, when he gave express permission to a select few, such as Michael Habermann and Yonty Solomon, to play his music in public. His works are often on a grand scale and written with superb fluency, skill and wit. Their sheer quantity, both in notes and in length, is such as to mesmerise the listener and give the impression of a veritable cataract of sound: the *Organ Symphony* of 1924 is written for the most part on four staves for a soloist with seemingly six hands, while the *Opus Clavicembalisticum* (1929-30), written at times on five staves and lasting four hours, appears in the Guinness Book of Records (though it is by no means the longest of his works for piano). Despite their complexity, however, these works retain a warmth and appeal that cry out for performance.

The details of Sorabji's life are difficult to sort out, as the composer himself has provided conflicting accounts. He was born at Chingford in Essex, son of a Parsi businessman and a Spanish-Sicilian singer. Rumours that he was baptised 'Leon Dudley' have been denied by himself. In his 'teens he familiarised himself thoroughly with the works of Busoni, Schoenberg, Bartók, Scriabin and many other progressive composers who were not at all fashionable in Edwardian England. A prodigious pianist himself, he performed his own works in public until 1936, when he withdrew from the public eye. He attracted attention as an uncompromising reviewer and published two books of musical criticism, 'Around Music' (1932) and 'Mi contra fa' (1947).

Sorabji's works include five piano concertos, *Jāmī* Symphony for baritone, chorus and orchestra (a massive work running to over 800 pages), other symphonic works, five numbered piano sonatas and other piano pieces, chamber music and songs.

SPARK, William
28 Oct. 1823 – 16 Jun. 1897

William Spark was born at Exeter, where his father was a lay-vicar at the Cathedral. He studied with S.S. Wesley and followed a career as a writer and organist, holding positions successively at Leeds, Tiverton, Daventry and Winchester. He returned to Leeds in 1850 as organist of St George's for thirty years, and was also appointed organist of the Town Hall, whose organ he helped to design. While at Leeds he founded the town's Madrigal and Motet Society. Spark edited several journals (including 'The Organist's Quarterly Journal'), wrote a biography of his friend Henry Smart, and composed oratorios, cantatas, anthems, services, glees and organ pieces. He died in Leeds.

SPEAIGHT, Joseph
24 Oct. 1868 – 20 Nov. 1947

Joseph Speaight was born in London. He was a pupil at the Guildhall School of Music, taking piano with Ernst Pauer and Li Calsi, and composition with R. Orlando Morgan. Though he played the violin and organ, Speaight was primarily a pianist, and in 1894 toured as accompanist to Madame Patey. He taught for some time at Wellington College, then was appointed a professor at the Guildhall School of Music. In 1919 he joined the staff of Trinity College of Music. His compositions include two symphonies, symphonic poems and suites, a piano concerto, string quartets and quintets, songs and part-songs, works for voice and orchestra, and pieces for violin, cello, and piano.

SPEER, Charlton Templeman
21 Nov. 1859 – 1921

Charlton Speer was born at Cheltenham and studied at the Royal Academy of Music with G.A. and Walter Macfarren for piano, and with Charles Steggall for organ. He held various posts as organist, and composed operas, works for chorus and orchestra (of which *The Day Dream* on texts by Tennyson had several successful performances), a symphonic poem, songs, piano pieces and church music.

SPEER, William Henry
9 Nov. 1863 – 31 May 1937

Cousin of the above, W.H. Speer was born in London, and took organ lessons with Walter Battison Haynes and Charles Harford Lloyd in the West Country, then with Parry and Stanford before attending the Royal College of Music. He was later organist at Bexhill Parish Church. He composed a symphony, an overture, an orchestral rhapsody, a string quartet, a ballad for chorus and small orchestra (*The Jackdaw of Rheims*) and organ and piano pieces. He died in Sidmouth, Devon.

SQUIRE, William Henry
8 Aug. 1871 – 17 Mar. 1963
W. H. Squire was born at Ross-on-Wye in Herefordshire. He won a cello scholarship to the Royal College of Music in 1883 and studied there with Edward Howell, also studying composition with Parry. As a cellist he appeared frequently as soloist at major festivals, and with the Queen's Hall Orchestra and LSO. He was a professor at the RCM and the Guildhall School of Music, and a vice-chairman of the Performing Rights Society. He was also for a time, from 1885, Keeper of Printed Music at the British Museum. His compositions include two operettas, a cello concerto and other orchestral works, numerous pieces for cello and piano, and songs – several of which became well known. Squire died at St John's Wood in London.

STAINER, John
6 Jun. 1840 – 31 Mar. 1901
John Stainer was born in Southwark, London. He studied harmony with William Bayley and counterpoint with Charles Steggall, and was a choirboy at St Paul's Cathedral. At sixteen he became organist at St Michael's College, Tenbury, and thereafter held several posts including those at Magdalen College, Oxford (at the age of nineteen), and St Paul's Cathedral (from 1872, succeeding Sir John Goss). He was Principal of the National Training School for Music, and Professor of Music at Oxford, writing textbooks and performing much valuable  research. His *Dufay and his Contemporaries* is still a seminal work. Stainer was decorated with the French Legion of Honour in 1880, and received a knighthood in 1888, by which time his sight was failing. He composed oratorios, cantatas, anthems, church services and organ pieces. His *Crucifixion* is still performed widely. (His sister Ann Stainer was a noted organist, holding a post in London for fifty years without missing a service.) John Stainer died in Verona while on a trip to Italy, and there is a memorial to him in St Paul's Cathedral. He is buried in Holywell Cemetery, Oxford.

STANFORD, Charles Villiers
30 Sep. 1852 – 29 Mar. 1924
Although the names of Parry and Stanford have always been linked as the architects of the late nineteenth century English musical renaissance, the relationship between the sensitive, genteel Englishman and the acerbic, often bad-tempered Irishman was for many years a fractious one.

Stanford was born in Dublin where he studied music privately with Sir Robert Prescott Stewart and Michael Quarry. In 1870 he went up to Cambridge on a classical and organ scholarship to Queen's College, then went to Germany as a pupil of Carl Reinecke and Friedrich Kiel. His lifelong mentor was, however, Joseph Joachim. As conductor for twenty years of the Cambridge University Musical Society, he introduced many new works to English audiences, including several of his own

compositions. But his name first came to public attention through his music to Tennyson's *Queen Mary* in 1875, and in the following year his first symphony won second prize to that of F.W. Davenport in the Alexandra Palace competition. At the opening of the Royal College of Music in 1883 he was appointed a professor of composition and orchestral playing, and in 1887 he succeeded Sir George Macfarren as Professor of Music at Cambridge. Stanford also conducted the Bach Choir, the Leeds Philharmonic Society and Leeds Triennial Festival chorus. At the RCM his pupils included Vaughan Williams, Hurlstone, Coleridge-Taylor, Ireland, Holst, Bridge, Howells, Jacob, Boughton, Goossens, Bliss, Benjamin and Gurney, as well as other names.

Stanford's work was justly rewarded with honorary doctorates from Oxford, Cambridge, Durham and Leeds, a knighthood in 1902, and membership of the Royal Academy of Arts in Berlin, being the only English composer ever to achieve this honour. Stanford's compositions were many and varied, and include seven symphonies, orchestral overtures, concertos for clarinet, piano (three) and violin (two), much chamber music (including eight string quartets), incidental music, a *Requiem* (to rival any) and other choral works, church services, songs and part-songs, five organ sonatas, pieces for piano and for violin, and nine operas (including *The Veiled Prophet of Khorassan*, *Savonarola*, *Shamus O'Brien*, *The Canterbury Pilgrims*, *Much Ado about Nothing*, *The Critic*, *The Travelling Companion*). Stanford suffered a stroke on St Patrick's Day in 1924, and died twelve days later. He is buried at Westminster Abbey.

STANSBURY, George Frederick
1800 – 3 Jun. 1845
Born in Bristol, Frederick Stansbury studied with his father, and in 1819 toured as accompanist to the soprano Angelica Catalani. He was also a flautist and noted tenor. He conducted at the Theatre Royal, Dublin, before appearing in London as a singer and theatre conductor. He composed operas and musical dramas (*Waverley*, *Puss in Boots*, *Elfin Sprite*) and songs.

STANTON, Walter Kendall
29 Dec. 1891 – 30 May 1978
Walter Stanton, born at Dauntsey in Wiltshire, studied at Lancing College and Merton College, Oxford. He taught at St Edward's School, Oxford, and at Wellington College, then joined the music department of Reading University. From 1937 to 1945 he worked for the BBC Midland Region, and edited the BBC Hymn Book. In 1947 he was appointed Professor of Music at Bristol University, remaining there until 1958, when he became conductor of the Bristol Choral Society. He composed anthems, motets and part-songs.

STATHAM, Heathcote Dicken
11 Jan. 1889 – 29 Oct. 1973
Heathcote Statham was born in London and studied at Caius College, Cambridge, and at the Royal College of Music. He was organist at Calcutta Cathedral, St Michael's College, Tenbury, and Norwich Cathedral (a post he held for thirty-eight years), and

for many years conducted the Norwich Festivals and the Norwich Philharmonic Orchestra. He composed some noteworthy organ works, including *Rhapsody on a Ground*, songs and church music He was awarded the CBE in 1967.

STEEL, Christopher Charles
(15 Jan. 1939*) – 31 Dec. 1991
That Christopher Steel's music is not more widely known could be a result of his having written most of it to satisfy his own creative urges rather than in response to commissions. That said, the quality of his output merited performances at the Three Choirs Festival, and broadcasts by the BBC of some of his symphonies. Soon after the outbreak of the war the infant Christopher was evacuated with a nanny to Canada, only to be reunited with his parents at the age of four. He attended Beaudesert Park School in Minchinhampton, before going to Shrewsbury School where his early leanings towards music were nourished. In 1957 he entered the Royal Academy of Music, studying with John Gardner and Denis Murdoch. A scholarship in 1961 enabled him to spend time at the Hochschule für Musik in Munich with Harald Genzmer (a pupil of Hindemith). Returning to the United Kingdom he taught at Cheltenham College Junior School from 1963 until he was appointed Director of Music at Bradfield College. His early retirement in 1981 was the result of ill health. (The rare genetic blood condition that brought him down was not diagnosed until much later.) Retirement did give him a much greater opportunity to compose, and he filled in the spare time by taking pupils for piano and composition, and serving as organist at Leckhampton.

Christopher Steel wrote seven symphonies, the fourth inspired by the Romantic poets, the sixth for choir and orchestra and the last unfinished. Among his other works are concertos for cello, organ, recorder, and string quartet with orchestra, an *Island Overture* (based on Huxley's novel), cantatas, a mass, a children's opera (*The Selfish Giant*) and other children's works, brass band music, songs, church anthems, and pieces for recorder, violin and for piano. Several of his organ works have been published: the *Dancing Toccata* is fun, and *Fantasy on a Theme of Purcell* to the tune *Westminster Abbey* ('Christ is made the sure foundation ...') is impressive.

* This is the date on which the baby was adopted by Brigadier Charles Steel of the Royal Engineers and his wife Elizabeth (née Chenevix Trench). Place and date of birth are not known, though Longdon near Shrewsbury and 31 Dec. 1938 has been suggested.

STEGGALL, Charles
3 Jun. 1826 – 7 Jun. 1905
Father of Reginald Steggall (see below) Charles was born in London and studied at the Royal Academy of Music with Sterndale Bennett, with whom he retained a lifelong friendship. After gaining his Mus.D. at Cambridge he became organist at various London churches including Lincoln Inn's Chapel. He was one of the founders of both the Royal College of Organists and Trinity College of Music, Hon. Secretary to the Bach Society, and also an influential teacher for many years at the Royal Academy of Music. He composed anthems and other church music. Charles Steggall died in Notting Hill, London.

STEGGALL, Reginald
17 Apr. 1867 – 16 Nov. 1938
The youngest son of Dr Charles Steggall, Reginald, like his father, was born and died in London. He went to Westminster School and the Royal Academy of Music, where he was a pupil of G.A. Macfarren, Ebenezer Prout, Henry Eyers and Oscar Beringer. He held various important posts as organist, and gave recitals in London and the provinces. In 1895 he was appointed professor of organ at the RAM. Reginald Steggall composed two symphonies, *Variations on an Original Theme* for orchestra, a *Concertstück* for organ and orchestra, orchestral suites, a wind quintet and other chamber works, church music, songs, and pieces for piano and organ.

STEPHEN, David
1869 – 1946
David Stephen was born in Dundee, and became one of the most representative of Scottish composers in the early part of this century. After studying in London he returned to Scotland to become an organist in Dundee, then Glasgow. He was a schoolteacher, organ recitalist, and conductor of the Arbroath and Dundee Choral Unions, later becoming the first director of the Carnegie Trust. David Stephen composed orchestral pieces, choral and chamber works, and edited collections of Scottish songs.

STEPHEN, Edward
1822 – 10 May 1885
A Congregational minister and amateur geologist, Edward Stephen (born Edward Jones Stephen) was born near Ffestiniog. Known by his bardic name 'Tanymarian', he was a conductor and poet as well as the composer of the first ever oratorio in Welsh, *Ystorm Tiberias* (The Storm of Tiberius) of 1852. He also wrote anthems and hymn-tunes. As a singer, he was much in demand in Wales, singing his own compositions. He was also an adjudicator at eisteddfodau. Stephen died at Tal-y-bont, Llanechid.

STEPHENS, Charles Edward
18 Mar. 1821 – 13 Jul. 1892
Charles Stephens was born in London and studied with Cipriani Potter, J.A. Hamilton and Henry Blagrove (the last for violin). He was an organist at several London churches, and wrote two symphonies (his G Minor symphony, *The Elegiac* of 1875, is noteworthy), five orchestral overtures, string quartets and trios, anthems and church services, songs and ballads, and piano pieces. Stephens died in London.

STEVENS, Bernard George
2 Mar. 1916 – 2 Jan. 1983
Bernard Stevens, who taught at the Royal College of Music from 1948 to 1981, expressed an individuality in his music that stemmed in part from a strongly Marxist aesthetic. He was able to incorporate popular elements into his serious works. Yet, despite this, his music has never had a wide following – though it by no means deserves to be consigned to obscurity. Stevens was born in London and received free piano lessons from Harold Samuel, who instilled in the youngster a lasting appreciation of

Bach. In his late teens he studied with E.J. Dent and Cyril Rootham, then entered Cambridge University, graduating in music and English literature. Lessons with Tovey followed, then a period at the RCM with R.O. Morris (for composition), Arthur Benjamin, Gordon Jacob and Constant Lambert. Stevens's early works were written during his six years in the army, and after demobilisation in 1946 he settled in London, composing for films and amateur choirs. His compositions include two symphonies, concertos for violin, cello and piano and other orchestral works, cantatas and other choral music, two string quartets and various trios, violin sonatas, piano pieces, songs and film music. Bernard Stevens died in London.

STILL, Robert
10 Jun. 1910 – 13 Jan. 1971
A descendant of John Still, bishop of Bath and Wells and author of one of the first English farces, Robert Still was born in London. He went to Eton, then studied History and French at Trinity College, Oxford, with the intention of following the family vocation in the legal profession. But, almost inevitably, other familial callings to music took over and he enrolled at the Royal College of Music to study with Kitson, Walker, Jacob and Keller. He was also a pupil of Alcher and Dyson. Before the war Still taught at Eton and occasionally lectured at the Royal Academy of Music, but after serving in the Royal Artillery he eventually settled at Bucklebury in Berkshire and devoted himself to composition. His studies of Mahler's music were the subject of radio broadcasts. He wrote articles on a variety of subjects ranging from crime and society through music and painting to psychoanalysis, and was a founder member of the Imago Society. (He extended Freud's ideas on the sublimation of infantile eroticism to the appreciation of music). He was a keen sports enthusiast and was an Oxford blue at royal tennis.

Among Robert Still's compositions are four symphonies, concertos for piano and for violin, an opera (*Oedipus*), a concerto for strings, *Ballad of the Bladebone Inn*, an *Elegie* for baritone, chorus and orchestra, other choral works, four string quartets and other chamber works, pieces for piano, and several songs. He died at Bucklebury.

STIRLING, Elizabeth
26 Feb. 1819 – 25 Mar. 1895
Elizabeth Stirling was born at Greenwich in London. She studied piano and organ with W.B. Wilson and Edward Holmes, and harmony with G.A. Macfarren, giving her first recital at the age of eighteen. Her organ recitals were much admired and often included works by J.S. Bach, a composer who was little-known in England at the time. Organist of All Saints, Poplar, for nineteen years, and St Andrew's, Undershaft, she wrote pedal fugues and other pieces for organ, songs, duets and part-songs and an unpublished opera (*Bleakmoor for Copseleigh*). In 1856 she submitted for an Oxford music degree a setting of Psalm 130 for large chorus and orchestra under the name of 'E. Stirling, Esq.'. The work achieved the required standard, but she was refused a degree on grounds of gender (Oxford only began to recognise women for degrees in 1921). In 1863 Elizabeth married Frederick Albert Bridge, another organist. In her later years she published many arrangements of Bach, Handel and Mozart for the organ. She died in London.

STOKES, Walter
28 Jun. 1847 – 25 Nov. 1916
Born at Shipton-upon-Stour, Worcs., Stokes was destined to become a school teacher. He received all his musical training from local teachers, then with Charles Swinnerton Heap of Birmingham for composition. Having graduated later in life with his Mus.D. at Cambridge, in 1882, he remained in Worcestershire. His compositions include a cantata, a large number of songs, and pieces for violin, piano and organ. He died in Worcester, and a scholarship at the RAM was established in his name.

STORER, John
18 May 1858 – 1 May 1930
Born at Hulland near Derby, John Storer studied with Dr John Naylor (organist at York Minster) and in 1878 graduated with a Mus.Bac. from Oxford. He was an organist, first at Scarborough, where he conducted the local orchestral society, then at Folkestone, where he converted to the Roman Catholic church, and in London. He conducted at various London theatres before becoming musical director at St Gregory's, Bath. As well as being a music critic for various papers, he found time to compose two symphonies, two operettas, an overture, an oratorio, masses, anthems and church services, songs, and pieces for organ and for piano. Storer died at Berwick-upon-Tweed.

STRATTON, Stephen Samuel
19 Dec. 1840 – 25 Jun. 1906
Born in London, Stephen Stratton studied composition with Charles Lucas and organ with Charles Gardner. He settled in Birmingham in 1886 as a teacher and organist, where he established the Popular Concerts, bringing new music to the public. He was also a music critic as well as a member of the Philharmonic Society and the Musical Association. As a composer he wrote of a number of part-songs and piano pieces, but his greatest contribution to his profession was in compiling, with the noted librarian James Duff Brown, 'British Musical Biography' (1897), and in writing books on the life and work of Mendelssohn and Paganini. Stratton died in Birmingham.

STUART, Leslie
15 Mar. 1856 – 27 Mar. 1928
Thomas Barrett, to give Stuart his birth name, was born at Southport and, in his youth, was organist at the Roman Catholic Cathedral, Salford, then moved to the Church of the Holy Name in Manchester. His initial success was as a composer of popular songs such as *Rip van Winkle, Louisiana Lou, Soldiers of the Queen* (popular during the Diamond Jubilee of Queen Victoria, and the second Boer War), *Lily of Laguna, Little Dolly Day-dream*, etc., before he turned to operettas (*Florodora, The Silver Slipper, Havana, Captain Kidd*, among others). Stuart died at Richmond, Surrey.

SULLIVAN, Arthur Seymour
13 May 1842 – 22 Nov. 1900
Arthur Sullivan's comic operas, mostly to libretti by W.S. Gilbert, are enormously popular even today, whereas his serious music, the subject of his real ambitions, is

virtually unknown. Sullivan was born at 8 Bolwell Terrace, Lambeth, son of a bandmaster and clarinet teacher at Kneller Hall. He displayed a musical talent at a very early age, and became a chorister at the Chapel Royal. Winning the first Mendelssohn Scholarship, he went to the Royal Academy of Music, then to Leipzig to study with Rietz, Moscheles and David. He was organist at St Michael's, Chester Square, and a highly successful conductor (especially at the Leeds Festivals and London Proms).

In 1876 Sullivan was appointed Principal of the National Training School for Music. He was knighted seven years later, having already been awarded the Legion of Honour and the Order of Saxe-Coburg-Gotha. In addition to the comic operas he composed a symphony (*The Irish*), a cello concerto (reconstructed Mackerras) and other orchestral pieces, incidental music to Shakespeare plays, oratorios and cantatas, anthems and hymn-tunes (incl. *Onward, Christian Soldiers*), piano pieces and chamber works. One of his most moving works is the orchestral overture *In Memoriam*, written in memory of his father. Sullivan's stage works and his often stormy relationship with Gilbert are extensively documented elsewhere. His little-known serious opera, *The Beauty Stone* of 1898, was written in collaboration with other librettists, as was his romantic opera *Ivanhoe*. Sullivan died in London, and is buried in St Paul's Cathedral.

SUMMERS, James Lea
1837 – 8 Jul. 1881
Blind from birth, Summers was a pupil of Kate Loder and G.A. Macfarren at the Royal Academy of Music. As a pianist, he appeared at Crystal Palace concerts on occasions. His works include a concert overture and other small orchestral works, a string quartet and some other chamber music, anthems, piano pieces and duets, and songs.

SUMSION, Herbert Whitton
19 Jan. 1899 – 11 Aug. 1995
Herbert Sumsion is remembered with some affection by several generations of church musicians for his anthems, services and organ music. His creative output lasted well into his eighties. 'John', as he was affectionately known, was born at Gloucester, and joined the Cathedral choir there when he was nine. He studied organ with Herbert Brewer, becoming his assistant at the Cathedral after two years in the Forces. In 1922 he took the organ stool at Christ Church Lancaster Gate, in London, and was appointed Director of Music at Bishop's Stortford College. From 1926-28 he was Professor of Theory and Composition at the Curtis Institute of Music in Philadelphia USA, finding himself a mate in the process. On returning to Britain he became organist at Gloucester Cathedral, remaining there for thirty-nine years, while serving concurrently as Director of Music at Cheltenham Ladies' College for most of that period.

Sumsion's career as a composer only began in 1935 with his *Te Deum* in G, and most of his church anthems were written when he was in his eighties. They are conservative in outlook, but sensitive and with some personal identity. In addition to the church music Sumsion wrote a rather fine cello sonata and a piano trio. He died at Frampton-on-Severn, his Gloucestershire retirement home.

SWAIN, Freda
31 Oct. 1902 – 29 Jan. 1985
Born at Portsmouth, Freda Swain studied with Dora Matthay and at the Royal College of Music with Stanford and Arthur Alexander, whom she married in 1921. In 1924 she joined the staff of the RCM, and in 1926 founded the British Music Movement to promote the works of young composers and artists. Just before the war she toured with her husband in South Africa and Australia, giving recitals, broadcasting and lecturing. She composed a one-act opera (*Second Chance*; another opera, *The Shadowy Waters*, remained unfinished), a piano concerto, a concertino for piano and strings and other orchestral pieces, two string quartets and many other chamber works, songs and song cycles, choral and church music, a *Suite for Six Trumpets*, and a great variety of instrumental pieces – all suffused with a rich Romanticism, and expertly crafted.

SWINSTEAD, Felix Gerald
25 Jun. 1880 – 14 Aug. 1959

Felix Swinstead was born at Stoke Newington. He won the Sterndale Bennett and Thalberg Scholarships to study with Tobias Matthay and Frederick Corder at the Royal Academy of Music, where he later became an examiner and professor of piano. In addition to over 200 piano works, many of which were valuable teaching pieces, Swinstead composed a *Scarlatti Suite* for piano and strings, and some pieces for violin.

TALBOT, Howard
8 Mar. 1865 – 12 Sep. 1928
Richard Lansdale Munkittrick was born in New York, but came to London as a medical student before going to the Royal College of Music to study with Parry. He adopted British citizenship and changed his name to Talbot. His output consisted of musical comedies (*Old Wapping Stairs*, *Monte Carlo*, *A Chinese Honeymoon*, *The White Chrysanthemum*, *The Belle of Brittany* and *The Blue Moon*) and he collaborated in several more with Monckton, Rubens and others. Talbot died penniless in Reigate, Surrey, having lost a fortune, invested in Russian oil, as a result of the 1917 Revolution.

TATE, Phyllis Margaret Duncan
6 Apr. 1911 – 27 May 1987
Phyllis Tate preferred the more intimate chamber medium than full orchestral writing, having contributed a valuable and varied repertoire for vocal and instrumental ensembles. She was born at Gerrards Cross in Buckinghamshire and received little schooling after being expelled for singing a bawdy song. Jazz was an early influence, and Tate taught herself the ukelele, writing foxtrots and blues. Later in her life she would arrange and compose lighter pieces under the sobriquet Max Morelle. At seventeen she enrolled at the Royal Academy of Music, studying piano and timpani, and composition with Harry Farjeon. Several of the works she had performed while at the RAM (including an operetta, *The Policeman's Serenade*), together with a symphony and a cello concerto, were among those early works that she disowned after World War Two, claiming them to be 'immature'.

After the RAM, fortune, in the guise of OUP and the Macnaghten-Lemare concerts, smiled on her. She eventually married Alan Frank, Head of OUP's Music Department. By the mid 1950s Phyllis Tate was involved with local music groups as well as the Composers' Guild and the Performing Rights Society. She wrote much of her music during this period for the local groups. Tate's acknowledged compositions include a Concerto for Alto Saxophone, *Panorama* for strings, several works for vocal and/or choral forces with orchestra or instrumental ensemble (*A Secular Requiem, All the World's a Stage, St Martha and the Dragon, Seven Lincolnshire Folk Songs*, etc.), an opera (*The Lodger*), string quartet, a splendid Sonata for Clarinet and Cello, many other instrumental and small ensemble pieces, many part-songs and songs, and several works for amateur or school groups. She died at Hampstead in London.

TAYLOR, Laura
1819 – 1905
Laura Barker was born at Thirklebury in Yorkshire, where her father was the local vicar. She studied with Cipriani Potter, and her musical talents attracted the attention of Paganini when she was only twelve years old. After her marriage to Tom Taylor, a lawyer and keen amateur musician, their Sunday musical soirées were attended by many great celebrities. Mrs Taylor composed incidental music, a cantata (*Enone*), string quartets and other chamber works, choral music, songs, glees and madrigals, and pieces for piano. She died at Coleshill in Buckinghamshire.

TEMPLETON, Alec
4 Jul. 1910 – 28 Mar. 1963
The whimsical piano piece *Bach Goes to Town* and the nonsense song *Three little fishes* are familiar to many, though their creator's name may have escaped notice. Alec Templeton was born at Cardiff in Wales, though he settled in the United States in 1935. Blind from infancy, he studied at the Royal College of Music and the Royal Academy of Music, leaving the latter with the highest possible accolades. In the States he appeared as a piano recitalist with all the major orchestras, and gained a following as a radio broadcaster. Templeton composed two piano concertos, some chamber music, songs, and much instrumental music.

TERRY, Richard Runciman
3 Jan. 1865 – 18 Apr. 1938
A distinguished organist whose career took him from Elstow School to St John's Cathedral, Antigua, then to Downside Abbey before his twenty-three years at Westminster Cathedral, Richard Runciman Terry was born at Ellington in Northumberland, and obtained a music scholarship to King's College, Cambridge. He lectured at Birmingham and Dublin Universities, and was editor of the Catholic Hymnal. In 1911 he received an honorary doctorate from Durham, and was knighted in 1922. Sir Richard was a renowned authority on sea shanties and carols, and did much to revive and promote English Tudor and medieval music. In 1929, while on a short voyage to the Arctic coast of Norway, he completed the harmonisation of Calvin's Psalter of 1539 and the Scottish Psalter. He composed five masses, a requiem, many motets, and some other church music. His carol *Myn Liking* is an excellent example of his understanding of the true carol.

THALBEN-BALL, George
18 Jun. 1896 – 18 Nov. 1987
George Thalben-Ball is probably little known outside the narrow field of organ and church music. But his work as a composer for and recitalist on the organ earned him considerable respect and affection. He was born George Thomas Ball in Sydney, Australia, but grew up in London, where at some time he prefixed his mother's maiden name. He studied at the Royal College of Music under Parry, Stanford, Frederick Bridge and Charles Wood. In 1919 he became a professor of organ at the Royal College of Music and organist at the Temple Church, London (where he stayed until 1981). Curator of the Royal Albert Hall organ, civic organist of Birmingham and Birmingham University from 1949, and conductor of the BBC Singers, Thalben-Ball composed works for chorus and orchestra, church anthems and services, and fanfares. His *Elegy* was played at the funeral of Diana, Princess of Wales. He married twice, his second wife being the organist Jennifer Bate.

THIMAN, Eric Harding
12 Sep. 1900 – 13 Feb. 1975
A self-taught musician who gained his FRCO at the age of twenty-one and his D.Mus. at London University six years later, Eric Thiman was born in Ashford, Kent. In 1939 he was appointed a professor of harmony and composition at the Royal Academy of Music, a post he held for over thirty years. Renowned as an improviser, he became organist of the City Temple in London in 1958. Although he wrote a few short works for orchestra and some piano and organ miniatures, his compositions are mainly for church choirs and suitable for amateur performance. His cantata *The Last Supper* is perhaps his most well-known work. Thiman died in London.

THIRLWALL, John Wade
11 Jan. 1809 – 15 Jun. 1875
John Thirlwall, born at Shilbottle in Northumberland, was musical director at the Durham Theatre before moving to London, where he held similar posts at the Drury Lane, Haymarket, Olympic and Adelphi theatres. In 1864 he became conductor of the Royal Italian Opera. A music critic as well as composer, he wrote songs (*Sunny Days of Childhood* being the most memorable), violin solos and other instrumental pieces. Thirlwall died in London.

THOMAS, Arthur Goring
20 Nov. 1850 – 20 Mar. 1892
Arthur Thomas, whose life ended tragically during a bout of manic depression when he threw himself under a train at West Hampstead Station, was born at Ratton Park in Sussex. He studied with Durand in Paris and with Sullivan and Prout at the Royal Academy of Music. He was also a pupil of Max Bruch. Thomas's compositions include operas (*The Light of the Harem, Esmeralda, Nadeschda*, and the unfinished *The Golden Web*). His choral ode *The Sun-Worshippers*, was produced at the Norwich Festival in 1881. Other works include cantatas, concert 'scenas', a Suite de Ballet for orchestra, a violin concerto, songs and duets, and some instrumental pieces. After his death a scholarship was established at the RAM in his memory. Thomas is buried in Finchley cemetery.

THOMAS, John
1 Mar. 1826 – 19 Mar. 1913
'Pencerdd Gwalia' (Prince of the Minstrels) was born at Bridgend in Glamorganshire, and demonstrated his musical abilities at an early age by playing the piccolo as well as winning a triple-stringed harp at the Abergavenny Eisteddfod when he was eleven. Through the kindness of the Countess of Lovelace, Lord Byron's daughter, he was sent to the Royal Academy of Music where he studied harp with J.B. Chatterton, piano with C.J. Read, and composition with RAM principals Cipriani Potter and Charles Lucas. He toured Europe as a harpist and played at Her Majesty's Theatre in London under Balfe. In 1871 he succeeded Chatterton as harpist to Queen Victoria. Professor at the Royal College of Music, Royal Academy of Music and the Guildhall School of Music, John Thomas composed two symphonies, two operas, two harp concertos, overtures, cantatas and instrumental pieces. He also edited old Welsh melodies and, after much strenuous effort, founded a Welsh Scholarship at the RAM.

THOMAS, Robert Harold
3 Jul. 1834 – 29 Jul. 1885
R.H. Thomas was born at Cheltenham and studied at the Royal Academy of Music with Sterndale Bennett, Potter and Henry Blagrove. He followed a brief career as a concert pianist, then became a professor of piano at the RAM and the Guildhall School of Music. Thomas composed three orchestral overtures (incl. *As You Like It* and *Overture to a Comedy*), songs and piano pieces. He died in London.

THOMAS, Vincent
4 Dec. 1872 –
Born in Wrexham, Thomas's debut as a conductor was at the Queen's Hall, when he conducted Liza Lehmann's *Endymion* in 1898. An amateur musician and a London banker, he composed several operas in the first two decades of the twentieth century, which were performed under the direction of Dan Godfrey and Alick Maclean, and bases mostly on themes connected with Arthurian legend (*Eos and Gwevril, Enid, The Sword of Glydwr*). He was for many years conductor of the Westminster Choral Society.

THOMSON, John
28 Oct. 1805 – 6 May 1841
Born at Sprouston, Roxburghshire, John Thomson was elected the first Reid Professor at Edinburgh University in 1839. He studied at Leipzig, maintaining a friendship with Mendelssohn, whom he had met in Edinburgh in 1829, and Schumann. Thomson composed three operas, songs, piano pieces and other instrumental works. He died in Edinburgh.

THORNE, Edward Henry
9 May 1834 – 26 Dec. 1916
Edward Thorne was born at Cranbourne, and studied with George Elvey at St George's Chapel, Windsor. He was an organist at Henley-on-Thames, Chichester Cathedral, then in Hove and on to London, where he was organist at several churches. It was here he took over from Joseph Barnby in reviving J.S. Bach's music. He

was a founder member of the Musical Artists Society, and composed a great many orchestral works (of which the overture *Peveril of the Peak* is the most notable), chamber music, church services, songs and part-songs, and pieces for piano and for organ. His hymn-tune 'St. Andrew', sung to *'Jesus calls us o'er the tumult'*, is well-known today.

TIPPETT, Michael Kemp
2 Jan. 1905 – 8 Jan. 1998

If only for their international renown, two names stand head and shoulders above those of their contemporaries: Benjamin Britten and Michael Tippett. Tippett was born in London, but spent most of his childhood in Wetherden, Suffolk. His father was a lawyer and his mother a novelist, Labour party member and suffragette. Tippett's uncomfortable two years' boarding at Fettes School in Edinburgh were followed by a happier stint at Stamford Grammar School, before he entered the Royal College of Music to study composition with Charles Wood and C.H. Kitson, and conducting with Adrian Boult and Malcolm Sargent. He later had private lessons with R.O. Morris, developing a knowledge of counterpoint that would inform much of his output. After four years teaching French at a preparatory school near Limpsfield, where he was very active in local music groups, he retired and settled in Surrey. He discarded many of his works prior to 1940 (including a symphony), but the premiere of his *Concerto for Double String Orchestra* in that year was well received. He had already written the oratorio *A Child of Our Time*, but it would not be heard until 1944 – a passionate statement against persecution and tyranny that stemmed from Tippett's deep commitment to social justice and radical causes. In 1943 he was imprisoned at Wormwood Scrubs for three months as a conscientious objector, which interrupted eleven highly successful years as musical director at Morley College, London, where he presented the first modern performance of Tallis's 40-part *Spem in Alium*. In the mid-1960s he took over the directorship of the Bath Festival, saving it from bankruptcy.

From 1951, with his first symphony already under his belt, Tippett concentrated on composition, completing his first opera, *The Midsummer Marriage*. His international reputation had to wait until he was in his sixties, and from then on he travelled worldwide, conducting and following performances of his works well into his eighties. He died peacefully at home after a bout of pneumonia contracted during a visit to Stockholm. His contributions to music in Britain were rewarded with a CBE, a knighthood, Companion of Honour and the Order of Merit. His autobiography, *Those Twentieth Century Blues*, was published in 1991. *Moving into Aquarius*, a collection of essays and poems, explores his thoughts about music in a technological age.

Michael Tippett's music was informed by popular musical movements as well as by contrapuntal techniques, the Elizabethan period and a wide range of literature – especially that of Classical Greece. It includes four symphonies, the Concerto for Double String Orchestra, Concerto for Orchestra, a piano concerto, a triple concerto for violin, viola, cello and orchestra, a Suite in D for the birthday of Prince Charles, and several other orchestral works, the last of which was *The Rose Lake*. Outstanding among British operas are his *The Midsummer Marriage*, *King Priam*, *The Knot Garden*, *The Ice Break*, and *New Year*. Other major choral works include *The Mask of Time*, *The Shires Suite*, and *The Vision of St. Augustine*. Among his vocal works are

Boyhood's End, The Windhover, The Heart's Assurance, Crown of the Year, Songs for Ariel and *Songs for Dov*. Five string quartets, four piano sonatas, a sonata for guitar and a few pieces for brass band rank amongst his chamber or instrumental pieces.

TOLHURST, George
1827 – 18 Jan. 1877
A teacher in London, Tolhurst was born in Maidstone, Kent. The family moved to Australia, where George was for a time organist at Melbourne Cathedral. He moved back to England in 1866, and died at Barnstaple in Devon. His oratorio *Ruth*, his one major composition, was performed (conducted by his father) in Melbourne in 1864 and in England four years later (conducted by C.E. Horsley). Although *Ruth* had regular private performances in Oxford in the 1950s 'after a good dinner', the work was revived in 1973, being reorchestrated and performed at the Royal Albert Hall, broadcast live by the BBC, and billed as 'the worst oratorio of all time'. Elgar described the work as 'a fountain of joy' and Donald Tovey (see below) was reputedly thrown out of the British Library Reading Room for laughing too loudly when consulting the score. The reviewer in the Musical Times of 1868 says: 'We know nothing of Mr Tolhurst and should have been pleased to know nothing of his oratorio. The choruses . . . are in some portions perfectly unendurable'. They have, however, continued to delight many for generations after.

TOVEY, Donald Francis
17 Jul. 1875 – 10 Jul. 1940
Sir Donald Tovey is regarded as one of the greatest writers on music, a reputation which overshadows his accomplishments as a composer. He was born at Eton (where his father taught classics at Eton College) and studied privately with Parratt, Higgs and Parry, before winning a scholarship to Balliol College, Oxford. He subsequently made his debut as a concert pianist at the age of twenty-five. He conducted the Reid Orchestra and was appointed Reid Professor of Music at Edinburgh in 1914. In 1935 he received  a knighthood. He was a champion of the two-manual piano invented by Emanuel Moór in the 1930s. Tovey composed a piano concerto, a cello concerto (both of which have had recent revivals), a symphony, an opera (*The Bride of Dionysus*), incidental music, two string quartets and a quintet, a suite for wind instruments, songs and piano pieces, and sonatas for violin, cello and clarinet. His compositions, however, have been overshadowed by his reputation as a writer, his 'Essays in Musical Analysis' achieving considerable status in the years following his death in Edinburgh.

TOYE, Geoffrey
27 Jan. 1889 – 11 Jun. 1942
Brother of Francis (below), Geoffrey Toye was born at Winchester and studied at the Royal College of Music. He conducted theatre and concert orchestras and, while a member of the Stock Exchange, founded the Lloyd's Choir. He composed an opera (*The Fairy Cup*), a masque (*Day and Night* – in partnership with his brother), a

symphony and songs. His ballet *The Haunted Ballroom* still earns a place in the orchestral repertoire. Toye died in London.

TOYE, John Francis
27 Jan. 1883 – 31 Oct. 1964
Like his brother Geoffrey (above), Francis Toye was born at Winchester. He graduated from Trinity College, Cambridge, and studied with Waddington and Dent. He joined the Morning Post in 1925 as a critic and in 1936 went to Florence as Director of the British Institute, returning from Italy when war broke out. He later spent some time in Rio de Janeiro with the British Council. Toye wrote critical biographies of Verdi and Rossini, and a musical novel (*Diana and Two Symphonies*). He composed a masque, a sonata for piano and flute (performed in 1910), and some songs. Toye died in Florence.

TURLE, James
5 Mar. 1802 – 28 Jun. 1882
James Turle was born at Somerton, Somerset, into a musical family. He became a boy chorister at Wells Cathedral, then moved to London, holding several appointments before undertaking the position of assistant organist and choirmaster at Westminster Abbey in 1819. In 1831 he succeeded to the senior post, retaining his musical connection with the Abbey for sixty-three years. His skill as a teacher is well attested, and he composed many church anthems, hymn-tunes and chants, some still in use, of which the best known is probably *Winchester*. Turle died at his house in the cloisters of Westminster Abbey and was buried in Norwood Cemetery.

TURNBULL, Percy Purvis
14 Jul. 1902 – 1976
Percy Turnbull was born at Old Benwell in Newcastle upon Tyne. He was a chorister there and at the cathedral church of St Nicholas. Unable to take up a scholarship to Armstrong College of Art owing to the onset of the war, he later won a Founder's Scholarship to the Royal College of Music, where he twice gained the Mendelssohn Scholarship and won the Arthur Sullivan Prize. Turnbull studied with Holst, Vaughan Williams, Ireland, Dyson, Dunhill and R.O. Morris. He worked in publishing and piano-roll editing, played the piano in theatre; and after 1945 taught at the Surrey College of Music. His compositions include an orchestral suite, chamber music, choral works, piano pieces and songs. *The rainy day*, a setting of Longfellow, is a particularly good example of the last genre. Turnbull was an accomplished painter, specialising in watercolours, and as a writer displayed a witty and entertaining style.

TURPIN, Edmund Hart
4 May 1835 – 25 Oct. 1907
Born at Nottingham, Edmund Turpin studied with C. Noble and in London with Hullah and Pauer. He was organist at St George's, Bloomsbury, and at St Bride's, Fleet Street. He conducted the London Orchestra at the Cardiff Eisteddfod in 1883 and edited The Musical Standard and Musical News. His compositions include oratorios, cantatas, much church music, a symphonic overture, chamber music, piano pieces and songs. Turpin died in London, having suffered from paralysis for many years.

VAUGHAN THOMAS, David
15 Mar. 1873 – 15 Sep. 1934

David Vaughan Thomas was born at Ystalyfera in Glamorganshire. He went to Swansea to study with Dr Joseph Parry, then won a scholarship to Exeter College, Oxford, to read mathematics. He taught that subject for a time in Bath, until he was appointed assistant music master at Harrow School. In 1909 he gained a doctorate at Oxford. Vaughan Thomas played the organ, lectured and adjudicated. His compositions, which were often influenced by Welsh folk music and literature, included orchestral pieces, choral works, two string quartets, songs and instrumental music.

VAUGHAN WILLIAMS, Ralph
12 Oct. 1872 – 26 Aug. 1958

Of all the English composers active in the twentieth century, none is of greater importance than Vaughan Williams. His pre-eminence stems from the extent and variety of his works, his dominant role in the English folk-song movement, and from his teaching activities. He was born at Down Ampney in Gloucestershire, son of a parson. After the death of his father, he grew up with his mother at Leith Hill, near Dorking, and went to Charterhouse School. After two years at the Royal College of Music as a pupil of Parry and Stanford he went to Cambridge, where he gained a doctorate in music. He settled in London as an organist and choirmaster until, in 1896, he went to Berlin to study with Max Bruch. On his return to England he joined the Folk-Song Society and started to teach at the RCM, remaining there for the rest of his life (except for a few months of study with Ravel and three trips to the United States). He did, however, enrol for service in World War One with the Royal Army Medical Corps. Although much of his time was spent at his home in Chelsea until 1929, for most of the later part of his life he lived at The White Gates, Dorking, where he helped to develop the Leith Hill Music Festival and other amateur musical activities in the area. Upon his marriage to Ursula Wood, he moved to London for his last five years.

Vaughan Williams remained very much an individualist, refusing to follow fashion, and his music has inspired several generations of younger composers. In his autobiography he pays special tribute to his friend Gustav Holst, who for many years was his mentor.

Among Vaughan Williams's many works were nine symphonies, concertos for piano, violin, oboe and bass tuba, a suite for viola and orchestra, operas (*The Shepherds of the Delectable Mountains, Hugh the Drover, Sir John in Love, The Poisoned Kiss, Riders to the Sea* and *The Pilgrim's Progress*), incidental music, *Job* (a masque for dancing), fantasias for strings (*Fantasia on a Theme by Thomas Tallis* is regarded as one of his best works), a partita and a concerto grosso for strings, two string quartets and other chamber works, several choral/orchestral works (*Dona Nobis Pacem* and *Flos Campi* are splendid examples), a Mass in G minor, songs and part-songs, church music, organ and piano pieces, and music for wind band.

Vaughan Williams was greatly influenced by his rediscovery of Elizabethan music and he instilled a similar enthusiasm in others. In 1935 he was awarded the Order of Merit, having refused a knighthood. He died at Hanover Terrace in London and is buried in Westminster Abbey.

VEALE, John Douglas Louis
15 Jun. 1922 – 16 Nov. 2006
John Veale's music is approachable, romantic and lyrical. It is no wonder then that, after a promising early start (one work, *Panorama*, was given a performance at Proms in 1955) his work was eclipsed as William Glock at the BBC concentrated on composers writing in a more progressive idiom. For twelve years Veale ceased writing, but resumed working in 1981 with his Violin Concerto. In that decade his music was championed by Lewis Foreman and began to be heard more. His cause was furthered by David Wright, then by Max Keogh in Australia.

Veale was born in Shortlands in Kent. He went to the Dragon School in Oxford, then to Repton, where he developed his interest in music. There followed a degree in modern history at Corpus Christi College, Oxford, during the course of which he took private lessons with Egon Wellesz. During World War Two he served in the army's Education Corps, and found time to continue lessons with Wellesz and begin studies in counterpoint and harmony with Sir Thomas Armstrong. He also managed to sketch out his first symphony (completed in 1947). After demobilisation Veale returned to Oxford (and Wellesz) to read music. He also began to write music for films (e.g. *The Purple Plain, No Road Back, The Spanish Gardener, High Tide at Noon* and *Portrait of Alison*). In 1949 a scholarship enabled him to study in the USA with Roger Sessions and Roy Harris. Two years later he returned to a Senior Fellowship at Corpus Christi. Soon afterwards the death of his four-year old daughter led to his *Elegy* for flute, harp and strings, which was adopted by the Boyd Neel Orchestra.

From 1965-80 he was film critic and film correspondent for the Oxford Mail (he was sacked as a result of his support for trade unionism) and from 1968-87 a copy editor for Oxford University Press. Success came his way again with several performances and a consequent creative impetus. Veale wrote three symphonies, concertos for clarinet and violin, *Panorama* (inspired by San Francisco from his US days), *Demos Variations* and other orchestral pieces. Choral works include *Kubla Khan* for baritone, chorus and orchestra, the erotic *Song of Radha* for soprano and orchestra and, inspired by his atheistic outlook, *Apocalypse* for chorus and orchestra. On a smaller scale are the highly regarded String Quartet and pieces for guitar duet commissioned by Max Keogh. Veale died in Bromley after a long struggle with prostate cancer.

VERNE, Mary.   See **WURM**, Marie

VINCENT, Charles John
19 Sept 1852 – 28 Feb. 1934
Vincent was born at nearby Houghton-le-Spring and became a Durham Cathedral chorister. He then continued his studies at the Leipzig Conservatoire before returning to Oxford to gain his Mus.Doc. After a move to a teaching and organ position at Tavistock, Devon, be settled in Hendon, London, in 1883, establishing the firm of Rogers, the piano manufacturers. He was also instrumental in developing a novel system of teaching harmony to students. Vincent's compositions include an oratorio (*Ruth*), an overture *The Storm*, masses and numerous part-songs. He died in Monte Carlo.

VINTER, Gilbert
4 May 1909 – 10 Oct. 1969
Well known for his extensive catalogue of works for brass and military bands, Gilbert Vinter was also recognised as a conductor of light music and an authority on folk music. He was born in Lincoln and went to the Cathedral School there, later studying at Kneller Hall and the Royal Academy of Music. In 1938 he became a professor of bassoon at the RAM, and later accepted the conductorship of the BBC Midlands Orchestra, then the International Light Orchestra. In addition to his brass and military music, Vinter composed a ballet, a saxophone concerto, *Piaculium* for soprano and orchestra, several overtures and other orchestral works and arrangements. Best known may be his *Hunter's Moon* and *Per Ardua ad Astra*. Vinter died at Tintagel in Cornwall.

WADDINGTON, Sidney Peine
23 Jul. 1869 – 2 Jun. 1953
Born at Lincoln, Sidney Waddington studied at the Royal College of Music, where he later became a professor of harmony and counterpoint, and in Germany and Vienna. For ten years he was pianist at Covent Garden. He composed a piano concerto, an operetta for children (*Whimland*), a cantata, a string quartet and trio, a quintet for piano and wind, sonatas for violin and for cello, an overture, *Ode to Music* (for soprano, chorus and orchestra), choruses, and piano pieces. Waddington completed the score of Goring Thomas's *Golden Web*. He died at Uplyme in Devon.

WALEY, Simon Waley
23 Aug. 1827 – 30 Dec. 1875
An active member of the Jewish community, Simon Waley Waley (his full given names) was a broker on the Stock Exchange. A gifted amateur musician and pianist, he had lessons with Moscheles and Sterndale Bennett, and theory and composition with Charles Horsley and Bernhard Molique. As well as performing regularly, he composed a piano concerto, piano trios, marches and caprices and miscellaneous piano pieces, as well as music for Jewish services.

WALKER, Ernest
15 Jul. 1870 – 21 Feb. 1949
Born in Bombay, Ernest Walker studied classics at Oxford, then joined the staff of Balliol College at the age of twenty, serving there for thirty-four years and eventually becoming Director of Music. In addition to publishing many learned books, including the acclaimed 'A History of Music in England', he composed orchestral music, choruses (his *Ode to a Nightingale* for baritone, chorus and orchestra of 1909 was enthusiastically reviewed at the time), many chamber works, sonatas for violin, viola and cello, a *Stabat Mater*, songs and part-songs, and pieces for organ and for piano. Percy Scholes described him as 'a delicate master of musical craftsmanship'. Walker died in Oxford.

WALLACE, William
3 Jul. 1860 – 16 Dec. 1940
Born at Greenock, William Wallace went to Fettes College. He gave up an exhibition scholarship at Edinburgh and entered Glasgow University, gaining an M.D. Later he resigned from a successful career as a research ophthalmologist and practitioner at London and Glasgow hospitals to study music at the Royal Academy of Music, though he did practise during World War One while a lieutenant in the Royal Army Medical Corps.

Besides contributing articles to medical journals Wallace wrote books on Wagner and Liszt, and on the development of the art of music and its psychological aspects. He translated several operas and served on various committees, including those of the Royal Philharmonic Society and the Society of British Composers. He was also involved in the Royal Commission on copyright. Claims that Wallace was the first British musician to compose a tone poem, *The Passing of Beatrice* of 1892, are incorrect, as Henry Cotton Nixon beat him by ten years. The rest of Wallace's output includes five other tone poems, five symphonies (including the programmatic *Creation Symphony*), orchestral suites and preludes, songs and song-cycles, and some chamber music.

WALLACE, William Vincent
1 Jun. 1814 – 12 Oct. 1865

William Wallace led an adventurous life that must be unique among composers, though his own accounts of his life may well be exaggerated. At the age of twenty-one Wallace left his native Ireland for New South Wales, where he was paid one hundred sheep for his first concert. He travelled extensively in Tasmania, New Zealand, Nepal and South America, experiencing several narrow escapes at the hands of native populations. He became a whaler for a time, later relating to Berlioz stories of cannibals and native girls, then went to America for three years. He was nearly blown up in a steamboat and lost all his savings through poor investment in tobacco and in piano manufacturing.

Wallace was born at Waterford. He played the violin in Dublin theatres, taking to the organ bench at Thurles Cathedral, Tipperary, where he briefly married and separated. He composed a violin concerto, symphonies, many operas (*Maritana* and *Lurline* were both highly successful), songs, and light piano pieces which were once much sought after. He also had successes in Mexico (a *Grand Mass*) and New Orleans. Eventually Wallace's health broke down and he was sent to the Pyrenees, where he died at the Chateau de Bagen.

WALMISLEY, Thomas Attwood
21 Jan. 1814 - 17 Jan. 1856
T.A. Walmisley was born in London and studied with his father, the composer Thomas Forbes Walmisley, and with Thomas Attwood, who was his godfather. For three years Walmisley was an organist in Croydon, then at Trinity and St John's Colleges, Cambridge, where he also studied mathematics and wrote poetry. (As a keen organist, he is recorded as playing for eight different college services on Sundays, often taking his choir with him). In 1836 he was appointed Professor of Music at Cambridge University, though it was not until 1848 that he managed to gain his

doctorate there. With S.S. Wesley, Walmisley was responsible for the Bach revival in this country. He composed odes, anthems, services, madrigals, chants and songs, and pieces for oboe and piano, and for organ. He died in Hastings.

WALSWORTH, Ivor
1909 – 2 Nov. 1978

The name of Ivor Walsworth is usually associated with the BBC, which he joined in 1936, later becoming Music Transcription Organiser. But he composed a wide variety of music, including five symphonies, concertos for piano, violin, viola da gamba and cello, three string quartets and other chamber works, sonatas for flute, piano, violin, and flute with harpsichord, songs and film music, and some electronic works (e.g. *Contrasts Essconic* in collaboration with Daphne Oram). Walsworth was born in London, and studied at the Royal Academy of Music and later in Munich, Budapest and Vienna. He married the concert pianist Joan Davies.

WALTHEW, Richard Henry
4 Nov. 1872 – 14 Nov. 1951

Richard Walthew was born in London. He studied at the Guildhall School of Music, and at the Royal College of Music with Parry and Stanford. In 1907 he became Professor of Music at Queen's College, London, later becoming conductor at the Guildhall School of Music and of the South Place Orchestra, Finsbury. Walthew composed choruses with orchestra, operettas (*The Enchanted Island* and *The Gardeners*), a piano concerto, violin concerto, orchestral suites and overtures, quintets, quartets and trios, instrumental music, songs and part-songs. He died at East Preston on the Sussex coast.

WALTON, William Turner
29 Mar. 1902 – 8 Mar. 1983

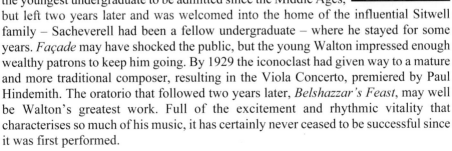

Now a musical monument, Sir William Walton first came to the fore with his anarchic and shocking (by the standards of the day) *Façade*, a setting of Edith Sitwell's experimental poetry to musical parodies. He was born at Oldham in Lancashire. As a boy chorister at Christ Church Cathedral, Oxford, he was encouraged by H.G. Ley and Hugh Percy Allen. As a composer he was largely self-taught, though he acknowledged valuable advice given by Busoni and Ansermet.

He had entered Oxford University at the age of sixteen, the youngest undergraduate to be admitted since the Middle Ages, but left two years later and was welcomed into the home of the influential Sitwell family – Sacheverell had been a fellow undergraduate – where he stayed for some years. *Façade* may have shocked the public, but the young Walton impressed enough wealthy patrons to keep him going. By 1929 the iconoclast had given way to a mature and more traditional composer, resulting in the Viola Concerto, premiered by Paul Hindemith. The oratorio that followed two years later, *Belshazzar's Feast*, may well be Walton's greatest work. Full of the excitement and rhythmic vitality that characterises so much of his music, it has certainly never ceased to be successful since it was first performed.

In 1948 Walton travelled to Argentina, where he met his future wife Susana Gil. They settled on the island of Ischia in the Bay of Naples, and remained there for the rest of their married lives. During this period Walton produced many more important works. He was knighted in 1951, awarded the Order of Merit in 1968, and received several honorary doctorates. Among his compositions are two symphonies, two operas (*The Bear* and *Troilus and Cressida*), concertos for viola, violin and cello, some chamber music including two string quartets, overtures and other orchestral works, ceremonial music, film scores, choral music and songs.

WARD, John Charles
27 Mar. 1835 – 1919
A chorister at the Temple Church, Ward was born in Upper Clapton, London. Although primarily an organist, Ward's claim to fame was as a virtuoso player of the concertina, giving many concerts on the instrument. He studied the instrument with the leading player of the time, George Case, though he first earned his living as an organist at various London churches, and was also organist and assistant conductor to Henry Leslie's choir for many years. His compositions include a cantata (*The Wood*), church music (including *In Memoriam Henry Leslie*), and organ music, (notably *A Nautical Symphony* and a *Prelude and Fugue on Westminster Chimes*), as well as solo and ensemble pieces for concertina, including a piece for eight concertinas!

WARLOCK, Peter
30 Oct. 1894 – 17 Dec. 1930
'Peter Warlock' was one of several pseudonyms used by Philip Heseltine, who wrote under his real name as a critic and as a contributor to various musical journals and encyclopaedias, concentrating especially on the music of his close friend Delius. He founded and edited a magazine, 'The Sackbut', and published collections of Elizabethan lute music and songs. Philip Heseltine was born in London and, after some music lessons at a preparatory school in Broadstairs, he went to Eton. As a composer he was largely self-taught, having begun a Classics course at Oxford, but he was greatly influenced by Delius, Vaughan Williams and Bernard van Dieren, as well as the Elizabethan lutenists and English folk-song.

His lasting contribution to English music lies in more than 120 solo songs and choral pieces, some of the finest yet written in Britain. His song cycle *The Curlew* is his most extended work, and arguably his masterpiece. Warlock also composed three orchestral works and some piano pieces. After his education at Eton, then a move to Zennor in Cornwall and a brief period in Ireland during World War One (he was a conscientious objector and classed as unfit for service) followed by travels abroad, he moved to live at his family home in Montgomeryshire. For three of his last five years he lived with E.J. Moeran in Eynsford, Kent. Often subject to fits of depression, Philip Heseltine almost certainly took his own life at the age of thirty-six, thereby depriving English music of one of its finest song composers.

WARNER, Harry Waldo
4 Jan. 1874 – 1 Jun. 1945
Waldo Warner was best known as a viola player and composer of chamber music, some of which won a Cobbett award in Britain and the Coolidge Prize in the States.

He was born at Northampton and studied at the Guildhall School of Music under Gibson and Morgan, later becoming a professor there until he joined the London String Quartet in 1920. Warner wrote orchestral suites, an opera (*The Royal Vagrants*), several works for string quartet, solo works for violin, piano, viola, and cello with piano, and over 100 songs and part-songs.

WATERS, Charles Frederick
1895 – 1975
Born at Epsom, C.F. Waters studied music privately and followed a career as a civil servant. He held various posts as an organist, contributed to Musical Opinion and wrote 'The Growth of Organ Music'. He gained a doctorate at London, and received the CBE in 1955. He specialised in the performance of new works by British composers. His own works include orchestral miniatures, instrumental suites, a cantata, anthems and organ pieces. His communion service, *Missa Sancti Phillipi*, was once widely used.

WATERSON, James
1834 – 13 Oct. 1893
James Waterson, a pupil of James Waddell, was a distinguished military musician who taught at Kneller Hall and became bandmaster of the Life Guards in 1876, serving under two Indian Viceroys, Lord Ripon and the Duke of Connaught. He was also editor of *British Bandsman*. Waterson composed a dramatic overture (*Sidonia*) and a great deal of music for the clarinet, including a wind quintet, four quartets, three trios, duets, studies and other solo pieces.

WEBBER, Amherst
25 Oct. 1867 – 25 Jul. 1946
Born of English parents in Cannes, Amherst Webber graduated from Oxford and studied music with Nicode in Dresden and Guiraud in Paris. He was accompanist and conductor at Covent Garden and the Metropolitan Opera (assisted de Reszke in Paris.) In 1925 he co-founded the Webber-Douglas School of Singing and Dramatic Art in London, and composed an opera (*The Ladder*), a comic opera (*Florella*), a symphony and songs. He died in London.

WELLESZ, Egon
21 Oct. 1885 – 9 Nov. 1974
A renowned musicologist specialising in Byzantine studies, early polyphony and Baroque opera, Egon Wellesz came to England in 1938, uprooted by the spread of Hitlerism. He was born in Vienna and studied with Schoenberg at the university there, later becoming a lecturer, then professor. In England he accepted a lectureship at Oxford and was made a Fellow of Lincoln College. In 1948 he became Reader in Byzantine music. In his own works Wellesz used the serial techniques of the modern Viennese school – but in a limited way, preferring to create his own individual idiom. He wrote nine symphonies, many operas (*Princess Girnara, Alkestis, Scherz, List und Rache, Achilles auf Skyros, Die Opferung des Gefangenen, Die Bakchantinen, Incognita*, etc.), ballets, orchestral and choral/orchestral works, nine string quartets, songs, piano pieces and other chamber works. In 1957 he was awarded a CBE. Wellesz died in Oxford.

WESLEY, Samuel Sebastian
14 Aug. 1810 – 19 Apr. 1876

The illegitimate son of Samuel Wesley (b. 1776), Samuel Sebastian can be considered as one of the major figures of English church music in the earlier years of the nineteenth century. He did much for both the Bach revival in this country and for the escape of our native church music from its stagnating cathedral traditions. He was born in London and was a chorister at the Chapel Royal, Windsor. After a period as organist of four London churches, he was appointed as organist at Hereford Cathedral in 1832, then Exeter Cathedral in 1835 before taking an position as organist of Leeds Parish Church from 1842 to 1849. After a move to Winchester Cathedral, he settled at Gloucester Cathedral, where he remained until his death.

Wesley's various posts can hardly have given him much happiness. His constant irascibility and railing against the dreary cathedral music of his time made him very unpopular with his employers. He did, however, gain considerable pleasure from his angling pursuits. Wesley composed mostly church anthems and services, hymns, secular choral works, glees and songs, and pieces for piano and organ. Wesley's works are generally regarded as being of considerably better quality and more imaginative than that of most of his cathedral contemporaries. He is buried in the Old Cemetery at Exeter Cathedral. Wesley's sister Eliza was also a noted London organist for many years.

WESTBROOK, William Joseph
1 Jan. 1831 – 24 Mar. 1894

Joseph Westbrook was born in London and studied with R. Temple. He held various posts as organist (including St. Bartholomew's, Sydenham), conductor and examiner, and published many arrangements and text translations. His compositions included an oratorio (*Jesus* submitted for his Mus.Doc.), madrigals, canons, songs and part-songs, and organ sonatas, voluntaries and arrangements. His 'Practical Organ Tutor' was popular in its day. Westbrook died at Sydenham.

WESTLAKE, Frederick
25 Feb. 1840 – 12 Feb. 1898

Frederick Westlake was born at Romsey in Hampshire. He studied with both Walter and George Alexander Macfarren at the Royal Academy of Music, where he later became a professor of piano. He also played the organ in various London churches. He composed a mass, other church works, a duet for cello and piano, songs and part-songs, solo piano pieces and hymn-tunes. Westlake died in London.

WESTROP, Henry John
22 Jul. 1812 – 23 Sep. 1879

Born at Lavenham in Suffolk, Henry Westrop was a pianist, singer, organist and choral conductor – largely in London, where he lived and died. He was a violinist in the Italian Opera and the Philharmonic Society. Westrop composed two operas (*The Maid of Bremen* had some success), a symphony, string quartets, quintets and trios, sonatas for piano, viola and flute, church music, songs, and some orchestral works.

WHETTAM, Graham
7 Sep. 1927 – 17 Aug. 2007
Despite his having had no formal training in composition, Graham Whettam's music gained recognition as early as 1951 with his *Sinfonietta for Strings*, although he discarded a number of early works. Thus the Clarinet Concerto No. 1 of 1959 became his first acknowledged opus. His dramatic and excellently crafted music was broadcast frequently by the BBC until the 1980s, but from then on Whettam's music was heard more abroad than in Britain.

Whettam was born in Swindon, Wiltshire, and then entered St. Luke's College, Exeter, to read English. After graduation he taught for a short time in Spalding, Lincolnshire. In 1958, following a divorce from his first wife, he moved to Coventry where he composed the Coventry Service in 1962 for the consecration of the new cathedral. He then married again, established Meriden Music to publish his own works, and composed his *Sinfonia Contra Timore*. This latter, his first acknowledged symphony, was dedicated to 'Bertrand Russell and all other people who suffer imprisonment or other injustice for the expression of their beliefs, or the convenience of politicians and bureaucracies'. Sadly, this statement caused the scheduled premiere to be abandoned. The work had to wait until 1965 for a first performance.

In 1973 an invitation to the biennale in Berlin led to a spate of performances in East Germany and to the composition of *Sinfonia Intrepida*, dedicated to those slaughtered in World War Two and to the rebuilding of bombed communities. In the 1970s he began teaching at the Colchester Institute, eventually moving to Ingatestone in Essex. His final home was in Woolaston, Gloucestershire. At various times Whettam was Chairman of the Composers' Guild of Great Britain, a director on the boards of the Mechanical Copyright Protection and Performing Right Societies, and vice-chairman of the British Copyright Council.

Of his five symphonies, the *Intrepida* was revised in 1977 and the fifth, the *Promethean*, was a massive reworking of his discarded *Sinfonia Stravagante*, which the BBC had broadcast in its original form. Other orchestral works include the *Introduction and Scherzo Impetuoso 'Benvenuto Cellini'* (revised 1977), three *Ballade Hebraique*s (one each for violin, viola and cello with orchestra), and the *Concerto Drammatico* for cello and orchestra. There are several works for string orchestra, a clarinet concerto, *Sinfonia Concertante*, and a *Concerto Ardente* for horn and strings. He also wrote piano pieces, organ solos, three violin sonatas and many other chamber works. Choral music, songs, percussion pieces (including a marimba sonata), and works for children also appear in Whettam's portfolio.

WHITE, Felix Harold
27 Apr. 1884 – 31 Jan. 1945
Felix White (the family name was Weiss) was a self-taught musician, though he had some guidance from his mother. His music was performed at London Promenade concerts. He composed 250 songs – some with orchestral accompaniment, others with violin – part-songs and a great deal of piano music. He also left manuscripts of much chamber, orchestral and instrumental music, including a trio for oboe, violin and piano, a study (*Dawn*) for twelve cellos, an operetta for children (*The Cockle Boat*) and many children's songs. His *The Nymph's Complaint* for oboe, viola and piano has been described as his finest work. Felix White died in London.

WHITE, Maude Valérie
23 Jun. 1855 – 2 Nov. 1937
Maude White was born at Dieppe to English parents, and, between her extensive travels lived mainly in England and Sicily. She studied at Heidelberg and Paris, first with Oliver May and W.S. Rockstro, then at the Royal Academy of Music with Francis Davenport and G.A. Macfarren, and finally with Robert Fuchs in Vienna in an abortive attempt to move away from song writing. She worked as a translator, published two volumes of memoirs and composed an opera (unfinished), a ballet (*The Enchanted Heart*), a mass, vocal quintet and piano pieces. She is chiefly remembered for her songs, many of them settings of Shelley and Herrick. In 1879 she was the first woman to be awarded the Mendelssohn Prize, and a year later success was assured when she accompanied Charles Santley in two of her own songs. Before long her songs were being performed by many famous singers; notable among the songs were *We'll go no more a-roving* and *To Althea from prison*. During World War One White organised many charity concerts. She arranged *Five Serbian Dances* (for full orchestra with bass clarinet, double bassoon and a battery of percussion) in aid of the Serbian Relief Fund; these were conducted by Sir Henry Wood. Being of frail health, Maude Valérie White spent much time touring and living in warmer climates, though for the last few years of her life she returned to England. She died in London.

WHITE, Robert le Rougetel
1908 – 1979
'Robin' le Rougetel White was born in Lancashire, and at an early age showed promise under Dr Aldous at St Bees School. While reading architecture at Liverpool University he continued his musical studies with Dr Pollitt, and after graduating, entered the Royal Academy of Music. He served with the Royal Navy during the war, and returned from the Middle East to take up a position in Cumberland as a town and country planner. He composed piano pieces and songs, some of which have been recorded.

WHITLOCK, Percy William
1 Jun. 1903 – 1 May 1946
An outstanding organist and composer for the instrument, Percy Whitlock was born at Chatham. He attended Rochester School, then King's School, and won scholarships to the Guildhall School of Music and the Royal College of Music. He held various posts in Kent before moving in 1930 to Bournemouth, where he became Municipal Organist, and spent the rest of his life there. Whitlock composed services and anthems, motets and hymn-tunes, an organ symphony and many other organ works. The Percy Whitlock Trust has been engaged in republishing his works and sponsoring recordings of them.

WHITTAKER, William Gillies
23 Jul. 1876 – 5 Jul. 1944
William Gilles Whittaker (known amongst his circle of friends as W.G.W.), was a man whose musical talents won the admiration of friends and contemporaries like Vaughan Williams and Holst, and whose energetic life bespoke the title of 'The Viking' awarded him by the sculptor Jacob Epstein. He was born at Newcastle upon Tyne, and studied there at Armstrong College, where in 1899 he joined the staff, eventually becoming

Director of Music. During this period he founded the Newcastle Bach Choir, achieving a standard of choral training and conducting unrivalled in his time. In 1929 Whittaker accepted the Professorship at Glasgow University, and concurrently the Principalship of the Scottish National Academy of Music. While in Glasgow he founded the Bach Cantata Choir, and in 1930 visited Uppsala University to unearth, edit and publish the sonatas of the English Restoration composer William Young.

Whittaker was a collector of northern folk-songs, an author of much respected books on the music of J.S. Bach, and a companion of the use of the gramophone in education and research, as well as a well-travelled examiner in music. Perhaps all his other activities have occluded Whittaker the composer, though a centenary festival in 1976 redressed the balance somewhat. His works include a prelude for orchestra, a piano concerto and other orchestral works, quartets, a trio, a wind quintet, many other chamber and instrumental works, choruses (best of which is his setting of *Psalm 139*), songs and church anthems. Roussel and d'Indy were important developmental influences. Whittaker died on Orkney.

WHYTE, Ian
13 Aug. 1901 – 27 Mar. 1960
A highly respected conductor who specialised in Scandinavian music, Ian Whyte received an OBE for his services to music. He was born at Crossford in Fifeshire, and won a scholarship to the Carnegie School in Dunfermline, then to the Royal College of Music, where he studied with Vaughan Williams and Stanford. His first musical appointment was as music organiser for Lord Glentanar, but by 1931 he had become Musical Director for Scotland, conducting the BBC Scottish Orchestra from its inception. Whyte composed two symphonies, concertos for violin and for piano, three ballets, two operettas (*The Forge* and *The Tale of the Shepherds*), an opera (*Comala*), two overtures, a piano quintet, a string quartet, choral music, and sonatas for violin and for piano.

WIENIAWSKA, Irene Regine. See **POLDOWSKI**

WILLAN, Healey
12 Oct. 1880 – 16 Feb. 1968
Though born at Balham in Surrey, Healey Willan spent the last fifty-five years of his life in Canada, where he was an organist in Toronto and taught at the university and conservatory there, becoming Professor of Music in 1950. As a boy he attended choir school in Eastbourne. He held posts as organist in Wanstead, then Holland Park, continuing to study (with fellow pupil Leopold Stokowski) under Stevenson Hoyte. As a church musician he was notable in returning to plainsong traditions in the liturgy, setting English words of introits, graduals, offertories and communions. He eventually produced the Plainsong Edition of the Canadian Psalter, and earned a reputation as a recitalist.

Willan composed two symphonies and other orchestral works, two radio operas (*Deirdre* was later adapted for the stage), incidental music (including for the Chester Mysteries), a piano concerto, choral and chamber music, marches and ceremonial music, songs, and a great many organ works (his *Introduction, Passacaglia and Fugue* has been described as 'one of the great organ works of our time').

WILLIAMS, Bryn
1924 – 1976
Bryn Williams was born at Merthyr Tydfil and studied at the Cardiff College of Music
and Drama. He taught music at secondary and further education levels, played the
organ and conducted local amateur orchestras. He composed a clarinet concerto, music
for strings, other orchestral works, two string quartets and other chamber works, choral
music, songs and part-songs, and piano pieces.

WILLIAMS, Charles
9 May 1893 – 7 Sep. 1978
Isaac Cozerbreit, to use his birth name, was a Londoner who started as a theatre and
cinema violinist. He later studied with Norman O'Neill at the Royal Academy of Music,
and afterwards was with Gaumont Films as a composer. As well as *The Dream of
Olwen*, his many works for films and radio shows followed, but his fame was made
not only as the first conductor of the Queen's Hall Light Orchestra but as the composer
of the *Devil's Galop* – the signature tune of the long-running radio series 'Dick Barton,
Special Agent'. He also wrote signature tunes for 'Friday Night is Music Night' and
Pathé News. He retired with his wife to Findon near Worthing, where he died.

WILLIAMS, Charles Francis Abdy
16 Jul. 1855 – 27 Feb. 1923
Abdy Williams was born at Dawlish in Devonshire. He studied music privately and
in Leipzig, then gained a Cambridge BA in 1878 and a B.Mus. in 1891. He spent some
time in Auckland, then returned to England to teach, becoming organist at Dover
College, and subsequently head of music at Bradfield College. He specialised in
researching ancient Greek music and plainsong, and wrote several articles and books
on the theory and history of music. His works include a string quartet, choral music
(including a number of sacred cantatas – *Music, a choral song*, was composed for the
Leeds Festival), a cello sonata, four canons for clarinet, violin and piano, and church
music.

WILLIAMS, Grace Mary
19 Feb. 1906 – 10 Feb. 1977
Grace Williams, daughter of a music teacher and conductor, was born at Barry, South
Wales. She graduated at University College, Cardiff on a scholarship, then went to the
Royal College of Music where she studied with Vaughan Williams. She was also a
pupil of Egon Wellesz in Vienna, having won a travelling scholarship. She taught for
some time at Camden School for Girls before returning to her native Glamorganshire.
Her compositions include two symphonies, an opera (*The Parlour*), a trumpet concerto,
violin concerto, sinfonia concertante for piano and orchestra, several works for chorus
and orchestra (such as the *Missa Cambrensis*, written for the 1971 Llandaff Festival),
other orchestral pieces with a Welsh flavour, incidental music for the radio and cinema,
anthems and songs, and pieces for piano and for harp. Her orchestral fanfare *Castell
Caernarfon* was performed at the Investiture of the Prince of Wales. She also made
several arrangements of Welsh folk-songs. Modest to a fault, Grace Williams refused
several honours, despite her considerable success as a composer. She died in Barry.

WILLIAMS, John Gerrard
10 Dec. 1888 – 7 Mar. 1947
Gerrard Williams, born in London, was largely self-taught as a composer, having
practised architecture until 1920. He did however receive some guidance from
Walthew. The first recital of his works was given in 1922 at the Aeolian Hall in London.
His compositions include operas (e.g. *Kate, the Cabin Boy*), operettas (*The Story of
the Willow Pattern Plate* was for children), orchestral and choral works, string quartets
and other chamber music, songs and piano pieces. He died at Oxted in Surrey.

WILLIAMSON, Malcolm Benjamin Graham Christopher
21 Nov. 1931 – 2 Mar. 2003
Master of the Queen's Music from 1975, succeeding Sir Arthur Bliss, Malcolm
Williamson was born in Sydney, Australia, where his father was an Anglican priest.
He attended Barker College, New South Wales, before entering the Sydney
Conservatorium, studying composition with Sir Eugene Goossens. He also studied
horn and became an accomplished pianist. Realising that the new European music had
not yet reached Australia, he came to London in 1953 to study with Erwin Stein, and
encountered the music of Olivier Messiaen. The latter proved the inspiration for him
to teach himself to play the organ. In 1954 his first published piece appeared – two a
cappella motets – but commissions were thin on the ground, so he found employment
in a publishing firm and played the piano in a nightclub. After he gave the premiere
of his First Piano Sonata at the Aldeburgh Festival in 1956 matters began to improve,
and in 1957 Boult conducted his First Symphony, albeit in a private concert. By 1965
an organ concerto, piano concerto and two operas (*Our Man in Havana* and *The Happy
Prince*) had appeared. He would go on to write seven more operas and eight miniature
operas for audience participation. In 1976 he was awarded the CBE, and in 1987 the
Order of Australia for his services to music and the mentally handicapped.
 Williamson's music never attained universal acclaim, and he was criticised
for his eclecticism and the shallowness of some of his music. Openly scathing about
other composers – Benjamin Britten and Andrew Lloyd Webber were two on the list
– and notoriously late with one royal commission, he made critical enemies. In addition
to works already mentioned, Williamson composed seven symphonies (including an
organ symphony and a choral symphony), several ballets (incl. *The Display*), a violin
concerto and two more piano concertos, concertos for harp and for two pianos, and
other orchestral works, several with solo voice. Chamber and instrumental pieces are
well represented, and he wrote much church music (he converted to the Roman Church
in 1952). Of his vocal output, *The Musicians of Bremen* is an amusing miniature gem.

WILSON, John Anthony Burgess
25 Feb. 1917 – 23 Nov. 1993
The film of the book *A Clockwork Orange* raised some controversy and gained its
author some considerable fame. Though known mainly as a satirical novelist, John
Burgess Wilson would probably have preferred to be known as a composer. He
produced three symphonies (the second based on Malayan themes), a *Sinfonietta* for
jazz combo, a symphonic poem (*Gibraltar*), concertos for piano and for flute,
Passacaglia for orchestra, *Song of a Northern City* for piano and orchestra, *Concertino*

for piano and percussion, three guitar quartets, *Partita* for strings, piano sonatas and cello sonatas, *Ludus Multitonalis* for recorders, several short piano pieces and some songs. He also wrote some light music including incidental music for plays, a ballet (*Mr. W.S.*) and an operetta, (*Blooms of Dublin*). As an author, John Burgess used a variety of pseudonyms to the extent that one publisher sent him one of his own novels to review.

John Burgess Wilson was born in Manchester, the son of a pub pianist. He was educated at Xaverian College before reading English language and literature at Manchester University. During World War Two he served in the Royal Army Medical Corps. He taught at Birmingham University from 1946 to 1950, and spent some time on the staff at Banbury Grammar School before taking up a post in 1954 as an education officer in Malaya and Brunei – a period that greatly influenced his novels and some of his music.

WILSON, Thomas Brendan
10 Oct. 1927 – 12 Jun. 2001

Thomas Wilson, one of Scotland's great composers, was born in Colorado, USA, to British parents who moved back to Glasgow when he was seventeen months old. Apart from school, university, military service and three years in France, he spent the rest of his life there. His schooling at St Mary's College, Aberdeen, was followed by three years in the RAF (1945-48), then a music degree course at Glasgow University, studying with Ernest Bullock and Frederick Rimmer. He joined the staff at the university in 1957 and was appointed Reader in 1971, then Professor six years later. He played a prominent role in British musical life, being at various times actively involved in the Arts Council, the New Music Group of Scotland, The Society for the Promotion of New Music, the Composers' Guild of Great Britain, and The Scottish Society of Composers. In 1990 he was awarded the CBE, and in 1991 was made a Fellow of the Royal Scottish Academy of Music. In the same year he accepted an Honorary Doctorate of Music at Glasgow University, and Edinburgh elected him a Fellow of its Royal Society.

The 1950s witnessed Wilson's espousal of atonalism, with his Third String Quartet. Subsequent works, often in the same vein and culminating in serialist techniques, gained him an international reputation. Many of them show a concern for humanity's impending catastrophes, as exemplified by his *Sequentiae Passionis* of 1974 for chorus and orchestra, which juxtaposes aleatoric percussion effects with plainsong. He was to use similarly disparate elements in many of his subsequent works. He was awarded a CBE in 1990.

Thomas Wilson composed five symphonies, the fourth being subtitled *Passeleth Tapestry*, concertos for orchestra, piano, viola and guitar, and other orchestral works, (his *St Kentigern Suite* being probably the most well known). He wrote two operas: *The Charcoal Burner* and *The Confessions of a Justified Sinner*, involving a bawdy song, a pastiche seventeenth century harpsichord minuet, quotations from Mozart, and some electronics. Wilson wrote many choral works, a ballet (*The Embers of Glencoe*), pieces for brass band, songs, and many chamber and instrumental works.

WINGHAM, Thomas
5 Jan. 1846 – 24 Mar. 1893
Thomas Wingham was a student at the Royal Academy of Music with Sterndale Bennett and Harold Thomas, becoming a professor of piano there in 1871. Most of his short life was spent in London where he was born and where he died. In addition he was organist at All Saints, Paddington, and Musical Director at the Brompton Oratory until his death. Wingham composed four symphonies (of which the third has a choral finale), six overtures, a piano concerto and other orchestral works, an opera, two string quartets and a septet, and much choral and church music (some for Antwerp Cathedral) including *Elegy on the death of Sterndale Bennett*.

WISHART, Peter Charles Arthur
1921–1984
Peter Wishart followed an academic career, teaching at the Guildhall School of Music and King's College, London, Bath University of Technology, Birmingham School of Music, Birmingham University, and finally as Professor of Music at Reading University. He was born at Crowborough in Sussex, and studied with Hely-Hutchinson at Birmingham and Nadia Boulanger in Paris. He composed two symphonies, operas (*Two in the Bush, The Captive, The Clandestine Marriage, Clytemnestra, The Lady of the Inn*, all to libretti by D.J. Roberts), ballets, two violin concertos and other orchestral works, choral music, two string quartets and other chamber works, and some instrumental music.

WOLSTENHOLME, William
24 Feb. 1865 – 23 Jul. 1931
William Wolstenholme was born at Blackburn in Lancashire and studied at the Worcester College for the Blind and at Oxford University. Though blind from birth, he displayed considerable practical musical talent at an early age, and was organist at several London churches. He composed some orchestral music, a choral ballad (*Lord Ullin's Daughter*), anthems, songs and part-songs, string quartets, quintets and trios, and solo pieces for violin, viola, cello and piano. His organ works are still played. Wolstenholme died in London.

WOOD, Charles
15 Nov. 1866 – 12 Jul. 1926
Charles Wood's music is seldom heard today, save for his church anthems, which show an originality not shared by many of his contemporaries. He was born in Armagh, and studied with Marks and with Stanford, Bridge and Taylor at the Royal College of Music. After teaching harmony for some time at the RCM, Wood took his doctorate at Cambridge, serving as organist at Gonville and Caius College and conducting the university's music society and band. He later joined the staff there, eventually succeeding Stanford as Professor of Music in 1924.

    In addition to his church anthems (*Expectans expectavi* and *O Thou, the central orb* are still used) Wood wrote a one-act opera (*Pickwick Papers*), symphonic variations, odes for solo, chorus and orchestra (*Ode to the West Wind, Ode to Music*), a piano concerto, seven string quartets, choruses, songs, and some chamber works. He also arranged folk-songs. He died in Cambridge.

WOOD, Haydn
25 Mar. 1882 – 11 Mar. 1959
Haydn Wood is remembered as a violinist and as a composer of light, popular ballads. He was born at Slaithwaite near Huddersfield, and started to learn violin with his brother before going to the Royal College of Music as a pupil of Stanford, Arbos and Caesar Thomson. In addition to the ballads, Wood composed several orchestral overtures, suites, rhapsodies and entr'actes etc., a piano concerto, variations for cello and orchestra, a violin concerto, *Lochinvar* for chorus and orchestra, music for strings, about 200 songs (including *Roses of Picardy*, *A brown bird singing*, and *Love's garden of roses*) and song-cycles. Haydn Wood died in London.

WOOD, Thomas
28 Nov. 1892 – 19 Nov. 1950
Thomas Wood was born at Chorley in Lancashire. He studied with Dr E. Brown of Barrow and went to Exeter College, Oxford. In 1918 he became a pupil of Stanford and Fryer at the Royal College of Music. After an Oxford doctorate he was appointed music master at Tonbridge School, then a lecturer and Precentor at his old college. In 1928 he retired to compose, though he served on several committees of musical importance. Wood's father was a master mariner, as might be guessed from a glance at the titles of many of his works (*The Merchantmen*, *Forty Singing Seamen*, *Master Mariners*, etc.). In addition to such songs and choruses, Wood composed some short orchestral pieces, incidental music, and about sixty smaller works for voices, piano, organ, woodwind, brass and military bands. He wrote books on musical education, and the autobiographical *True Thomas*. He died at Bures in Suffolk.

WOODFORDE-FINDEN, Amy
1860 – 13 Mar. 1919
Born in Valparaiso, Chile, where her father was British consul, Amy Ward's family moved to London, where she studied piano and composition privately with Amy Horrocks. She then travelled to India and, while in Kashmir, she married a cavalry medical officer, Lt-Col. Woodforde-Finden. After their return to London she wrote her unashamedly romantic *Four Indian Love Lyrics* in 1902, for which she will be remembered, if for nothing else. A number of other songs and collections followed, all inspired either by her South American birthplace or by her Indian travels.

WOODGATE, Herbert Leslie
15 Apr. 1902 – 18 May 1961
Leslie Woodgate is remembered as a highly respected chorus master. He was born in London and went to Westminster School and the Royal College of Music. His earliest musical experiences were as a chorister at Holy Trinity, Sloane Square, and he spent several years as organist and choirmaster at various London churches. In 1934 he became chorus master to the BBC, at the same time conducting the LNER Musical Society, for which he wrote many of his choral works. He founded the BBC Theatre Orchestra. Woodgate composed a great many choral works, including an oratorio and a *Cornish Miracle Play*, songs, a few orchestral pieces, some chamber music and a few works for organ. He also arranged folk-songs, spirituals and carols for choir.

WORDSWORTH, William Brocklesby
17 Dec 1908 – 10 Mar. 1988

Son of a clergyman and a descendant of the poet's brother, William Wordsworth was born in London. He studied with George Oldroyd at St. Michael's, Croydon, and at Edinburgh with Donald Tovey, to whom he dedicated his Second Symphony (1949). In the 1930s he was an active pacifist for the Peace Pledge Union and the Hindhead Fellowship of Reconciliation Group. Most of his life was spent at Hindhead in Surrey, and he was also an energetic campaigner for contemporary British music.

In 1955 he was elected to the executive committee of the Composers' Guild of Great Britain, becoming chairman in 1959. Two years later he settled in Kincraig, at the foot of the Cairngorms, and became active on the Scottish musical scene as chairman of the Scottish branch of the CGGB. By 1980 he had helped found the Scottish Society of Composers. Wordsworth's early music met with considerable success, his first String quartet winning the Clements Memorial Prize and his Second Symphony winning the Edinburgh International Festival Competition. But in the 1950s European music took off in directions unacceptable to him, and his music fell out of favour. He established his own publishing company, Speyside, to provide an outlet for his music.

Wordsworth's compositions include eight symphonies, concertos for piano, violin and cello, orchestral overtures, choral works and anthems, six string quartets and a great deal of other chamber works, incidental music for radio, instrumental music, songs, and educational music. Though Wordsworth may have eschewed more progressive compositional techniques, his music has a strong identity and great variety of mood and texture, ranging from the sadness of *Valediction* (for piano) and the tension of the overture *Conflict* to the spiky exuberance of the Fifth Symphony and the sublimity of *Adonais* (for five singers, piano, cymbals and bells). The last two works place Wordsworth indisputably in the twentieth century, despite comments by critics such as Peter Pirie. Wordsworth was a gardener, bee-keeper, skilled carpenter, angler and keen rock climber, and his work, unashamedly romantic, often exhibits the grandeur and spaciousness of his final resting place in the Cairngorms.

WURM, Marie J.A.
18 May 1860 – 21 Jan. 1938

Marie Wurm was born in Southampton, and studied piano and composition at the Stuttgart Conservatorium with Franklin Taylor, Clara Schumann and Joachim Raff, and in London with Stanford, Sullivan and J.F. Bridge. She held the Mendelssohn Scholarship at the RAM, became a brilliant improviser, and gave many recitals in England and Germany. She also organised the first women's orchestra in Berlin, and raised a few eyebrows when she conducted it. Her compositions (sometimes written under the name of Mary Verne) include an opera, (in German) a piano concerto, an orchestral overture, a string quartet, a cello sonata, and numerous piano pieces, as well as part-songs to both English and German texts. She died in Munich.

WYLDE, Henry
22 May 1822 – 13 Mar. 1890
Born at Bushey in Hertfordshire, Henry Wylde was a pupil of Moscheles and Potter at the Royal Academy of Music, where he afterwards became a professor of harmony. He was appointed Gresham Professor of Music in 1863. He was also founder of the New Philharmonic Society, which he conducted (after some arguments with Berlioz) from 1858 for more than twenty years, during which time he, together with Wilhelm Ganz (who took over from him in 1881) helped to promote performances of music by contemporary British composers. He founded the London Academy of Music, and supervised the building of St. George's Hall in Langham Place to house it. He composed an oratorio (*Paradise Lost*), cantatas, a piano concerto, songs and solo piano works, finding time also to write several books on music. Wylde died in London.

YOUNG, John Matthew Wilson
17 Dec. 1822 – 4 Mar. 1897
Born in Durham, Young, after teaching at York and Ripon Training College, became organist of Lincoln Cathedral in 1850, where he remained for forty-five years. Young was a composer of sacred music, and his cantata *The Return of Israel to Palestine* was composed with a prominent organ part, designed to show that the organ could be satisfactorily combined with the orchestra as a solo instrument. He moved to London in his retirement, where he died.

His younger brother, **William James Young** (1835-1913) was Assistant Organist at Lincoln Cathedral under his brother for a short while, and a composer of numerous part-songs and some songs with orchestra.

YOUNG, Percy Marshall
17 May 1912 – 9 May 2004
In the West Midlands, where he spent most of his life, Percy Young will be most remembered as an active supporter of the football team Wolverhampton Wanderers, writing articles about their performances and progress as well as a history of the club, *Centennial Wolves*. He also wrote books on football in Sheffield and Merseyside. Those whose culture extends beyond the terraces will remember his life's work in musical education – his choral and orchestral concerts with little known works by Handel featuring prominently – and his musical talks on BBC radio for children. A prolific writer, Young also penned a study of Handel for Dent's *Master Musicians* series, a study of that composer's operas, critical biographies of Vaughan Williams, Elgar, Bach, Schumann, Sullivan and Kodaly, a *Critical Dictionary of Composers and their music,* a history of British music, a volume on the choral tradition in Britain, contributions to *The New Grove,* a biography of Grove himself, and several other books on music.

Percy Young was born at Northwich in Cheshire, and attended Christ's Hospital school, Horsham. An organ scholarship took him to Selwyn College, Cambridge, where he read English, Music and History. He taught in Northern Ireland for a brief period before completing a Doctorate at Trinity College, Dublin. In 1937 Young became Music Adviser for Stoke-on-Trent education authority and seven years later he was appointed Musical Director at Wolverhampton College of Technology.

Young's main musical interest was in Elgar and his music, and he completed Elgar's unfinished opera, *The Spanish Lady*, from fragments given to him by Elgar's daughter. He was a prolific composer in his own right, producing many choral motets, some lieder, a song cycle based on R.L. Stevenson's *A Child's Garden of Verses*, chamber works, a *Festival Te Deum* for massed voices, semi-chorus and organ, and an *Elegy* for string orchestra.

ZAVTRAL (Zavertal, Zavrthal, Zaverthal), Ladislao J.P.P.
29 Sep. 1849 – 29 Jan. 1942

From 1881 to 1906 Ladislao Zavtral was Bandmaster of the Royal Artillery Band, Woolwich, where he composed the march *Loyal Hearts* for the Diamond Jubilee of Queen Victoria. He was born in Milan, son of a Bohemian composer, but emigrated to Glasgow in 1872, soon becoming conductor of the Glasgow Amateur Orchestra and other orchestras in the Glasgow suburbs of Hillhead and Pollockshields. In London he conducted the first performance (probably a private run-through) of Dvořák's *New World* Symphony and in 1895 inaugurated and conducted Sunday Concerts in the Royal Albert Hall. He became a naturalized British subject the following year, and in 1901 was made a Member of the Royal Victorian Order. Zavtral's works include two symphonies, the operas *Tita* and *Una notte in Firenza*, and other marches.

ZIMMERMANN, Agnes Marie Jacobina
5 Jul. 1847 – 14 Nov. 1925

Born in Germany, Agnes Zimmermann was brought to England by her family. At the age of nine she took piano lessons with Cipriani Potter and harmony tuition with Charles Steggall at the Royal Academy of Music, and later with G.A. Macfarren. Apart from two successful tours in Germany, she spent her life in England, and died in London. She was much in demand as a concert pianist, and was instrumental in organizing a series of piano recitals and chamber music concerts at prominent London venues. Although she is known to have had a performance of a concert overture at a RAM concert, much of her music is for piano. She also wrote a cello sonata, three violin sonatas and a piano trio, all composed between 1872 and 1879. Her songs, however, were less successful than her instrumental music. Her editions of the Mozart and Beethoven piano sonatas and Schumann's piano music were important in their time.

ZOELLER, Carli
28 Mar. 1840 – 13 Jul. 1889

Although Zoeller spent the first thirty-two years of his life in Berlin, he came to London to complete his studies at the Royal Academy of Music, later working as Bandmaster to the 7th Queens Own Hussars. His major compositions are a wind quintet, a string quartet and a piano trio, the lyric drama *Mary Stuart of Fotheringay*, overtures, a violin concerto, masses, a cantata (*Qui Sedes Domine* with viola d'amore obbligato), songs and piano pieces. His claim to fame, however, lies in his furtherance of the repertoire for the viola d'amore, preceding Montague Cleeve's work on the instrument's revival in Britain by some sixty years. He wrote several works for the viola d'amore, as well as a tutor and a history of the instrument.

Chronology
and
Appendices

A. Chronology of Composers listed in the Profiles

1800	BLOCKLEY, John		POLE, William
	GOSS, John		SALAMAN, Charles K
	RODWELL, George H		WALMISLEY, Thomas A
	STANSBURY, George F	1815	JACKSON, William J
1801	BUCKLEY, Olivia		LAZARUS, Henry
	ELLERTON, John Lodge		PEARSON, Henry H
	SEVERN, Thomas H		PRAEGER, Ferdinand
1802	ANDREWS, Richard H	1816	ANGEL, Alfred
	BARNETT, John		BENNETT, W Sterndale
	LEE, George A		ELVEY, George J
	TURLE, James		PHILLIPS, William L
1803	BECHER, Alfred J	1817	ANDREWS, Jenny
1804	BENEDICT, Julius		RICHARDS, H Brinley
	FORBES, Henry	1818	HOPKINS, Edward J
1805	GAUNTLETT, Henry J		LITOLFF, Henry Charles
	THOMSON, John		REINAGLE, Caroline
1806	OSBORNE, George A	1819	ALBERT, Prince Consort
1807	CALLCOTT, William H		LONGHURST, William H
1808	BALFE, Michael W		MONK, Edwin G
	COSTA, Sir Michael		MOUNSEY, Elizabeth
	CROUCH, Frederick N		OBERTHÜR, Charles
	LUCAS, Charles		STIRLING, Elizabeth
	NORTON, Caroline		TAYLOR, Laura
	PARISH-ALVARS, Elias	1820	BARNARD, Charlotte
1809	d'ALBERT, Charles L		MELLON, Alfred
	ALLEN, Henry R	1821	MACIRONE, Clara
	HATTON, John L		MORI, Frank
	MUDIE, Thomas M		SAINTON-DOLBY, Charlotte
	THIRLWALL, John W		STEPHENS, Charles E
1810	HILES, John	1822	ALLEN, George B
	WESLEY, Samuel S		HOPKINS, John
1811	MOUNSEY, Ann S		HORSLEY, Charles E
1812	BARKER, George A		LAMBETH, Henry A
	HOLMES, William Henry		LESLIE, Henry D
	HULLAH, John P		LUTZ, Wilhelm M
	KNIGHT, Rev Joseph P		REAY, Samuel
	PYE, Kellow John		STEPHEN, Edward
	RUSSELL, Henry		WYLDE, Henry
	WALLACE, William V	1823	CHIPP, Edmund T
	WESTROP, Henry J		DYKES, Rev. John B
1813	ASPULL, George		JEWSON, Frederick B
	DAVISON, James W		ROCKSTRO, William S
	GREATHEED, Samuel S		SPARK, William
	LODER, Edward J	1824	ADAMS, Thomas J
	MACFARREN, George A		AGUILAR, Emanuel
	SAINTON, Philippe Prosper		BEXFIELD, William R
	SMART, Henry		FAWCETT, John Jnr
1814	MAY, Oliver	1824	FITZWILLIAM, Edward F

	MACFARREN, Emma		LEVEY, William C
1825	BALY, William		SUMMERS, James Lea
	GABRIEL, Virginia	1838	ARCHER, Frederick
	LODER, Kate		BARNBY, Joseph
	PÂQUE, Guillaume		CLAY, Frederic
1826	BEST, William T		COBB, Gerard
	HILES, Henry		NAYLOR, John
	LAHEE, Henry		ROECKEL, Joseph
	MACFARREN, Walter C	1839	HOLMES, Henry
	STEGGALL, Charles		SMITH, Alice Mary
	THOMAS, John		SMITH, E Sydney
1827	CALKIN, John B	1840	CLARK, Rev. Frederick S
	OLD, John		CLARKE, James Hamilton
	PHILP, Elizabeth		JORDAN, Charles W
	TOLHURST, George		STAINER, John
	WALEY, Simon		STRATTON, Stephen
1828	GILBERT, Alfred		WESTLAKE, Frederick
	MARTIN, George William		ZOELLER, Carli
1829	GOLDSCHMIDT, Otto	1841	PARRATT, Walter
1830	BARRY, Charles A		PARRY, Joseph
	OAKELEY, Herbert S		ROBERTS, John Varley
1831	ASCHER, Joseph	1842	BACHE, Walter
	BANISTER, Henry C		CALDICOTT, Alfred J
	CUMMINGS, William H		COULDERY, Claudius H
	ROBINSON, Fanny		GADSBY, Henry R
	WESTBROOK, W Joseph		JEKYLL, Charles S
1832	ARNOLD, George B		NIXON, Henry Cotter
1833	BACHE, Francis E		PRENTICE, Thomas R
	CUSINS, William G		PRESCOTT, Oliveria
	KETTLE, Charles		SULLIVAN, Arthur
	PRENDERGAST, Arthur H	1843	MACLEAN, Charles D
1834	BERGER, Francesco	1844	ADAMS, Stephen
	BUNNETT, Edward		BERINGER, Oscar
	GARRETT, George Mursell		BRIDGE, John F
	O'LEARY, Arthur		CELLIER, Alfred
	SANTLEY, Charles		CRESER, William
	THOMAS, Robert Harold		MARTIN, George Clement
	THORNE, Edward H		PEACE, Albert L
	WATERSON, James	1845	GLADSTONE, Francis E
1835	ASPA, Edwin	1846	PAGE, Arthur J
	OUSELEY, Rev. Frederick		WINGHAM, Thomas
	PROUT, Ebenezer	1847	DAVENPORT, Francis W
	TURPIN, Edmund H		HEAP, Charles S
	WARD, John Charles		ILIFFE, Frederick
1836	ANDERTON, Thomas		MACKENZIE, Alexander
	ARMES, Philip		ROGERS, Roland
	CARRODUS, John T		STOKES, Walter
	FARMER, John		ZIMMERMANN, Agnes
1837	BARNETT, John F	1848	ALLISON, Horton Claridge
	CLIFFE, Frederic		ALLITSEN, Frances
	COLBORNE, Langdon		JENKINS, David
	GAUL, Alfred R		NICHOLL, Horace W
	HOLMES, Alfred	1848	PARRY, C Hubert H

ROBERTS, John Henry

1849 COWARD, Henry

LLOYD, C Harford

SHAKESPEARE, William

ZAVTRAL, Ladislao J. P.P.

1850 BEAZLEY, James C

FANING, Eaton J

MANN, Arthur H

THOMAS, Arthur G

1851 CARMICHAEL, Mary

FOSTER, Myles Birket

HILL, Lady Arthur

1852 CLIFTON, Henry R

CORDER, Frederick

COWEN, Frederick H

CROOK, John

DELIUS, Frederick

STANFORD, Charles V

VINCENT, Charles J

1853 BRIDGE, Joseph C

HOLLANDER, Benno

SELBY, B Luard

1854 CRUIKSHANK, William A C

EDWARDS, Henry J

1855 HERVEY, Arthur

HUGHES, Edward J

HUGHES, Richard S

WHITE, Maude Valérie

1856 BENNETT, Frederick J W

BEVAN, Frederick C

HOPEKIRK, Helen

MACBETH, Allan

PEARCE, Charles W

STUART, Leslie

1857 ASTLE-ALLAM, Agnes

ELGAR, Edward

ELLICOTT, Rosalind F

KENNEDY-FRASER, Marjory

SAWYER, Frank J

1858 BARNES, Frederick E

CARR, Frank O

DARE, M Marie

DARKE, Harold E

DE LARA, Isidore

FORD, Ernest

MATTHAY, Tobias

MAUNDER, John H

SMYTH, Ethel Mary

STORER, John

1859 ASHTON, Algernon B

FLOOD, William H G

HADOW, William H

HARWOOD, Basil

HAYNES, W Battison

SPEER, Charlton T

1860 AMES, John C

ANCLIFFE, Charles

DACRE, Henry

FORRESTER, James C

WALLACE, William

WOODFORDE-FINDEN, Amy

WURM, Marie

1861 ALCOCK, Walter G

ANDERTON, Howard O

CARYLL, Ivan

JONES, Sidney

MONCKTON, J Lionel

SHARPE, Herbert F

1862 AYLWARD, Florence

BYNG, George W.

CHEVALIER, Albert

GERMAN, Edward

LEHMANN, Elizabeth

1863 ARKWRIGHT, Marian

BENNETT, George John

BOYCE, Ethel

BRIGHT, Dora E

BUNNING, Herbert

GODFREY, Arthur E

MERRITT, Thomas

SOMERVELL, Arthur

SPEER, William Henry

1864 d'ALBERT, Eugene F C

ALLON, Henry E

BROWN, Henry A

BROWNE, J Lewis

GRIMSHAW, Arthur E

HUME, J Ord

PARRY, Joseph Haydn

1865 BREWER, Alfred H

COLLISSON, Rev. William A H

HOLLINS, Alfred

LEMARE, Edwin H

MACPHERSON, C Stewart

MILES, Philip

TALBOT, Howard

TERRY, Richard R

WOLSTENHOLME, William

1866 ALDRIDGE, Amanda

CLUTSAM, George H

DRYSDALE, F. Learmont

DUNCAN, William E

MADDISON, Adela

1866 PROTHEROE, Daniel

	WOOD, Charles		AUSTIN, Ernest
1867	BEDFORD, Herbert		BAIRSTOW Edward
	BRYSON, Ernest R		BARNS, Ethel
	BUCALOSSI, Ernest		GATTY, Nicholas C
	HAWLEY, Stanley		HART, Fritz
	HORROCKS, Amy		HOLST, Gustav
	NAYLOR, Edward W		ROBERTON, Hugh S
	NOBLE, Thomas T		WARNER, H Waldo
	ROSSE, Frederick	1875	COLERIDGE-TAYLOR, Samuel
	STEGGALL, Reginald		KETÈLBEY, Albert W
	WEBBER, Amherst		KLEAN, Bluebell
1868	AITKEN, George B		NICHOLSON, Sydney H
	BANTOCK, Granville		O'NEILL, Norman
	BROOME, William E		ROOTHAM, Cyril B
	D'ERLANGER, Baron Frederic		SHAW, Martin
	IVIMEY, John W		TOVEY, Donald F
	JOHNSON, Bernard		WATERS, Charles F
	LAMOND, Frederic A	1876	BRIAN, Havergal
	MACCUNN, Hamish		HENLEY, William
	MCEWEN, John B		HENSCHEL, Isidor George
	SPEAIGHT, Joseph		HURLSTONE, William
1869	ALLEN, Hugh		REED, William H
	ATKINS, Ivor		RUBENS, Paul A
	BARCLAY, Arthur		WHITTAKER, W Gillies
	BOTTING, Herbert W	1877	AMERS, Henry G
	DAVIES, H Walford		BONAVIA Ferruccio
	HINTON, Arthur		BRUCKSHAW, Kathleen
	STEPHEN, David		DUNHILL, Thomas F
	WADDINGTON, Sidney P		GARDINER, H Balfour
1870	ARNOTT, Archibald D		GARRATT, Percival M
	FELLOWES, Rev. Edmund H		PEEL, G Graham
	MACPHERSON, Charles		QUILTER, Roger
	McALPIN, Colin		SCOTT, Marion
	PITT, Percy	1878	BOUGHTON, Rutland
	WALKER, Ernest		CARSE, Adam
1871	BUCK, Percy C		DAVIES, Evan T
	HARRIS, Clement H G		FARJEON, Harry H
	SQUIRE, William H		HOLBROOKE, Josef C
1872	AUSTIN, Frederic		HOLLAND, Theodore S
	BOROWSKI, Felix		IRVING, Ernest K
	FINCK, Herman		ROBERTS, Caradog
	LYON, James		SANDERSON, Wilfrid E
	MACLEAN, Alexander	1879	BRIDGE, Frank
	PHILPOT, Stephen R		CORDER, Paul W
	THOMAS, Vincent		FLETCHER, Percy E
	VAUGHAN WILLIAMS, Ralph		HARTY, Hamilton
	WALTHEW, Richard Henry		IRELAND, John
1873	BELL, William H		SAMUEL, Harold
	CLARKE, Robert C		SCOTT, Cyril
	RONALD, Landon		SHAW, Geoffrey
	VAUGHAN THOMAS, David		BAYNES, Sydney
1874	ANSELL, John	1880	AGATE, Edward

BAINTON, Edgar
CARR, Howard
1888   FOULDS, John H
LLOYD, J Morgan
POLDOWSKI
SCOTT, Francis G
SWINSTEAD, Felix G
WILLAN, Healey

1881 ALFORD, Kenneth J
GEEHL, Henry E
ISAACS, Edward
KELLY, Frederick S
SMITH, J Leopold

1882 BRAHAM, Philip
CHIGNELL, Robert
COATES, Albert
CRIPPS, Alfred R
GIBSON, Henry
GRAINGER, Percy
LUCAS, Mary A
MARTIN, F J Easthope
O'BRIEN, Charles
WOOD, Haydn

1883 BATH, Hubert
BAX, Arnold
BERNERS, Gerald, Lord
BRAITHWAITE, Sam H
CAREY, Francis C S
DYSON, George
HARRIS, William H
LLOYD, David J de
TOYE, J Francis

1884 BOWEN, York
REYNOLDS, Alfred C
WHITE, Felix H

1885 ANTHONY, Evangeline
BUTTERWORTH, George
COLAHAN, Arthur
DALE, Benjamin J
FARRAR, Ernest B
GRAY, Alan
HARRISON, Julius
WELLESZ, Egon
WILLIAMS, C F Abdy

1886 CLARKE, Rebecca
COATES, Eric
FRISKIN, James
MERRICK, Frank
MORRIS, Reginald O
OLDROYD, George
PHILLIPS, Montague F

1887 COLLINGWOOD, Lawrence A
DIEREN, Bernard van

HEATH, John R
LEY, Henry G
1888 BESLY, Maurice
BROWNE, W C Denis
COLES, Cecil F.G.
WILLIAMS, J Gerrard

1889 BRENT-SMITH, Alexander
CHAPLIN, Charlie
GIBBS, C Armstrong
GREENWOOD, John D H
HAY, Norman
HENRY, Leigh Vaughan
JENKINS, Cyril
LEWIS, Idris
RHODES, Harold W
STATHAM, Heathcote D
TOYE, Geoffrey

1890 BULLOCK, Ernest
CAMPBELL, Colin M
GURNEY, Ivor
PRICE, Richard M

1891 ALEXANDER, Arthur
ANDERSON, William Robert
BERNARD, Anthony
BLISS, Arthur
BURROWS, Benjamin
DAVIDSON, Malcolm
FENNEY, William
LANG, Craig S
MORRIS, Haydn
OWEN, Morfydd
SAINTON, Philip Prosper
STANTON, Walter K

1892 ANDERSON, William Henry
COLLINS, Anthony
HOWELLS, Herbert
REDMAN, Reginald
ROWLEY, Alec
SORABJI, Khaikosru Shapurji
WOOD, Thomas

1893 BENJAMIN, Arthur
BRIDGEWATER, E Leslie
CUNDELL, Edric
DAVIES, Hubert
GOOSSENS, Eugene
GOW, Dorothy
NOVELLO, Ivor
ORR, Charles W
WILLIAMS, Charles

1894 ANSON, Hugo V
BLOWER, Maurice
1894 CLEEVE, S Montagu

MILNER, Arthur F
MOERAN, Ernest John
WARLOCK, Peter
1895 CONNELLY, Reg
COOPER, Walter T Gaze
GRAY, Cecil
JACOB, Gordon
KLEIN, Ivy F
NICHOLAS, John M
PALLIS, Marco
PROCTOR-GREGG, Humphrey
1896 DANN, Horace
GERHARD, Roberto
JACOBSON, Maurice
PETERKIN, G Norman
SLATER, Gordon
THALBEN-BALL, George
1897 ADAIR, Yvonne
CHRISTOPHER, Cyril S
HEWARD, Leslie
1898 ARMSTRONG, Thomas
ARUNDELL, Dennis
COWARD, Noel
DEMUTH, Norman
FOSTER, Arnold W A
HAMILTON, Janet
HOWELL, Dorothy
MARK, Jeffrey
RANKL, Karl
ROOPER, Jasper B
1899 BAINES, William
BARBIROLLI, John
CURZON, Frederic E
EDMUNDS, Christopher
FOSS, Hubert J
HADLEY, Patrick
SUMSION, Herbert W
1900 BRYDSON, John C
BUSH, Alan Dudley
ELKINGTON, Lilian
HEAD, Michael D
JOHNSTONE, Maurice
THIMAN, Eric
1901 BARSOTTI, Roger
BUSCH, William
BYE, Frederick E.
DUNLOP, Isobel
FINZI, Gerald
GREENBAUM, Hyam
HELY-HUTCHINSON, Victor
RUBBRA, Edmund
WHYTE, Ian

1902 LONGMIRE, John B H
SWAIN, Freda
TURNBULL, Percy P
WALTON, William
WOODGATE, H Leslie
1903 BALL, Eric W J
BERKELEY, Lennox
COLERIDGE-TAYLOR, Avril
COX, Desmond
FOGG, C W Eric
GOLDSCHMIDT, Berthold
HALL, Richard
LUCAS, Leighton
MILFORD, Robin
PITFIELD, Thomas
RAINIER, Priaulx
WHITLOCK, Percy W
1904 ADDINSELL, Richard
AGER, Laurence M
BENBOW, Charles E
CARR, Michael
CHISHOLM, Erik
CLIFFORD, Hubert J.
RICHARDSON, Alan
1905 ALWYN, William
BRODSZKY, Nicholas
CENTER, Ronald
CHAGRIN, Francis
DARNTON, Christian
GUNDRY, Inglis
LAKE, Ian T
LAMBERT, Constant
LEIGH, Walter
PLUMSTEAD, Mary
POSTON, Elizabeth
RAWSTHORNE, Alan
SEIBER, Mátyás
TIPPETT, Michael
1906 BAGA, Ena Rostra
COOKE, Arnold A
DOLMETSCH, Rudolph
FRANKEL, Benjamin
LUTYENS, Elisabeth A
LYDIATE, Frederick
WILLIAMS, Grace M
1907 CREITH, Guirne
HOLST, Imogen
MACONCHY, Elizabeth
NAYLOR, Bernard
1908 FERGUSON, Howard
GREEN, Russell
LE FLEMING, Christopher
WHITE, Robert le Rougetel

	WORDSWORTH, William		SALZEDO, Leonard
1909	EASDALE, Brian		SIMPSON, Robert
	FULTON, Norman R		WISHART, Peter C A
	KEAL, Minna	1922	CARWITHEN, Doreen
	MURRILL, Herbert		HAMILTON, Iain
	ORR, Robin K		MOORE, Timothy
	RAYNOR, John		SMITH, Ronald
	VINTER, Gilbert		VEALE, John
	WALSWORTH, Ivor	1923	BANKS, Don
1910	BINGE, Ronald		DRING, Madeleine
	FISKE, Roger		LANCHBERY, John
	REED, William L	1924	BUNTING, Christopher E
	STILL, Robert		GOW, David
	TEMPLETON, Alec		WILLIAMS, Bryn
1911	ASHFIELD, Robert James	1925	CARY, Tristram
	BATE, Stanley		GOODWIN, Ronald A
	REIZENSTEIN, Franz		MILNER. Anthony
	ROSS, Colin		ORAM, Daphne
	TATE, Phyllis	1926	BROCKLESS, Brian
1912	COKE, Roger Sacheverell		OLDHAM, Arthur W
	HARKER. Clifford A	1927	BARLOW, David
	YOUNG, Percy		BULLER, John
1913	BLACK, Stanley		JOSEPHS, Wilfred
	BRITTEN, E Benjamin		WHETTAM, Graham
	DAVIE, Cedric Thorpe		WILSON, Thomas
	LLOYD, George W S	1928	HURD, Michael
1914	CHACKSFIELD, Frank	1929	HODDINOTT, Alun
	LLOYD WEBBER, William		JEFFREYS, John
	PANUFNIK, Andrej		LEIGHTON, Kenneth
	RICHARDSON, Arnold	1930	BART, Lionel
1915	ALLIN, Steuart		MAYER, John
	COCKSHOTT, Gerald	1931	WILLIAMSON, Malcolm
	PIGGOTT, Patrick	1932	BLYTON, Carey
	SEARLE, Humphrey		JESSETT, Michael
1916	ApIVOR, Denis		SHERLAW-JOHNSON, Robert
	ATHERTON, Robert	1933	SANDERS, John
	STEVENS, Bernard G	1934	MATTHIAS, William
1917	ARNELL, Richard		RIDOUT, Alan
	BAINES, Francis	1935	MAW, Nicholas
	SMITH BRINDLE, Reginald	1936	CARDEW, Cornelius
	WILSON, John A Burgess	1937	ARDLEY, Neil
1919	DEL MAR, Norman		DERBYSHIRE, Delia
	DUARTE, John W	1938	STEEL, Christopher
	HORDER, T Mervyn		STOKER, Richard
1920	ADDISON, John M	1939	HOLD, Trevor
	BUSH, Geoffrey	1941	BURGON, Geoffrey
	FRICKER, P Racine	1942	DAVIS, John D
	HEMING, Michael S		FANSHAWE, David A
1921	ARNOLD, Malcolm	1943	DAVIES, Hugh S
	BLEZARD, William		SOUSTER, Timothy
	CRUFT, Adrian	1948	BODMAN, Christopher
	GIPPS, Ruth	1950	OLIVER, Stephen

B. British Societies and some London Venues

The following is a selective list of organisations and main concert venues mentioned in the Profiles

1719	Three Choirs Festival
1775	Hanover Square Rooms (–1874)
1754	Society of Arts (Royal Society of Arts 1847)
1813	Philharmonic Society (Royal Philharmonic Soc. 1912)
1834	Society of British Musicians (–1865)
1852	New Philharmonic Society (–1879)
1855	Crystal Palace (–1936)
1858	St James's Hall (–1902)
1858	Musical Society of London (–1867)
1858	Monday Popular Concerts (–1898)
1871	Royal Albert Hall
1873	Alexandra Palace
1873	Carl Rosa Opera Company
1874	Musical Association (Royal Musical Association 1944)
1876	Bach Choir
1878	Musical Artists Society (–c.1891)
1882	Incorporated Society of Musicians
1889	Associated Board of the RAM and the RCM
1893	Queen's Hall (–1941)
1895	First Promenade Concerts
1901	Wigmore Hall (orig. Bechstein Hall)
1903	Aeolian Hall , London (–1943)
1905	Society of British Composers (–1918)
1908	Music Teachers' Association
1911	Society of Women Musicians (–1972)
1918	British Music Society (–1933)
1921	British National Opera (–1929)
1922	International Society for Contemporary Music
1927	Royal School of Church Music
1929	Rural Music Schools Association
1931	First Macnaghten Concerts (–1994)
1936	Workers' Music Association
1940	Council for the Encouragement of Music and the Arts (later Arts Council)
1943	Society for the Promotion of New Music (now Sound and Music)
1945	Composers' Guild of Great Britain
1951	Royal Festival Hall, London
1978	The British Music Society
1985	British Music Information Centre (also now Sound and Music)

C. British and Foreign Conservatories of Music

		First Principal/Founder
1795	Paris Conservatoire	
1811	Prague Conservatory	
1813	Brussels Conservatory	
1817	Vienna Conservatory, originally (Gesellschaft der Musikfreunde)	Antonio Salieri
1822	Royal Academy of Music, London	William Crotch
1843	Leipzig Conservatory	Felix Mendelssohn
1848	Royal Irish Academy of Music, Dublin	
1850	Berlin Hochschule für Musik	
1850	Cologne Conservatory	Ferdinand Hiller
1857	Royal Military School of Music	Henry Schallehn
1864	College of Organists, London (Royal 1893)	
1869	Tonic Sol-fa College	John Curwen
1872	Trinity College of Music, London	H. Bonavia Hunt
1872	Royal Normal College for the Blind, S. London	FJ Campbell, R Armitage
1873	National Training School for Music (later RCM)	Sir Henry Cole
1877	Frankfurt Conservatory	Joachim Raff
1880	Guildhall School of Music, London	Thomas H. Weist-Hill
1883	Royal College of Music, London	Sir George Grove
1885	Morley College, London (part-time classes)	Gustav Holst (1907)
1887	Birmingham and Midland Institute School of Music	Granville Bantock
1887	London College of Music	Alfred J. Caldicott
1890	Athenaeum School of Music, Glasgow (later Royal Scottish Academy of Music and Drama, Now Royal Conservatoire of Scotland)	Allan Macbeth
1893	Royal Manchester College of Music (later Royal Northern Sch. of Music)	Sir Charles Hallé
1903	Royal Marines School of Music (orig. Portsmouth, moved to Deal 1930)	
1912	Royal Academy of Music moves to present building	
1920	Northern School of Music (merged with Royal Manchester College of Music in 1973)	
1949	Welsh College of Music and Drama, Cardiff	

There were also a number of smaller suburban and provincial British conservatoires and schools of music, many of which have not stood the test of time, such as at:

Blackheath (1881) – now The Conservatoire, Brighton (1883), Croydon (1883), Huddersfield, Leeds (1898), South London Institute (1869), Watford, Woodford, etc.

Appendix A
Some Foreign Teachers mentioned in the Profiles

The following is a selective list of teachers referred to in the Profiles, with their main place of work. p.=piano, c.=composition, v.= violin, hc.=harmony and counterpoint, o.=organ, vc.= cello.

BOULANGER, Nadia	(1887–1979)	[v,c]	Paris Cons.
BÜLOW, Hans von	(1830–1894)	[p]	Berlin, then dir. of Munich Cons.
DANNREUTHER, Edward	(1844–1905)	[p]	Moved to London 1853, taught at RAM
DAVID, Ferdinand	(1810–1873)	[v]	Leipzig Cons. 1843–
DOEHLER, Theodor	(1814–1856)	[p,c]	Much travelled; Florence 1848–56
GARCÍA, Manuel	(1805–1906)	[s]	B. Spain, taught Paris Cons. and RAM (1850)
GRÜTZMACHER, Freidrich	(1832–1903)	[vc]	Leipzig Cons. 1849–60, then Dresden
HAUPTMANN, Moritz	(1792–1868)	[v, c]	Leipzig 1842–68
HILLER, Ferdinand	(1811–1885)	[c]	Founder of Cologne Cons. 1850
JADASSOHN, Salomon	(1831–1902)	[c,p,hc]	Leipzig Cons. 1852–
JOACHIM, Joseph	(1831–1907)	[v[	Berlin from 1866 (several visits to London)
KNORR, Iwan	(1853–1916)	[c]	Hoch Conservatory, Frankfurt and privately
KREUTZER, Conradin	(1780–1849)	[c]	Switzerland
KREUTZER, Leon	(1817–1868)	[p]	Berlin Hochschule
LAMPERTI, Francesco	(1813–1892)	[s]	Milan Cons. 1850–75
LEICHENTRITT, Hugo	(1874–1951)	[c]	Berlin, privately
LESCHETIZKY, Theodor	(1822–1916)	[p]	Taught in Vienna
MOLIQUE, Bernhard	(1803–1869)	[v, c]	London 1849–66
MOSCHELES, Ignaz	(1794–1870)	[p]	Moved to London in 1822
NAVA, Gaetano	(1802–1875)	[s]	Milan Cons. 1837–
PAER, Ferdinando	(1771–1839)	[c]	Taught in Venice
PAUER, Ernst	(1826–1905)	[p]	Taught London 1851-96 at RAM and NTS
PETRI, Egon	(1881–1962)	[p]	Manchester Coll. (1905-11), Berlin Hochschule (1921-26)
PIXIS, Johann Peter	(1788–1874)	[p]	Vienna (1806), Paris (1823), Baden (1840)
PLAIDY, Louis	(1810–1874)	[p]	Leipzig Cons. 1843–65
RAFF, J. Joachim	(1822–1882)	[p]	Director of Frankfurt Cons. 1877–82
REINECKE, Carl	(1820–1910)	[p,c]	Leipzig Cons. 1860–1902
RICHTER, Ernst F.E.	(1802–1879)	[hc.]	Leipzig Cons. 1843–
RIVARDE, Achille	(1865–1940)	[v]	Taught at RCM 1899–1936
SAURET, Emile	(1852–1920)	[v]	Taught at RAM 1890–1903; at TCM 1908
SCHNEIDER, Johann G	(1789–1864)	[o]	Org. Leipzig Univ., Dresden
SCHWEIZER, Otto	(1846–	[p,c]	Leipzig Cons., taught in Edinburgh from 1870
THALBERG, Sigismond	(1812–1871)	[p]	Much travelled; Naples 1858–71
WILHELMJ, August	(1845–1908)	[v]	Taught at GSM and privately from 1894

Appendix B
Some British Universities
and their Degrees

Oxford
Until 1911 the Mus.Bac. and Mus.Doc. were awarded externally on submission of a composition (plus a substantial fee), with a performance at the university (usually at the expense of the candidate). In 1870 two written examinations were included and the requirement for a performance of the submitted composition was dropped for the Mus.Bac. in 1878 (1891 for the Mus.Doc.). Only in 1911 (under Sir Walter Parratt) was three years' residence made compulsory, with some instruction provided. Women were not able to be awarded degrees (although they could submit exercises and sit the examinations) until 1921. Professorships, until this time, were non-resident, and only required attendance at meetings and supervision of submissions, with the occasional lecture.

Cambridge
Examinations for its degrees (Mus.B. and Mus.D.) were instituted earlier, in 1857. In 1875 the Professor (now G.A. Macfarren) was required to give lectures during the year, and candidates' work was assessed by a Board of examiners rather that just by the Professor. The requirement for performance of the exercise was dropped at the same time as Oxford. The examinations, however, were particularly rigorous at that time, limiting the number of awards. Compulsory three-year residence was required for the Mus.B. as early as 1893.

London
In 1858 the Faculty of Music was formed, but degrees were not instituted until 1878. These were more rigorously academic than those for Oxford and Cambridge, requiring examinations in acoustics, traditional harmony and counterpoint, as well as the submission of an exercise for the B.Mus. and D.Mus. The London music colleges formed links with the University, and full-time students at the RAM, RCM and TCM were able to take London University academic external degrees, although as late as the 1950s this was not widely encouraged. These colleges' own degree programmes were introduced much later in the twentieth century. The Music Department was not established until 1964, under Thurston Dart.

Durham
Durham's degrees, like Oxford and Cambridge, from their inception in 1831 were external, but considerably cheaper. Its music degrees were not introduced until 1890, and required the submission of an exercise as well as a written examination of competence in English, Geography and Arithmetic. The awarding of degrees to women at Durham was in advance of Oxford and Cambridge – in 1910.

Appendix C
Significant articles on British composers that have appeared in British Music Society publications

Most issues of the British Music Journal (later *British Music*) are available from the British Music Society. Newsletters are not available but Gerald Leach will photocopy required material on receipt of a donation to the British Music Society.

Key to Sources:
J   British Music Society Journal/British Music
N   British Music Society Newsletter
Composers' names in the titles are given as initials only.
Titles in brackets indicate subject matter when the title is vague.

Composer	Title	Source
Agnew, Roy	R.A.	N73
Alford, Kenneth	K.A. & Hubert Bath	J17
Allin, Steuart	A.S. (1915-2002)	N97
Alwyn, William	W.A. A brief chronology	N122
Alwyn, William	W.A. at 100	J27
Aplvor, Denis	An unsung modernist	N91
	Yerma. A somewhat closer look. D.A.'s magnum opus	N85
April, Elsie		N128
Arnell, Richard	R.A at 75	J14
	R.A. A little 90th birthday tribute	J29
Arnold, Malcolm	M.A. and John Lord	N76
	M.A. at 80	J23
	M.A. in Cornwall	N109
	M.A. The symphonies Pt 1	N92
	M.A. An appreciation on his 65th birthday	N32
	Scott & A. Is the symphony out-dated?	J27
Ashton, Algernon	A.A. 1859-1937	J14
	The Music of A.A.	N104
Austin, Frederic	F.A. 'A most versatile Musician'	J26
	The music of F.A.	N93
Baines, William	W.B. (1899-1922)	J21
Bainton, Edgar	Dr. E.L.B.	N114
	E.B.	J12
Bantock, Granville	B. meets the press; new music before WWI	J25
	B.'s *Sappho* Fragments	N73
	G.B. and Ernest Newman: Role of a press champion	J29
	G.B. Recalled	N56
	G.B. The Hebridean Connection	N72
Bate, Stanley	S.B. Forgotten International Composer	J13
	S.B.	N47
Bath, Hubert	H.B. & Kenneth Alford	J17
Bax, Arnold	A B. by any other name . . . Dermot O'Byrne	J32
	B.'s *Grania & Diarmid*	N127
	Bax's Last Golden Twilight	N95

Acknowledgements

The authors acknowledge with thanks the help given by Pamela Blevins, for her advice on the entries for Denis Browne, Marion Scott and Ivor Gurney; Professor Jeremy Dibble, for help with the Parry and Stanford entries; Rob Barnett, for some corrections; Wendy and Andrew Hiscocks and Martin Cotton for their assiduous reading of the text and for making various corrections and suggestions, and above all to John Talbot, for his invaluable proof reading.

Cover photographs:
Doreen Carwithen: photograph taken by Doreen Carwithen's cousin W. Alec Davison; used by the family's permission. Sir Malcolm Arnold: photo by Fritz Curzon.

The following cover photographs are reproduced by permission of the Royal Academy of Music, London:
Sir Arnold Bax: portrait by Vera Bax, 1933; Sir Lennox Berkeley: photograph by Clive Barda, February 1983; York Bowen: photograph by Herbert Hughes, 1935; Gordon Jacob: photograph 1976 (bequeathed by Norman McCann); Sir John McEwen; Sir Arthur Sullivan: photograph by Walery, undated; Maude-Valérie White: photograph (from the McCann collection).

The following images have been reproduced by permission of the Royal Academy of Music, London:
Michael Balfe, Granville Bantock, Lord Berners, Samuel Coleridge-Taylor, Frederick Corder, Michael Costa, Frederick H. Cowen, Benjamin Dale, Frederick Delius, Myles Birket Foster, Edward German, Josef Holbrooke, Albert Ketelby, Elisabeth Lutyens, George A. Macfarren, Walter C. Macfarren, Tobias Matthay, Ivor Novello, Morfydd Owen, Walter Parratt, Hubert Parry, Roger Quilter, Brinley Richards, Prosper Sainton, Charles Santley, Ethel Smyth, Charles V. Stanford, Charles Steggall, Arthur Sullivan, Felix Swinstead, Donald F. Tovey, William Walton, William V. Wallace, S.S. Wesley.

The following images have been reproduced with permission from the Royal College of Music, London:
Ethel Barnes (photo by Iona Connell), Algernon Ashton, William Hurlstone.

The following images have been reproduced with thanks to Stainer and Bell:
Adam Carse, Sir George Dyson, Edmund Rubbra.

The following are also acknowledged:
William Alwyn: by permission of the William Alwyn Foundation; Denis Aplvor: courtesy of Len Mullinger: John Barnby: from the Lewis Foreman Collection: Arthur Benjamin, photo by Frank Otley, courtesy of Boosey and Hawkes: Rutland Boughton: with

acknowledgement to the Rutland Boughton Music Trust: Havergal Brian, bronze by Robert Thomas, ARCA, FRBS, 1967, courtesy of Havergal Brian Society: Denis Browne, with thanks to Pamela Blevins: Benjamin Burrows: with thanks to Brian Blyth Daubney: George Butterworth, reproduced by permission of the English Folk Dance and Song Society: Eric Coates, photo by Ian Graham-Jones: Bernard van Dieren: photo by Alvin Langdon Coburn, courtesy of George Eastman House, International Museum of Photography and Film; Rudolph Dolmetsch: courtesy of Dr Brian Blood; Lilian Elkington: courtesy of David J. Brown; E.H. Fellowes: courtesy of the Dean and Canons of Windsor; John Foulds: photo by Malcolm MacDonald; David Gow: by permission of Margaret Gow; Percy Grainger: reproduced by kind permission of the Estate of Percy Aldridge Grainger; Ivor Gurney: by permission of the Ivor Gurney Estate; Julius Harrison: courtesy of Len Mullenger; Gustav Holst: photo by permission of the Dean and Chapter, Chichester Cathedral; Dorothy Howell: with thanks to Merryn Howell and the Dorothy Howell Trust; Michael Hurd: photograph by Robert Carpenter Turner; Kenneth Leighton: from Kenneth Leighton Trust (University of Edinburgh); George Lloyd: with thanks to George Lloyd Music Library; Alexander Mackenzie: from the Lewis Foreman Collection; Thomas Pitfield: photograph reproduced courtesy of Royal Northern College of Music. The Pitfield verses are reproduced ©The Pitfield Trust. Elizabeth Poston: photograph © Margaret Ashby, reproduced with permission; Alice Mary Smith: by permission of V. Carse with acknowledgments to West Sussex Record Office and the County Archivist; Sydney Smith: courtesy of The Royal Society of Musicians of Great Britain; Edward J. Thorne: by permission of the Dean and Chapter, Chichester Cathedral; William B. Wordsworth: courtesy of The Scottish Music Centre.

The following images were taken from the sources listed below:
Emanuel Aguilar: from Jewish Music Information Centre; Ivor Atkins: from auspostalhistory.com (Australian Postal History and Social Philately); William Baines: from wildyorkshire.co.uk; J.F. Bridge: from hymntime.com; Cornelius Cardew: from Opendemocracy.net; Walford Davies: from boyschoirs.org; Charles Heap: from Lazarus editions (ed. Martin Harlow, Colin Bradbury); Imogen Holst: photo by Brian Heseltine from 'Imogen Holst at Dartingon' (The Dartington Press 1988); Nicholas Maw: from The Daily Telegraph, 19 May 2009; Elias Parish-Alvars: from parishalvars.com (portrait by Joseph Kriehuber, Vienna , 1839); Luard Selby: from The Musical Times, Mar. 1908.

THE BRITISH MUSIC SOCIETY
President: John McCabe CBE

The aim of the British Music Society is to encourage and renew world-wide enthusiasm for much British music of the last two centuries which may appear these days to be undeservedly neglected. The Society endeavours to achieve this aim through the dissemination of recordings and printed publications issued under its own imprint, and the promotion of lecture-recitals and live concert performances for which the Society acts as sponsor.

The Society's recordings, which are listed on its website and in a printed Compact Disc Catalogue, are currently produced on two labels: the main **BMS** label and its subsidiary **BMS Historic** label, both available for general sale as well as to members (the latter at discounted rates). Recordings of piano music of Lennox Berkeley and John McCabe have each received *Gramophone* Critics' Choice awards, as has the BMS Historic release of Noel Mewton-Wood's famed performances of piano concertos by Bliss, Stravinsky and Shostakovich. A number of other CD releases have recently been designated as *Gramophone* Recommended Recordings. The BMS recordings programme is now supported by funds received from the Michael Hurd Bequest.

The BMS publishes annually one Journal (**British Music**) and four Newsletters (**News**), which are all distributed free to members. It also publishes a series of Monographs and other occasional books – listed on the website and in a printed Catalogue of Publications – which members may purchase at discounted rates.

The Society's principal live-music activity has been its biennial BMS Awards competition, open to young musicians studying at one of the eight major British music colleges. Other occasional concerts, lecture-recitals and musical events are also organised, notably in conjunction with the Society's Annual General Meeting each June.

Enquiries concerning BMS membership can be found on The Society's website: **www.britishmusicsociety.co.uk**

Registered Charity No. 1043838